INSIDERS' GUIDE®

✓ W9-BPM-468

INSIDERS' GUIDE® TO
PENNSYLVANIA DUTCH COUNTRY

MARILYN ODESSER-TORPEY

INSIDERS' GUIDE®

GUILFORD, CONNECTICUT
AN IMPRINT OF THE GLOBE PEQUOT PRESS

The prices and rates in this guidebook were confirmed at press time. We recommend, however, that you call establishments before traveling to obtain current information.

INSIDERS' GUIDE®

Text design by LeAnna Weller Smith
Maps by XNR Productions, Inc. © Morris Book Publishing, LLC

ISSN: 1559-9582
ISBN-13: 978-0-7627-3550-1
ISBN-10: 0-7627-3550-3

Manufactured in the United States of America
First Edition/First Printing

CONTENTS

CONTENTS

Directory of Maps

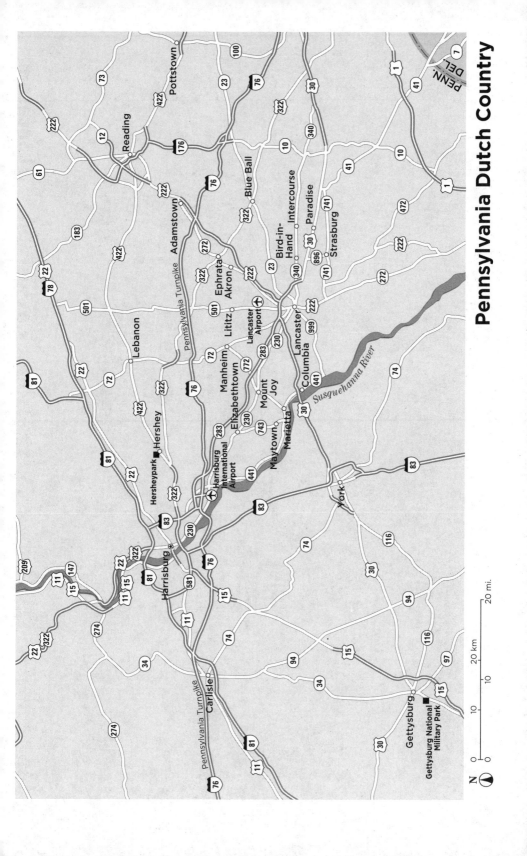

Pennsylvania Dutch Country

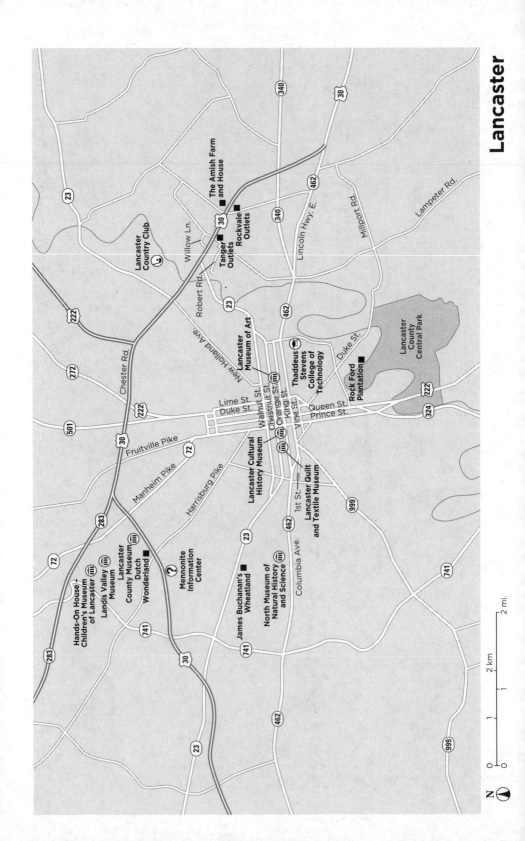

Lancaster

York

N

0
0

1

2 km

1

2 mi.

Hershey

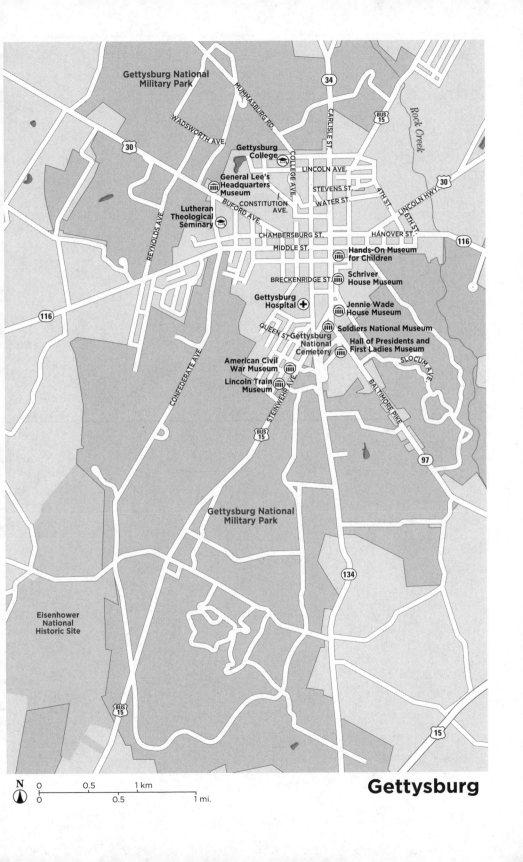

Gettysburg National Military Park

34

BUS 15

Rock Creek

MUMMASBURG RD.

WADSWORTH AVE.

30

CARLISLE ST.

30

Gettysburg College

LINCOLN AVE.

COLLEGE AVE.

General Lee's Headquarters Museum

STEVENS ST.

4TH ST.

LINCOLN HWY.

CONSTITUTION AVE.

WATER ST.

6TH ST.

BUFORD AVE.

Lutheran Theological Seminary

REYNOLDS AVE.

CHAMBERSBURG ST.

HANOVER ST.

116

MIDDLE ST.

Hands-On Museum for Children

116

BRECKENRIDGE ST.

Schriver House Museum

Gettysburg Hospital ✚

Jennie Wade House Museum

QUEEN ST.

Gettysburg National Cemetery

Soldiers National Museum

CONFEDERATE AVE.

American Civil War Museum

Hall of Presidents and First Ladies Museum

SLOCUM AVE.

Lincoln Train Museum

STEINWEHR AVE.

BALTIMORE PIKE

BUS 15

97

Gettysburg National Military Park

134

Eisenhower National Historic Site

BUS 15

15

N

0   0.5   1 km

0   0.5   1 mi.

Gettysburg

To Dana and Kristen, once my little girls,
now my best friends

PREFACE

Many visitors come to south-central Pennsylvania looking for a place where farms, homes, and businesses are still fueled by wind and water instead of by amps and watts, and transportation runs on horsepower of the hay-munching rather than gas-guzzling variety. First timers are often confused by the sight of sprawling big-brand shopping outlets, the razzle-dazzle of theme parks, the bright lights of theaters, and the profusion of fast-food emporia that line the major arteries of Pennsylvania Dutch Country.

Where are all the horses and buggies? The windmills? The distinctively named delicacies such as shoofly and whoopee pies, chowchow, schnitz and knepp? Above all, where are the Amish?

They're all here, if you know where to look.

Turn off just about any main highway and you'll discover the back roads, country byways that meander for miles, winding their way past fields, farms, and home-based barn and basement businesses advertised by small, hand-lettered signs. You'll see eggs gathered from the henhouse that morning; cider pressed from apples ripened in the sunny orchards; ears of corn just picked from their stalks; and cookies, cakes, pies, and apple turnovers baked from family recipes passed through generations. At stores large and small you'll find quilts stitched with care into centuries-old patterns that weave together history and artistry, as well as hand-hewn wooden furniture and toys destined to become heirlooms.

The traffic moves slower back there; horses don't have odometers. But if you're not in a hurry, the steady clip-clop pace of the old-fashioned buggies gives you time to get a good glimpse of a very different lifestyle. (Some of those buggies are carrying tourists, but most are filled with resident farmers and their families just going about their daily routines.)

You can find restaurants that offer the authentic flavor of Pennsylvania Dutch cooking and family-style dining. Some Amish families will even invite you to share a family breakfast or dinner on the farm (you can find out how to make the arrangements in the "Dining Deutsch Style" chapter of this book).

Pennsylvania Dutch Country is not a living history museum, frozen in a time centuries past. It is a living culture, one that has remained stable at its core amid an onslaught of technological, ideological, and theological change. And the influence of the Amish on their surroundings—and vice versa—continues to evolve.

While interest in the Amish is undoubtedly a major reason why more than eight million visitors travel to Lancaster County every year, it's definitely not the only one.

If it's greener pastures you're after, you can book a stay at a working dairy, produce, or horse farm where the resident rooster can roust the kids at chore time, while you just snuggle in your feather bed. Perhaps the only birdie you want to see is on a score card. For you, there is a galaxy of stellar golf courses and resort-style facilities that make them family-friendly.

Find out how the tiny towns of Intercourse, Blue Ball, and Bird-in-Hand got their colorful names, and discover each one's unique personality and charm. Walk in the footsteps of the soldiers who fought in the Battle of Gettysburg and of the townspeople whose lives were also swept up in the raging tides of the Civil War.

For railroad aficionados, all tracks lead to Strasburg, where you can still take a steam train to Paradise, visit the Railroad Museum of Pennsylvania, and check out the National Toy Train Museum. Or you can take to the sky for a whole new perspective on the countryside from the basket of a hot air balloon.

Is this heaven, or do I just smell chocolate? Both. Pennsylvania Dutch Country is the home of two world-class confectioners: Wilbur's in the town of Lititz and Hershey in the town of, well, you know. The aromas wafting from these factories are so sweet, the air itself must be caloric. So if you're going to breathe it in anyway, you might as well let your taste buds in on the fun.

You can work off those chocolate calories during your shopping spree. Whether you're looking for discounts or priceless antiques (with hundreds of individual and co-op shops, Adamstown, in northeastern Lancaster County, is widely recognized as the "Antiques Capital of the United States"), artisan crafts or imported luxuries, you'll find opportunities in abundance to give your credit cards a good workout. Come in spring and join the Amish at their annual "Mud Sales," special fund-raising events held at community firehouses, where locals and visitors can bid on and buy everything from livestock to farm equipment, furniture to housewares, homemade quilts to shoofly pies.

So savor the slower pace of a horse-and-buggy lifestyle, but don't dismiss Pennsylvania Dutch Country as a one-trick pony. It's rural, sophisticated, peaceful, exciting, away from it all, and in the middle of everything.

It's all here . . . if you know where to look.

ACKNOWLEDGMENTS

For their wealth of information and infinite patience with all of my questions, I want to, first and foremost, thank Cara O'Donnell and the staff of the Pennsylvania Dutch Convention and Visitors Bureau. My gratitude also to the helpful and knowledgeable folks at the multitude of helpful visitor centers, chambers of commerce, and historical societies in the City of Lancaster and in each of the towns and villages in Lancaster County.

The Convention and Visitors Bureaus of Gettysburg, York County, and Brandywine Valley, Pennsylvania, provided strong basic factual foundations to set me on my personal explorations. My appreciation, too, to Hershey Entertainment Resorts and Hershey Community Archives for maintaining and providing access to such comprehensive historical data.

Thank you to Jim Smucker, owner of Bird-in-Hand Family Restaurant, for giving me so many tasty tidbits about Pennsylvania Dutch cooking and its heritage. My deepest gratitude and everlasting affection to the famous cookbook author Betty Groff and her wonderful husband, Abe, for opening their Mount Joy home to me, inviting me to their table and introducing me to some of the best-kept secrets of their native neighborhoods. Last but not least, a very special thank you to the many members of the Pennsylvania Dutch Amish and Mennonite communities who so graciously shared their history and traditions with me.

HOW TO USE THIS BOOK

As a native Philadelphian, I thought I knew all about Pennsylvania Dutch Country when I first began the research for this book. I was absolutely wrong. The Pennsylvania Dutch experience with which I had grown up was pretty one-dimensional, involving a single community with a culture that, while undeniably unique, was only one of many reasons to visit this multidimensional area of gentle green hills, fertile farmland, quaint historic villages, and thriving cities in the south-central section of the state.

Although many people think Pennsylvania Dutch Country begins and ends in Lancaster County, they're only half right. The area also encompasses Hershey in Dauphin County and Gettysburg in Adams County, two locales that have flavors (particularly Hershey, where there's even chocolate in the air), histories, and distinctive allure all their own.

Wherever you are, the "Getting Here, Getting Around" chapter will make it easy for you to find your way to the area and any and all of its attractions. It will also help you to easily arrange visits to multiple locations adjacent to one another or along the same route. Another chapter introduces you to the people who live in Pennsylvania Dutch Country, focusing in on "The Plain People"—the Amish, the Mennonites, and the Brethren—communities that have given Pennsylvania Dutch Country its name and some of its most distinctive characteristics.

Before you head out, check out the "Area Overview" chapter for a look at the physical parameters of Pennsylvania Dutch Country; some general geographical groupings of its most popular towns, cities, and villages; landscape and climate; primary products; peak seasons, and other basics. Then read about the histories and personalities of the various areas that comprise Pennsylvania Dutch Country in the chapters entitled, "Cities, Towns, Villages, and Back Roads," "Gettysburg," and "Hershey."

Because food is such an important part of the Pennsylvania Dutch experience, dining options are divided into two separate sections. The first, "Dining Deutsch Style," tells where you can find Amish and Mennonite farm favorites. Many of these restaurants serve buffet- or family-style, but often also offer a la carte options. But Pennsylvania Dutch Country is much more than scrapple and shoofly pie. Sophisticated contemporary and international eateries also abound, as well as casual sandwich spots and bistros, dinner theaters, and even railroad repasts. Some of the best are described in the chapter entitled "Other Area Restaurants." In both chapters, listings are broken down by town or city location.

Whether the sun is shining or the stars provide the illumination, you'll find plenty to do in our "Attractions," "Tours," "Parks, Recreation, and Golf," and "Annual Events" chapters. (If you have a particular place or activity in mind, just check out the index at the back of the book.) To make these chapters as easy as possible for you to use, I have broken out the attractions into various categories, beginning with the all-important Visitor Information Centers (where you can collect maps and learn about the area's events du jour), Amusement Parks (Dutch Wonderland and Hersheypark are two big family draws), Animals (which includes zoos and horse farms), Art (including a hidden-away Gettysburg mural), Factory Tours (whether hands-on or simulated, they're interesting and educational), Films and Historic Productions (learn about the people and places through screen and stage reenactments and presentations), Fun and Games (everything from go-karts to Lasertron to minigolf), Historic Homes and Gardens (from presidential homes to wartime headquarters to Amish farmhouses), Museums (displays of locally made quilts, watches and clocks, antique cars, an animatronic one-room schoolhouse, and the largest living history village depicting Pennsylvania Dutch life), Natural Wonders (from caverns to corn mazes), and Railroads (take a ride back through history). Under these general headings, you will find the attractions subdivided by the city or town in which they are located.

You can find any tours you may want to take in the chapter with that heading. Self-guided, guided, and "step-on" tours (you pick up your guide at a designated point and drive in your own car) are each listed separately, as well as modes of available transportation such as buses and motor coaches, hot air balloons, horses, carriages, and bicycles. Due to their number and popularity, ghost tours and horse-and-buggy rides are broken out by geographic location (listed in alphabetical order).

The chapter "Annual Events" categorizes events by the months in which they occur to enable you to plan your visits according to your interests.

After dark, the footlights come up and the nightlife begins. The chapter "Theaters and Nightlife" is divided into two categories—one for concerts/music and opera and another for theater. The listings are further broken down by town or city and ordered alphabetically.

In the "Parks, Recreation, and Golf" chapter, golf courses are listed by city or town. Public recreational facilities such as city and state parks, swimming pools, gardens, wildflower and nature preserves, wildlife management preserves, and rail trails are also divided by geographical areas. (Because it is such a multidimen-

sional site, the information about Gettysburg National Military Park is included in the "Attractions" chapter rather than in this one.) Spectator sports such as hockey, baseball, and motor sports are designated by type of activity.

No matter how much energy you have, you're going to have to sleep sometime. We give you plenty of choices of places to lay your head. To help you find the exact type of accommodation you want, we have broken them out into five different chapters. In "Hotels and Motels," we'll tell you where to find the familiar chains and some one-of-a-kind family-owned and -operated hideaways. Make yourself at home at one of the area's cozy bed-and-breakfasts, which you'll find in the chapter "Bed-and-Breakfasts and Inns," experience country life, ranging from rustic to luxe, by checking "Farm Stays"; or follow your pioneer instincts to a campground or cabin (you'll find everything in "Campgrounds," from primitive to amenity-abundant). There are plenty of posh properties here as well, as you'll see in the chapter titled "Resorts." In each chapter, each accommodation can be found alphabetically, listed by city or town.

Renowned for its farm stands and home workshops, Pennsylvania Dutch Country has an abundance of "home-grown and homemade" offerings (see the chapter of the same name), ranging from field-ripened fruits and veggies to home-baked goodies to hand-carved furniture and toys and hand-woven or quilted textiles. In "Shopping" you'll find every kind of retail establishment, from mom-and-pop stores to big-name outlets. Listings are divided into types of products, then alphabetically by the name of the shop. Because the categories are so much broader (for example, Antiques, Art, Books, Clothing, Gifts and Collectibles, Home Accessories, Furniture, Jewelry, Teddy Bears and Dolls, and Factory Outlets and Multiunit Centers), the listings have been subdivided into geographic designations as well.

Thinking of moving to Pennsylvania

Dutch Country? You'll get more than research in the "Relocation" chapter; you'll have the benefit of personal experience—mine. In this chapter, you'll find everything from real estate and rentals to retirement communities, and all about health care, education, child care, the media, and emergency numbers to keep on hand.

During the course of writing this book, I came to love Pennsylvania Dutch Country so much, I decided to move here. I am now a proud resident of Lititz.

AREA OVERVIEW

Although the term *Pennsylvania Dutch Country* is usually associated with the cities, towns, and villages of Lancaster County, the Pennsylvania Tourism Office also usually includes two locations to the west—Hershey in Dauphin County and Gettysburg in Adams County—under the same destination umbrella.

LANCASTER COUNTY

As the heart of Pennsylvania Dutch Country, Lancaster County is a natural starting point for any trip to this area. Situated about 70 miles west of Philadelphia, 34 miles southeast of Harrisburg, and 87 miles north of Washington, D.C., this 956-square-mile county in the south-central part of the Keystone State is made up of 60 independent boroughs, townships, and a city. Close to the center of the county is Lancaster City, a bustling urban center that is a good place—geographically and historically—to begin your acquaintance with this area.

All told, Lancaster County is only 46 miles at its widest and 43 miles at its longest, so you can drive to any point within its boundaries in about an hour or less. Many of the most popular Amish-oriented tours and attractions are located just east of Lancaster City, in the towns

During the American Revolution, Lancaster City was the capital of the United States for one day. On September 27, 1777, the Continental Congress, which had fled Philadelphia just ahead of invading British troops, convened in Lancaster before continuing across the Susquehanna River to the city of York, around 25 miles to the southwest.

and villages of Bird-in-Hand, Intercourse, Paradise, and Ronks. Also in this eastern portion of the county is Christiana, famous as a hotbed of antislavery activity in the period before the Civil War.

North of the city are numerous small communities—including Leola, New Holland, Akron, Ephrata, Denver, Lititz, Manheim, and Adamstown—many of which blend the pastoral beauty of rolling farmlands with quaint main street business districts and a combination of lovingly preserved old and chic new residential areas.

Western Lancaster County offers the charming Susquehanna River towns of Columbia, Marietta, and Wrightsville, as well historic Maytown, scenic Mount Joy, and collegiate Elizabethtown a little farther inland. In southern Lancaster County are the railroad-centric town of Strasburg, the towns of Quarryville and Willow Street, and miles of preserved natural areas, recreational parks, and state park land.

The primary symbol on the seal used by the County of Lancaster is a folk art rendition of a heart within a heart. That's a fitting image for the vibrant center of a thriving, constantly growing entity. It is also a reminder of some 300 years of commitment to providing a place where people can find religious freedom, spiritual peace, and the support of community.

Also on the seal, a Conestoga wagon, which had its origins in this area, stands for the ingenuity and pioneering spirit that have characterized this county and its people. Corn piled high acknowledges the gifts of the earth and the work and tenacity of the generations who have sown, tended, and harvested the crops that have sustained their neighbors and the nation.

Farmers are still the backbone of the economy in Lancaster County. In fact, Lancaster is acknowledged as the most productive nonirrigated farming county in the

United States, according to the Lancaster Chamber of Commerce and Industry. It is also ranked No. 1 among all U.S. counties for farmland preservation, with 55,000 acres (15 percent of the total farmland) currently under preservation.

Of the 255,400 members of the Lancaster County workforce, 51,289 jobs (one in five) involve the agricultural industry. Of those jobs, 10,499 are in farming.

Over 99 percent of the 5,293 Lancaster County farms are family owned. The average farm size is 78 acres. Dairy is the focus of many of these farms, but you'll also find plenty of poultry and pigs as well as produce and other crops flourishing in the fields.

According to U.S. Census Bureau estimates for 2003, about 482,775 people live in Lancaster County. Over the last 50 years, the area has demonstrated a steady growth pattern of roughly 50,000 residents per decade.

Lancaster County's agricultural diversity—and appeal as a year-round tourism destination—is supported by a climate in which each of the four seasons brings its own distinctive weather patterns, beauty, and activity opportunities.

Spring is planting time for farmers and gardening hobbyists, so, even though the flowers and fields aren't yet in full bloom, there are plenty of colorful sights to see. As you pass by the farms, keep an eye out for the baby calves, sheep, and foals wobbling as they try out their legs under watchful parental supervision.

For the most part, you can expect the roads to be emptier, the lines to be shorter, and the lodging rates to be lower from March through mid-June. But keep in mind that seasonal festivals, limited openings of certain outdoor attractions, art shows, craft fairs, local auctions, and just the opportunity to ramble along budding country roads often bring out fair numbers of pleasure seekers. Spring temperatures can range from the 50s to the 70s Fahrenheit, so keep an eye on the local forecasts if you plan to visit, and pack a sweater or light jacket, just in case.

Lancaster was the home of the only Pennsylvania-born (and only bachelor) president of the United States, James Buchanan. His mansion, Wheatland, where America's 15th president spent 20 years, served as Democratic headquarters during the 1856 presidential campaign. Wheatland has been restored and is open for public tours.

Summer is peak season, not just for tourism, but for sunshine and temperatures that average in the low 80s Fahrenheit, but have often been known to rise into the 90s. Mid-June to early December can be pretty humid here, too, which is great for the crops, but may cause you to wilt if you spend too much time out in the heat. You're never too far, though, from shade, shelter, or a refreshing drink of homemade birch beer (a carbonated root beer–type concoction made from birch tree bark extract instead of sassafras—it's usually redder in color than root beer and can pack a flavorful punch, which, in some cases, may be reminiscent of wintergreen). And where there are dairy farms, there must be ice cream, the good stuff that you can only get from real country cream.

Fields and orchards are full to bursting with veggies and fruit ripe for the picking: fat ears of corn; juicy red and yellow tomatoes; peppers in just about every color you can imagine; sweet strawberries and raspberries; fragrant herbs; and a sumptuous salad of lettuce, cucumbers, and other produce. You can pick all you want at the farm stands that spring up like wildflowers on just about every back road.

Fall in Lancaster County is generally crisp and cool (actually, it can range from the warmth of an Indian summer to an early winter chill), like the apples that come from its orchards. Farms and vineyards are in full harvest mode. Pumpkins proliferate in the fields and at the farm stands for jack-o'-lantern making and pie baking.

In late September and early October, leaf peepers will love the golden and

---

Witness, *the Oscar-winning 1985 Paramount Pictures film starring Harrison Ford and Kelly McGillis, was partially filmed in Intercourse, Lancaster County. One of the most famous scenes in the movie involved the telephone outside* **W. L. Zimmerman & Sons General Store** *(3601 Old Philadelphia Pike, Intercourse; 717–768–8291), which still provides a hitching post out front and buggy parking in the rear for its many Amish customers.*

---

flame-colored foliage. After the harvest, in November and early December, look for the blue dresses of the Amish brides.

Some winters are whiter than others (average snowfall for the season is 26.4 inches), but from mid-December through February, there are mugs of steaming mulled cider, Currier and Ives–type scenery, horse-drawn sleigh rides, and warm, snuggly inns with fireplaces and feather beds to keep you cozy. Shopping is an all-season sport and holiday shopping an all-star event whether you're looking for something homespun or haute couture. Temperatures can plummet (low 30s and below), so button up and break out the long johns.

HERSHEY

Located about a 40-minute drive from Lancaster City is a place that is known by many names, including "Chocolatetown U.S.A." and "The Sweetest Place on Earth." Like Lancaster County, this area is characterized by its agricultural heritage and Pennsylvania Dutch ancestry.

An interesting tidbit is that the town of Hershey doesn't really exist because it was never officially incorporated. The people who live there are actually citizens of Derry Township—that's where they pay their taxes and send their children to school. But if you send a letter addressed to Hershey, it will arrive because the post office does bear the name of the famous chocolatier who built the town.

The history of Milton Hershey and the place and company that bear his name are further explored in the "Hershey" chapter of this book.

GETTYSBURG

Before there was a Battle of Gettysburg, often described as the turning point of the Civil War, there was a town surrounded by peaceful farmland where families lived and worked for generations. According to the Pennsylvania Tourism Office, this agrarian, family-oriented culture, so like that of Lancaster County, is as important a part of the heritage of Adams County as the battlefield that made it so famous.

Located a little more than 50 miles from Lancaster City, Gettysburg is a "must-see" destination for visitors to central Pennsylvania. Even more than geographic proximity, the Gettysburg and Lancaster areas are linked by their prominence in the shaping of American history.

In a separate chapter entitled "Gettysburg," the past and present of this historic city are explored in more detail.

GETTING HERE, GETTING AROUND

Whether you're making the trip by car, plane, train, or bus, getting to Lancaster is pretty much a snap, especially when you consider that early-18th-century traders and travelers from Philadelphia used to slog for four days along bumpy, rut-pocked, mired-in-mud "roads." Although that route had the regal name of "King's Highway," it was really nothing more than a glorified dirt trail.

The construction of the nation's first turnpike, which opened in 1795, significantly smoothed the way, allowing stagecoaches to make the journey from Philadelphia in around 12 hours. Sharing the turnpike were Conestoga wagons (which, by the way, were invented in Lancaster County) drawn by horses specially bred to haul hefty loads of produce from Lancaster farms to Philadelphia markets. Lancaster also became a primary "Gateway to the West" for settlers on their way to the Allegheny Mountains.

GETTING HERE

By Car

Turnpike driving has changed a lot since the 18th century, but it's still the quickest way to get to Lancaster. The Pennsylvania Turnpike (U.S. Route 76) travels in an east–west direction across the northern part of Lancaster County. Exit 266/Lancaster–Lebanon (old exit 20) will take you into Lancaster via Pennsylvania Route 72, exit 286/Lancaster–Reading (old exit 21) via U.S. Route 222.

All of Lancaster County's major highways (except the Pennsylvania Turnpike) come together in Lancaster City, so it's a perfect geographical launching point for a grand tour of Pennsylvania Dutch Country, as well as a worthy historic and entertaining destination on its own.

You can take your time and soak in all the scenery because the entire county is only 46 miles wide and 43 miles long. That means you can be anywhere you want to be in an hour or less.

ROUTE 30 NORTH TO COLUMBIA WITH CONNECTIONS TO MARIETTA, MOUNT JOY, MANHEIM, AND ELIZABETHTOWN

From Lancaster, you can jump on U.S. Route 30 (also known as Lincoln Highway) going west and meander your way down to the peaceful, yet wonderfully hospitable towns along the Susquehanna River. First you'll come to Columbia, then it's less than 4 miles northwest along the river on Route 441 to Marietta.

Route 441 also intersects with Route 772, one of the area's most scenic roads winding through miles and miles of farmland. Less than 5 miles northeast of the intersection is Mount Joy; stay on 772 East for a little over 7 miles and you'll arrive in Manheim.

Right around Mount Joy, you can also branch off Route 772 onto Route 230 and head northwest a little less than 7 miles to Elizabethtown.

ROUTE 30 EAST TO PARADISE WITH CONNECTIONS TO STRASBURG, BIRD-IN-HAND, AND INTERCOURSE

Route 30 East from Lancaster City is the quickest way to Paradise, but before you get that far, you can make a right at the intersection of Routes 30 and 896 for a

CLOSE-UP

Peak of the Pike

Next time you're waiting in a line of cars to pay your toll on a turnpike, consider this: Due to the high cost of building a crushed stone road that would be able to hold up to high volumes of traffic passing between Philadelphia and Lancaster, state planners had the bright idea to privatize the construction. The builders were granted permission to levy a "reasonable" toll on every vehicle that used the road to raise money to pay off investors.

In 1792, 1,000 shares of stock were issued at $300 apiece to fund the building of the Lancaster Pike, America's first major planned paved road. Two additional stock offerings were made, one in 1795 for 200 shares and another for 100 in 1796. By the time it was completed, the road had cost a total of $465,000 to construct. In today's dollars, that amount would equal $60 million.

To enable the builder to collect tolls, the company erected nine gates, or "pikes," at intervals between the first and last stops. Horse-and-wagon drivers paid about 25 cents at each gate. After the money was paid, the gatekeepers would turn their "pikes" aside to allow the vehicles to pass—thus the word *turnpike*.

During peak summer seasons, those toll takers would be pretty busy. It was not unusual for at least 1,000 wagons to use the turnpike each day. Too bad there was no such thing as E-ZPass (or FasTrak, if you're a West Coaster)!

The use of railroads and canals for shipping freight brought a period of decline to the turnpike around the middle of the 19th century. While the widespread use of the automobile later revived turnpikes, Lancaster Pike was never the same, although you can still get to Lancaster from Philadelphia by way of its modern-day descendant, Route 30. But with all the little towns and stoplights along the way to impede any reasonable amount of speed, doing so would be the equivalent of taking a slow boat to China.

quick jaunt north to Strasburg at the intersection of Routes 896 and 741. From 30 East, you can also connect to Route 340 (Old Philadelphia Pike), which will take you through villages with such eyebrow-raising names as Bird-in-Hand and Intercourse.

ROUTE 30 WEST TO HERSHEY AND GETTYSBURG

To get to Hershey, about a 40-minute drive from Lancaster City, take Route 30

to Route 283 West for about 16.6 miles, then take the right-hand fork in the road to get onto Route 743 North. You can also get to Hershey from Lancaster by taking Route 72 North to Route 322 West and following 322 for about 12 miles.

For Gettysburg, follow Route 30 West for about 53 miles.

ROUTE 501 NORTH TO LITITZ

A little less than 9 miles north of Lancaster on Route 501 is Lititz (if you miss the sign, you certainly won't miss the smell of Wilbur's Chocolate Factory located in the middle of town).

ROUTE 23 EAST TO LEOLA, NEW HOLLAND, AND BLUE BALL

About 8 miles east of Lancaster City on Route 23 is Leola, followed by New Holland and Blue Ball.

ROUTE 222 NORTH WITH CONNECTIONS TO EPHRATA

Route 222 North from Lancaster will connect with Route 322, just under 11 miles from Lancaster. Turn left on 322 and drive another 2 miles or so to find Ephrata.

ROUTE 272 NORTH TO AKRON AND ADAMSTOWN

About 12 miles northeast of Lancaster on Route 272 is Akron; a little more than 10 miles farther on is Adamstown.

By Air

LANCASTER

Lancaster County has its own airport, located at the intersection of Route 501/Lititz Pike and Airport Road in Lititz 6 miles north of Lancaster City (717–569–1221; www.lancasterairport.com). There may be no such thing as a free lunch, but there is free parking at Lancaster Airport—all day, every day, no matter how long you stay.

Daily flights on U.S. Airways Express (800–428–4322; www.usairways.com) offer connections to more than 200 domestic and worldwide destinations.

Not quite as close by, but still convenient to Lancaster City (about a 40-mile drive east on Route 283) is Harrisburg International Airport (510 Dauphin Drive, Middletown 17057; 888–442–5387; www.flyhia.com). Harrisburg International Airport is served by seven major airlines offering nonstop daily service to 13 domes-

tic and one international destination along with one-stop service to cities around the world:

Air Canada
Reservations: (888) 247–2262
www.aircanada.ca
All Air Canada flights at this airport are handled by United Airlines. This includes check-in and baggage.

American Eagle
Reservations: (800) 433–7300
www.aa.com

Continental Airlines
Reservations: (800) 525–0280
www.continental.com

Delta Airlines
Reservations: (800) 221–1212
www.delta.com

Northwest Airlines
Reservations: (800) 225–2525
www.nwa.com

TMA (TransMeridian Airlines)
Reservations: (866) 435–9862
www.tmair.com

United
Reservations: (800) 241–6522
www.ual.com

Route 30 in Lancaster County can be a bumper-to-bumper, slow-going crawl during peak tourist times in summer or fall. You can get a preview of whether you can expect smooth sailing or should seek an alternate route by checking out the live Route 30 cam sponsored by Lancaster Newspapers on the Web site http://visit.lancasteronline.com. Located at some of Route 30's busiest exists—to the Fruitville, Lititz, and Oregon Pikes—this traffic-tracking technology provides both east and west perspectives of the road.

US Airways
Reservations: (800) 428–4322
www.usairways.com

HERSHEY

Harrisburg Airport (MDT) is about a 15-minute drive from Hershey. (If you're staying at one of the Hershey Resorts, shuttle service to and from the airport can be arranged for a reasonable fee.) Baltimore/Washington Airport (BWI) is about 90 minutes away by car.

GETTYSBURG

Harrisburg International Airport is approximately 42 miles from Gettysburg; Baltimore/Washington Airport is about 61 miles.

By Train

LANCASTER

Amtrak operates two rail lines with stops at the Lancaster Amtrak Passenger Station (code LNC) in the city's downtown area (53 McGovern Avenue; 800–USA-RAIL or 800–872–7245; www.amtrak.com). Lancaster Station offers an enclosed waiting area with ATM and Quik Trak Automated Ticketing System availability.

Amtrak's Keystone Service, which provides daily service between New York City and Harrisburg by way of Philadelphia, stops at stations in Harrisburg, Elizabethtown, Mount Joy, and Lancaster. The Three Rivers line, which travels daily between New York City and Chicago via Philadelphia, Harrisburg, and Pittsburgh, stops at Lancaster Station.

Taxis and rental cars are available from Lancaster Station.

HERSHEY

The Harrisburg Train Station (station code HAR), serviced by Amtrak, is a 15-minute drive from Hershey (Fourth and Chestnut Streets, Harrisburg 17101; 800–USA-RAIL

or 800–872–7245; www.amtrak.com). Guests of Hershey Resorts may arrange for a reasonably priced shuttle service to their particular accommodation.

GETTYSBURG

Harrisburg is also the closest train station (around 36 miles) from Gettysburg.

By Bus

LANCASTER

Greyhound Bus Lines (53 McGovern Avenue; 800–231–2222, 717–397–4861) offers daily service to Lancaster.

HERSHEY AND GETTYSBURG

Greyhound Bus Lines at the Harrisburg Train Station (Fourth and Chestnut Streets, Harrisburg 17101; 800–229–9424, www.greyhound.com) is the closest station to both destinations. Hershey Resort guests may arrange for a reasonably priced shuttle service to their particular accommodations.

GETTING AROUND LANCASTER CITY AND COUNTY

Car Rentals

LANCASTER

Both Avis (717–569–3185) and Hertz (717–569–2331) have rental facilities at Lancaster Airport. If you are arriving at Harrisburg International Airport, you'll find Avis (717–948–3720), Budget (717–944–4019), Enterprise (717–795–0900), Hertz (717–944–4081), National (717–948–3710), and Thrifty (717–944–9024).

Most major car rental companies also have locations throughout Lancaster County. To reach them, call Alamo (800–327–9633), Avis (800–831–2847), Budget (cars and trucks—717–519–0111), Dollar (800–800–4000), Enterprise

(800-736-8222), Hertz (800-654-3131), and National (800-227-7368).

HERSHEY AND GETTYSBURG

The following rental companies have locations in or near Harrisburg International Airport:

Avis Rent-A-Car
(717) 944-4401, (800) 230-4898

Enterprise Rent-A-Car
(717) 944-6566, (800) 736-8222
Services the airport via shuttle bus.

Hertz Rent-A-Car
(717) 944-4088, (800) 654-3131

National Car Rental
(800) 227-7368 at the airport,
(800) 328-4567

Thrifty Car Rental
(717) 948-5710, (800) 847-4389

Parking

LANCASTER

A number of downtown Lancaster hotels, motels, bed-and-breakfasts, and inns offer free off-street parking for overnight guests. For day-trippers, there are plenty of strategically located parking lots, garages and meters.

Parking Garages
The Lancaster Parking Authority (717-299-0907) operates five garages. The three largest and most convenient to city attractions, shopping, and dining costs $1.00 per hour or any part of an hour:

Prince Street Garage
111 North Prince Street

King Street Garage
25-51 East Vine Street

Duke Street Garage
2828 South Duke Street

If you're driving, the major streets of downtown Lancaster are two lanes but in only one direction. If you want to head south, use either Prince or Duke Streets; to go north, use either Queen or Lime Streets. It's westward on Orange and Walnut Streets, eastbound on King and Chestnut Streets.

The following two garages cost $2.00 per day:

Cherry Street Garage
Cherry and Madison Streets

Water Street Garage
220 North Water Street

Parking Lots
Hagar Parking (717-397-6445) operates two surface lots, 37 West King Street and 33 North Prince Street. Both are conveniently situated close to Central Market, Fulton Opera House, and other downtown attractions. Parking will cost you $1.35 per hour. Fees are calculated on an hourly basis, with no incremental discounts. That means, whether you park for 10 minutes or a full 60, you will pay $1.35.

Parking Meters
On-street metered parking is available for 50 cents a half hour. Meters are free after 6:00 P.M. and all day on Saturday and Sunday.

HERSHEY

Most of the major attractions, accommodations, and dining spots have parking lots on their premises. Some charge a parking fee, depending on the site and time of year.

GETTYSBURG

Parking Lots
Racehorse Alley Parking Plaza (behind Lincoln Station and accessible from the first block of Carlisle Street north of Lin-

If you park your car in one of the Lancaster Historic Area public garages, be sure to take your ticket when you tour. Many downtown merchants will validate parking garage tickets. Just ask wherever you shop or dine.

coln Square or the first block of North Stratton Street, north of York Street; 717-334-4390). Vehicles for visitors with special needs are available. Public restrooms are available at the plaza entrance and on the lower lever behind Lincoln Train Station. Cost is 50 cents per hour or $12 for the day.

Parking Meters
Metered parking is available on every street within the Gettysburg Visitors' District. Parking on Lincoln Square and up to 2 blocks out is considered short-term parking (up to 2¼ hours), and the cost is a quarter for 20 minutes or a dime for 10. Long-term parking begins 2 to 3 blocks from Lincoln Square, and these meters go up to 12 hours (1½ hours costs a quarter, 30 minutes a dime).

Taxis, Limos, Passenger Vans, and Private Charter Buses

LANCASTER COUNTY

Expressions Limousine of Lancaster
107 Buchland Road, Ephrata
(717) 556-5466

Friendly Transportation Service
625 East Orange Street, Lancaster
(800) 795-FAST, (717) 392-2222
www.friendlytransportation.com
Friendly offers all of the above for business or pleasure, whether you just need a lift to the airport or a regal chariot for a night out on the town. Friendly provides

24-hour, seven-day-a-week taxi service or chauffeur-driven Lincoln Town Cars or passenger vans. Wheelchair-accessible buses are available.

Keystone Limousine Service
988 Stony Battery Road, Lancaster
(717) 892-1240

Lancaster County Taxi Service
114 Noble Street, Lititz
(717) 626-8294

Lancaster Yellow Cab Co. Inc.
1278 Loop Road, Lancaster
(717) 397-8100

Public Transportation

LANCASTER

Red Rose Transit Authority (RRTA)
47 North Queen Street
(717) 397-4246
www.redrosetransit.com
RRTA operates 17 bus routes that serve Lancaster City and County. In the city, bus stops are marked by signs. If you're traveling outside the city, make sure you have a schedule with you to note the route of the bus you want. If you want to get on and there is no sign nearby to indicate a regularly scheduled stop, just wait at a safe spot (that is, out of the path of traffic) on the side of the road and wave when you see a bus approaching. The travel will stop to allow you to board. Each RRTA bus is clearly marked on the front, sides, and back with a route number and a name. Fares are determined by zone, beginning at $1.15 to a maximum of $2.25. Transfers are an additional 5 cents. Persons with special physical needs and those under age 65 with a Medicare card can ride for half fare during off-peak hours (peak hours are 7:00 to 8:00 A.M. and 4:30 to 5:30 P.M. weekdays). To qualify, passengers must show a Half Fare ID card (available to qualified individuals from RRTA). Students (kindergarten through grade 12) are

eligible for a student rate; high schoolers must show proof of student status to obtain the discount rate. Children ages five and under ride free when accompanied by a full-fare paying passenger.

Senior citizens age 65 and older with a transit ID or Medicare card ride free every weekday, except between the hours of 7:00 and 8:00 A.M. and 4:30 and 5:30 P.M. (on selected holidays, RRTA allows seniors to ride free all day). Persons with special physical needs who obtain an ID card from RRTA can ride for half price during these same periods. ID cards may be obtained at RRTA's Downtown Information Center (47 North Queen Street) or RRTA Operations Center (45 Erick Road—off Dillerville Road between Fruitville and Manheim Pike). For more information, call RRTA at (717) 397-4246.

To get you to some of the more popular area locations, RRTA's Route 13/White Horse bus travels through Bird-in-Hand and Intercourse on Route 340, where many of the Amish attractions can be found. For shopping, the Route 14/Rockvale Square will take you along Route 30 to the outlets. The Route 11/Ephrata combines history with upscale retail with stops at the Ephrata Cloister and Doneckers. You can visit Lancaster County's Susquehanna River towns by hopping on the Route 17/Columbia bus to Columbia and Marietta. If your quest is farther west, take the Route 18/Elizabethtown to Elizabethtown and Mount Joy. Buses require exact fare.

Bicycling

LANCASTER COUNTY

Lancaster County's back roads are just made for long, leisurely bike rides. If you have a basket on your handlebars, you can stock up on just-picked produce from the farms that tend to pop up all along these less-traveled trails. There's no better way to tour the county's famous covered bridges. For weekend athletes looking for

Need some directions or information while you're touring the historic heart of Lancaster City? Look for any shop, restaurant, or other business displaying the red-and-white DOWNTOWN FRIENDLY sign in its window. The folks inside are indeed visitor-friendly and will be happy to help you find your way around.

an easy ride, keep to the flatter areas around Bird-in-Hand and Leola. More challenging are the hills south of Strasburg and Route 741. Lancaster County has more miles of road than any other county in Pennsylvania, most of which remain untainted by motorists and commercial establishments. The Lancaster Bike Club has graciously detailed more than 25 of its members' favorite scenic routes on its Web site (www.lancasterbikeclub.org) to help you plan a ride to remember. When you access the site, click on the heading "Scenic Tours of Lancaster County" and scroll down through tours with such whimsical names as "Red Rose Pedal," "Tick Tock Trek," "Mount Joy Jaunt," and "Undiscovered Amish."

Touring downtown Lancaster is a bargain when you leave your car at the Red Rose Transit Authority's Park 'n Ride lot (¼ mile south of Route 30 right over the Fruitville Pike bridge near Liberty Place) and hop on the Historic Downtown Trolley shuttle. Parking at the lot is free for trolley passengers, and an all-day ticket to ride costs only $2.50 (regular per-ride ticket price is $1.15). The trolley leaves the lot every 15 minutes Monday through Friday during peak hours. Stops for pickup and drop-off also include the Amtrak Station and Greyhound Bus Terminal and the Downtown Lancaster Visitors Center. The trolley runs from 7:10 A.M. to 6:30 P.M.

THE PENNSYLVANIA "DUTCH"

Despite the working windmills that still power a number of the farms that dot the rolling green hills of Lancaster and surrounding counties, the term *Pennsylvania Dutch* refers to neither Holland nor the Netherlands. Historians tend to agree that *Dutch* is an Anglicized version of the word *Deutsch,* meaning "German," a reference to the language spoken by many of the settlers who came here in the early 1700s.

While many people associate Pennsylvania Dutch with the Old Order Amish, a religious group that differentiates itself from others by dressing in simple, dark clothing, eschewing the use of electricity in their homes, and choosing the horse and buggy as their primary mode of transportation, there is actually a wide range of other nationalities and religions represented here. This diversity is what actually gives Pennsylvania Dutch Country its unique flavor. But it is still the Amish and the other "Plain People" who give the area its special mystique.

THE PLAIN PEOPLE

For many tourists, the sight of bearded men in broad-brimmed hats and women in aprons and bonnets, horse-drawn buggies, and windmills may be a novelty. But for about 75,000 of the total 460,000 residents of the Pennsylvania Dutch heartland, this no-frills lifestyle is a matter of faith that has been passed down through generations over hundreds of years.

Plain People is a term commonly identified with the most conservative members (or "Old Older") of the religious group known as the Amish. In reality, the Amish make up only about one quarter of the area's total "Plain" population. There are also other denominations, such as Mennonites and members of the Brethren, who base their lifestyles on modesty and humility.

According to Merle and Phyllis Good, codirectors of The People's Place in Intercourse, an educational and heritage center about Amish and Mennonite faith and life, and authors of a book entitled *20 Most Asked Questions About the Amish and Mennonites,* Lancaster County has the world's largest Mennonite and second-largest Amish communities. In his book *The Riddle of Amish Culture,* Donald B. Kraybill, a professor at Messiah College in Pennsylvania, notes that the area is also home to the oldest surviving Amish settlement in the world.

In another of his books, *Who Are the Anabaptists?,* Kraybill explains: "In general, the more conservative the group, the longer the beard, the wider the hat brim, the darker the color of clothing, the larger the head covering for women, the slower the singing, the longer the sermons, the greater the use of a Swiss or a German dialect, and the more traditional the technology."

The Amish, Mennonites, and Brethren all have their roots in the 16th-century

---

For more information about the history or present-day lives of the Amish and Mennonites, or to conduct your own genealogical search, visit the Lancaster Mennonite Historical Society, 2215 Millstream Road, Lancaster (717–393–9745; fax 717–393–8751; e-mail lmhs@lmhs .org). It's open Tuesday to Saturday, 8:30 A.M. to 4:30 P.M.; closed major holidays.

Family members of all ages pitch in for the harvest. PENNSYLVANIA DUTCH CONVENTION & VISITORS BUREAU

Protestant Reformation. Although the Reformation challenged many of the basic tenets of the Catholic Church, some Christians did not think it went far enough.

Among the most critical points of contention was baptism, which both the Catholic and Protestant Churches agreed should be done in infancy. Believing in a more literal interpretation of the Scriptures, a group called the Swiss Brethren pointed out that the Bible made no reference to infant baptism. They believed that joining the church should be a conscious and voluntary act and therefore a choice that could only be made by an adult.

As an expression of their faith in "Believer's Baptism," these adult Brethren, who, as Christians, had already been baptized as infants, chose to baptize themselves again. As a result, they became known as "Anabaptists," or rebaptizers. Today, Anabaptist sects baptize only once, when each individual reaches adulthood, usually somewhere between the ages of 18

and 22. Baptism is still a voluntary act and is a decision that results from years of thought and soul searching.

A second major sticking point was the Anabaptists' insistence on the separation between church and state. While that belief is a common one to us now, it was considered heresy back then. The Anabaptists were punished for their dissenting views with banishment from their homelands, imprisonment, torture, and even death.

The Anabaptists wouldn't be swayed, but they couldn't fight. Their belief in nonresistance or pacifism would not allow them to take up a sword to defend themselves, their families, or their homes. Nonresistance is still a central tenet in all Anabaptist sects. It is a tenet that has survived through centuries of war.

The histories of believers killed during the 16th through mid-17th centuries have been preserved in a book called *Martyrs Mirror*, which was published in 1660. Many

Unless you're invited into someone's home, the best glimpse you'll get of "Plain" living is at the Amish Farm and House, located at 2395 Route 30 East in Lancaster (717–394–6185, www.amish farmandhouse.com). On a guided tour of the 1805 farmhouse, you'll see furnishings and clothing indicative of the "Old Amish" lifestyle. The 25-acre working farm, which dates from 1715, features a stone bank barn, waterwheel, windmill, early Americana museum, and live animals. Seasonal events include blacksmithing and quilting demonstrations, sheep shearing, a corn maze, and kerosene lamp tours. Open year-round; hours vary according to the season. Cost: $6.95 per adult (ages 12 and up), $6.25 (seniors 65+), and $4.25 (ages 5 to 11).

present-day Anabaptists keep a copy of the book in their homes.

Even today, members tell of a Dutch Anabaptist of the late 1560s named Dirk Willems, who, while running to escape from a persecutor seeking to arrest him for his beliefs, crossed an icy river. Although Willems made it across safely, the other man fell through the ice. Instead of continuing to run, Willems went back to rescue the man from the freezing water. Willems was later imprisoned and burned at the stake.

To escape persecution, many Anabaptists fled into the mountains of Switzerland and southern Germany, where they lived quietly, farming the land. For safety, they held secret worship services in one another's homes or in nearby caves.

Many Anabaptist leaders died during those bloody years. But others sprang up to carry the movement forward throughout Europe. In 1536, Menno Simons, a former Catholic priest from Holland, joined the Anabaptist movement and became an influential teacher whose followers became known as "Mennists" or "Mennonites."

Toward the end of the century, a Swiss Mennonite named Jakob Ammann took issue with what he viewed as a lack of sufficient discipline of church members who had strayed from their baptism vows. In 1693, Ammann split from the Swiss Mennonite church. His followers became known as the "Amish" (pronounced AH-mish).

Continued persecution throughout Europe resulted in the emigration of groups of Anabaptists across the Atlantic to the colony of Pennsylvania, particularly in the early 1700s. For them, William Penn's "Holy Experiment" of religious tolerance offered hope of a life of peace and freedom. So many German-speaking immigrants settled in the south-central area of the state that it became known as Pennsylvania "Deutsch," or "Dutch," Country.

THE AMISH

Over the centuries, immigrants from all over Europe brought their religions and customs to Lancaster County and it continues to be a diverse and constantly evolving area today. All live physically side by side, but the "Old Order" Amish and Mennonites remain separate.

Wonder what those crops you see growing on Amish farms are? The main ones are corn, hay, wheat, tobacco, soybeans, barley, potatoes, and vegetables, along with grasses for livestock.

"Be ye not conformed to the world," says the Bible. The conservative "Old Order" Amish and Mennonites do everything they can to keep the influences of the outside world from influencing their way of worship and their way of life. They even have a separate name for anyone who is not a member of the Amish faith—"English" (or "Englishers").

Within their own communities, the Amish live, work, and worship as a tightly knit unit. Every aspect of their lives is governed by a set of rules called the *Ordnung* ("order"). This code of ethics is not written down; rather, it is learned from childhood through the behaviors, activities, and rituals of the daily and ceremonial life of the community.

Separation means that, although an "Old Order" Amish man may serve as a leader in his church (ministers are selected by a drawing of lots), he cannot run for or hold a public office. Participation in public affairs violates the basic principles of separation of church and state and of the Amish community from the rest of the world. (They do, however, pay the same taxes as everyone else, with the exception of Social Security and workers' compensation, from which self-employed Amish individuals are exempt.)

It may seem odd that in a country where individuality is so prized the Amish live according to a code that places such emphasis on obedience to God and yielding to the general will of the community. The German word *Gelassenheit* is often used to describe this submission of self. While this way of life may seem foreign and even harsh to outsiders, to the Amish it is a means of preserving a culture that is based on humility and brotherhood, in which neighbors and generations take care of one another. For example, if a neighbor has a fire, the community gets together at a barn raising to help rebuild. When one member is ill or disabled, other community members immediately pitch in to help with chores and, if necessary, finances.

Any perception of the Amish life as all work and no play would not be correct. It's

If you see a lot of celery growing in an Amish family's garden in the spring, you can bet there's a future bride living there. In Amish tradition, the parents of a bride-to-be plant hundreds of extra stalks of celery to prepare for their daughter's fall wedding feast (Tuesdays and Thursdays in November and December, after the harvest, are prime times for nuptials out here). At the reception, celery is served raw, creamed, and in the dressing for the chicken, and jars of leafy stalks may even decorate the table in lieu of flowers.

just that these people have learned to combine fun with function. Sometimes a frolic is gender-specific, as is the case when women get together for a day of quilting, canning, or baking (these occasions are often referred to as "bees"). Men may form a "threshing ring" to help harvest one another's crops, and all will participate in the building of a new home or school. Such get-togethers offer members a chance to socialize as they work toward a common goal.

Generations remain together, with senior family members living in *Grossdaadi* ("Grandpa") houses on the farm and continuing their active roles in the work, social, and religious activities of the community. Programs such as Social Security, Medicare, Medicaid, and other public subsidy programs administered by the government are totally opposite to the self-sufficiency that characterizes the Amish community.

Kraybill points out that, while an estimated 85 percent of the Amish adhere to Old Order traditions and beliefs, there are actually four different groups within the Amish faith. Like their "Old Order" neighbors, "New Order" Amish dress plainly, use horses and buggies as their primary mode of transportation, and hold their worship services in one another's homes. However, this group will use electricity and tele-

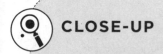
Mind the Sign

Along the back roads of Pennsylvania Dutch Country, you'll often see yellow diamond-shaped signs with a black horse-and-buggy silhouette in the middle. These are more than quaint reminders of a bygone era when traffic was slower paced. They're serious reminders that, in this part of the world, it often still is.

Horse-drawn buggies remain the primary transportation for Amish families, and you'll often see them interspersed with car and bus traffic on area roads. It's important for visitors to remember that these horse-drawn vehicles travel at top speeds of 5 to 8 miles per hour, so, if you're traveling behind one, give it lots of leeway.

Only pass where road markings indicate (never on a curve, when you can't clearly see in front of you). Horses are usually used to traffic, but they can still be spooked by honking horns and gunning motors.

Although many of the Amish regard flashing lights, headlights, and red and yellow reflective safety triangles as gaudy, they abide by state law to display these warning signals at night. However, a report by the Ohio Department of Transportation (the largest Amish population in the world is located in Holmes, Ohio) found that more than half of all buggy/motor vehicle accidents occur in the daylight. At least 60 percent are caused by cars following too closely. So give the buggy drivers plenty of road, and if you slow down, you'll see much more of the beautiful countryside.

For Amish families, horse-drawn buggies are still the primary means of transportation. PENNSYLVANIA DUTCH CONVENTION & VISITORS BUREAU

phones in their homes and modern farming equipment, including tractors, in their fields. The two other Amish subdivisions, the "Beachy Amish" (named for Bishop Moses M. Beachy of Somerset, Pennsylvania, in 1927) and Amish Mennonites (whose beliefs and customs are influenced by both the Amish and Mennonites), are permitted to drive cars, have telephones, and use electricity.

Capes and Caps

The Amish do not wear dark colors because they are a somber people. Again, one of the major reasons they dress in "Plain" style is to emphasize their separateness. Modesty is another.

Adult "Old Order" Amish women wear one-piece, solid-colored dresses (conservative Mennonite women may wear fine prints, according to the Goods) fastened in the front with straight pins or snaps. But they don't always have to be black; they may also wear gray, blue, green, purple, or wine. Skirts are full rather than fitted, hemlines always cover the knees, and a triangular cape covers the bodice of the dress.

According to Amish law, women must not cut their hair; most adults twist it into a bun at the nape of the neck. From infancy, females are expected to keep their heads covered at all times, and the most common covering is the *kapp*, a linen or organdy cap in black or white, depending upon age, marital status, and context (at home, in a social situation, at worship services, etc.).

Men wear straight-cut coats, "broadfall" pants (no hip pockets or zippers) held up by suspenders, and solid-colored shirts, vests, and plain suit coats without lapels. Shirts may have buttons, but vests and suit coats are usually held closed with hook-and-eye fasteners.

After marriage, men grow their beards long but keep their upper lip clean-shaven because, to the Amish, a mustache is a symbol of the European military. Broad-

brimmed black wool or felt hats cover their heads in winter, straw hats in summer. Neither the women nor the men wear any jewelry.

Language

English is learned at school and spoken with non-Amish neighbors and others outside the immediate community. Religious services are held in High German. Among themselves, they speak a German dialect that has come to be known as "Deitsch," "Pennsylvania German," or "Pennsylvania Dutch."

One-Room Schoolhouse

Like all other citizens of Lancaster County, the Plain People pay school taxes, even though they don't use the public schools anymore. Until the 1950s, the Amish and Mennonite children did attend public schools, but state consolidation of small country schools, the introduction of subjects such as sex education and evolution, and other activities that focused on "worldly" pursuits prompted parents to withdraw their children and set up their own system.

Today, formal education is conducted in one-room schoolhouses and goes up to eighth grade. About 30 pupils attend school at any given time. Teachers are members of the community who have also been educated in the Amish system.

Subjects are selected according to their practical application to adult life. In his book *Amish Society*, author and minority group researcher John A. Hostetler explains that basic subjects usually consist of English (including reading, grammar, spelling, penmanship, and some composition), arithmetic, health, history, and geography. Some schools may substitute agriculture for history and geography. For-

Amish children attend class in one-room schoolhouses through eighth grade. PENNSYLVANIA DUTCH CONVENTION & VISITORS BUREAU

mal religious teaching is saved for the home.

After years of discussion and debate, in 1972 the U.S. Supreme Court exempted the Amish and other related groups from state compulsory attendance laws beyond the eighth grade. As Supreme Court Chief Justice Warren E. Burger said:

> *The Amish have a legitimate reason for removing their children from school prior to their attending high school. The qualities emphasized in higher education (self-distinction, competitiveness, scientific accomplishment, etc.) are contrary to Amish values. Additionally, attendance in high school hinders the Amish community by depriving them of the labor of their children and limiting their ability to instill appropriate values in their adolescents. A state's interest in universal education must be balanced against the legitimate claims of special groups of people.*

Amish and Mennonite sects that are not "Old Order" usually choose to send their children to public or their own schools. Many young people attend high school and go on to college.

The Amish and Technology

In today's world, technology often determines how we live our daily lives. Not so for the Amish. That doesn't mean that they automatically reject every new innovation. For them, every technological advance requires a great deal of examination to determine how and to what degree it might fit in with—or disrupt—the community's overall lifestyle.

Take automobiles, for example. According to Amish law, members may not have a driver's license let alone own, drive, or finance a car. However, they are permitted to ride in cars, vans, and buses owned by nonmembers and often rent drivers (often non-Amish neighbors who refer to themselves as "Amish taxis"). But horse and buggy continues to be the premier mode of transportation.

Far from being a contradiction, this example demonstrates how technology can be integrated into Amish life on a limited basis. Because the church prohibits car ownership, there is no concern about the division of the community into haves and have-nots. The difficulty of long-distance horse-and-buggy travel also serves to keep members close to home.

Telephones have also found a place in Amish life, even though they are still not allowed in the home. Members are permitted to use public or community-owned telephones (often housed in sheds or shanties) for a variety of purposes, including business, medical emergencies, and contacting family members who live in distant areas. Social chatting is not encouraged for fear that it will replace face-to-face communication.

Whenever possible and practical, the Amish continue to use waterwheels and windmills to power their homes, farms, and businesses. You won't see them plugging into public electric power lines, but, for certain purposes such as running milking machines and cooling units (required by state sanitation laws) or providing power to operate a home-based craft, produce, or other business, they may use diesel-powered generators.

Other acceptable alternative fuels are bottled gas for heating water and natural gas or kerosene lanterns for lighting.

Worship

Unlike most Christian sects, the Amish do not worship in churches, nor do they meet every Sunday.

Congregations are determined by "church districts," each of which is comprised of about 30 or 35 families living within close geographical proximity to one

To accommodate worshippers, special "bench wagons" transport portable seating from house to house as it is needed.

another. This proximity is important because worship services are held in the district members' homes every other Sunday. (Alternate Sundays are for visiting friends and family.) Responsibility for hosting the service rotates among the families in the district.

Whether or not worship services are scheduled, there is no business conducted on Sundays. Services generally last over three hours and include hymns sung from the *Ausbund*, a 900-page book rooted in 16th-century Germany. Historians believe it is the oldest Protestant hymnbook in continuous use. The *Ausbund* is written as poems, with no musical notation. The melodies are simply passed down orally through the generations.

Keeping the faith is the number one concern of the Amish church, so those who stray from its precepts know that they must answer for their indiscretions. First, they are encouraged to repent before the church.

If all other attempts fail, the church will administer what is considered its harshest punishment—the *bann* ("ban"). Translated from the German, a *bann* is the excommunication of a congregant. Once a *bann* is issued, the individual may attend worship services but must leave right after. He or she may not participate in other community activities or dine at the same table as other church members, even family. This practice of avoiding an excommunicated individual is known as *Meidung*, or "shunning."

For people whose lives are so bound up in community, losing the sense of belonging, even temporarily, can be devastating. And, in most cases, the *bann is* temporary. Excommunicated individuals can—and usually eventually do—repent. When they do, the *bann* is lifted, shunning ceases, and they are welcomed back to community life.

CLOSE-UP

Rumspringa

Just because the "Old Order" Amish choose to separate themselves from the rest of the world doesn't mean they have no experience with it. From the age of 16 until they choose to be (or not to be) baptized, youngsters are given the opportunity to "flirt with the world," as Donald Kraybill, author of *The Riddle of Amish Culture*, describes the tradition known as rumspringa, or the "running around years."

During rumspringa, boys and girls join "gangs," social groups that may include over 100 of their peers from various church districts. Each gang has a distinctive personality and determines its own activities. Some like to enjoy sports and dances, others take their freedom further by shucking their "Plain" clothes and hairstyles. Some boys even buy cars to transport them to places they've never seen and are not likely to see again after rumspringa.

In 2002, rumspringa came to the forefront of national controversy with the release of a documentary by filmmaker Lucy Walker entitled *Devil's Playground*. In the film, Amish youngsters talk about some of the extreme behavior—including drug use, drinking, and sexual activity—that they and some of their peers experienced during rumspringa.

For many "Old Order" Amish, rumspringa remains an important tradition. Non-Amish people may assume that tasting the temptations of the outside world will lure great numbers of Amish young people from the "Plain" life. The reality is quite the contrary. Over the past 20 years the Amish population has actually doubled, according to the Pennsylvania Dutch Convention and Visitors Bureau. Some of this growth can be attributed to average family sizes of 7 to 10 children, but, just as important, it seems that people who are born Amish usually choose to remain Amish. The general consensus among experts is that between 80 and 90 percent of the young people opt for baptism, despite the fact that there is no threat of shunning if they don't.

Photographs

Ironically, the modes of dress, transportation, education, work, and religious practice that are supposed to separate the Amish from the rest of the world are also the things that pique the curiosity of tourists from all over the world. But, while these people may be almost irresistibly photogenic, they (children included) really don't want to be part of your vacation scrapbook. Some visitors have been known to offer money or other bribes for photo opportunities. Others have snapped away in secret. Neither is polite.

Some experts say that their camera shyness is based on the biblical commandment "Thou shalt not make unto thyself a graven image." Photographs also encroach on their privacy and may be viewed as a violation of their humility-based culture. Whatever their reason, the Pennsylvania Dutch Country Convention and Visitors Bureau offers this basic rule of etiquette: "While you talk and mingle with the Amish, please remember that they are not actors or spectacles, but ordinary people who choose a different way of life. Please respect their privacy and refrain from trespassing on their land or taking photographs."

MENNONITES

Like their Amish counterparts, the Old Order Mennonites wear plain dress, reject the need for higher formal education, and believe in separating themselves from the world outside their religious communities. They use some technology on their farms, and, while many still travel by horse and buggy, some do drive cars. According to Donald Kraybill, a total of 10 percent of the total Mennonite population is Old Order. Another group of Mennonites, the "Conservatives," put fewer restrictions on technology for agriculture or business, allowing telephones and electricity (but still eschewing some modern marvels such as computers, the Internet, and video games). About two thirds of total Mennonites are "Assimilated" or "Contemporary," embracing modern dress; technology, including television and computers; higher education (there are some Mennonite-run universities in the United States); and interaction with the rest of the world.

THE BRETHREN

German-born Alexander Mack Sr. led another Anabaptist group out of Europe to escape religious persecution in the 1700s, coming to Pennsylvania at the invitation of William Penn. Unlike other Christian sects, including the Amish and Mennonites, who all used a sprinkling or pouring of water during the rite of baptism, Mack and his followers strongly

After Amish worship services, members usually congregate for a light meal. This sweet spread is often found on the table accompanied by freshly baked bread.

AMISH PEANUT BUTTER OR CHURCH SPREAD
1/2 cup creamy peanut butter
1/4 cup Marshmallow Fluff or other marshmallow cream
1 cup light corn syrup (or molasses)
In a mixing bowl, stir all the ingredients together until combined. Place in a covered container. Store in refrigerator. Bring to room temperature to serve as a bread spread or ice cream topper. Makes about 1 1/2 cups.

believed in "baptism by trine immersion," meaning that the ceremony involved three immersions in water to symbolize the Father, the Son, and the Holy Spirit. Although formally known as the German Baptist Brethren, the practice of trine immersion earned Mack's group the nickname of "Dunkers," or "Dunkards."

In those early days, the German Baptist Brethren shared the plain dress code of their Anabaptist neighbors. But as the group grew and spread out, the members became more assimilated in their clothing; in their acceptance of technology, including automobiles and electricity; and in their encouragement of higher education (Elizabethtown College in Lancaster County is a Brethren-operated liberal arts school).

However, another group of Brethren, founded around 1800 by Swiss Mennonite refugees John and Jacob Engel, has maintained the plain garb of its ancestors. This group, which settled in the northwestern section of Lancaster County on the banks of the Susquehanna River near the town of Marietta, became known as the "River Brethren in Christ." Today the members of this church, now known as Brethren in Christ, continue in the Plain tradition.

CITIES, TOWNS, VILLAGES, AND BACK ROADS

I t's easy to get lost in Pennsylvania Dutch Country, not because the directional signage isn't good, but because of the many bends in the road that constantly beckon you off the beaten track. Go ahead; put away the map and just follow the gentle hills and curves through tiny towns and villages, each with a history and character all its own. Stop off, take a stroll, don't worry about what you might be missing somewhere up the road. Most of these places have been here for more than a hundred years. Whenever you get there, they'll be waiting.

LANCASTER CITY

When it comes to longevity, Lancaster City holds the record, at least the official one as the nation's oldest inland city "founded" in 1730. But long before the first Europeans set foot here, this area was settled by the Susquehannock and other First Nation Native American tribes. Sometime around 1709, the first "Deutsch" (German) immigrants settled in the south-

---

> *Lancaster is known as "The Red Rose City," a nickname that actually has its roots in the 15th-century War of the Roses in England. During that long-ago struggle for the English throne, the two contenders—the Houses of Lancaster and York—both had roses as their emblems. The House of Lancaster's was red, York's was white. (York, about 25 miles from Lancaster, calls itself "The White Rose City.")*

---

central part of William Penn's colony bounded by the Susquehanna River on its north and west, naming the area "Hickory Town" for its groves of trees.

Later, prominent citizen John Wright suggested that the name be changed to "Lancaster" after the place in England where he formerly lived. From the mid-1700s through the early 1800s, Lancaster was the largest inland city in America. It served as a major munitions center during the Revolutionary War and was the capital city of the American colonies for one day—September 27, 1777—and was the capital of Pennsylvania from 1799 to 1812 (at that time it was reputed to have "taverns without number and numerous houses of worship").

Much of the activity in Lancaster centers on Penn Square, with its easily recognizable Soldiers and Sailors Monument that dates to 1874. One block west of the square is the nation's oldest operating theater, the Fulton Opera House, built in 1852 and named for inventor Robert Fulton, a native son who built the first proficient steamboat, the *Clermont*. A National Historic Landmark Theater, the Fulton hosted such performers as the Barrymores, Sarah Bernhardt, and Al Jolson. The venue continues to offer a range of classical and modern dramatic, comedic, and musical productions and is home to the Lancaster Symphony Orchestra.

ADAMSTOWN

Any town that promotes itself as "Antiques Capital USA" had better have the collectibles to back up its claim.

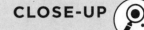

CLOSE-UP

Lancaster City Firsts

- After an unsuccessful first try—lasting only a few months—in Utica, New York, Frank Winfield Woolworth opened a first "five-cent store" in downtown Lancaster in 1879. Profits on opening day were $127. By 1911, Woolworth's concept—by now expanded to the "five and dime" price range—had spawned more than 1,000 stores.

- In 1859, Lancaster-born scientist, inventor, and aeronaut John Wise attempted the first airmail delivery via hot air balloon, ascending from Lafayette, Indiana, with a sack of official U.S. mail that included 123 letters and 23 pamphlets. He had hoped to take his special delivery all the way to New York City but had to land about 25 miles away from his launch point due to technical difficulties. But the U.S. Post Office honored him with a special commemorative stamp 100 years later anyway. (Wise also was the first to observe "the great river of air which always blows from east to west" in higher regions of the atmosphere—what we call the jet stream. He also invented the para-

chutists' best friend, the rip cord.) A monument to Wise stands at the corner of North Lime and East Marion Streets in Lancaster.

- Renowned chocolatier Milton Hershey—who would later found his own eponymous manufacturing town nearby—apprenticed for four years with a Lancaster candy maker. After failed attempts at establishing his own business in Philadelphia, Chicago, and New York, he opened his first successful operation, the Lancaster Caramel Company, here in 1883.

- The Hamilton Watch Company in Lancaster introduced the Ventura, the world's first battery-operated or electric wrist watch, in 1957 and Pulsar, the world's first digital watch, in 1979.

- Also close by is America's oldest publicly owned, continuously operating farmers' market, built in 1889 (the site itself was used as a market as far back as the 1730s). The Central Market is a great place to check out the local ingredients and characteristic cuisine.

Adamstown definitely does. More than 5,000 dealers in all manner of items ranging from the reminiscent to the rare, from the 18th through 20th centuries, line the "Adamstown Antique Mile," which runs north and south along Route 272, a short way from the Route 286 exit of the Pennsylvania Turnpike.

Originally named "Addamsburry" after William Addams, who developed its layout in 1761, the town first became associated

with antiques in the early 1960s, when a local dealer named Charles Wiek began holding outdoor flea markets in a lovely wooded area called Shupp's Grove on Sundays during the summer. These events attracted a tremendous amount of attention from sellers and buyers, many of whom hauled their wares from other states for the Sunday sales. In the mid-1960s, Terry Heilman, manager of a local farmers' market called Renningers and a regular at

Shupp's Grove, recognized the potential of turning the area into a year-round antiques marketplace and began offering sellers an indoor venue where they could continue their operations throughout the colder seasons.

The transformation of Renningers summer farmers' market into a four-season antiques market inspired other similar enterprises, including one opened in 1971 by restaurateur/antique aficionado Ed Stoudt in the basement of his Black Angus steakhouse.

Since then, Stoudt's resulting "antiques mall" has grown to house 500 dealers. A second building called Clock Tower Antique Center, built in the complex that operates under the umbrella name of Stoudtburg, features dealers in approximately 100 showcase settings plus 10 individual shops.

As time went on, other antiques dealers got together to form co-ops, where each operates a separate open booth, and showcase shops, in which items are displayed in glass cases. Dealers specializing in a particular genre, era, or item have also opened individual shops along the "Mile." Many of these operations are open seven days a week.

Three times a year, the town teems with thousands of collectors looking for the ultimate find at weekend-long "Antique Extravaganzas."

AKRON

In Greek, the word *akros* means "a high place." But it was German immigrants who were the first Europeans to settle here in the late 1700s. They originally named the area "New Berlin" but changed it to Akron in the early 1800s in recognition of its position at the highest point of the Ohio & Erie Canal.

During the course of its history, Akron has been a center for cigar making (in the 1880s, close to half of the town's population was involved in this industry, and one of the major streets is still called Tobacco

Road). In the early 1900s, leather shoes became the staple of the area's economy.

Today, Akron's major employer is the Mennonite Central Committee (MCC), which is a globally involved relief, service, and peace agency. Each year, the MCC raises more than $61 million from donations, grants, and sales at its thrift stores.

BIRD-IN-HAND

Legend has it that sometime in the 1730s, after a day of working on the layout of the Old Philadelphia Pike (Route 340) between Lancaster and Philadelphia, two road surveyors were debating about whether to spend the night at a nearby inn or continue on to find accommodations in Lancaster. "A bird in the hand is worth two in the bush," one of the men was said to have reasoned.

What is known for a fact is that once the Old Philadelphia Pike became the "gateway to the West" for stagecoaches and Conestoga wagons, inns began popping up every few miles along the way to provide overnight accommodations to travelers en route to and beyond the Allegheny Mountains. Because many of these travelers were recent immigrants from Europe whose command of the English language might range from minimal to nonexistent (and even the native-born wagon drivers usually did not have the education to read well), innkeepers needed to use signage that would be universally understood.

Most used hand-painted pictures, including one inn along the Old Philadelphia Pike that featured on its sign a rendering of a man with a bird in his hand and a bush nearby in which two birds were perched. By 1734, the "Bird-in-Hand Inn," as it came to be called, was a popular stop, so popular, in fact, that the village that grew up around it took the name as well.

Technically, Bird-in-Hand is a village rather than a town, because it has no governing body. Historians have traced the native population to the Shawnee and Conestoga tribes through unearthed artifacts such as tomahawks and arrowheads. English Quakers and Swiss Mennonites were among the Europeans who settled here, but, as in much of this area of Pennsylvania, the predominant culture and the one that still colors the life of the village today is German ("Deutsch").

Travelers on the still-busy Route 340, today's name for the Old Philadelphia Pike, still take their rest at the 18th-century brick inn, now listed on the National Register of Historic Places and renamed the Village of Bird-in-Hand Inn & Suites. The village bustles with commerce and tourists but still offers a number of old-fashioned pleasures, including a farmers' market with more than 25 stands filled with locally produced bakery items, fruits and vegetables, candies, smoked meats and cheeses, jams and jellies, relishes, and handicrafts.

BLUE BALL

Blue Ball's the kind of little town where the local fire company raises funds with $5.00 all-you-can-eat community breakfasts, $10.00 ham suppers, and Christmas tree and fruitcake sales. Situated at the intersection of Routes 23 and 322 in eastern Lancaster County, this quiet farming community was settled by Welsh immigrants, followed by Germans.

Probably what intrigues visitors most about Blue Ball is its name. The *blue* probably originated from natural springs that were so abundant that they inspired the Native American tribes who came to the area to call it "Blue Google," meaning gurgling or running waters. In later years, settlers would build their homes over these springs so they could have water available inside. The *ball* part came much later, probably around 1766, when a hotel was built to the landscape. Its distinctive identifying mark? A large copper ball painted blue.

COLUMBIA

A drive along the Susquehanna River in the western part of Lancaster County will reveal yet another facet of Pennsylvania Dutch Country personality. Not part of prime tourist territory, this gentle little borough on Route 30 still has its share of attractions, from the natural to the historically notable.

Established more than 260 years ago by English Quakers, including John Wright, an innovator whose transportation enterprise gave the area its original name of Wright's Ferry, Columbia's British-inspired architecture and overall flavor are epitomized in the 18th-century mansion built by Wright's daughter Susanna. With its laid-back attitude, it may be hard to envision this town as a hotbed of Civil War activity. But it was a key "stop" on the Underground Railroad, and its population activists who, on June 28, 1863, burned down their own bridge—then the longest covered bridge in the world—to halt the easterly advance of Confederate troops to Philadelphia.

Some of the area's most dramatic scenery can be found in Chickies Rock County Park, Lancaster County's second-largest regional park that stretches between Columbia and its riverside neighbor to the north, Marietta. Chickies Rock itself is a massive outcropping of quartzite that soars 200 feet above the river, making it a magnet for adventure-seeking rock climbers and a destination for view-seeking visitors.

Other unique sights can be found inside Columbia's museums, particularly the Watch and Clock Museum, featuring a collection of more than 8,000 timepieces that spans the globe and more than four centuries, and the 1850s First National Bank Museum, the only known bank in the United States still preserved in its original setting. You can also watch artisans hand cut designs of function and fantasy from crystal at the Susquehanna Glass Factory, just as they have been doing for three generations.

ELIZABETHTOWN

Located in northwestern Lancaster County, Elizabethtown was established as a trading post called the Bear Tavern in 1730. Twenty-three years later, it was renamed by new owner Barnabas Hughes, an immigrant from County Donegal, Ireland, in honor of his wife, Elizabeth. When modern roads paved the way between Lancaster and Harrisburg, Elizabethtown, conveniently located along a major turnpike, continued to grow as a hub of commerce.

In 1899, the area also became a center of education with the opening of Elizabethtown College by members of the Church of the Brethren, an Anabaptist organization with origins in Germany. Today, the college offers 45 majors and more than 60 minors/concentrations in the humanities, arts and sciences, and professional disciplines.

EPHRATA

The name, derived from the Bible, means "fruitful," and the 18th century Cloister at Ephrata, founded in 1732, did produce prodigious amounts of original art and music, particularly in the 1740s and 1750s, when about 300 members worked and worshipped here. But life inside the medieval-looking walls of this religious community in northeastern Lancaster County was based on asceticism, with the Brothers and Sisters eschewing even the basic comforts for benchlike beds of hard wood with wooden block "pillows." A

National Historical Landmark, the Cloister is open to the public for tours.

From the ascetic to the abundant, Ephrata is also home to the renowned Green Dragon Farmers' Market, where more than 400 local growers, merchants, and crafters have come every Friday since 1932 to display their wares.

INTERCOURSE

Following the common practice in the area, this town, founded in 1754 11 miles east of Lancaster, took its early name, Cross Keys, from the symbol on a local tavern sign. The origin of Intercourse, the eyebrow-raising moniker it adopted 60 years later, is not quite so certain.

One explanation centers on the town's location at the intersection—or intercourse—of two famous roads, the King's Highway (now Old Philadelphia Pike/Route 340) and the Old Newport Road (now Route 772). The raciest story suggests that the name may have derived from "Entercourse," what the locals called the long stretch of road that led to the entrance to a race track just east of town. A third possibility is that in the early 19th century the word intercourse was to describe everyday social *interaction*, and that this area was the center of local life.

Even though all three of its possible origins are totally innocent, the name *Intercourse* does get people's attention. But it's the town's innate charm that makes it a definite "must-visit" part of any Pennsylvania Dutch tour.

If you're looking for a good introduction to the Amish and Mennonite beliefs, lifestyles, and cultures, visit the People's Place to view its long-running documentary, *Who Are the Amish?*, and its interactive "20 Questions" discovery museum. In the multimedia production *Jacob's Choice* at the Amish Experience Center, you can follow one young man's experience as he wrestles with the decision of whether to accept baptism into his family's faith or break away for a new life in the modern world.

---

i *Noodledoosie may not be an easy place to find on any map, but it's definitely a hard name to forget. According to the Landis Valley Museum in Lancaster, there have actually been two areas called Noodledoosie in Pennsylvania Dutch Country, and one still exists not far from Ephrata.*

The name "Intercourse" often induces giggles from visitors, but the town's charm is what keeps them smiling. PENNSYLVANIA DUTCH CONVENTION & VISITORS BUREAU

LITITZ

When it was founded in 1756, only members of the Moravian Church could live in Lititz, a small town located along Pennsylvania Route 501 about 7 miles north of Lancaster City. The Moravian church, quite possibly the oldest organized Protestant sect, was founded by the followers of European religious reformer John Hus in ancient Bohemia and Moravia (now the Czech Republic) in the year 1467, 60 years before Martin Luther began his reformation and 100 years before the establishment of the Anglican Church.

In 1756, a local farmer donated more than 490 acres of farmland to the Moravian Church to begin a religious community after hearing one of its missionaries, Count Zizendorf, preach. Zizendorf named the area "Lititz" (or "Litiz," its early German

spelling) after Lidice Nad Citadelou, a castle in the eastern part of the current Czech Republic that provided refuge to persecuted Moravians. The Lititz Moravian Church, built in 1787, still stands on Moravian Square on Main Street.

When the town was opened to outsiders in 1856, it attracted settlers from around the country. One of its most famous residents was General John Augustus Sutter, founder of Sacramento, whose land became the epicenter of the California Gold Rush. In 1871, Sutter built a home here, and in 1880 he was buried in the Moravian Cemetery nearby, even though he was a Lutheran.

Lititz is one of those towns you could find with your eyes closed. That's because of the sweet scent that emanates from the Wilbur Candy Americana Museum and Store on North Broad Street. Inside, you'll

CLOSE-UP

Auld Lang Syne

In New York City, the dropping of a huge lighted ball marks the stroke of midnight on New Year's Eve. But some Pennsylvania Dutch Country towns and villages have their own novel notions of celebration.

Lancaster, which adopted the red rose as its symbol hundreds of years ago, commemorates the moment with the raising of one big blossom (actually a 6-foot-tall rose replica) in the middle of the town square.

Elizabethtown, which owes its chocolate-scented breezes to its M&M/Mars manufacturing plant, sends a gigantic version of the colorful candy sailing down into its Center Square.

Harrisburg "drops" an 8-foot-high lighted strawberry from a downtown highrise (the shopping mall across from the State Capitol building is called Strawberry Square).

Hummelstown (in Dauphin County, between Hershey and Harrisburg) lowers a 9-foot-high lollipop.

see artisans hand-dipping chocolates just as they did when the factory first opened in 1865, and you can still buy the company's famous Wilbur Buds (melt-in-your-mouth morsels that predated the Hershey Kiss by 14 years).

A couple of blocks away on East Main Street is the Sturgis Pretzel House, where Julius Sturgis opened the first commercial bakery in the United States. The original recipe treats are still hand-twisted and baked in the facility's 200-year-old ovens.

At the head of East Main Street is Lititz Springs Park, first landscaped by the Moravians in the 1700s and maintained as a public park for residents and visitors to play and picnic. This lovely spot (recognized by the American Society of Landscape Architects for its beauty) is the epitome of small-town understatement except on the Fourth of July, when thousands of candles are lit along the stream and fireworks color the skies to the strains of classical music. Begun in 1843, Lititz Springs Park's Independence Day shindig is the oldest continuing celebration in the nation.

MANHEIM

Although this tract of land in northern Lancaster County was originally presented as a gift in 1734 to William Penn's secretary, James Logan, by Penn's widow, Hannah, and her sons, its beginnings as a town are actually credited to three German businessmen who purchased it 28 years later. One of these men was iron master-turned-glassmaker Henry William Stiegel, who would make Manheim (named after the town of Mannheim in Germany) his manufacturing center from 1764 to 1775.

A colorful man who lived an elaborate lifestyle, Stiegel was nicknamed "Baron" by his neighbors, which explains why he is often referred to in writings and discussions as Baron Von Stiegel. And while his glasshouse may have lasted only a little over a decade, Stiegel achieved fame by building schools to educate his workers' children and by giving the local Lutheran congregation ground on which to build a church "for five shillings" and annually in the month of June the rent of "One Red Rose." To this day, congregants at the Zion Lutheran Church in Manheim dutifully "pay" that same rent to a descendant of Henry Stiegel at the town's Festival of the Red Rose.

On Tuesdays, Root's Market & Auction, the oldest single-family-run market in the county, continues its 80-year tradition of displaying the edible, wearable, and otherwise desirable grown and made by local producers. There's a produce auction plus more than 200 stands for browsing and buying.

MARIETTA

Back in the early 19th century, the building of the Pennsylvania Canal and Railroad brought commerce and growth to Susquehanna River towns such as this one in western Lancaster County, which took its early name, Anderson's Ferry, from a local family's enterprise. In 1812 a member of that same family combined the names of his two daughters, Mary and Henrietta, and redubbed the town Marietta.

Prosperous residents built many homes and mansions in the grand Colonial, Federal, and Victorian architectural styles. Their owners entertained lavishly, providing high-class hospitality to the era's rich and famous, including U.S. presidents Grant and Cleveland.

Fortunately, these majestic abodes proved to be sturdy enough to withstand the passing years, even as the local economy's momentum stalled with the dwindling of river trade. Even Hurricane Agnes, which blew through in June 1972, couldn't destroy the structures, but the storm and the federal disaster relief funds that followed did spark a major restoration effort that continues today.

With a rejuvenated spirit and 45 percent of the town officially designated as a National Historic District, Marietta proudly displays its preserved treasures. One favorite stop in this area is Le Petit Museum of Musical Boxes, a magical collection of antiques housed in a late-18th/early-19th-century Federal town house.

MAYTOWN

Just north of Marietta along the Susquehanna River is another small residential area where preservation is prized. In Maytown, the architecture ranges from Colonial-era log cabins to 19th-century structures made from locally produced brick.

Founded on the first day of May in 1760 by a German Mennonite couple, the 150-acre village became an important fur-trading center populated initially by Scottish-Irish immigrants, but later and most predominantly by German settlers.

MOUNT JOY

It's not situated on a mountain, so don't call it *Mt.* Joy. The Scottish-Irish Presbyterians who settled in this area in western Lancaster County in the 1730s actually took the name from Englishman Lord Mountjoy, who served under Queen Elizabeth I.

Tucked throughout this tranquil residential town are restorations that allow visitors to experience the life and times of centuries past. For example, President McKinley's great-grandfather found the countryside around Mount Joy to be such an appealing rural retreat that, in 1805, he built a mansion there. That painstakingly preserved mansion (it's listed on the National Register of Historic Places), set on 15 acres of lawns, rose gardens, and woodlands, now offers guests a taste of early-19th-century elegance as Cameron Estate Inn Bed and Breakfast.

CLOSE-UP

Underground Railroad

Some called it "Freedom Line," "Lightning Train," "Freedom Train," "the Mysterious Tracks," or "the Trackless Train." Most commonly the network of freed slaves and abolitionists who harbored, guided, and otherwise bucked laws and sympathies to help somewhere between 50,000 and 100,000 slaves escape to freedom between the early 1800s and the end of the Civil War is known as the Underground Railroad. Several of its most traveled "routes" ran through Lancaster County, Pennsylvania.

To aid the escapees, some say local residents would hang quilts in the windows or on backyard clotheslines to send coded messages. For example, a "Bear's Paw" pattern might warn that the area is unsafe, while the black triangles in a "Flying Geese" design might point out a direction to follow.

One of the most active Underground Railroad "stations" in the area was the Bethel African Methodist Episcopal

(A.M.E.) Church in Lancaster City. Every Saturday from February through December, the church presents a production called *Living the Experience,* which tells the story of the Underground Railroad through reenactments and the singing of spirituals that slaves used to guide them along the treacherous paths to freedom.

In Christiana, a town located in the southern part of the county, a bloody clash of Northern and Southern philosophies, which many consider to have been the first battle of the Civil War, was fought on September 11, 1851. The "Christiana Resistance," or the Fugitive Slave Rebellion, ignited when slaveholders from Maryland went to the home of William Parker, a free black man, to retrieve four Underground Railroad escapees.

Parker's refusal to cooperate was viewed as an act of civil disobedience against the Fugitive Slave Act of 1850, which had legalized the pursuit of slaves wherever they fled. An alarm was

Beer lovers can drain a draught or two at Bube's Brewery, one of the only breweries left intact from the 19th-century heyday of German-style lager. Built in 1876 by German immigrant Alois Bube, the single small brewery expanded into a complex of buildings that eventually also incorporated a Victorian hotel to accommodate overnight guests.

After Bube's death in 1908, the brewery continued to produce until around 1917, just prior to Prohibition. His family continued to live in the complex until the 1960s,

changing very little and removing almost nothing. In 1968 restoration efforts began, and in November 2001 Bube's began producing its eponymous microbrews once again, this time in the old icehouse portion of the complex. (The pretty Beirgarten at Bube's and the Victorian hotel bar in its white-tablecloth venture Alois are perfect places to enjoy the old-style new brews in authentic surroundings. Alois is also renowned for its Martini Bar, for aficionados who crave variations on that particular cocktail.)

The Bethel African Methodist Episcopal (A.M.E.) Church was a center of antislavery activity during the Civil War. PENNSYLVANIA DUTCH CONVENTION & VISITORS BUREAU

sounded, bringing neighbors running to Parker's aid. The ensuing struggle left one of the slave owners dead and prompted the federal government to send in troops to investigate. Thirty-seven men were arrested and charged with treason, but at a trial in which they were represented by famed abolitionist Thaddeus Stevens, they were declared not guilty.

For further information about Lancaster County's role in the Underground Railroad, a free map and guide are available at www.lancasterheritage.com.

PARADISE

Some people spend their entire lives looking for Paradise; Pennsylvania Dutch country folk know it's right here along Route 30 east of Lancaster. A pretty place set beside the Pequea Creek, the town is believed to have taken its name from early-19th-century mapmaker Joshua Scott, who is said to have suggested it because the beauty of the surrounding farm country made it "seem like a paradise."

Others believe the name came from Mary Fierre (also spelled Ferree), a French Huguenot who, along with her son Daniel and his family, found sanctuary here in 1712 from the religious persecution that had driven her from her European homeland. The Fierres were believed to have been among the first 5,000 of 150,000 Huguenots to arrive in America.

A third theory credits David Witmer, a wealthy business and community leader as well as reputed friend of George Washington, for choosing the name later in the

Railroad aficionados should make tracks to Strasburg. STRASBURG RAIL ROAD

century. The same legend goes on to point out that other members of Witmer's family disapproved, preferring either Pequea, after the nearby creek, or Tanawa, in honor of a local Native American chief.

Even if Witmer didn't do the naming, he did establish a little piece of Paradise in the form of his circa 1781 home, now the Creekside Inn B&B. Another idyllic spot was a former tavern and stagecoach overnight stop along the Philadelphia-to-Lancaster turnpike route called the Sign of the Spread Eagle in the mid-18th century, now known as the Revere Tavern. A Paradise dining institution, the building was the home of the Reverend Edward V. Buchanan and his wife, Eliza Foster Buchanan, sister of "Oh, Susannah!" com-

poser Stephen Foster. Foster is believed to have written some of his most memorable songs while visiting here.

Later, the building was purchased by Buchanan's brother James, the 15th president of the United States. Today, guests can dine in the original tavern, built in 1740, and spend the night in one of three buildings, including a 1790 farmhouse.

STRASBURG

If the whistle of a steam train is music to your ears, the village of Strasburg in southeastern Lancaster County at the intersection of Routes 896 and 741 is a locomotive lover's dream. America's oldest short-line steam train, the Strasburg Rail Road was founded during the first term of President Andrew Jackson, incorporated by a special Act of the Pennsylvania Legislature in 1832, and had its maiden chug sometime in 1851.

Back then, the 4½-mile track was used to carry passengers and freight. Now it takes riders on a 45-minute trip to Paradise (the town, that is) aboard an authentically restored coal-burning steam train, with a stop for a leisurely lunch in a pretty shaded grove along the way.

Just across the street from the East Strasburg station is the Railroad Museum of Pennsylvania, with more than 100 historic trains and a bonanza of memorabilia of the state's glory days of train travel.

Less than a mile away at the National Toy Train Museum, the locomotives in the five working layouts spanning more than a century may be lilliputian, but they're just as carefully restored.

After your railfest, make tracks for Strasburg's downtown area, where old-time brick sidewalks take you past 18th-century homes, one-of-a-kind shops, and quaint inns and taverns. Founded by French Huguenots but later more prodigiously populated by English and Pennsylvania "Deutsch" who came into the area, it took its name from a French city on the Rhine River. But it didn't always have quite such a melodic moniker: In its early days, Strasburg was better known to locals as Poodlehausie (Beggartown) or Hell's Hole.

GETTYSBURG

It may have been war that brought Gettysburg to the attention of the world, but long before the Union and Confederate troops had their accidental meeting here in July 1863, the peaceful green fields of what is now the center of Adams County in south-central Pennsylvania were home to the Iroquois. In 1736 the family of William Penn purchased the land from the Native Americans. Scottish-Irish and German immigrants who had fled persecution in their homelands came to build their farmsteads in what became known as the Marsh Creek Settlement, named for the waters that flowed through the area.

In 1761 one of these early settlers, Samuel Gettys, established a tavern on part of his 381 acres of the settlement. Following the Revolutionary War, Gettys's middle son, James, purchased 116 of his father's acreage and, by 1786, had laid out a lot around a center square (now known as Lincoln Square, it is still the focal point of the historic downtown district).

By 1806, the area was incorporated as the Borough of Gettysburg. The growing borough's location in the middle of Adams County (itself legislated into being only six years before) made Gettysburg the logical county seat. When Gettysburg was incorporated as a borough there were 80 houses on the tax rolls.

Three years before the fighting of the Civil War came to its fields, Gettysburg had a population of 2,400 residents. It seemed that all roads led into the town—and at least 10 of them actually did. The

Gettysburg Railroad also provided a key link to other towns and other markets.

By the time the battle began, Gettysburg was a lively community with 450 buildings and a number of small businesses in addition to its farms. The meeting between the 97,000-man Army of the Potomac under General George G. Meade and the 75,000-man Army of Northern Virginia led by General Robert E. Lee on the morning of July 1, 1863, was not part of either military force's original strategic plan.

Lee had actually planned to destroy the railroad bridge at Harrisburg, then "turn my attention to Philadelphia, Baltimore, or Washington as may seem best for our interest." As the troops made their way north, brigades were dispatched to neighboring farms and communities to scout for supplies. On July 1 one of Lee's brigades spotted a column of Meade's cavalry on a ridge a mile west of the town of Gettysburg. Meade's troops had been trailing Lee's army as the Confederates headed north. The Union troops' primary mission was to protect the nation's capital from invasion.

Under orders not to engage the Union soldiers, the Confederate brigade reported to their commander, General A. P. Hill, what they had seen. Hill sent out a column to investigate. When a Union cavalry officer at McPherson Ridge spotted the Confederate troops, he fired the first shot, setting off the three-day battle.

Although they were outnumbered, the Union cavalry was able to hold its position and, when reinforcements arrived, even drive the Confederate army back as the morning progressed. However, in the afternoon, additional southern troops arrived and pushed the northern soldiers through the town. Many members of the Union army were captured as they struggled to reach Cemetery Hill, south of town. Those

Throughout Gettysburg, wayside markers tell the stories of historic sites such as Gettys' Homestead (Race Horse Alley), where James Gettys, the town's founder, lived in a log-and-weatherboard building.

who did manage to make it to that rallying point worked far into the night building defenses against the second wave of invasion that would most certainly come the next day.

When July 2 dawned, the two armies faced one another from parallel ridges nearly a mile apart. Union troops stood in a "fish hook" configuration stretching from Culp's Hill to Cemetery Ridge, Confederate forces on Seminary Ridge to the west. That day, sites such as the Peach Orchard, "Bloody Run," the "Devil's Den" at the base of Little Round Top, and Culp's Hill saw much of the fiercest fighting. Although the Union troops had firmly entrenched themselves on East Cemetery Hill and Culp's Hill, the Confederate Army was only a few hundred yards from taking the Union's supply trains—they just didn't know it. During a nighttime assault on Culp's Hill, darkness, confusion, and unceasing musketry fire convinced the southern commander that his force was heavily outnumbered. As a result, he halted his attack to wait for reinforcements.

The struggle for possession of Cemetery Ridge resumed the next afternoon, but the Union army maintained its stronghold. The last major attempt to break the Union lines is known in history by a variety of names. Probably the most accurate of those names is "Longstreet's Grand Assault," because it was actually coordinated by General James Longstreet (albeit reluctantly; he had tried to warn General Robert E. Lee of the futility of this strategy). But the most commonly used designation for this last-ditch battle strategy is "Pickett's Charge," although General George Pickett was only one of the three divisional commanders who were chosen to lead it. (The other two were Generals J. Johnston Pettigrew and Isaac R. Trimble.)

More than 12,000 men made the charge across a mile of open field, under heavy barrage of Union fire. A small number of soldiers reached their goal and partially breached the Union's first line of defense at "The Angle," a low stone wall with a right-hand turn that marked the

When President Lincoln came to town to dedicate the Gettysburg National Cemetery, he made a point to meet the "Hero of Gettysburg," John Burns, a 69-year-old cobbler who, upon hearing the sounds of battle on the morning of July 1, volunteered to join the Union forces. Burns fought with the Seventh Wisconsin regiment, was wounded three times in one day, and recovered after a neighbor brought him home.

northern troop line. This penetration is now known as the "High Water Mark" and is designated by a monument on the field.

Within 50 minutes, about 50 percent of the Confederate soldiers who had begun the charge were dead, wounded, or captured. The next day, July 4, General Robert E. Lee led the Confederate retreat. Over the course of the three-day battle, more than 50,000 soldiers from both sides lost their lives or were wounded, captured, or missing. More men fought and died here than in any other battle ever fought before or since in North America. During the second and third days of fighting, the Confederate army occupied the town of Gettysburg, using its homes, shops, and other buildings as lookout posts, sharpshooters' nests, military headquarters, and hospitals.

Consecrated in 1853 (the present facade was added in the 1920s), Saint Francis Xavier Catholic Church at 42 West High Street housed around 250 wounded soldiers during the Civil War. One of the plaques outside the main entrance honors the Sisters of Charity from Emmitsburg, Maryland (later known as the "Angels of the Battlefield"), who tended wounded soldiers in this and other "hospitals" throughout the town. Inside the church is a stained-glass panel depicting the days following the battle.

At 6 Lincoln Square is the Wills House, where Abraham Lincoln spent the night on November 18, 1863, and polished the second draft of his Gettysburg Address. The house was built in 1814.

Two weeks after the battle, President Lincoln wrote this poem, which he entitled "General Lee's Invasion of the North":

In eighteen sixty three,
with pomp, and mighty swell,
Me and Jeff's Confederacy,
went forth to sack Phil-del,
The Yankees they got arter us,
and giv us particular hell,
And we skedaddled back again,
and didn't sack Phil-del.

To properly bury the soldiers who had died in July's battle, Pennsylvania Governor Andrew Curtin commissioned Gettysburg attorney David Wills to purchase 17 acres of land for a permanent resting place. President Abraham Lincoln was invited to offer "a few appropriate remarks" at the dedication of the Gettysburg National Cemetery on November 19, 1863. Accounts of the day noted that the 272-word, two-minute length of Lincoln's speech so shocked his audience (another speaker at the dedication had already orated for two hours) that there was little initial response at its conclusion. Lincoln, himself, despaired of his Gettysburg Address as "a

Gettysburg National Cemetery is not the only historic resting place in town. Lincoln Cemetery, located on Long Lane, was established in the mid-19th century as an African-American burial site. Of the nearly 400 individuals who are buried here, 30 fought in the Civil War.

flat failure." In a note following the event, the day's other speaker, Edward Everett, put the power of Lincoln's speech into clearer perspective when he wrote, "I should be glad if I could flatter myself that I came as near to the central idea of the occasion in two hours as you did in two minutes."

Gettysburg National Cemetery is the resting place for more than 6,000 honorably discharged servicemen and their dependents from the Civil War, Spanish American War, World Wars I and II, and the Vietnam War.

The battlefield itself was christened Gettysburg National Military Park on February 11, 1895, and dedicated as a memorial of those who fought there. Included in the nearly 6,000-acre park are 26 miles of roads and over 1,400 monuments, markers, and memorials.

But the Civil War was not the only conflict to have an impact on the Gettysburg community. In 1917, Camp Colt was set up adjacent to Emmitsburg Road to train Army Tank Corps troops for battle in World War I. The camp, long gone, but acknowledged with a commemorative tree and marker where it once stood, was commanded by Captain Dwight D. Eisenhower.

Many years later (in 1950), then-President Eisenhower and his wife, Mamie, would purchase the nearby Allen Redding farm adjoining Gettysburg National Military Park. The Eisenhowers expanded the 189-acre farm into a 230-acre estate, which they used as a weekend retreat, meeting place for international leaders, and, from 1961 to 1969, retirement residence. Visitors can tour the Eisenhower National Historic Site, now administered by the National Park Service.

During World War II, a field on the west side of Emmitsburg Road was the site of a compound where 300 German prisoners of war were held for a period of six months in 1944. During their internment, the prisoners worked picking and processing fruit, cutting and milling lumber, and making road and trail improvements in

Adams County. No reminders of this camp remain.

Close to two million people visit Gettysburg National Military Park each year. Located less than two hours' driving time from Washington, D.C., and Baltimore, Maryland, and about two and a half hours from Philadelphia, Gettysburg sits at the crossroads of two national highways, U.S. Route 30 (formerly Lincoln Highway) and Route 5. It is a town where history waits in many of its doorways and around just about every corner.

Although most are not open to the public, many Civil War–era buildings in Gettysburg remain in good condition. These buildings are marked with dated bronze plaques.

Today, the Borough of Gettysburg has a population of a little over 7,890 (the total population of Adams County is 98,322).

HERSHEY

For chocoholics, Hershey is not just a vacation destination, it's a pilgrimage. You won't need a map to know you're there, not when the major intersection of the town is at Chocolate and Cocoa Avenues, the street lamps are shaped like candy Kisses, and an unmistakable sweetness fills the air.

Located in Dauphin County, Hershey's proximity to the state capital of Harrisburg (12 miles to the west) makes it part of Pennsylvania's "Capital Region" (which also includes the city of Carlisle). But its proximity to Lancaster (20 miles to the south) and heritage make it very much Pennsylvania Dutch.

The Township of Derry was incorporated on August 1, 1729, and by 1787 the population of Scottish-Irish, Germans, and Swiss Germans who had migrated to this rural community seeking religious freedom and a livelihood for their families had grown to 198. Today, more than 21,000 people call Derry home, according to the township's Web site (www.derrytownship .org). Hungarian and Italian immigrants plus African Americans from Virginia came later, in the 1800s, to work in the local limestone and brownstone quarries as laborers and stonecutters.

Derry Township was well positioned for trade, with the Horseshoe and Reading Turnpikes (now known as Routes 322 and 422), the Union Canal (which brought together the Schuylkill and Susquehanna Rivers), and the Lebanon Valley Railroad connecting the area to the rest of the state. By 1860 the population of Derry had soared to 2,300.

In 1896 Milton Hershey bought back his family's original homestead in Derry Township and in 1909 made it the first location of his school for orphan boys.

The Hershey family saga in Derry Township began in 1826, when Isaac and Anna Hershey bought 350 acres of local farmland. On September 13, 31 years later, their great-grandson Milton Snavely Hershey was born here to Henry and Veronica ("Fanny") Hershey. Both Henry and Fanny (nee Snavely) were born into Mennonite families. Only Fanny maintained her deep religious ties and the Plain dress of her faith. Henry Hershey, a dreamer, found it hard to settle into any ordered way of life or find a consistent way to produce income to support his family. During Milton's youth, the family moved constantly as Henry pursued one business opportunity after another. In 1877 the family farm had to be sold to pay off the family's debts.

So many moves during the early years of his life meant that he changed schools seven times over his total eight years of formal education. He never went beyond the fourth grade. Instead, in 1871, he was briefly apprenticed to a local printer who published a German-English newspaper, then to a confectioner named Joseph Royer in Lancaster County. After four years with Royer, Milton Hershey decided to open his own candy business in Philadelphia, in 1876, at the age of 18 with $150 borrowed from his aunt, Martha Snavely. It failed.

Hershey moved to Denver, Colorado, to try mining silver with his father. When that didn't "pan" out either, he took a job with a Denver confectioner who taught him how to make caramels using fresh milk (many candy makers at that time were using paraffin to make caramels, so the taste difference amazed Hershey). Taking the process to New York, Hershey tried to break into the candy business on his own again. But even that failure, and the fact that he was 28 years old and virtually penniless, did not stop him from returning to Lancaster for one more try.

In 1886 he opened the Lancaster Caramel Company. Like his other ventures, this one was likely destined for failure because Hershey did not have sufficient capital to make his production volume profitable. Unlike the other times, a British candy importer agreed to market Hershey's caramels abroad, and, with that large order, the Pennsylvania confectioner was able to secure bank financing for expansion. Within four years, Hershey was operating one of the leading caramel manufacturing companies in America and employing about 1,400 people.

Chocolate came into the picture when Hershey visited the 1893 Columbian Exposition in Chicago and decided to purchase some German machinery to produce chocolate coatings for his caramels. He soon began marketing the chocolate itself and at one time was making more than 100 different novelty items. These items were made of "sweet chocolate," which was actually dark chocolate. At that time, only the Swiss knew how to make the lighter and more delicate "milk chocolate," a product so expensive it could only be afforded by the wealthy. Milton Hershey worked for many years to come up with a combination of milk, sugar, and cocoa that could rival the coveted Swiss recipe.

In 1900 he perfected his formula, and the Hershey Bar was born.

That same year, he sold Lancaster Caramel Company to a local competitor for $1 million, so he could concentrate on manufacturing chocolate. Expansion plans for his chocolate company brought him back to Derry Township, which offered a supply of fresh milk from neighboring farms and access to a substantial labor pool. Also available were transportation resources for bringing in raw materials such as cocoa beans and sugar from major ports such as Philadelphia and New York and sending out finished product. Building of the new factory began in 1903 and was completed two years later.

The Derry Church School, one of the many one-room schoolhouses Milton Hershey attended during his early years, sits next to the entrepreneur's High Point Mansion, which he built after his success in the business world.

More than just the factory, Hershey wanted to build a model town in Derry, with well-constructed, affordable homes, a quality public school system, and a variety of recreational and cultural options for his employees.

Although the town that Hershey built never became an incorporated entity (it's still part of Derry Township, and its children attend Derry Township schools), it did have its own post office. To find a name for that post office, Milton Hershey held a contest with a $100 prize. Of the thousands of submissions, the name "Hersheykoko" was chosen, but the U.S. Post Office rejected it on the grounds that it sounded too commercial. In 1906 the post office—and the surrounding town—was simply named Hershey.

In the center of the town, Hershey planned to have a picnic area. Opened in 1907, its amenities, which included a playground, baseball field, and band shell, soon drew visitors from outlying communities as well. In 1908 a merry-go-round was the first actual amusement ride at the site of what is now Hersheypark. Today Hersheypark covers 110 acres with more than 60 rides, shows, and attractions, including 10 major roller coasters, and attracts more than two million visitors a year.

While clearing the five-acre field in Derry for Hershey's new factory, a great number of rocks were unearthed. Many ended up being used in the construction of the factory and other buildings in the town.

Each day, Hershey produces more than 80 million Kisses at its chocolate factories in Hershey and California. It takes 99 Kisses to equal 1 pound of chocolate. Due to a rationing of silver foil during and immediately after World War II, Hershey halted the production of Kisses from 1942 through 1949.

The year 1907 also marked the introduction of the Hershey's Kiss, a flat-bottomed, conical milk chocolate candy individually wrapped in little squares of foil. It is believed that Kisses got their name from the sound or motion of the chocolate being deposited during the manufacturing process. The famous (and, eventually, trademarked) paper plume or flag coming out of the point of the Kisses was introduced when the wrapping process was automated in 1921.

With his wife Catherine ("Kitty"), whom he had married in 1898, Hershey set about building his own residence on a hilltop overlooking his town. By any standards, High Point Mansion, completed in 1908, is a magnificent building. Surprisingly, however, the construction, furnishings, and landscaping are estimated to have cost $100,000 (as compared, for example, to Biltmore, the 400-room mansion constructed by George Vanderbilt in Asheville, North Carolina, which cost around $10 million).

The Hersheys preferred to focus a great deal of their wealth on the establishment of a boarding school for orphan boys

From November 17, 1942, to October 1, 1943, The Hotel Hershey was closed to the public and served as a place of internment for diplomats from the Vichy government of Nazi-occupied France. The American government had chosen the hotel partly because of its remote location and its defensibility.

(the couple had no children of their own) at The Homestead, Milton's birthplace, with its 486 acres of farmland. In 1909 the Hershey Industrial School was opened with an enrollment of 10 students. In 1918 (Kitty had died three years earlier) Milton Hershey transferred his ownership in his chocolate company and other enterprises to the Hershey Trust, to be held for the school.

Today, more than 1,300 students—girls as well as boys—live on the 9,000-acre campus and attend the institution, which was renamed the Milton Hershey School in 1951 and accepted its first female students in 1976. These students are provided with a free education from kindergarten through 12th grade, along with board and medical care.

The Trust's assets now include 30 percent of ownership in The Hershey Company and 100 percent ownership of Hershey Entertainment and Resorts Company (HERCO). Among the properties currently owned and operated by HERCO are Hersheypark, Hersheypark Arena, Hersheypark Stadium, and The Star Pavilion, ZooAmerica North American Wildlife Park, Hershey Bears AHL Hockey Club, The Hotel Hershey, The Hershey Lodge & Convention Center, Hershey Highmeadow Campground, the Giant Center.

In 1963 the Hershey Trust contributed $50 million and land to Pennsylvania State University to establish the Penn State Milton S. Hershey Medical Center. With more than 500 physicians, the Penn State College of Medicine (opened in 1967), and a children's hospital, the Milton S. Hershey Medical Center, has become one of the nation's most renowned and respected health care facilities.

To raise more capital for his company's expansion, Milton Hershey took his company, renamed Hershey Chocolate Corporation, public in 1927. Opening price for the initial offering of 250,000 shares was $61.50.

During the Great Depression, Hershey kept his employees working, not just in the chocolate factory, but in continuing to build up their hometown. In the 1930s, many of the town's landmark buildings were constructed, including a headquarters for the chocolate corporation, the Hotel Hershey, the Hershey Sports Arena, and the Hershey Stadium. Construction of the grand hotel—based on a design Milton Hershey and his wife had seen during a trip to the Mediterranean—alone required over 600 workers. Commentator and author Lowell Thomas described the Hotel Hershey as "a palace that out-palaces the palaces of the maharajas of India."

At the same time, Milton Hershey created the M. S. Hershey Foundation to fund local educational and cultural activities. The nonprofit foundation continues to fund the Hershey Theatre, Hershey Museum, Hershey Gardens, and Hershey Community Archives.

New products, such as Mr. Goodbar (1925), Hershey's Syrup (1926), chocolate chips (1928), and the Krackel bar (1938), continued to build the brand and generate new revenues. As a result of the popularity of these products as well as the new construction and activity in the model town built around its factory, Hershey began to make its mark as a tourist destination during the 1930s. In subsequent years, Hershey has been referred to by a number of nicknames, including "Chocolate Town, U.S.A." and "The Sweetest Place on Earth."

Even after the death of its founder at the age of 88 in 1945, the brand and the town of Hershey continued to flourish. In 1963 the company purchased H. B. Reese Candy Co., another local operation that had been making chocolate-covered peanut butter cups since 1928 (Hershey's had always supplied the chocolate coating for Reese's cups).

Diversification continued with the acquisition of San Georgio Macaroni and Delmonico Foods in 1966 and other confectionery brands such as Twizzlers licorice in 1977, Peter Paul/Cadbury's U.S. candy operations (Almond Joy and Mounds) in 1988, and Ronzoni Foods in 1990. Hershey

During World War II, Hershey's developed Field Ration D to fill the U.S. Army's requirement for a 4-ounce, high-energy bar that would not melt in the extreme heat and, while palatable, would not taste so good that soldiers would eat them right away rather than saving them for emergencies. By the end of the war, the company had produced more than a billion of these bars.

built additional chocolate plants in Ontario, Canada (1963), and Oakdale, California (1965).

Now called The Hershey Company, Milton S. Hershey's lifelong labor of love is the leading North American manufacturer of chocolate and nonchocolate confectionery and grocery products, with net sales in excess of $4 billion. The company has about 13,700 employees, exports products to over 90 countries, and maintains licensing agreements with partners in South Korea, Japan, the Philippines, and Taiwan (Hershey's Kisses are extremely popular in Japan). On a dollar basis, The Hershey Company's sales are roughly 75 percent chocolate and 25 percent nonchocolate.

With more than two million square feet of floor space, the Hershey Company's hometown plant is the largest chocolate and confectionery manufacturing facility in the world. According to the company, the main storage facility holds more than 90 million pounds of cocoa beans, enough for about five and one half billion Hershey's milk chocolate bars.

Could a Kit Kat be Kosher? Yes, this and many other Hershey treats, including 5th Avenue, Almond Joy, Mr. Goodbar, and Reese's peanut butter cups and pieces, as well as the famous milk chocolate bar and Kisses, are approved by the Kashruth Division of the Union of Orthodox Jewish Congregations of America.

HOTELS AND MOTELS

Whether in the middle of the city or in the heart of the country, in a Civil War–era hotel or on the deck of a steamboat moored on its own private lake, a romantic hideaway for two or a family-size vacation accommodation, there's a place for any preference and price in Pennsylvania Dutch Country.

Many hotels and motels are smoke-free, but some, particularly chain operations, still offer smoking rooms. Others may designate special areas of their facility as smoking lounges. We will note hotels and motels that accommodate smokers.

Many accommodations prohibit pets. We will specify pet-friendly lodging facilities.

If you don't have a reservation upon your arrival in the area, most times the Greater Lancaster Hotel and Motel Association will be able to help you find one on the spur of the moment. Call them at (866) 729–5132 or log on to the Web site at www.padutchlodging.com. In addition to saving you time and aggravation, the association guarantees that it will get you the lowest available published rate.

Although rates are subject to change, we use the following pricing code to indicate the average rate for a one-night stay, in season, for two adults. Note that these rates do not include taxes, gratuities, or add-on services such as room service or premium TV channels unless otherwise indicated. Off-season rates are, of course,

lower. October (especially weekends) and June through August are usually considered peak seasons.

$	Less than $65
$$	$66–$95
$$$	$96–$150
$$$$	$151–$200
$$$$$	More than $200

In Pennsylvania Dutch Country, you'll find just about every major name in lodging, from Hilton to Holiday Inn Express; however, there are many not-so-familiar family-operated options here that can save you money and provide a more local flavor. Don't be shy about pulling in and asking for a look around.

BIRD-IN-HAND

Amish Country Motel $$
3013 Old Philadelphia Pike
(800) 538-2535, (717) 768-8396
www.bird-in-hand.com/amishcountry/
You can soak in the surrounding ambience of Amish farmland or splash in the indoor or outdoor pools located at its nearby sister property, Bird-in-Hand Family Inn. Guests also receive a complimentary two-hour guided Amish back roads tour on a climate-controlled bus.

Standard rooms have two double beds, and refrigerators are available for a nominal cost. King rooms ($10 additional) feature king bed, love seat, and fridge, and a two-room family suite ($40 to $50 additional) comes with two double beds, sitting room with queen-size sofa bed, two TVs, refrigerator, and microwave. Cots and cribs are available for an additional cost.

If you're staying for two nights, check out the motel's special package that includes accommodations, two breakfasts at the Bird-in-Hand Family Restaurant &

Check-out time may be at 10:00 or 11:00 A.M., but if you want to squeeze in a little more sightseeing or shopping or maybe a farewell buggy ride, ask the front desk staff if they will store your luggage for a few extra hours. Many offer this service as a customer courtesy.

Smorgasbord, one meal at another local family-style restaurant, a treat from the Bird-in-Hand Bakery, and discounts or other offers from several area shops.

AmishView Inn & Suites $$$$–$$$$$
3125 Old Philadelphia Pike (Route 340)
(866) 735-1600
www.bird-in-hand.com

Recently built, these 50 luxe rooms and suites are set in the heart of Plain & Fancy Farm, a complex that also includes the educational Amish Experience Theater and Amish Country Homestead, Plain & Fancy Farm Restaurant, and a lot of shopping. All of the units have oversized Pulaski mahogany furniture, high-speed Internet access, HBO and Disney channels, and kitchenette with refrigerator and microwave. Suites have whirlpool and/or fireplace. If you didn't bring your laptop, there's an Internet kiosk in the common room called the Great Room where you can check your e-mail or access the Web. The common room is also where your complimentary country-style breakfast (including made-to-order eggs and waffles; fresh fruits, breads, and muffins; and baked oatmeal) is served.

An indoor pool and spa provide all-weather fun, as does an on-premise arcade (open 24 hours). Also open 24 hours are the fitness center (equipped with treadmills, elliptical machine, recumbent bike, universal gym, dumbbells, and mats) and a guest laundry. On selected Movie Nights, a featured film is shown on the inn's large-screen TV.

Guests can stop by the front desk or use the "Restaurant" button on their in-room phone for priority seating at Miller's Smorgasbord and other local dining hotspots. Money-saving specials include winter midweek packages (two nights' accommodation with breakfast buffet, one family-style meal at Plain & Fancy Farm Restaurant, and selected shopping and attraction discounts) and other seasonal one- and two-night deals.

Before you hit the theme parks, museums, or shopping outlets, be sure to check for discounts at the front desk. Many hotels and motels will reserve tickets to entertainment venues in advance, eliminating waits in line as well as saving you money.

Bird-in-Hand Family Inn $$–$$$
2740 Old Philadelphia Pike
(800) 537-2535, (717) 768-8271
www.bird-in-hand.com

There are lots of perks for the price here, including a complimentary two-hour guided back roads bus tour, two heated indoor pools and outdoor pool with walk-in entrance, hot tub, lighted tennis courts, and playground and game room. There's also an 18-hole miniature golf and Bird-in-Hand Family Restaurant & Smorgasbord. All rooms and suites come with refrigerators.

Choose from a standard room with two queen or double beds, king rooms with one king bed, efficiency with two double beds and a kitchenette, or two-room family suites with two queens or one king bed, queen-size sofa bed, kitchenette/sitting room, and two televisions. Pool building suites cost extra. Cots and cribs are available for a nominal cost.

Check out special midweek and other one- and two-night packages including meals, treats from the Bird-in-Hand Bakery, and shopping discounts.

GETTYSBURG

Best Western—Gettysburg Hotel $$$–$$$$
One Lincoln Square
(800) 528-1234, (717) 337-2000
www.gettysburg-hotel.com

This hotel has a lot of history, going all the way back to 1797, when it was opened as a tavern by James Scott. It stood in the summer of 1863 while Union and Confederate troops fought the Battle of Gettysburg in the surrounding streets and fields, and nearly a century later during the cold war it served as President Dwight Eisenhower's national operations center while he recovered from a heart attack at his nearby farm.

Located on Lincoln Square in the center of town, the hotel is convenient to everything. There's even a free shuttle to the Battlefield Bus Tour. There's an outdoor pool, cocktail lounge, full-service English-style pub (McClellan's Tavern), and casual fine-dining restaurant (Centuries on the Square) on the premises. Afternoon tea service is complimentary.

Standard rooms (available smoking and nonsmoking) have two double beds. Higher priced queen (two beds) or king (one) are also available. King or queen suites also have microwave, refrigerator, sofa bed, and work desk with high-speed Internet access. Some rooms have fireplaces and hot tubs. Wheelchair-accessible rooms are available. Cribs and rollaway beds are available for a nominal fee. Dry cleaning and guest laundry provide extra convenience.

After check-in, take a couple of minutes to tune in the free Pennsylvania Dutch Country video tour that many lodging spots play continuously over their in-room televisions.

James Gettys Hotel $$$–$$$$
27 Chambersburg Street
(888) 900–5275, (717) 337–1334
www.jamesgettyshotel.com

Listed on the National Register of Historic Places and located in the center of downtown Gettysburg, this hotel was established in 1804 as the Sign of the Buck tavern and roadhouse for travelers on their way to and beyond Pennsylvania's western frontier. By the mid-1850s the lodging spot was known as the Union Hotel. In 1863, it served as a hospital for

soldiers wounded in the Battle of Gettysburg.

Today, the lobby's original chestnut staircase gives the lobby the ambience of a European boutique hotel from yesteryear. The 11 sophisticated suites, named primarily for businesses that have existed in or near the building over the past two centuries, come with sitting rooms and kitchenettes with refrigerator and microwave. Fresh seasonal flowers and in-room continental breakfast are also included, and same-day laundry and dry-cleaning services are available. You can pick up a free self-guided walking tour brochure or ask the concierge to help you make travel and tour arrangements. Two restaurants—The Blue Parrot Bistro and Thistlefields Tea Room—are located on the premises.

Quality Inn Larson's at
General Lee's Headquarters $$$–$$$$
401 Buford Avenue
(717) 334–3141
www.thegettysburgaddress.com

(Mention the Web site when making reservations and get 10 percent off regular room rates, excluding suites.) Guests also receive free (retail value $3.00 per person over age 15) admission to General Lee's Headquarters Museum (April–November) and transport to battlefield tour pickup.

Located on Seminary Ridge overlooking the battlefield, this hotel is adjacent to a small stone house built in the 1830s. At the time of the Civil War it was owned by noted statesman and abolitionist Thaddeus Stevens. General Robert E. Lee established his personal headquarters here during the Battle of Gettysburg.

Over its history, the hotel has hosted historic figures, ranging from General George Patton to President Dwight Eisenhower to the last surviving Confederate widow.

Both the Upper and Lower Dustman Suites of the hotel were part of a field hospital during the Battle of Gettysburg. The two-story, two-bedroom Inn on Seminary Ridge Suite has a back porch view of

McPherson's Ridge, where the first skirmish of the Civil War turned into a full-fledged battle. The two-story General Buford Suite features a master bedroom balcony with a sweeping view of the town.

Amenities include complimentary continental breakfast and an outdoor pool. Some rooms have two-person Jacuzzis, wet bars, queen-size sofa sleepers in addition to beds, and microwaves and refrigerators or full kitchens. Smoking and nonsmoking rooms are available. Appalachian Brewery & Restaurant is on-site.

HERSHEY

Hershey Lodge
(see Resorts chapter)

Hotel Hershey
(see Resorts chapter)

Milton Motel $$–$$$
1733 East Chocolate Avenue
(866) MILTON4, (866) 645–8664,
(717) 533–4533
www.miltonmotel.com
The rate range noted for this accommodation really applies to the peak summer season; the rest of the year you can get a room with a double or queen bed for as low as $39 or $49. About a 1½ miles from all things Hershey (Hersheypark, Chocolate World, Hershey Gardens, ZooAmerica, outlet shopping, and the Giant Center), this is a great base for seeing and doing it all. Guest rooms are pleasant and feature such niceties as refrigerator, microwave, and free HBO as well as 60+ channels. Suites include two separate rooms, one with queen-size bed, fully furnished kitchenette, and breakfast nook, the other with two queen-size beds, breakfast bar, microwave, and refrigerator. The Milton deluxe efficiency has a king-size bed, living room, queen-size sleeper sofa, fireplace, fully furnished full-size kitchen, outdoor deck, and private yard.

With so many great farmers' markets and roadside stands in the area, why not stock up on some fresh fruits, veggies, and home-baked goods to stow in your room for snacking? Beats the prepackaged stuff in any vending machine! If you have a fridge, stock up on some just-squeezed cider or Pennsylvania Dutch birch beer (nonalcoholic, like root beer with its own tangy kick).

For recreation, there's a heated outdoor pool, picnic/play area, and inside game room. Parking is provided. Duke's Bar and Grill is located right next door, the Palmdale Cafe across the street.

Spinners Inn $$–$$$$
845 Chocolate Avenue
(800) 800–5845, (717) 533–9157
www.spinnersinn.com
One thing I've always really liked about Spinners is the fact that, although it has been providing comfortable accommodations to Hershey visitors for more than 50 years, it always looks fresh and inviting inside and out. Standard accommodations feature single queen or two double beds and come with complimentary continental breakfast of coffee, juice, pastries, doughnuts, and muffins served in the game room.

For families, the deluxe queen is a good fit, with its two queen-size beds, built-in refrigerator, and microwave. Connecting rooms are available.

The property has a seasonal outdoor heated pool; gym (guests must be 18 or older) equipped with treadmill, exercise bike, and Nautilus-style weights; coin-operated laundry; and the What If . . . Restaurant on the premises. Discounts to Hersheypark, Hershey Gardens, and Hershey Museum are available, as well as special accommodation, dining, and Hershey attraction packages.

INTERCOURSE

**Best Western Intercourse Village
& Inn** $$-$$$
Routes 340 and 772
P.O. Box 40
Intercourse, PA 17534
(800) 717-6202
www.amishcountryinns.com

Barn-style exteriors with Pennsylvania
Dutch hex signs and antique-style lamps
outside the doors give the hotel an out-in-
the-country ambience that fits its surroundings in picturesque Intercourse.
Check in, then park your car in the lot and
forget it. You're within easy walking distance of everything in this charming village, including museums, shopping, and
dining. There's also a restaurant on the
premises where you'll be served a complimentary breakfast and which also offers
local specialties on its lunch and dinner
menus (the all-you-can-eat specials are
popular).

Choose from standard rooms with
double-, queen-, or king-size beds or suites
with extra queen-size sofabed and kitchenette with microwave and refrigerator.
Cribs and rollaway beds are available. Free
high-speed wireless Internet access is
offered, and, if you don't have your laptop,
there's a computer in the lobby for guest
use.

Save time in line and buy local amusement park or theater tickets and arrange
for buggy rides or other sightseeing tours
at the hotel.

---

*If you stay at the Amish Country Motel
in Bird-in-Hand or The Travelers Rest
Motel in Intercourse, a two-hour guided
bus tour of Pennsylvania Dutch Country
is included with your stay at no additional charge. Several stops will be
made along the way, including one to
an Amish-owned quilt shop.*

Kitchen Kettle Village $$$-$$$$
Route 340 East
(6½ miles from Route 30)
(800) 732-3538, (717) 768-8261
www.kitchenkettle.com

You can shop 'til you drop in Kitchen Ket-
tle Village's 32 stores, then rest up in your
accommodation right in the Village. While
you're taking a shopping break, check out
the surrounding farmland vistas from the
porch of the Grand View Suite, a two-
bedroom unit with king-size and full-size
beds, living room with pull-out sleeper
sofa, and fully equipped kitchen. The two
guest rooms in The Cottage (each with
two double beds) share a fenced-in back-
yard. All rooms feature a minifridge and
microwave.

Kling House Restaurant, a Lancaster
County institution, is on the premises. Ask
about seasonal "Sleep Over, Eat Free"
packages.

The Travelers Rest Motel $-$$
3701 Old Philadelphia Pike
(800) 626-2021, (717) 768-8731
www.bird-in-hand.com

Start the day with a continental breakfast,
then board the climate-controlled bus for
your complimentary two-hour guided
back roads tour. Get to know the lively little town of Intercourse, just a few minutes
outside your door, with its many attractions, shops, and dining spots within walking distance. Discount tickets to American
Music Theatre, Dutch Wonderland Amusement Park, and the Strasburg Rail Road
are available at the front desk.

Choose from a standard room with
two double beds or one king. All rooms
have refrigerators.

LANCASTER

Continental Inn $-$$
2285 Lincoln Highway East
(717) 299-0421
www.continentalinn.com

For sunny days, enjoy Dutch Wonderland,
which is right next door, and a seasonal

outdoor swimming pool with lovely countryside views for breaks from the theme park frenzy. For rainy afternoons, there are a neighboring four-screen movie theater and a heated indoor pool (with kiddie pool for them, sauna for you) just steps from your door.

Two lighted tennis courts as well as equipped areas for basketball, volleyball, shuffleboard, badminton, and tetherball provide lots of athletic alternatives. For kids, there are video games, Ping-Pong, and pool.

Most of the 158 guest rooms and four suites on the nine-acre property are non-smoking, but there are a limited number of rooms with double beds that are designated for smoking. Standard rooms are available, with choice of one king or two double beds.

A full hot breakfast—either a la carte or buffet, depending on the day's service—at the on-site restaurant La Fleur is included with overnight stay. La Fleur also serves dinner. There is also an on-premise cocktail lounge with big-screen television.

Ask in advance or check at the front desk for discount coupons for local attractions. Specially priced golf, Dutch Wonderland, Hersheypark, and American Music Theatre and Amish Experience packages are also available.

Eden Resorts Inn and Suites $$$–$$$$
222 Eden Road
(717) 569-6444
www.EdenResort.com

For just the two of you, or for the whole bunch, the generous-size (276 units) facility has rooms for all. Most of the standard kind are available with either one king, two queens, or two double beds. All have refrigerators, pay-per-view movies, Nintendo Games, and high-speed wireless Internet access. Pet-friendly rooms are available.

Bring your bathing suit, no matter what the weather or the season. There's a large free-form pool outside plus a tropical-themed indoor oasis with pool and whirlpool spa. If that doesn't provide enough exercise, there's a lighted tennis court, fitness trail, and 24-hour fitness center with Finnish sauna. Kids have their own game room.

On-premise dining options are just as diverse. Garden-themed Arthur's serves breakfast, lunch, and dinner; Garfield's has a weekday lunch buffet as well as its regular menu; and the Encore Lounge offers light fare along with beer, wine, and cocktails. Eden Resorts Inn's Champagne Sunday Brunch (in the Courtyard) is an elegant repast.

Special packages are built around two of the area's most popular sports—golf and shopping. For golfers, the all-inclusive gives you accommodations, breakfast and dinner, greens fees at one of the seven nearby courses, and guaranteed tee times and cart. Shopper's specials add discounts for area outlets to overnight lodging, hot breakfast buffet, and dinner.

Some hotels offer babysitting referrals upon request.

Fulton Steamboat Inn $$$
Routes 30 and 896
P.O. Box 333
Lancaster, PA 17602
(717) 299-9999
www.fultonsteamboatinn.com

There's a steamboat moored on a lake just outside Strasburg, next to an Amish farm and across the street from Rockvale Outlets. It's not transportation, but rather an accommodation that honors the accomplishments of inventor Robert Fulton, who was born in a farmhouse just a few miles away, in 1765. Fulton's *Clermont*, built in 1807, was the first successful steam-powered boat, regarded as a marvel of modern technology from the time of its maiden voyage from Albany to New York City.

Guests enter through an extravagant Victorian-style lobby and proceed to one of the three decks to their nautical-themed cabins. The Promenade Deck features family units with either two queen or queen-plus bunk beds. Second-floor Observation Deck cabins are extra spacious with separate sitting rooms. Top-level Sun Deck units (reserved exclusively for guests age 11 and older) are state room–sized and lavishly appointed with a king or two queen beds, rocking chairs and recliners, in-room whirlpool tubs, and private garden with bistro table. Wheelchair-accessible rooms are available.

All of the rooms have refrigerators and microwaves, and all are nonsmoking. There is, however, a smoking lounge that's accessible to guests any time.

To make sure every stay is a pleasure cruise, the hotel has an indoor atrium pool and Jacuzzi, plus a Universal fitness room, game room, and children's playground. Breakfast, lunch, and dinner are available at the full-service Robert Fulton Room (it has a special children's menu) and cocktails and casual fare at the Clermont Lounge.

Parking is provided. Two on-premise shops (Chandler's Nook for collectibles and the Emporium for souvenirs) are fun to browse.

Holiday Inn Express at Rockvale $$
24 South Willowdale Drive,
Rockvale Outlets
(Routes 30 and 896)
(800) 524–3817, (717) 293–9500
Bargain-savvy shoppers come for miles to check out the bargains at Lancaster's

---

Unless you're set on hitting the amusement parks such as Dutch Wonderland and Hersheypark in high season, you'll find that you can save a bundle on accommodations during off-peak spring, fall, and winter months (holiday periods excepted). To sweeten the pot and fill their rooms during these times, many places put together some very nice seasonal packages combining lodging, dining, and sometimes even entertainment.

Rockvale Outlets, but you'll only have to walk outside your door if you stay at this lodging spot in the middle of the action. Get in some training for your shopping marathon at the on-site fitness center (cycle, stair climb, and treadmills), or just get a good night's sleep and be the first one in the door when the outlets open in the morning. It's clean, it's comfortable, and it's about as close to the stores as you can get.

Ramada Inn Brunswick $$–$$$
151 North Queen Street
(North Queen and Chestnut Streets)
(800) 821–9258, (717) 397–4800
www.hotelbrunswick.com
Although the current building dates to 1966, the history of hospitality on this site actually reaches back hundreds of years. The first accommodation on the spot was the Hofnagel Hotel in 1776. It has gone through many physical and nominal changes since, but one thing that has remained constant is its prime setting in downtown Lancaster, across the street from the railroad station. In 1861 Abraham Lincoln addressed the residents of Lancaster from the balcony (it was named the Heister House at that time) during a stop-off between his home in Springfield, Illinois, and Washington, D.C., for his first inauguration. A little more than a half century later, former president Theodore Roosevelt addressed a large gathering from the balcony of the building called the Imperial Hotel that then occupied the site.

The first Hotel Brunswick, built on this spot in 1914, was renowned for its luxurious accommodations and fine service. This incarnation, downtown Lancaster's only full-service hotel, has rejuvenated that reputation.

Complimentary enclosed parking allows you to leave your car and stroll the streets of Lancaster to the Central Market, museums, theater, and dining. Other amenities include a sky-lit heated indoor pool, 24-hour fitness center, guest laundry, lobby bar (Bernhardt's Lounge) with billiard table, and Maxwell's Restaurant, a casual breakfast-through-dinner eatery on the premises.

Fully wheelchair-accessible rooms with roll-in shower are available. Guests may choose from smoking and nonsmoking rooms.

LEOLA

Zook's Motel $
103 East Main Street
(717) 656-3313
You're only 8 miles east of Lancaster and all of the area's attractions, but you'll feel far from the bustle of city living in this very small (nine rooms), very quiet accommodation set behind the owner's home. In warm weather, there are lots of birds and flowers to provide background color and music. Rooms come with refrigerators and microwaves. It's one of those comfortable, homey places that fits even the tightest budget.

RONKS

The Olde Amish Inn $-$$
33 Eastbrook Road
(Route 896, ¼ mile north of Route 30)
(717) 393-3100
www.OldeAmishInn.com
Amish farmers at work outside your window; clean rooms with queen beds inside; complimentary coffee and pastry in the morning. This economy-minded accommodation's location between Bird-in-Hand and Strasburg puts you in easy reach of attractions, shopping, and entertainment, but the setting is pure country. Discounts for seniors are often available.

STRASBURG

Carriage House Motor Inn $-$$
144 East Main Street
(Routes 896 and 741)
(717) 687-7651
www.amishcountryinns.com

Cots and cribs (one per family) are free here, and there's a playground on the grounds, so you know this place loves families. (The grown-ups get to cuddle up in double-, queen-, or king-size beds.) Small pets are also welcome, so no one has to stay at home.

Hershey Farm Inn $$-$$$
Route 896
P.O. Box 159
Strasburg, PA 17579
(800) 827-8635
www.hersheyfarm.com
Is it a farm stay or a motel? Actually, it's a little of both. Set on 23 acres, the Hershey Farm Inn has fruit and vegetable gardens, a fishing pond, a 1-mile wooded walking trail featuring a waterfall, and thousands of flowers. Signs posted among the plantings offer do-it-yourself instructions for floral fans who want to re-create some of the scenery at home. You'll even find a how-to for the waterfall. Friendly farm animal residents include turkeys, goats, rabbits, roosters, and exotic chickens.

The lodging part of the property is more motor lodge than farm home, although the 58 guest rooms are prettily themed in "Amish Farmhouse," "Country Meadow," and "Carriage House" styles. Family-size quarters with two separate bedrooms and two suites with jet stream baths are available. For other liquid recreation, there's an outdoor pool with separate baby pool. Make room reservations online and you'll save $5.00 per night. AARP members also save $5.00 a night.

You can taste the farm's freshly grown produce at the breakfast buffet at the on-premise Hershey Farm Restaurant. It comes with your overnight stay. You can also pick up some home-baked goodies for later at the on-site Gift Shop/General Store.

Special lodging and dining packages are available. The inn also offers guests the opportunity to purchase advance discount tickets to Dutch Wonderland, Discover Lancaster County History Museum,

American Music Theatre, and other attractions.

Netherlands Inn & Spa   **$$$$**
One Historic Drive
(800) 872-0201, (717) 687-7691
www.netherlandsinn.com
Although it is surrounded by 18 handsomely landscaped acres, it's more than property size that sets this gracious inn apart. It's also the full-day spa offering a range of body and beauty services from basic manicures and pedicures to age-defying facials and full body wraps.

Whether or not you visit Spa Orange for services, the Netherlands Inn has lots of other relaxation-inducing features, including an outdoor pool with Jacuzzi, full fitness room with sauna, and Adirondack chairs for rocking in a shady spot and admiring the scenery. You can relax about the kids, too, because there's plenty of room for them to run and play in the outdoor playground. Rent bicycles (available at the inn) and take a family ride. Don't worry about any of the details—the inn has a concierge to do that for you.

Rooms with country-side views come with double- or queen-size beds or one king (there's a two-room suite with two queen beds for more space). Full breakfast comes with each room or suite. An on-premise restaurant, The Bistro, offers lunch and dinner indoors or alfresco, and the adjacent Lounge with its living room ambience complete with fireplace serves cocktails and light fare.

Packages combining accommodations, spa treatment, or outlet shopping discounts and dining are available.

BED-AND-BREAKFASTS AND INNS

L odging at a bed-and-breakfast is a lot like staying at a friend's home. Unlike most hotel and motel chains, there is little standardization as far as room layout and decor. Some have live-in owners, others do not. Some offer rooms in their main residence, where you can mingle and socialize with other guests in common rooms and dining areas. Others offer the option of complete privacy in converted carriage houses or other separate facilities. For the budget-minded, you can find a cozy room with shared bathroom in the hall. (Private baths are available at most accommodations; shared baths will be indicated in the accommodation description.) Or you can book a deluxe suite with in-room amenities, including whirlpool bath.

While bed-and-breakfast accommodations usually serve meals only to overnight guests, inns open their dining rooms to the general public and frequently offer lunch and dinner as well as breakfast.

If you need a phone in your room, or can't live without a television or high-speed Internet connection, check with the accommodation before booking. Some guests prefer to totally relax out of range of today's sometimes intrusive technologies.

"Breakfast" can mean anything from a buffet spread of muffins, cold cereals, and coffee to a multicourse candlelight feast. Some vary the format according to the day of the week. All kinds of refreshments, ranging from midday tea to a help-yourself cookie jar to an elegant nightcap liqueur, may be included. If you're going to be on the go all day, some owners will even fix you a boxed lunch to take along.

Some bed-and-breakfasts and inns are not set up to accommodate young children. Others accept young guests above a particular minimum age. And some welcome children with special amenities such as cribs, high chairs, play areas, and kid-friendly snacks and breakfast foods. Each accommodation description will spell out the specifics.

If you have any particular physical, dietary, or other lifestyle restrictions or requirements, call ahead to make sure the operator can handle them. Most bed-and-breakfasts and historic inns prohibit smoking indoors. Since that ban is so widespread, we will designate any lodgings that do permit smoking.

Many bed-and-breakfasts and inns have their own resident pets but are unable to accommodate additional animals, no matter how well trained. So if you are allergic to dogs or cats, be sure to check to determine if your accommodation of choice already has a pet. Accommodation descriptions in this book will also indicate if there is room at the inn (or B&B) for your Fido or Fifi.

Credit cards are welcome in many bed-and-breakfasts and inns, but some smaller lodging places may prefer traveler's or personal checks, or even cash. Check before you book.

Some accommodations have two-night stay requirements for weekends, particularly during peak seasons. Holidays may also require minimum two- or three-night stays.

Finally, as members of their communities, operators usually have great connections for dining and other activities. In

Pennsylvania Dutch Country, many hosts can arrange for you to have dinner in an Amish home, a countryside bus tour, tee time at the local links, or a romantic winter sleigh ride.

Although rates are subject to change, we use the following pricing code to indicate the average rate for a one-night stay, in season, for two adults. Note that these rates do not include taxes, gratuities, or add-on services, such as room service or premium TV channels, unless otherwise indicated. Off-season rates are lower. October (especially weekends) and June through August are usually considered peak seasons. Many accommodations offer seasonal packages that may include dining, theater, golf, tours, and other extras.

$	$59–$75
$$	$76–$99
$$$	$100–$149
$$$$	$150–$199
$$$$$	$200 and more

ADAMSTOWN

**The Barnyard Inn B&B and
Carriage House**   **$$$**
2145 Old Lancaster Pike
P.O. Box 273
Adamstown, PA 19501
(888) 738-6624, (717) 484-1111
www.barnyardinn.com
Inside it's an elegant bed-and-breakfast; but some of the neighbors, well, there's no other way to say it, they're pigs (potbellied, no less). They're also cows, llamas,

alpaca, pygmy goats, mini horses and donkeys, and other animals who live right outside on the two-and-a-half-acre wooded property that surrounds the restored schoolhouse. The guest rooms are named for animals, too, and themed for fun. For example, the Llama Room features handcrafted wall hangings imported from Peru, as well as llama pictures and figurines. The Pig Room (which is pink, of course) has an old-fashioned tin ceiling and a deck from which you can view the animals. For families or couples who want a place all their own, there's a detached three-room carriage house suite (priced at about $165 and sleeps four) with a carved Depression-era bedroom set with a queen-size bed, eat-in kitchen with '50s fridge, microwave, coffeepot, and the old-fashioned cast-iron sink. This carriage house can accommodate children of any age, while the rest of the bed-and-breakfast is appropriate for the over-12 crowd. All rooms have wireless Internet, and a computer in the common room is available for guest use. Breakfast is a big deal here because owner Jerry Pozniak is a retired chef who has owned and operated restaurants, catering facilities, banquet halls, and hotels. Expect specialties such as eggs Florentine, strawberry waffles dipped in Belgian chocolate, Lancaster County smoked bacon, and zucchini and parmesan quiche (Jerry is happy to share recipes). In-room massage by a certified therapist is available with advance reservation.

Inns of Adamstown   **$$–$$$$**
62 West Main Street
(800) 594-4808, (717) 484-0800
www.adamstown.com
Two distinctive lodging options are available here, both surrounded by colorful flower gardens.

Combining the best of 1800s Victorian splendor and 1920s rejuvenation, The Adamstown Inn is the perfect roost for history hunters who come to Pennsylvania's Antiques Capital. Stand-out features include handsome chestnut woodwork and leaded beveled glass. Guest room walls are hand sculpted; others are adorned with paper from eras past. Sleep tight in an antique rope, oak, or canopy bed. Snuggle into a two-person Jacuzzi, sink into a soft feather bed, or snuggle in front of a cozy stove or fireplace. Awake to a light-filled morning in the seven-window Sun Room.

The Amethyst Inn is a circa 1830s bed-and-breakfast situated high on a hill overlooking Main Street. If you think the view from the veranda is striking, take a look at this Victorian "painted lady" herself, all decked out in shades of amethyst, gold, lavender, and forest green. The five guest rooms are named for jewels—topaz, cobalt, garnet, jade, and ruby—and offer a variety of individual treasures, such as a hand-painted wardrobe, antique rope bed, private balconies with old-fashioned porch swings, featherbeds and down comforters, stained-glass doors, and other surprises.

Both accommodations welcome "well-behaved children over the age of 12." There is a resident dog, but no other pets are permitted.

Ask about weekday specials at both accommodations and themed romance, massage, and golf adventure packages. Additional themed packages include room-delivered baskets just made for romantic couples (choice of champagne or sparkling cider, wine glasses, gourmet chocolate, photo album, and camera; $60), chocoholics (gourmet chocolates to milk chocolate soaps; $45), and antiques lovers (tote bag filled with the latest antiques guide book, maps of the area, magnifying glass, and snacks for the road; $75).

BIRD-IN-HAND

Bird-in-Hand Village Inn
& Suites　　　　　　　　**$$–$$$$**
2695 Old Philadelphia Pike
P.O. Box 253
Bird-in-Hand, PA 17505
(800) 914–BIRD, (717) 293-8369
www.bird-in-hand.com/villageinn
Listed on the National Register of Historic Places, this inn, originally owned by a

Quaker named William McNabb, was the home-away-from-home of the surveyors involved in the building of Old Philadelphia Pike in 1734. Local legend says that the images depicted on its hand-painted sign inspired the name of the entire village. In recent years, the Smucker family, descendants of a local early-20th-century farmer, have created a hospitality "village," with the original inn as its centerpiece. Following the renovation of two historic houses and a carriage house across the street, the complex offers 24 period-furnished rooms, including nine luxury suites. Some of the rooms include whirlpools, kitchenettes, fireplaces, and sitting rooms. Every morning, a complimentary continental-plus breakfast serves up goodies baked by the family's traditional bakery next door accompanied by assortments of fruits, yogurts, cold cereals, juices, and hot drinks. Complimentary evening snacks are also available. Other amenities include the use of an indoor/outdoor pool within walking distance of the complex and a free two-hour tour of the scenic Pennsylvania Dutch farmlands in a climate-controlled bus, while guides provide a background of Amish and Mennonite history and traditions.

Greystone Manor Bed
& Breakfast　　　　　　　**$–$$$$**
2658 Old Philadelphia Pike
(717) 393–4233
www.greystonemanor.com
Like Cinderella, this mid-1800s farmhouse blossomed into a graceful Victorian mansion when stained-glass windows, cut crystal and double-leaded glass doors, gleaming woodwork, and other regal accoutrements were added later in the century. If you're looking for a country feel more in keeping with Greystone Manor's Amish farm neighbors, stay in the Carriage House, created from the original barn and furnished in a more rustic style than the mansion. All of Greystone's 13 nonsmoking guest rooms and suites come with private baths; use of the pool, patio, and picnic areas; and complimentary

breakfast of seasonal fruits, juices, and freshly baked breads. You're also within a couple of minutes of the renowned Bird-in-Hand Farmers' Market and shops. Accommodations are wheelchair accessible. Family-friendly units are available.

Mill Creek Homestead $$$-$$$$
2578 Old Philadelphia Pike (Route 340)
(800) 771-2578, (717) 291-6419
www.bbhost.com/millcreekhomestead
For a really homey experience, book one of the four smoke-free guest rooms (three queen and one twin) in this 18th-century fieldstone farmhouse, one of the oldest residences in Bird-in-Hand. Ambience can be historic (the Colonial-style Patriot and authentically furnished Shaker Rooms) or romantic (the Garden and Magnolia Rooms). Mix with your hosts and other guests in comfy common rooms with fireplace or out by the pool. Eat your fill at the complimentary candlelight breakfast featuring such house specialties as baked apples, warm-from-the-oven cinnamon coffee cake, quiche, and freshly blended coffee. There's also a guest refrigerator and beverage station for midday and late-night snacking. For children over 10 who are wise to the ways of B&Bs, this is a warm, welcoming environment. Mill Creek is within easy walking distance of all of the shopping, dining, and sights of Bird-in-Hand.

CASHTOWN

Historic Cashtown Inn $$$-$$$$
1325 Old Route 30
P.O. Box 103
Cashtown, PA 17310
(800) 367-1797, (717) 334-9722
www.cashtowninn.com
In the late 1790s, the Cashtown Inn was built as the first stagecoach stop west of Gettysburg (it's located about 8 miles from the downtown district and 7 miles from the battlefield). During the Gettysburg campaign in 1863, the building served as the headquarters of Confeder-ate general A. P. Hill. Renowned artists, including Civil War specialist Dale Gallon, have depicted the July 1, 1863, meeting at the inn between General Robert E. Lee and General Hill. The building has also been featured in the film *Gettysburg*.

Four of the original 1797 guest rooms still provide comfort for overnight visitors. These and one of the three suites are set up to accommodate guests over the age of 12 (families with younger children are welcome to book the Pender or Anderson Suites). Full breakfast is included with overnight stays; the inn's on-premise restaurant is also a popular lunch and dinner spot (see the Other Area Restaurants section of this book for more details).

Ask about battlefield tours, Civil War–themed interactive murder mystery weekends, romance and holiday packages, ghost hunters' investigations weekends, and history weekends featuring Abraham Lincoln live and in person.

CHURCHTOWN

Churchtown Inn Bed and Breakfast $$-$$$
2100 Main Street
(800) 637-4466, (717) 445-7794
www.churchtowninn.com
Churchtown is too small to even have its own post office, making this tucked-away (but easy to find, on Route 23) village and, particularly, this 200-year-old National Register of Historic Places fieldstone mansion just right for a quiet getaway. Linger in a glass-enclosed garden breakfast room over course after course of such homemade specialties as apple, honey, and walnut compote; Amish baked oatmeal; "Guten Morgen" eggs; and Louisiana Lemon Crème Toast with Lancaster County wild strawberries. Or come back after a day of sightseeing and shopping to homemade lemonade and cookies in the garden. Handmade Amish quilts top the queen-size beds in the antique-filled guest rooms. Ask your hosts to arrange for dinner in a local Amish home or a Sat-

urday carriage ride through the surrounding farmland, or time your visit to coincide with one of the many themed weekends, such as the Victorian Ball, Amish Wedding Feast, and murder mysteries, that are held throughout the year. All of the new rooms feature high-speed wireless Internet connection. Accommodations are available for children over the age of 12.

COLUMBIA

Belsnickel Inn Bed & Breakfast $$-$$$
885 Old Chickies Hill Road
(717) 684-7399, (717) 669-3712
www.belsnickelbandb.com
Tucked into a natural setting on Route 441 about 1½ miles north of Columbia and 1 mile south of Marietta and surrounded by an extensive county park with hiking trails along the Susquehanna River, this four-guest-room English Country–style residence is a true rural retreat. Owner Barbara Frey is a professional decorator and decks out her home to suit the seasons. In winter, it's Belsnickel time, and Frey's treasured decorations depicting the German Christmas elf (he's the one that visits the naughty children) are everywhere. Well-behaved small dogs are permitted (Frey has two of her own) if they will be accompanying their owners on outings. In warmer weather, nature themes predominate, with tulip and hydrangea china on the breakfast table and artistically rendered bunnies on display. Breakfast garnishes come straight from the property's herb garden, and an extensive library offers books on decorating and cooking. English boxwoods surround the home, along with magnolia and holly, and there's a spring-fed pond with a waterfall to complete the idyllic scene.

The Columbian Bed & Breakfast $$-$$$
360 Chestnut Street
(800) 422-5869, (717) 684-5869
www.columbianinn.com
In a town rich with extravagant 19th-century architecture, this 1897 Colonial

Was your bed-and-breakfast meal so yummy that you'd like to try to duplicate it at home? You may be surprised to find out that many owners are happy to share their recipes (yes, even the "secret" family ones). Some keep photocopies of guests' favorites on hand just for that purpose, and some have even created their own cookbooks (usually available for sale at the front desk).

Revival mansion was considered to be a crown jewel, known to locals simply as "the mansion of Columbia." Enter through the wraparound porch, and the gleaming staircase, window seats, pocket doors, and original fireplaces will sweep you back into that genteel era. Four guest rooms and one suite are furnished for old-fashioned comfort, some with antique beds, gas-log fireplaces, and pedestal sinks and showers.

A full breakfast is included in your room rate, featuring recipes that have become such guest favorites that the innkeepers have assembled their own cookbook (on sale at the front desk for $7.00). For relaxation, there's a hammock to swing on and a peaceful garden with a stream, pond, and miniature railroad. For sport, there are horseshoes and croquet. Walk a block or two and you'll find yourself at the Susquehanna River or at Columbia's famous National Watch and Clock Museum. Children are welcome. Smoking is permitted outside on front and side porches. Ask the innkeepers about special two-night getaway packages that can include tickets to attractions, golf, tours, ski lift passes, and meals at local restaurants.

ELIZABETHTOWN

Conewago Manor Inn $$$$
2048 Zeager Road
(717) 361-0826
www.conewagomanorinn.com
Built in 1739, the brick portion of this

grand manor, built on a land grant from the William Penn family adjacent to the Conewago Creek, has seen service as a private residence, public house and inn, U.S. post office, and railway ticket office. In 1811 a new owner constructed a stone addition. The interesting combination of eras and materials carries through to the upholstered opulence of the Victorian front parlor, the leather and wood ruggedness of the library, and the breezy tropical wicker and palm of the sunroom. Nine guest rooms, with names such as Emma's Attic, Dr. Alexander Suite, and Gentleman Smith's Quarters, are inspired by the lives and times of people past. All have antique decor, fireplaces, and private whirlpool baths; most have private balconies. Guests receive full breakfast and have use of the fitness room. The hosts will provide transportation to and from Harrisburg Airport with prior notice. This is an adults-only accommodation.

If you're interested in sampling the local wine, chocolates, or other specialty foods produced in the area, a number of bed-and-breakfast owners and innkeepers will get the items of your choice or even make up entire gift baskets for you. Look on the accommodation's Web site or ask when you book your reservation.

West Ridge Guest House   **$$-$$$**
1285 West Ridge Road
(877) 367-7783, (717) 367-7783
www.westridgebandb.com
Located on 22 sprawling acres, West Ridge offers guests pastoral pleasures, with horses grazing in the front pasture near a sparkling pond. Three two-room suites in the 1894 European-style manor house have fireplaces and single or double Jacuzzis. Five additional rooms in the guest house are done in country, Victorian, wicker, Williamsburg, and romantic "anniversary" themes. Full breakfast and

use of the hot tub and exercise room are included. Adults only, no smoking. Look for seasonal midweek specials and anytime "Flowers and Chocolates" packages.

EPHRATA

The Inns at Doneckers   **$-$$$$**
318-324 North State Street
(800) 377-2206, (717) 738-9502
www.doneckers.com
With its art studios, upscale home and personal fashion shops, and renowned white-tablecloth restaurant, Doneckers is a vacation destination all by itself. The close to 40 guest rooms and suites of the inns are styled to represent local lifestyles and personalities throughout the centuries. But don't expect anything close to the hard wooden bench and stone pillow austerity of the historic Ephrata Cloister nearby. The Guesthouse, actually three adjoining Victorian structures with a total of 19 units, is lush with original inlaid wood floors, stained-glass windows, and a parlor/lobby furnished by Harrod's of London.

Hand-stenciled walls and antique furniture capture the period when Cloister clockmaker Jacob Gorgas resided in the building now called the 1777 House (no doubt he would be surprised by the gas fireplaces, Jacuzzi tubs, and wireless Internet access). These and other modern amenities update the decor and functionality of rooms, while special touches such as the wall of fully stocked bookshelves in schoolmaster Brother Obed's Study and the hand-crafted crewel-embroidered chairs in singing school head Sister Anastasia's Room retain their sensibilities for learning and beauty.

The original Donecker family residence has been converted into The Homestead, with four guest rooms and suites, each with a fireplace and/or Jacuzzi. These quarters are decorated with local antiques and textiles, accenting furnishings created by artisans from around the country.

All stays include an extended complimentary continental breakfast buffet. The innkeeper can suggest specific rooms best for accommodating infants and children. Ask about off-season rates as well as special midweek and seasonal shop-and-stay packages (50 percent off weekday stays and 15 percent off weekends).

Twin Pine Manor Bed & Breakfast $$$$–$$$$$
1934 West Main Street
(888) 266-0099, (717) 733-8400
www.twinpinemanor.com
For one of the most spectacular views of Pennsylvania Dutch Country at its rural best, check out the rooftop mahogany deck atop this quietly lovely expanded A-frame house that overlooks nearby farms. The building itself is set on 26 well-tended acres, which you can admire from a lower deck or, even better, from the outdoor Jacuzzi. The inside scenery is worth viewing as well, especially the cozy great room, with its soaring cathedral ceiling and stone hearth; exercise room equipped with treadmill, stationary bike, sauna, and steam bath; common room with pool table and big-screen television; and eight distinctively decorated guest rooms and suites. A full breakfast including two hot entrees is included. If you want to economize a bit, ask about the Amaryllis and Fox Hunt Rooms—they're both cute, cozy, and under $100.

GETTYSBURG

Baladerry Inn at Gettysburg $$–$$$
40 Hospital Road
(800) 220-0025, (717) 337-1342
www.baladerryinn.com
This circa 1812 farm, located at the edge of the Gettysburg Battlefield, served as a field hospital for the Army of the Potomac during the Civil War. Today it's a tranquil getaway with seven guest rooms and a suite in the Main House, 1812 House (the oldest part of the inn), and Carriage House. The Windflower Room in the 1812 House features a whirlpool tub. Full breakfast is included. Guests may use the on-

premise tennis court. Children over 12 are welcome. Off-peak discounts are available in January and February.

Battlefield Bed & Breakfast Inn $$$$
264 Emmitsburg Road
(888) 766-3897, (717) 334-8804
www.gettysburgbattlefield.com
Every day, guests at this 1809 bed-and-breakfast located on the South Cavalry Battlefield, five minutes from the visitors center, can participate in a different Civil War learning program focusing on topics that range from infantry, cavalry, and sharpshooter to battlefield medicine. Friday nights, gather in the summer kitchen parlor for ghost stories. On special occasions, reenactors demonstrate the lives and times of wartime Gettysburg. You can also contemplate the peace that reigns in the area today during a stroll of the property's 30 acres and pond area.

The four rooms and three suites at the inn are named and themed for the military units and leaders that fought at this little-mentioned site of Civil War action. Breakfast is served by a costumed staff, the Farm Potatoes are a house specialty, as are the raspberry cream crepes, red, white, and blueberry biscuits with whipped cream, and homemade apple cake.

"Considerate parents" are invited to bring their children. Military and emergency services personnel receive discounts with ID. Ask about special two-nights-for-the-price-of-one specials and other discounts on selected off-peak nights.

Brafferton Inn $$$–$$$$
44-46 York Street
(717) 337-3423
www.brafferton.com
Gettysburg's oldest residence is the original 1786 four-bedroom native brownstone home located about 1½ blocks east of Lincoln Square in the center of town. You can stay in the original building (as well as in expanded areas of the home that were added prior to the Civil War). During the Battle of Gettysburg, the Codori family, who resided there at the time, hid away in

the basement to escape flying bullets. One of those minié balls became lodged in the mantle above the fireplace in what is now a guest unit called The Battle Room. (The building is still known to many local residents as the "Codori House"—a fact to keep in mind if you're asking someone for directions.) History buffs will probably also particularly like the Loft Suite, situated on the third floor of the house, with its exposed stone walls, open rafter cathedral ceiling, and original wide pine board floors. Breakfast is served on Spode and Wedgwood china set with family silver and crystal. The owners say children over eight are "particularly welcome."

Because certain religious organizations prohibit the drinking of alcoholic beverages, some bed-and-breakfast owners request that guests refrain from bringing any beer, wine, or liquor into their homes.

The Doubleday Inn
Bed and Breakfast   **$$–$$$**
104 Doubleday Avenue (Oak Ridge)
(717) 334-9119
www.doubledayinn.com
Abner Doubleday is a name that many people equate more with baseball than with the military. Some even believe he invented baseball (which he didn't). Doubleday's real claim to fame came on the first day of the three-day Battle of Gettysburg during an encounter that many historians consider to be the turning point of the war.

A West Point graduate, he was a captain in the army when on April 12, 1861, Confederate troops fired on Fort Sumter, part of the defense for Charleston Harbor in South Carolina. It was on Captain Abner Doubleday's command that the first retaliatory Union shot was fired. After serving in a number of the Civil War's major campaigns, Doubleday assumed command of a division at Oak Ridge in Gettysburg, now the site of the Doubleday Inn. From there, he held off Confederate forces far outnumbering his own for seven hours, a feat that allowed the Union forces to regroup and gain the strategic advantage on the second day of the three-day battle.

The Doubleday Inn, a 1929 colonial white clapboard-sided home, is the only bed-and-breakfast on the Gettysburg National Military Park Battlefield. Surrounded on three sides by the Battlefield, the B&B is located a mile from Town Square. A second-floor deck, called The Porch on Oak Ridge, affords a panoramic view of 8 to 10 miles. Its nine guest rooms are done in English country style with period accents, Civil War memorabilia, and paintings by renowned local artist Dale Gallon. A full country breakfast is included. (Ask about reduced winter rates.)

When you make your reservation, you may also ask the innkeepers to arrange for a battlefield tour with a licensed guide. On selected evenings, the owners will invite a Civil War historian to the inn to lead what always turns out to be a spirited discussion.

Herr Tavern & Publick House $$$–$$$$
900 Chambersburg Road
(800) 362-9849, (717) 334-4332
www.herrtavern.com
Local lore suggests that this building may be haunted by spirits who, believers say, have ordered beer (and vanished before the tab could be paid . . . hmm), randomly appear and disappear, and otherwise make themselves known (particularly in Rooms 1 through 4 in the building's original section—maybe they like the Jacuzzis in Rooms 2 and 4).

Some say at least one of the ghosts may be that of former proprietor Frederick Herr, for whom the inn is named. If so, these ghostly glimpses wouldn't be the only reason why Herr, who bought the circa 1815 tavern in 1828, is a well-remembered personality in these parts. During the days of his ownership, whispers of counterfeiting downstairs and a brothel upstairs gave this accommodation a racy air. On the other hand, Herr also allowed his tavern to be used by the Underground Railroad prior to the Civil War. Ironically, in 1863 the building was captured by Southern troops and was turned into the first Confederate hospital. In the early 1900s, more than a half century after Herr's death, the property underwent another drastic personality change, this time becoming a peaceful dairy farm.

Painstaking restoration has given new life to this historic landmark. Children ages 12 and up are welcome. Full breakfast is included (if you're too comfy to get up on time, the innkeeper will oblige with a continental breakfast at your leisure). And if the thought of wandering spirits makes you a bit tense, head for the on-premise massage room for a Swedish, deep tissue, warm stone, or other therapeutic treatment.

INTERCOURSE

Amish Guest House and Cottage $$$
3625 Newport Road (Route 772 East)
(717) 768-8914

In the Amish culture, generations of family members live with or close to one another. Instead of moving away when they retire, older members move into smaller quarters called the *grossdaadi* or *dawdi haus* (pronounced DAH-dee HAHS), or grandparents' house, so they can continue to share in the lives and daily activities of their loved ones. The two-bedroom ranch-style residence built in 1951 was the first guesthouse in Intercourse. It sleeps six (one queen and one single bed in each bedroom), plus there are two extra roll-away beds if needed. The guesthouse has a full kitchen, living room, and dining room; an Amish sewing room with antique framed quilt; and a porch with a glider. The cottage, or *grossdaadi/dawdi haus,* sleeps six in its one "grand" room that is furnished with two queen beds and a sofa

bed. It comes with a refrigerator and microwave, sitting area with table and chairs, and porch with an Amish-made swing. Both family-friendly accommodations have full baths, interior hand-painted murals, authentic Amish antiques, and fenced-in backyards. Continental breakfast is provided.

Carriage Corner Bed & Breakfast $$
3705 East Newport Road (Route 772)
(800) 209-3059, (717) 768-0691
www.carriagecornerbandb.com

Although the busy little village of Intercourse is just a five-minute walk away, the setting here in this five-room residence with its homespun accents of handcrafted folk art is serene and idyllic. Relax in a queen-size bed, in front of the gas log stove in the common room or outside on the back deck or in the gazebo (smoking is permitted outside). Owner Gordon Shuit is very proud of his oatmeal pancakes, or he and his wife, Katie, might whip up an egg sausage souffle, baked oatmeal, and bran muffins or stuffed cinnamon French toast. Children over age eight are welcome. Winter rates are lower Sunday through Thursday, and the Shuits have dreamed up lots of special packages for romantic couples, theater lovers, bicycling or hot air ballooning enthusiasts, and those who lean more toward history or horticulture. Frequent visitors can earn one point per night booked; earn six and receive a gift certificate worth $50 toward your next stay. For an impromptu getaway, call within just 24 hours of a weekend in the months of December through March, or Sunday through Thursday in December through June and receive 10 percent off any available room.

Intercourse Village
Bed & Breakfast Suites $$$$–$$$$$
Route 340, Main Street
(800) 644-0949
www.amishcountryinns.com

Classic or country, take your pick. For those who revel in Victoriana, there's period décor—complete with queen-size poster or canopy bed and fireplace (gas-burning)—in a restored 1909 home. There's no television or phone in these two rooms, but who needs them? For the more casual-minded, there are four country-style suites just a short meander down a landscaped brick pathway. Decorated with local woodwork and beamed ceilings, the Country Homestead Suites do have TVs and phones (with data ports), as well as queen beds, gas-burning fireplaces, private sitting area with love seat, and wet bar with microwave, refrigerator, and coffeemaker. In the three Honeymoon/Anniversary Suites, there are king-size beds, and each has a Jacuzzi for two. All guests receive a five-course gourmet-style candlelight breakfast. For outdoor relaxing there's a lovely "wedding garden," with a tree-shaded gazebo and water-spouting statues.

Accommodations are for guests age 18 and over. For getaways *pour deux*, ask about the "I Love You" package, which delivers fresh flowers, Godiva chocolate, and a chilled bottle of nonalcoholic champagne, and "The Ultimate Romance," which includes all of the above plus a cheese, cracker, and fruit tray, along with an aromatherapy bath basket.

LANCASTER

Country Living Inn $$-$$$
2406 Old Philadelphia Pike
(717) 295-7295
www.countrylivinginn.com
Children under 15 are not only welcome here, they stay free. If you need a cot or crib, that's free, too. This homey bed-and-breakfast is situated across the field from a working Amish farm and one-room schoolhouse. Authentic Shaker furniture adds to the homespun atmosphere, with artistic touches provided by family antiques and examples of wall printing, an old German craft. Complimentary breakfast of coffee, tea, hot chocolate, and muffins is available daily.

E. J. Bowman House $$$
2672 Lititz Pike
(877) 519-1776, (717) 519-0808
www.ejbowmanhouse.com
Built as a physician's mansion in the 1860s, this Italianate Victorian home, known locally simply as "the Big Yellow House," is as colorful inside as it is outside. Fourteen murals in the foyer and along the formal staircase depict the ever-changing palette of the 19th-century Lancaster countryside. Musically inclined guests are invited to bring their own instruments or songs to share in front of the grand fireplace in the parlor/living room. Children over age 10 who are comfortable around antiques and musical instruments are welcome. Private baths have heated tile floors, and guest rooms have stove-fireplaces and queen, king, or two twin beds. (There's also a suite, available at a higher rate, which has a master bedroom with king-size bed, adjoining sitting room with two-person day bed, and bath with whirlpool.) Family-style breakfast specialties include fresh fruit clafouti, homemade pecan sticky buns, and red pepper jam–lined corn crepes with herbed eggs, cheese sauce, roasted corn, and more peppers. Special discounted rates may be available to quilters, farmers' market fans, "nonprocrastinators" (that is, guests who book any three consecutive nights at least two months in advance), teachers, nurses, and members of AARP.

O'Flaherty's Dingeldein House $$$
1105 East King Street
(800) 779-7765, (717) 293-1723
www.dingeldeinhouse.com
A little Southern hospitality in the midst of Pennsylvania Dutch Country, this circa 1910 Dutch Colonial house and later-built cottage are owned by Tennessee natives Nancy and Danny Whittle (Dingeldein was the name of former owners and O'Flaherty a nod to other owners of Irish origin). Originally built for members of the Armstrong family flooring tycoons, the residence offers five guest rooms, four of which have private baths. The fifth is a

suite (available at a higher rate) with a shared bathroom in the hall (but, emphasizes Nancy, you'll never wind up sharing the bathroom with strangers—she only rents these rooms to people who know one another). The airy, high-ceilinged cottage has two guest rooms. In season, Nancy's prized gardens bloom with pansies and perennials. Not surprisingly, breakfast is often Southern-style, with Kentucky ham (or Lancaster County sausage or bacon for a local twist), grits, or Nancy's own heart-shaped fresh blueberry pancakes or apple cream cheese–stuffed French toast.

Secret Garden $$–$$$
445 West Chestnut Street
(717) 399-9229
www.secretgardenpa.com

Parents of students at Franklin & Marshall College, located 5 blocks away, were among the first to discover this little hideaway in the city's historic district. But it's also a central spot for visitors who want to walk to any of the downtown area's attractions, including the Central Market District (4 blocks away), museums, shops, and restaurants. Owners Marianne and Amos Stolzfus both grew up on Lancaster County Amish farms, and they've managed to infuse the single guest room and three suites in their grand Victorian abode with country-style comfort. For privacy, there's the third-floor posh Red and Gold Suite; for fun, the Tropical Suite with live and silk greens, Spanish tile, Jacuzzi, and three southern-facing 10-foot-high windows for lots of light. The Garden Suite has an outdoorsy mural, Jacuzzi for two, fully equipped kitchen, and balcony overlooking the courtyard plants and flowers. The Victorian Room with its double canopy bed is just right for late sleepers because it's out of the direct morning sun. A full breakfast (think baked French toast topped with walnuts, homemade cheese Danish, and vegetable quiche) can be served in the candlelit dining room or alfresco in the garden. No credit cards; only personal and traveler's checks are accepted. Parking is free either in the off-street lot around the corner or on the street in front of the bed-and-breakfast.

1725 Historic Witmer's Tavern Inn–Bed & Breakfast $$
2014 Old Philadelphia Pike (Route 340) (0.2 mile east of the intersection of Routes 30 and 340)
(717) 299-5305

Back when Lancaster was known as Hickorytown and was a major stock-up stop for the Conestoga wagon trains heading west and south, travelers stayed at this inn made of blue limestone from a nearby quarry; so did members of the Continental Congress and officers of the Revolutionary War. Restored to its original rustic style, with much of the hardware and many of its architectural features still intact (it's listed on the National Register of Historic Places and is designated a Federal Landmark), Witmer's Tavern is Lancaster's oldest and only pre–Revolutionary War inn still lodging travelers. The dedication to authenticity during restoration included such details as researching original paint colors for the seven guest rooms and furnishing them with antiques from the period. Each room also has an original woodburning fireplace with old-fashioned popcorn poppers—and popcorn—supplied. A fireside continental-plus breakfast is included.

Walnut Lawn Bed & Breakfast $–$$
1027 Village Road
(717) 464-1382
www.walnutlawn.com

For people with allergies, asthma, multiple chemical sensitivity, or other environmen-

---

Most bed-and-breakfasts serve their morning meal between specified hours, particularly when they offer full, hot, multicourse repasts. Most operators will tell you about breakfast service when you check in, and many leave polite reminder notes in the rooms. Sometimes the fact is, if you snooze, you lose.

tal illnesses, travel can be a traumatic experience. While Dan and Erma Wenger can't guarantee perfection, they do their best to provide a comfortable oasis for these travelers by providing an environment free of smoke, pets, room deodorizers, and aerosol cleaning products and by using HEPA (or near-HEPA-quality) filters in their vacuum cleaners to maintain indoor air quality. Everything, from the bedding to the food (including hormone-free milk and eggs from Amish and Mennonite farms, as well as fruit and vegetables from the Wengers' own orchard and garden), has been chosen with guest sensitivity in mind, and special diets will be accommodated whenever possible with prior notice. Best of all, the Wengers have managed to do all of this without creating an aesthetically sterile environment. Just the opposite; they have decorated each of the four guest rooms in their 1909 two-story brick Colonial home with distinctive furnishings built around a distinctive theme. The Safari Room, for example, is done in the bright colors, animal prints, drums, and wood carvings that Dan, the son of missionaries, recalls from his birthplace of Tanzania. Erma's mom's handcrafting dexterity is celebrated in the Quilt Room, with its antique treadle sewing machine and old spools. If you want to learn more about Amish and Mennonite life and culture, there's a collection of films and local documentaries in the den. Better yet, settle in for a chat with Dan, a former world cultures and social studies teacher. (Although the address is Lancaster, the bed-and-breakfast is located just south of the city on Route 741, on the edge of the tiny village of Lampeter.)

LITITZ

Forgotten Seasons Bed & Breakfast **$$**
304 East Newport Road
(717) 626–3088
www.forgottenseasons.com
George Washington may not have slept here, but Count Zinzendorf did. Zinzen-

dorf, a Moravian missionary, also preached here so passionately in December 1742 that a local farmer was inspired to will his land to the church, leading to the development of the town of Lititz (named by Zinzendorf for a castle in the eastern part of the current Czech Republic that provided refuge to persecuted Moravians).

Known as Jacob Huber's Tavern when it was built in 1735, this white farmhouse, one of the oldest remaining homes in Lititz, has been lovingly preserved through the centuries, and each of the three present-day guest rooms has a story about the people who lived or stayed here. So don't look for a hot tub (Zinzendorf didn't have one either), but if you're a history buff, you'll feel right at home. Owner Dale Groff is a font of knowledge about the area's past and has amassed a wonderful library, which he is happy to share with guests.

After a full country breakfast of fresh fruit, baked blueberry French toast, Farmer's Casserole, or cheese strata and ham, and other accompaniments, take a walk in the Warwick Township Linear Park right next door to the bed-and-breakfast. In one direction, you'll find a 1-mile hiking and biking trail into the countryside, in the other the local ball fields. Be sure you take some time to peek into Barbara's Room, where the walls are covered with hand-painted artwork from the early to mid-1800s (this room is not available for overnight stays, but is being studied and documented).

General Sutter Inn **$$–$$$**
14 East Main Street
(717) 626–2115
www.generalsutterinn.com
Although non-Moravians could not live in Lititz until the mid-1850s, a few inns such as this one, which was built in 1764, were operated "for the necessary entertainment of strangers and travelers." Over the years, the building (originally called Zum Anker, or Sign of the Anchor) expanded and changed names, first to the Lititz Springs Hotel, then, in 1930, to the General Sutter Inn. The name change was a tribute to

John Augustus Sutter, of California gold rush fame and misfortune, who lived his last years and was buried in Lititz. Sutter's home stands across the street from the inn that bears his name.

This family-friendly (cots are available for $5.00, cribs for $10.00), pets-allowed (there's a $10.00 per pet nonrefundable fee) accommodation offers 15 Victorian- and country-themed rooms and suites. On-premise dining is offered at the General Sutter Inn, the landmark 1764 Restaurant, Pearl's (a Victorian bar), and the ZA (Zum Anchor) Cafe, for breakfast (included with your stay), lunch, or cappuccino break. Look for full descriptions of the restaurants in the Other Area Restaurants section of this book.

The Lititz House $$
301 North Broad Street
(800) 464-6764, (717) 626-5299
www.lititzhouse.com
Three blocks north of Main Street, this 1904 home has recently been totally refurnished in Scandinavian leather and teak, but maintains its original chestnut woodwork, pocket doors, and other features unique to early-20th-century residences. Each of the three guest rooms has a private entrance, and there's a two-bedroom suite in its own wing that's a bargain (about $130) for families or friends traveling together. Former caterer and gourmet cook Pat Erven, who owns the inn with husband, Jim, makes sure no one goes hungry (or thirsty). She sets up prebreakfast coffee and tea for early risers, followed by an elaborate eye-opener of a meal. In the early evening, she serves wine or other refreshments and hors d'oeuvres. In between, there's always a stash of cookies and glasses of lemonade. Two decks and a wraparound porch with rockers overlook the flowers in the yard. There's also an old-fashioned garden swing next to an antique fountain. The Ervens offer midweek discounts and special romance packages with wine or champagne, chocolates, and fresh flowers. Pat will also cook up a three-course gourmet dinner ($40 per person with wine, $30 without) for you from her extensive repertoire of recipes.

MOUNT JOY

The B&B at Groff's Farm $$$
650 Pinkerton Road
(717) 653-2513
www.groffsfarmrestaurant.com
You don't have to be a golfer to appreciate this accommodation, even though its location overlooking the first tee of a course created on former farmland is perfect for aficionados of the sport. Owners Betty and Abe Groff used to farm that land, and they are also some of the most hospitable hosts around. Just having the chance to chat with Betty, an internationally renowned chef, cookbook author, and authority on Pennsylvania Dutch cuisine, and digging into one of her hearty country breakfasts is reason enough to visit. The living room with its cozy fireplace is a great place to sit and chat. There won't be a crowd because there are only two guest rooms, both with private whirlpool baths, queen-size beds (plus queen-size sofa bed), and views of the golf course and Chiques Creek, with its graceful three-arch stone bridge.

If you are planning a late arrival or find yourself stuck in traffic or otherwise running behind schedule, it's a nice courtesy to call your bed-and-breakfast or inn to let them know. Many of these operations are small and/or in family residences and do not have 24-hour front desk staff like a hotel, motel, or resort would.

The Cameron Estate Inn $$-$$$
855 Mansion Lane
(888) 4-CAMERON, (717) 492-0111
www.cameronestateinn.com
Tucked away on 15 private acres (but only a few minutes' drive to other Mount Joy

area attractions), this 1805 mansion, now listed on the National Register of Historic Places and a Lancaster Historic Preservation Trust Site, was the rural retreat of financier, politician, and Secretary of War Simon Cameron, his son, James Cameron, who served as Ulysses S. Grant's secretary of war, and their descendants. Each of the 18 guest rooms features distinctive period furnishings, including canopy beds, and fireplaces (some original). The majestic Simon Cameron Room has a 10-piece Italian antique bedroom suite and original built-in cabinetry. The Lincoln Room (interestingly hidden behind a bookcase/door) has an antique king-size bed, marble bath with whirlpool, and separate shower. A full country breakfast is served in the Garden Dining Room, which overlooks the property's woods and streams. Children over 12 are welcome.

The Olde Square Inn $$$-$$$$$
127 East Main Street
(800) 742-3533
www.oldesquareinn.com

In the heart of Mount Joy, on the town's historic square and within easy walking distance of the shops on Main Street and Bube's Brewery (a must-visit multiple-concept dining spot), this accommodating brick home is imaginative in its decor and warm in its welcome. An in-ground pool invites seasonal splashing, and the movie library has more than 100 selections. Each of the five guest rooms has its own fireplace and a fanciful theme. One of the most fun is the Fantasy Island Suite, with its spa tub and lounge area with palm tree. Also worth mentioning is the Enchanted Cottage, with its centerpiece oversized raspberry-colored whirlpool for two, adjacent fireplace, ornate iron queen-size bed, double dressing area, wet bar, refrigerator, microwave, and private patio. (The cottage is wheelchair accessible.) Pile up your plates with homemade goodies at the breakfast buffet—special delivery is available for cottage guests. The entire bed-and-breakfast is pet friendly (there is a small fee, and animals must be

crated while alone in rooms and on a leash while on the property).

NEW HOLLAND

Rocking Horse Bed & Breakfast $$-$$$
285 West Main Street
(800) 208-9156, (717) 354-8674

Lancaster County is home to many premier woodcrafters, including Fred Dilworth and his sons, who live and work in the little town of New Holland, just 4 miles away from Intercourse. Their studio, where they create antique rocking horse reproductions, carousel animals, bedheads, and other works of art, is a renovated carriage house behind the 200-year-old stone Colonial home that Fred and his wife, Millice, operate as a bed-and-breakfast. Guests are welcome to watch the woodcarving process in the workshop. In the Cherub guest room, the headboard of the queen-size bed is one of Fred's creations. Also available are the Serenity and Victorian Lace Rooms and the Country Suite (a little bit higher price for this unit with separate sitting room, king-size bed, and balcony). Breakfast is served in front of a walk-in fireplace. Children over 12 are welcome.

PALMYRA

1825 Inn $$-$$$
409 South Lingle Avenue
(877) 738-8282, (717) 838-8282
www.1825inn.com

Situated on a quiet residential street only a few miles' drive from the town of Hershey and all of its attractions, this 1825 country-style home residence (formerly the Hen Apple Bed and Breakfast) has a fun, informal personality all its own. Antiques, reproductions, and "just plain old stuff" from local crafters make for comfortable surroundings in the six guest rooms, parlor, and game room. High-speed wireless Internet access is available, as well as a computer for guest use. Or

Want to know what accommodations are available without calling around or find a last-minute vacancy for an impromptu getaway? Try one of the following central reservation services.

Lancaster Lodging Reservations
(866) 729-5132
www.padutchlodging.com
Whether you're looking for a cozy bed-and-breakfast, stately inn, convenient hotel or motel, working farm, or spacious campgrounds, dial up the Call Reservations Center or click on to the Web site to find out what's available during your timeframe and within your price range. You can make your reservations online and learn about any special packages local accommodations might be offering. This service is free and guarantees that it will provide you with the lowest available published rate any of its more than 38 hotels and motels and over 4,000 room member accommodations. If you can find a lower published rate, the service will match it.

The Innkeepers of Authentic Bed and Breakfasts of Lancaster County Association
(800) 552-2632
www.authenticbandb.com
This organization of close to 25 bed-and-breakfasts/inns hosts a detailed Web site with descriptions of their individual facilities, business and personal amenities, available dates, price ranges, direct links to each accommodation, and online reservations. Before reserving, click on the "Specials" tab on the Web site's home page; you can often find a special discount coupon (a recent one was worth 20 percent off a two-night stay at any member bed-and-breakfast) to make your Lancaster County stay an even bigger bargain.

Lancaster County Bed & Breakfast Inns Association
(800) 848-2994, (717) 464-5588
www.padutchinns.com
Check out locations, amenities, prices (including specials), and available dates from around 14 local bed-and-breakfasts. Link directly with the accommodations of your choice and make your reservations online.

Inns of the Gettysburg Area
(800) 586-2216, (717) 624-1300
www.gettysburgbedandbreakfast.com
Twenty of the area's finest bed-and-breakfasts and inns housed in Federal, Victorian, and turn-of-the-20th-century buildings are members of this organization, which offers details about and direct Web links to each property.

totally escape from the high-tech life with a stroll through the herb garden or out to the stand of old fruit trees, a sit-down in the gazebo, or a snuggle in the swing for two. Full breakfast is served in the stenciled dining room or, weather permitting, on the screened-in porch. Owner William McQueen can arrange special rates at two of the area's top golf courses (the Country Club of Hershey–East and Dauphin Highlands) and will be happy to schedule tee times and arrange after-game refreshments. Advance discount tickets to Hersheypark are also available.

PARADISE

Frogtown Acres $$
44 Frogtown Road
(888) 649–2333, (717) 768–7684
www.frogtownacres.com

Why the name Frogtown Acres? You won't have to ask after you see all of the croaker-inspired creations that turn up all over this off-the-beaten-path estate. Owners Gloria and Joe Crawshaw have converted their property's 1810 carriage house into a four-guest room bed-and-breakfast, retaining the rustic feel of the original stone floors and wooden rafters, while adding all of the amenities for modern comfort. Comfortable family accommodations abound here—particularly in The Balcony Room, with its queen-size bed and two singles, and the lower-level Alcove Room, with its queen-size poster bed and pocket-door-separated alcove with single bed. A full breakfast garnished with herbs fresh from the garden is included. Some of the house specialties include pumpkin pancakes, outdoor-grilled big-link Amish sausage, and locally made scrapple (for anyone who is not familiar with this pork-based breakfast specialty, it's one of those don't-ask-what's-in-it, just-eat-it foods).

Family-style activities are also plentiful. The Crawshaws love to fire up their outdoor barbecue and invite guests to come out on the deck for some marshmallow toasting. In the summer, kids can help crank the old-fashioned ice-cream maker. There's good fishing in a nearby stream and an area to play quoits, the Amish version of horseshoes. Or just grab a swing or take a seat in the gazebo and soak in the serenity of Pennsylvania Dutch Country farmland.

STRASBURG

Limestone Inn Bed and Breakfast $$–$$$
33 East Main Street
(800) 278-8392, (717) 687-8392
www.thelimestoneinn.com

An architectural melding of medieval and Georgian styles makes this circa 1786 home one of the most unusual and, according to owners Richard and Denise Waller, one of the most photographed historic buildings around. Its location at the heart of Strasburg's Main Street means you can park your car (off-street parking is provided) and forget it as you walk to shops, restaurants, museums, and all kinds of other in-town attractions. Five of the six guest rooms have private baths. One of the most picturesque is Doc Tinney's Room, with its queen-size late-19th-century Dutch-style bedroom set, fireplace, and bath with claw-foot tub. The nighttime view of the town from the window of the Tower Room is worth the price of admission alone; add a full-size antique oak sleigh bed and a fireplace, and it's even better. (Two things to keep in mind about this room: If you want a private bath, the one down the hall can be reserved for your visit. Also, if you're over 6 feet tall, you may want to choose another room—the ceilings in this one are a little low.) Full breakfast in the formal dining room is included, as well as snacks of coffee, tea, cold drinks, cookies, and pastries in the Gathering Room, one of the four common rooms and the only room in the house with a television. This accommodation does not accept credit cards. Children over 12 are welcome.

FARM STAYS

Nature didn't intend for us to rise and shine every morning to the clanging of an alarm clock. That's why there are roosters. A farm stay can be a great wake-up call in more ways than one.

It's amazing how keen your sense of hearing becomes when it's not dulled by the honking of car horns and the shrilling of cell phones, when, instead of assaulting your senses, sound soothes with the music of bird and insect song and the rustling of leaves.

Even if we didn't grow up with grandparents in the country, experiencing a farm brings us back to something, a sense of childlike wonder and excitement about the most basic things in life. For children, a farm is a magical place filled with a myriad of memorable sights, sounds, and adventures.

If you think making your bed in the morning constitutes a chore, try getting up at the crack of dawn to milk the cows, feed the chickens, and collect the eggs. And that's just before breakfast!

When you're in Pennsylvania Dutch Country, you'll hear a lot about "plain and fancy," usually in reference to clothing and lifestyles differentiating the Old Order Amish and Mennonites and their more worldly neighbors. The phrase also accurately describes the range of accommodations you can find on Pennsylvania Dutch Country farms.

For a big helping of country living, you may want to stay in the farmhouse with your host family. Some offer totally posh suite setups for privacy and luxury. Architectural aficionados may prefer a converted barn complete with rustic charm and modern amenities. A family-size cabin might be fun, or maybe an efficiency apartment. The options are virtually endless.

As with so many accommodations in this area, smoking inside farm buildings is usually prohibited. We will point out in the listings any accommodations that do allow smoking.

If you need a phone in your room, or can't live without a television or high-speed Internet connection, check with the accommodation before booking. Some guests prefer to totally relax out of range of today's sometimes intrusive technologies.

While many farm lodgings accept major credit cards, some small, family-owned operations may prefer traveler's checks, personal checks, or even cash. We will try to designate those accommodations that do not accept credit cards. However, it is advisable to check before you book.

The general protocol for tipping is the same as for a bed-and-breakfast. Like B&B operations, many farms are family-owned and operated but hire part- or full-time staff to make sure accommodations are always guest-ready. Therefore, you'll probably want to tip as you would at a hotel or motel. Even if it is a family-only operation, everybody likes to be appreciated. If you're still in doubt, ask the owners.

Finally, as members of their communities, operators usually have great connections for dining and other activities. In Pennsylvania Dutch Country, many hosts can arrange for you to have dinner in an Amish home, a countryside bus tour, tee time at the local links, or a romantic winter sleigh ride.

Although rates are subject to change, we use the following pricing code to indi-

---

While a stay at a farm can be a delightful and educational experience for children, not all farms are equipped to accommodate very young ones. Be sure to check with the farm of your choice.

Feeding time on the farm is fun for the kids. PENNSYLVANIA DUTCH CONVENTION & VISITORS BUREAU

cate the average rate for a one-night stay, double occupancy, in season, for two adults. Note that these rates do not include taxes, gratuities, or add-on services such as room service or premium TV channels, unless otherwise indicated. Off-season rates are lower. October (especially weekends) and June through August are usually considered peak seasons. Many accommodations offer seasonal packages that may include dining, theater, golf, tours, and other extras.

$	$50–$89
$$	$90–$130
$$$	$131–$159
$$$$	$160–$199
$$$$$	$200 or more

GORDONVILLE

Beacon Hollow Farm Guest House $
130 Beacon Hollow Road
(717) 768–8218
Nothing fancy; just a clean, quiet two-bedroom cottage on a working Old Order Amish dairy farm (yes, there is electricity available to guests) situated 1 mile north of Intercourse. The cottage has queen-size, double, and single beds; a large kitchen with refrigerator and range; and a private full bath. Breakfast items are provided for a make-your-own meal. Ask in advance to arrange a tour of the farm. This accommodation accepts cash or traveler's checks only.

(Note: If no one answers when you call, leave a message. The owner will call you back.)

Eby's Pequea Farm Bed and Breakfast $
345 Belmont Road
(717) 768-3615
www.frontiernet.net/~ebyfarm

About halfway between Intercourse and Paradise is Gordonville, where Amish and Mennonite farms still make up most of the scenery. One of these is Eby's, a seventh-generation, 81-acre dairy farm (nearly 100 cows), built in the early 1800s on land that was part of a grant from William Penn. Since 1999, the farm has been run by Mike Eby and his wife, Lynette, who live in the 1814 brick farmhouse. In true Pennsylvania Dutch tradition, parents Mel and Joyce Eby didn't move far—in fact, they're just across the field in a modern Cape Cod of their own. And both families welcome guests to share their homes with them.

In the 1814 farmhouse, visitors may choose from three guest rooms, two with shared bath, one with a private bath. Or there's an efficiency apartment with a master bedroom with double bed, kids' room with bunk beds, a full kitchen, and a patio.

In the Cape Cod, one bedroom over-looking a covered bridge has a two-person Jacuzzi and is wheelchair accessible. Three additional rooms have private baths and share a family room and kitchen. Breakfast is included with all overnight stays.

The Ebys are happy to take you on a tour of their farm. Even better, you can pitch in. There are always hungry calves to feed, along with their moms. Milking is also something everybody should try at least once. The family grows corn, too.

Kids can burn off any excess energy bouncing on a trampoline or having fun in the playground. There's fishing and canoe-ing in the adjacent Pequea River, as well as a wood-carver's studio within easy walking distance of the farm.

The Ebys are a practicing Mennonite family who request that no alcoholic bev-erages be brought into their home. They also invite guests who want to experience Mennonite worship services firsthand to join them at their local church (the Par-adise Mennonite Church, built in 1806, the oldest in the township).

HUMMELSTOWN

**Inn at Westwynd Farm
Bed and Breakfast $$-$$$**
1620 Sand Beach Road
(877) WESTWYND, (717) 533-6764
www.westwyndfarminn.com

Horse lovers with a handful of carrots will make friends quickly with the ones that live here (not to mention the goats—they're pretty friendly, too). Located 3 miles north of Hershey on 32 pristine acres, the inn features fireplaces, antiques, luxuriously soft linens, and bountiful breakfast. But it's the inhabitants of the renovated 1858 classic Pennsylvania bank barn that really steal the show here. Equine enthusiasts will love the opportu-nity to get up close and personal with more than 20 resident steeds.

If you want to watch the horses strut their stuff, you'll have a bird's-eye view of the dressage ring and jump field from the inn's second-floor room named for Sea Gift–Phred–The Physic Chestnut (all seven guest rooms are named for equine friends of the family). The Killarney-John Room, done in a hunt motif, overlooks the pasture and pond. It comes with binoculars on the windowsill to help you spot the herons, egrets, and other winged wonders. The first-floor Fortune's Return–Radar, with its view of the east pasture, is wheelchair accessible and has a separate entrance. A particularly cost-friendly option for families (children over eight are welcome) or friends traveling together is a combination rental of the Roman Canon–Little John and Penny Power Rooms with shared bath. Most rooms with king-size beds can be

Click on www.afarmstay.com for descriptions and links to a large local association of farm accommodations.

replaced with two twins, and cots are available for larger rooms.

Guests can receive special rates at two of the area's top golf resorts—Country Club of Hershey–East and Dauphin Highlands—along with after-game refreshments. And you can save time and money on a visit to Hersheypark with discount tickets that you can reserve at the inn.

LANCASTER

Equestrian Estates Horse Farm
Bed & Breakfast $$–$$$
221 Schultz Road
(717) 464–2164, (717) 464–1345
www.equestrianbnb.com

David Stoltzfus was one of nine children raised in an Old Order Amish Pennsylvania Dutch home. David is currently pastor of the House of the Lord Mennonite Fellowship Church, and he, along with his wife, Linda, and their children, are happy to share the traditions of both faiths with guests in their circa 1800s brick farmhouse and carriage house. Guests are also invited to the worship services that are held in the barn every Sunday (dress is casual).

In the bank barn and stables, the Stoltzfus family raises show and quarter horses. Guests are invited to help feed the steeds or accompany their hosts to a horse auction or show. The silky, purry fluff balls that you'll see pouncing and playing are Himalayan cats that the family also breeds.

You can't get more country than a stroll through orchards bursting with fruit (apples, pears, and peaches, to name a few). Fresh-picked blueberries and strawberries often find their way to the breakfast table, along with an Amish-style baked oatmeal and other goodies. For lunch, you can pack a picnic to share in the meadow on a small island between two streams, under the willow trees, or in the Victorian gazebo in the orchard.

Guest rooms in the house are furnished with antiques. The Fireplace Room, in the

oldest part of the house, has a private entrance and porch, two-person Jacuzzi, and separate sitting room.

Higher priced accommodations on the property include the Carriage House ($179), a separate 1870 cottage with private screened-in porch with picnic table and chairs; two bedrooms with antique double beds, plus a sleeper sofa in the living room; and kitchenette equipped with a refrigerator, a microwave, and a dining table. The Stable Suite ($189) is a private hideaway that comes with a romantic dinner for two. The Victorian Honeymoon Suite (also $189) is the most deluxe accommodation, with its king-size canopy bed, entertainment center with Surround Sound, two Victorian sitting rooms, library, two-person Jacuzzi, private entrance and porch, and picture window (a telescope is provided to help you enjoy the view) overlooking the barns, orchards, and gazebo. Breakfast in bed for two is available to Victorian Suite guests for a small additional charge.

This is a cash-only accommodation.

Pheasant Run Farm $$–$$$
200 Marticville Road
(717) 872–0991
www.pheasantrunfarmbb.com

It's only about a 15- to 20-minute drive to downtown Lancaster, the surrounding colleges, and all of the other city attractions, but with 48 acres of farmland around you, all of that can be as far away as you'd like. Former teachers Bob and Vivian Abel, who live in the property's 1842 stone farmhouse, grow corn and alfalfa on close to half of the farm. And they offer four guest rooms in a beautifully restored 1809 stone bank barn. The Abels have done such a great job that they were presented with an award for Adaptive Re-use by the Historic Preservation Trust of Lancaster County.

Watch the sun rise over the meadow from your eastern-facing vantage point in Catharine's Room, named for a former owner of the farm. Other distinctive features in this room include a vaulted ceiling with exposed beams, an antique armoire, a gas fireplace, and a queen-size hand-made tiger maple canopy bed (even the quilt is special—it's a locally handmade piece with a "barn raising" motif). First-floor wheelchair-accessible Henry and Anna's Room (their names appear on the date stone of the farmhouse) has an ele-gant exposed stone wall, king-size poster bed, gas fireplace, whirlpool tub, and pri-vate door to the veranda overlooking the garden.

Breakfast at the pine farm table, with its locally made fan-back Windsor chairs, is served by candlelight on decorative dishes from Vivian's personal collection. Special dietary needs can be accommodated with prior notice.

Children 12 and older are welcome. This is a cash-only accommodation.

MANHEIM

Country Vistas Bed & Breakfast $
448 West Sun Hill Road
(717) 664–2931
www.countryvistas.net
Five acres of family fun are waiting at this hands-on farm just south of Manheim (halfway between Hershey and Inter-course). There are baby lambs and goats to pet; chickens, sheep, and other animals to feed; eggs to gather from the hen-house; and a big tabby cat appropriately named Cuddles for a companion. A large yard gives kids lots of safe space to run around and play; there are also swings, basketball hoops, and a tetherball. For quieter recreation, soak in the breathtak-ing view of the surrounding flower gar-dens, fruit orchard, pastureland, and woodland from the top of the ridge.

Breakfast is the definition of farm fresh, with fruit just picked from the orchard; asparagus, strawberries, or raspberries plucked from their patches; and eggs from the resident chickens. Enjoy it all in a sunny dining room with skylights and a large picture window.

The king- or queen-size bed in each of the four guest rooms can be supplemented with futons and cribs for the children upon request. For extra space, there's the two-bedroom Kwansan Cherry Suite at the end of its own separate hallway and the Pines Loft, a second-story room with a private entrance, furnished with bunk or twin beds in addition to a queen-size bed.

If you're going to visit Hersheypark, reserve your tickets with your farm hosts to save money and time. Golfers who stay here can also get special rates and reserve tee times at the Country Club of Hershey–East and Dauphin Highlands (along with after-game refreshments back at the farm).

---

i

B&B or DIY? Some farms include break-fast with overnight stays, some provide kitchens or kitchenettes stocked with do-it-yourself morning munchies, and others leave the food entirely to you. (Lots of farm hosts invite guests to help themselves to eggs from the hen-house for a truly authentic morning repast.)

Jonde Lane Farm Bed & Breakfast $
1103 Auction Road
(717) 665–4231
http://800padutch.com/z/jondelane
.htm
This brick farmhouse has been in the Niss-ley family since current owner John's great-great-great-grandfather built it in 1859. The Nissley family's Lancaster County history, however, goes back fur-ther than that, to when its first members sailed from Bern, Switzerland, in 1717. John and his wife, Elaine, are proud to talk about that history with guests who stay in the four rooms available in their home.

Most of the guest rooms share two hallway bathrooms. Private facilities are available in the only main-floor guest room, called the Hen House, which also has a private entrance from the back porch, refrigerator, microwave, lots of sleeping space (a queen-size bed, set of bunks, and a single sofa bed), and vintage-design hydrothermal massage tub.

Set far off the road, the farm is a protected haven for children and animals, such as Angel, the snow-white pony; Maybelline, the friendly St. Bernard; goats Millie, Lillie, and Billie; Flopsy, the bunny; sheep Wally, Polly, Dolly, and Molly; and kittens that love to be cuddled. Lots of the animals like to be hand-fed, a treat for kids. The pastures are also filled with Holsteins.

The back roads are so lightly traveled, say the owners, that they're perfect for walking and biking. There's also an off-road linear park.

A full hot breakfast is served every day except Sunday. But nobody will go hungry even then, because a generous continental breakfast is available.

When packing for your farm stay, tuck in at least one extra pair of shoes—the ground can get muddy, and there are animals. Old clothes are a must; farm work can be as messy as it is satisfying. For rainy days, throw in a couple of games, particularly if the kids are coming along, and good books.

Landis Farm Guest Home **$–$$**
2048 Gochlan Road
(717) 898-7028
www.landisfarm.com
What could be more relaxing than spending a sunny day at the old fishin' hole? Well, maybe a picnic in the pasture or a nap in a giant tire swing surrounded by flowering gardens and fertile fields. It's your choice at this 70-acre working farm set about 5 miles west of Lancaster City, off Route 283.

Earl and Evelyn Landis have restored a 200-year-old farm cottage, right down to the polished wide-plank floors, Indian door, and original Williamsburg colors, for guest rental. Two bedrooms (each with double bed) and a living room with a sofa that converts into another double provide ample room for family bunking. If that's not enough, the Landises offer sleeping bags for children. A full modern kitchen comes stocked with utensils, linens, and self-serve breakfast fixings.

Although this is no longer a dairy farm (Earl and Evelyn grow primarily corn, alfalfa, soybeans, and wheat), there are still cows—as well as goats, rabbits, and chickens—in the meadow. You can even leave the kids' toys at home. The farm has plenty of toys, including bikes, a Big Wheel, and a scooter, to keep them amused.

Stone Haus Farm Bed & Breakfast $–$$
360 South Esbenshade Road
(717) 653-8444
www.afarmstay.com/stone
Celery is an integral part of Pennsylvania Dutch cooking. To ensure that there is plenty on hand for year-round use, the ingenious farmers around these parts bury their harvested stalks in barrels or tile troughs, where the usually delicate veggie keeps for weeks. A happy side benefit of this storage—often called "bleaching" or "blanching"—is sweeter, crisper celery that has developed a loyal following of its own. At Stone Haus Farm, Merv and Angie Shenk devote 30 of their 100 total acres to growing celery hearts for bleaching (the rest of the land is dedicated to corn and soybeans). Guests are welcome to help in the seeding of the beds in April, the transplanting in June and July, and the harvesting in September through January (weeders are particularly welcome).

Otherwise, there are chickens to feed, eggs to gather, and bunnies and kittens to pet. The Shenks have three youngsters of their own, so kids will have plenty of company on the property's playground. Families can also just relax on a hayride to a local covered bridge; play tennis, volleyball, or croquet; or jog or bike along a quiet country road.

Accommodations in the 200-year-old farmhouse are spacious and have queen-size and single beds to comfortably fit families of four. The lower priced room has two bedrooms and shared bath, the higher price room has a private bath. No alcoholic beverages are permitted.

One breakfast specialty that's a favorite with both family and guests are Angie's shoofly cakes (like shoofly pie, but not quite as gooey, she explains).

(Accommodation rates based on family of four rather than double occupancy.)

MARIETTA

Olde Fogie Farm $$
106 Stackstown Road
(877) 653-3644, (717) 426-3992
www.oldefogiefarm.com

That's "olde" as in quaint, not ancient, joke the good-natured owners of this organic (been that way for about 40 years), free-range farm, who, by the way, are named Tom and Biz Fogie. Ever been kissed by a llama? Now's your chance. And the rest of the menagerie, which includes a potbellied pig, hens and baby chicks, cows, sheep, and dogs, can be pretty friendly, too.

A sense of humor is essential on this farm. Among the farm's multiple amenities, for example, are, according to "liberated farm wife" Biz, shoe scrapers, fly swatters, and "artifacts" ("stuff other people threw out").

The Fogies are an extremely warm couple, and they enjoy answering children's (and their parents') curious questions. Follow them along during chore time every morning; help out if you want to or just pet the animals (a little attention puts Wootsie, the pig, in hog heaven). Farmer Tom likes to tell stories and answer questions ("especially during chore time," says Biz, who, by her own admission, does a good deal of her own storytelling and some singing in her "cabaret"—aka the gathering room, a cozy common room in the house).

If you plan on sleeping in during your farm stay, don't expect the rooster to set his alarm clock. As the owner of Olde Fogie Farm in Lancaster County cautions, "If you've never slept in a farm setting, please know that a peacock 'in season' does not sound like a nightingale, and barnyard critters crow quite randomly and at all hours."

Bring bathing suits (and swim shoes) for splashing in the pond with three waterfalls. Then fire up the grill and picnic in the screened gazebo.

Two types of accommodations are available here: traditional bed-and-breakfast rooms and family efficiency suites. The Garden Room, with its white picket fence–painted mural, comes with a queen-size bed and private bath. The Pig Pen Room (which is anything but) has animal-stencil walls, a queen-size bed, and adjacent private bath facilities. Both come with full breakfast.

If you prefer to do your own cooking (the Fogies invite guests to gather their own free-range eggs, if they wish), both the Hayloft and Chicken Coop Suites come with kitchens. The third-floor Hayloft Suite also has a shaded deck overlooking the barnyard, a queen-size bed, a claw-foot tub, and a trundle bed for two little ones. The ground-floor Chicken Coop Suite has private entrances, front and back porches with rocking chairs, a full-size bed, and a sofa bed. Breakfast is not included with these suites.

September through April, senior citizens are eligible for a 12 percent discount on the price of accommodations.

MOUNT JOY

Green Acres Farm B&B $$
1382 Pinkerton Road
(717) 653-4028
www.thegreenacresfarm.com

Skip the kennel and pack up the pets.

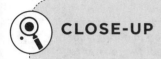

CLOSE-UP

Lights Out

If you really want to immerse yourself in the Old Order Amish lifestyle, ask owners Jacob and Sadie Zook to leave the electricity off in the guesthouse at their Starlit Acres Amish Farm (4021B Old Philadelphia Pike, Gordonville, PA 17529; 717–768–3774). For those who can't live without artificial lights and ceiling fans, there's a private electrical source available (the Zooks adhere to tradition and don't plug in), but the real experience is in using propane and candlelight like the locals have been doing for hundreds of years. The three-bedroom wood-frame guesthouse with private bath built sometime in the 1940s accommodates one family at a time. A large front yard gives kids lots of room for outdoor play in a safe setting sur-rounded by 80 acres of alfalfa, corn, and pumpkin fields. The Zooks also breed horses. This is not a hands-on farm, but farmer Jacob Zook says that guests may "tag along" as family members do their chores. He also says that they get lots of questions about the Amish lifestyle from guests and are happy to answer them as best they can. There are no televisions or radios, and the Zooks do not permit alcohol or smoking on their property. They also ask that guests refrain from using foul language and maintain a level of courteous "modesty" in their dress (shorts are fine as long as they're of moderate length). The Zooks want their guests to be comfortable but still respectful of Amish codes and customs.

You're never far from a farm in Pennsylvanina Dutch Country. PENNSYLVANIA DUTCH CONVENTION & VISITORS BUREAU

They're as welcome at Green Acres as the rest of your family. And they'll have lots of company with all the resident kittens, pygmy goats, sheep, peacocks, and pony.

Owner Wayne Miller will take you on a hayride down the back roads through a nearby covered bridge. Parents can relax and enjoy the pastoral view while the kids have the time of their lives in a playhouse and barn built especially for them, bouncing on the trampoline, soaring through the air on the swing set, or building the castles of their dreams in the sand. Of course, they're also welcome to share in the animal feeding, egg gathering, and other daily farm chores. Better yet, while away a sunny day fishing at the nearby stream.

Stay in one of Wayne and wife, Yvonne, Miller's seven guest rooms in their 150-year-old farm house, with its large antiques-furnished living room for lounging and big, bright kitchen for lingering over a full-course family-style farm breakfast. (Early risers can enjoy a prebreakfast cup of coffee starting at 7:00 A.M.)

This accommodation accepts credit cards to reserve rooms only—cash or check are required for payment at time of stay.

Rocky Acre Farm
Bed & Breakfast   **$$–$$$**
1020 Pinkerton Road
(717) 653–4449
www.rockyacre.com
Even the furniture is kid-proof in this family-friendly 200-year-old stone farmhouse that was once a stop on the Underground Railroad. All of the eight rooms have queen-size or double beds, with extra sleeping accommodations (including a loft in one room, trundle beds in another, and cribs and sleeping mats on request) for the young ones. The Efficiency Room on the third floor comes with a kitchenette equipped with stove/oven, microwave, sink, and refrigerator. Kids love the custom-made bunk beds in the Balcony Room (and adults love that quiet space overlooking the rolling hills).

Summer is prime time for farm stays, but no matter what the season, the scenery is always spectacular, and the livestock still needs tender loving care. Spring is planting season and the time when many baby animals make their world debut. Fall is a time of harvests and colorful foliage. Winter can be serene or a playground for building snowmen and taking sleigh rides. In other words, there's never a dull season down on the farm.

Owners Galen and Eileen Benner say that the most popular is the two-floor, two-bedroom apartment located in the oldest part of the farmhouse. The space retains such elements of Colonial architecture as a walk-in fireplace, exposed beams, and Indian door. Upstairs, two bedrooms (one with a queen-size bed and another with two doubles and a single) accommodate seven. Downstairs, a kitchen and living area provide ample elbow room.

For an even more private hideaway, there's the Guest House, tucked away in the woods, but close enough to the main residence to require a less-than-10-minute walk for breakfast. (It has a kitchen, too, if you want to dine solo—but with a spread of fresh scrambled eggs, pancakes, hash browns, homemade applesauce, toast with homemade preserves, and milk produced right on the farm, that's not terribly likely.)

After-breakfast pony, train, and tractor rides are only the beginning of a full day of fun. There are lots of animals (including cute-as-a-button miniature horses) to tend and pet. There are also a kid-size playhouse and old-fashioned swing set.

Bring your own fishing rods for the stream, but you can borrow all kinds of other outdoor equipment, including bikes, balls, a rowboat, and a charcoal grill. Golfing is only steps away at the 18-hole course next door. And a stroll along Little Chickies Creek through woodlands and fields can be a natural antidote for insomnia.

(Accommodations are priced for four guests rather than for double occupancy.)

NEW HOLLAND

Smucker's Farm Guest House $
484 Peters Road
(717) 354-6879

Farm owners Amos and Malinda Smucker are Old Order Amish, but they do provide electricity, air-conditioning, and other "worldly" amenities for guests on their horse farm located 3 miles north of Intercourse. The main-floor suite comes with a queen-size bed and private bath. Two rooms on the second floor with shared bath can accommodate up to eight people. Cots are available. Guests also have the use of kitchen and laundry facilities and picnic area. Continental breakfast is included. Traveler's checks are accepted.

PARADISE

Verdant View Farm Bed
& Breakfast $-$$
429 Strasburg Road
(888) 321-8119, (717) 687-7353
www.verdantview.com

OK, so it's really in Paradise, a mile east of Strasburg (and the Strasburg Rail Road runs through the field behind the farmhouse), but with 118 acres of lush green acreage waiting to be explored, there's no need—or time—to nitpick. This working dairy and crop farm has been owned by the Ranck family since 1916 (ancestors have actually lived in the area longer, having arrived in 1728, a year before Lancaster County was officially founded).

i

Aside from the expected cows, horses, and sheep, some Pennsylvania Dutch Country barns and pastures are home to some pretty exotic creatures. Think llamas, alpacas, exotic birds, and colorful fish.

Built in 1896, the farmhouse has interior door and window trim of gleaming American chestnut (constructed before widespread blight made this wood a rarity). Bank barn buffs will love this one; it's one of the largest barns in the area, built in 1923 with mortise-and-tenon joints and hickory pegs instead of nails.

Current owners Don and Ginny Ranck offer accommodations inside their farmhouse or across the meadow in a separate building they call the "Little White House by the Side of the Road." Inside the Rancks' residence, there are three rooms (two with semiprivate and one with private bath) and one two-bedroom suite with queen-size and bunk beds, a double futon, and private bath.

The White House, a five-minute walk down the lane, can be rented by the room or in its entirety ($277 to $337 for the whole house). It has one downstairs suite and two upstairs rooms, three full bathrooms (the two upstairs have air-jet tubs), and a kitchen. For convenience, the Rancks provide complete bedding and kitchen service for 18.

For an extra $5.00 per adult and $4.00 for children (age 12 and under), all guests are invited to share a bountiful farm breakfast that could include fresh milk, homegrown meat, local Amish-made yogurt, seasonal fruits, eggs from a neighboring farm, and a homemade dessert.

Hand milking a cow or bottle feeding a calf are not required (at least not for guests), but everybody's invited to lend a hand should they find themselves in the moo-d. Kids (and adults) who have never seen a fainting goat will get the surprise of their lives, and there's a charmer of a miniature donkey as well as the requisite bunnies, kittens, hens, roosters, swans, and, riding herd over all of them, Snipper, the terrier.

Stroll along the two natural springs that originate on the property. One flows into the farm's pond and is a great fishing spot for largemouth bass and bluegills. The other begins a stream that eventually flows into the Chesapeake Bay. For a longer walk, take the ½-mile hike to the "back 40."

RONKS

Cherry-Crest Tourist Farm   **$$**
150 Cherry Hill Road
(717) 687-6843
www.cherrycrestfarm.com

Situated just east of Strasburg, this farm, once owned by well-known Conestoga wagon maker Phillip Feree, was a popular stopover for travelers from Philadelphia who were headed to the Indian Outpost in Carlisle, just west of Harrisburg. Today Jack and Donna Coleman live in the restored 1774 limestone house on the property and operate a diversified farm consisting of 300 acres of crops, a "U-pick" fall produce operation, about 50 heifers, and thousands of chickens. Cherry-Crest Farm is also a lively center for "agritainment" from July through October, featuring the "Amazing Maize

Farm animals may be cute and look cuddly, but they're not always as pettable as you might think (I personally remember a certain bull on a dairy farm). Ask the owner for tips before touching.

Maze" (admission is separate and detailed in the Attractions chapter of this book).

Two separate lodging options are available at the Cherry-Crest guesthouse. One is family size, with two bedrooms, a large living room, bath, and fully equipped kitchen. The other is a one-bedroom unit with a king-size bed, large living area with sofabed, and bath. Each part of the guesthouse has its own private entrance but can be made interaccessible to accommodate large groups. There's a large front deck and yard with swing set, playhouse, and courts for basketball and volleyball.

RESORTS

In a place most closely identified with the humble austerity of its Old Order religious communities, it may seem surprising to find resorts with world-class golf courses, spas and other major amenities representing the epitome of luxury. But rather than being an anomaly, this coexistence of opposites is one of the main reasons why Pennsylvania Dutch Country has such a unique, multifaceted personality and appeals to such a broad spectrum of visitors.

Although rates are subject to change, we use the following pricing code to indicate the average rate for a one-night stay, in season, for two adults. Note that these rates do not include taxes, gratuities, or add-on services, such as room service and premium TV channels (unless otherwise noted). Off-season rates are lower. October (especially weekends) and June through August are usually considered peak seasons.

$	$85–$139
$$	$140–$189
$$$	$190–$250
$$$$	$251–$300
$$$$$	More than $300

ℹ️ *Gettysburg is where President and Mrs. Dwight D. Eisenhower owned a 230-acre country estate. During his presidency, the couple used the farm, which adjoins Gettysburg Battlefield, as a retreat and meeting place for world leaders. At the conclusion of Eisenhower's presidency, they retired there. (For details about the Eisenhower National Historic Site, see the Attractions chapter.)*

GETTYSBURG

Eisenhower Hotels, Conference Center & Resort $-$$
2634 Emmitsburg Road
(800) 776-8349, (717) 334-8121
www.eisenhower.com

Many people know the Eisenhower, a 10-minute drive north of downtown Gettysburg, as a huge full-service business conference center. But with its country setting, two hotels, Allstar Family Fun & Events Complex, and range of on-site dining options, the resort is perfect for families on vacations.

Together, the two Eisenhower Hotels have a total of 307 guest rooms. Eisenhower I offers a choice of double rooms; king leisure rooms with sleeper/sofa; executive kings with mini kitchen; and presidential suites with living room, bedroom, and refrigerator. An indoor tropical-themed courtyard with a sky dome that opens contains a swimming pool and Jacuzzi. There's also a fitness room with dry saunas.

Eisenhower II features queen leisure rooms that sleep six and have refrigerator and microwave and two executive suites with separate bedroom, living room, and kitchen areas and Jacuzzi bath.

Both also have access to tennis courts and lakeside walking or jogging trails. Business Express Office Center provides Internet access, personal computer, copier, and fax facilities (small fees are charged for these services).

For dining, there's the food court–like Marketplace, where you eat in or take out a sandwich, soup, salad, or snack. Richard's Restaurant American-Continental specializes in steaks, seafood, and Italian entrees. A wide-screen television and fireplace make Richard's Lounge a comfy place to watch sports or just relax.

HERSHEY
Hershey Resorts

What began as a project to keep construction workers gainfully employed during the Great Depression has evolved into a world-class resort facility that includes a European-style grand hotel, a lodge inspired by the natural rustic beauty of the southeastern Pennsylvania countryside, a full-service day spa (with an innovative menu of no-cal, chocolate-based body and soul soothers), a country club with two championship courses available to guests (and two public courses), and all manner of fun and fine-dining eateries.

Guests at both The Hotel Hershey and Hershey Lodge enjoy access to the country club's two 18-hole championship golf courses; free admission to the Hershey Museum, and, in season, Hershey Gardens; seasonal complimentary shuttle bus service to Hersheypark and other area attractions is also available.

Resort-style amenities include plush terry bathrobes, concierge service, 24-hour room service, dry-cleaning and laundry service, complimentary self-parking (valet parking is also available), airport and train station shuttle service, hotel limousine service, babysitting, HBO and in-room pay movies, and Hershey's Kisses on your pillow with evening turndown service.

Resort guests have access to the two private 18-hole golf courses at the Hershey Country Club (there are also two public courses on the premises). The par-73 West Course, with its sweeping view of the town and play high on the hill on the front lawn of Milton Hershey's estate, High Point Mansion, has hosted several LPGA and PGA tournaments. The par-71 East Course, designed by George Fazio, features three artificial lakes and more than 100 bunkers.

If you really want to immerse yourself in chocolate, The Spa at The Hotel Hershey gives you many multisensual ways to do it: Foaming Whipped Cocoa Bath, Chocolate Sugar Scrub, Cocoa Massage (classic Swedish massage with chocolate-scented

What could be better than a movie under the stars? How about a movie next to the pool? Check out the "Dive-In-Movie" at Hershey Lodge on selected evenings between Memorial Day and Labor Day (weather permitting).

massage oil), and Chocolate Fondue Wrap. There are also "Everything Chocolate" and "Chocolate Immersion" spa packages, so you can luxuriate all you want.

Hershey may be synonymous with chocolate, but there are other flavors, too, at The Spa. You can have a Strawberry Parfait or Peppermint Scrub, a CoffeeBean Polish or Milk & Honey Wrap. Even more exotic are the signature "Cuban Experiences" (in 1916, Milton Hershey paid a visit to Cuba and was so enamored of the island that he purchased sugar plantations and mills there to supply his Pennsylvania candy factory). "Treat"-ments include a Mojito Sugar Scrub; Green Coffee Body Wrap; and Noche Azul Soak, containing tropical flowers including *la Mariposa blanca* (white butterfly jasmine)—Cuba's national flower—hibiscus, and orange blossom.

Hershey Lodge   **$$–$$$**
West Chocolate Avenue
and University Drive
P.O. Box 446
Hershey, PA 17033
(800) HERSHEY, (717) 533–3311
Although this facility wasn't opened until 21 years after the death of Milton Hershey, its style and service definitely live up to his original standards. Originally opened in 1967 as Hershey Motor Lodge, it has grown

Teens need pampering, too, so The Spa at The Hotel Hershey has developed special treatments, including facials, manicures, pedicures, hair cut and styling, and makeup lessons, for 13- to 17-year-old luxury seekers.

into a major property in its own right, with 665 rooms, including 28 suites, and a 100,000-square-foot convention center.

Unlike the Mediterranean-style Hotel Hershey, the Lodge decor takes its cue from the Pennsylvania Dutch countryside and its heritage, with high post-and-beam ceilings, exposed stonework, regionally crafted furnishings, and local artwork. Indoor amenities include a health club equipped with treadmills, recumbent bicycles, EFX elliptical, Stairmaster, handheld free weights, and a variety of Cybex personal weight equipment. There's also a

game room for the kids.

Lodge guests play free at the 18-hole miniature golf course located on the property (weather permitting). Two outdoor swimming pools are open Memorial Day through Labor Day, plus there's a heated indoor pool, 1-foot wading pool, and whirlpool that are available year-round. Dry saunas are available at the recreation center.

Facilities and equipment are also available for basketball, tennis, volleyball, and shuffleboard. An on-site playground, appearances by Hershey's Product Characters, and an ever-changing roster of seasonal activities and programs add even more opportunities for fun.

On-premise dining ranges from the casual steak-and-seafood-focused Hershey Grill to Lebbie Lebkicher's Casual Buffet Dining (named for a longtime friend of Milton Hershey) to the Bears' Den Sports Bar (the Hershey Bears is the American Hockey League's oldest continuously operating franchise). Or, if you don't feel like going out, Mama Meoni's Pizza will deliver to your room.

The Hotel Hershey　　　　**$$$$-$$$$$**
Hotel Road
P.O. Box 400
Hershey, PA 17033
(800) HERSHEY, (717) 533-2171
www.hersheypa.com

Although the town of Hershey was built in the early 1900s to provide a community for the employees of the chocolate factory of the same name, its founder took great pains to make sure it didn't turn into just another factory town where workers toiled in anonymity and could lose everything as a result of any business whim or economic glitch. So when the Great Depression put the brakes on America's building boom and threatened the livelihood of the town's 600 construction workers, Milton S. Hershey figured that it was his moral obligation to either feed them or provide work for them.

Hershey Hospitality

Milton and Catherine Hershey were avid world travelers who took copious notes of designs and other items of interest that caught their eyes and imaginations. Prior to her death in 1915, Catherine, according to official Hershey history, had expressed the hope that she and Milton would model their hotel after the Heliopolis in Cairo, Egypt. Wanting to fulfill his late wife's dream, Milton figured he would find the architect of the Heliopolis and buy his plans . . . until he discovered that the cost of duplicating the Middle Eastern masterpiece would be $5 million.

Instead, Milton showed his architect and chief engineer a postcard of a hotel in which he and Catherine had stayed while traveling in the Mediterranean region. To create the ambience he wanted, Hershey pulled ideas from his and Catherine's travel notes, specifying a Spanish patio, tiled floors, and a fountain. The dining room should be circular, he said, because "in some places, if you don't tip well, they put you in a corner. I don't want any corners."

To construct the hotel, more than $2 million was spent, and 800 steelworkers, masons, carpenters, and other craftsmen and laborers were employed. Begun in 1932, the building was ready for its first guests in May 1933.

With building materials available at lowest prices, Hershey decided that this was the right time to build the hotel that he and his late wife, Catherine, had been planning for years. Fearing for his fortune during those economically turbulent times, Hershey's mother tried to dissuade him from the venture, but, in 1930, construction began on a hill overlooking the chocolate factory.

Today, The Hotel Hershey, a member of the Historic Hotels of America, spans 300 acres with 232 deluxe Mediterranean-inspired guest rooms (with one king-size, one queen-size, or two double beds) and 25 suites, all with views of the formal gardens, flowered terrace, or the velvet green valley below. Top of the line is the suite named for Milton Hershey, which includes a large central parlor, two bedrooms, a sunroom, and a veranda overlooking the town he built. Wheelchair-accessible rooms are available. Cribs and refrigerators are available on request.

Recreational facilities on the hotel grounds include two swimming pools (indoor and outdoor); a health and fitness center; nature trails; and basketball, bocce, and tennis courts. Bike rentals are available. For business events, the property offers 23,500 square feet of meeting and function space.

On-premise dining options range from the elegant white tablecloth Circular Dining Room to snacks and ice cream by the pool at the Club House Cafe & Creamery.

LANCASTER

**Lancaster Host Resort
& Conference Center** $
**2300 Lincoln Highway East (Route 30)
(800) 233-0121, (717) 299-5500
www.lancasterhost.com**

With three working Amish farms around it, Dutch Wonderland right across the street, and the outlet stores only a mile away, this 225-acre resort facility is both scenic and convenient. A big attraction right on the grounds is an 18-hole, par-71 championship golf course, which has been the site of Pro Am events and has hosted such major club wielders as Jack Nicklaus, Arnold Palmer, and Sam Snead. Special midweek golf packages, including accommodations and golf, can save you money. Weekend packages are also available.

Driving range and practice facility (including a night-lit putting green) provide lots of opportunities for honing stroke-shaving skills. Golf lessons (30- to 60-minute private sessions with a PGA professional instructor) are available on Tuesday and Thursday in June and July. There's also a miniature golf course so the entire family can take a swing.

Nongolfing recreational activities include indoor and outdoor swimming pools, a walking/jogging trail, bike rentals, Ping-Pong and pool tables, shuffleboard, and a game room. If you want to get around and see the sights, look into the Dutch Country Family Fun Package, which includes breakfast for two adults (up to three children per room ages 12 and under eat free), up to four tickets each to Dutch Wonderland Amusement Park, the Strasburg Rail Road, and Dutch Wonderland Mini Golf. Other packages include accommodations, breakfast, and tickets to either Dutch Wonderland or Hersheypark.

Lancaster Host Resort is pet-friendly. It has 330 standard, deluxe, and king rooms and family suites, all equipped with Web TV, first-run in-house movies, Internet access, music videos, and other amenities. Many of the rooms also offer pool, garden, or fairway views.

Dining options are plentiful here. The Vista Restaurant, with golf course views, serves a hearty Amish breakfast buffet and contemporary lunch selections. Legends is white tablecloth-sophisticated and serves regional specialties in a clublike setting with classic golf memorabilia decor. Good

Spirits, located in the resort's main lobby, has armchairs, a piano bar, and a "lite fare" appetizer and drinks menu for a little nibble. Or you can call up room service for private dining.

You can also pick up a burger at Mulligan's, located on the golf course's 10th tee, or a hand-dipped cone or sundae at Scoops at Mulligan's, an old-fashioned ice-cream parlor within the cafe. When pool season's in session, Splash's serves piña coladas and strawberry daiquiris.

Willow Valley Resort
& Conference Center $$
2416 Willow Street Pike
(800) 444-1714
www.willowvalley.com

First opened as a 30-unit motel on Route 222, Willow Valley Resort now has 324 guest rooms and banquet facilities for up to 1,000. The resort also includes a nine-hole public golf course, with special seniors and twilight prices available. (Golfers with established handicaps who are looking for a more challenging experience may arrange for access to the private 18-hole Meadia Heights Golf Club located less than 1 mile away.)

Other outdoor recreational options include a water playground (pool with slides, tubes, and other drenching diversions), bike rentals, wagon rides, and tennis and basketball courts. For a full workout, there's a well-equipped fitness center with free weights, treadmills, stair climbers, elliptical machines and stationary bikes, as well as saunas and whirlpools.

Resort guests also have access (and discounted pricing) to the spa services at the Cultural Center, located just a few minutes from the resort at the Willow Valley Retirement Community. This center is not open to the general public. Day spa services include therapeutic, hot stone, and reflexology hand and food massages; aromatherapy; wraps; facials and skin peels; manicures and pedicures; and deep-cleansing back facials for men and women. Special packages include "Total Body Bliss" and "Gentlemen's Escape."

Guest rooms in the South Wing, with a view of the duck pond, come with two queen-size beds (can accommodate up to five with a cot). Centre Building rooms have two queen-size beds (can add cot) or two queen-size beds and one queen-size pullout sofa, some with two bathrooms, fireplaces, and pool view. Atrium Building rooms are available with two queen-size beds with cot or queen-size pullout sofa or one king-size bed, one queen-size pullout sofa, and Jacuzzi. Some rooms offer Palm Court or outside views. All rooms have refrigerators.

For dining, guests with hearty appetites favor Willow Valley's Family Restaurant, with its all-you-can-eat smor-gasbords for breakfast, lunch, and dinner. On Sunday, brunch at Willow Valley's Palm Court is a big deal, with made-to-order omelets, carved round of beef, stir-fry and pasta stations, crab legs and shrimp, salads, homemade desserts, and much more.

Specially priced packages include a number of seasonal, holiday, or any day dine-and-stay options. Discount tickets to local attractions such as Dutch Wonderland and Hershey Park are available at the resort. Along with their accommodations and other amenities, guests of Willow Valley Resort receive a complimentary three-hour bus tour of Pennsylvania Dutch Country with stops for samplings of local food and culture.

CAMPGROUNDS AND CABINS

For some people, camping is a chance to air out the old tent and pitch it in a beautiful spot under the stars or to rough it in a primitive log cabin. To others, it's a comfortable road trip in a fully appointed RV. Some apply the term *camping* to accommodations that range from quaint cottages to amenity-loaded resorts. The only key factor that seems to define the camping experience for all is an abundance of opportunities to enjoy the great outdoors.

The wide-open countryside and cool, shaded forests of Pennsylvania Dutch Country make this area extremely popular with campers of all kinds. Some facilities offer a range of options, from primitive to posh, unplugged from electricity or cable television- and WiFi-ready, away from it all or in the middle of everything.

Many facilities are pet-friendly when it comes to their tent and RV sites but don't allow canine or feline companions (with the exception of Seeing Eye dogs) in cabins and cottages. If you do bring your pets, most campgrounds ask that they be crated or temporarily boarded at a local kennel (a list of recommended kennels is usually available) if you plan to be gone for the day.

While visitors are permitted on many campgrounds, they are usually asked to register, pay a daily fee, and honor designated visiting hours. Most facilities also ask guests to keep all noise at a minimum during designated night and early morning "quiet hours."

Campers can find facilities open year-round. Listed rates do not include tax, unless otherwise specified.

ELIZABETHTOWN

Elizabethtown/Hershey KOA
1980 Turnpike Road
(800) 562-4774, (717) 367-7718
www.campwithrusty.com, www.koa.com
Open from April through early November, this 50-acre tree-filled property offers accommodations ranging from tent and RV sites to cabins with the basics or the works. Facilities include a swimming pool, stock catch-and-release fishing pond, playground and game room, minigolf, baseball, basketball, horseshoes, sand volleyball, convenience store, laundry, and clean rest rooms. Leashed pets are welcome.

Activities include free hayrides, crafts, bonfires, movies, campfires with hotdog and marshmallow roasts.

Pull-throughs for big rigs as well as water and 20/30/50 amp electric hookups are available. Rates are based on a family of two adults and three children or grandchildren, 17 years of age or younger. Basic tent site (no hookup) runs from $25.00 to $28.50; tent site/pop-up with water and electric, $27.00 to $31.50; trailers and motor homes, $33.00 to $42.50; pull-through campsite, $36.00 to $44.00. Stay seven or more nights and get 15 percent

---

A number of campgrounds offer free camping space (some also offer the option of a discount on a cabin or cottage) plus other perks (for example, a free homemade chili dinner and karaoke party) to energetic individuals who are willing to spend a designated Saturday morning in early April tidying up the grounds for the big season kick-off. Bring your own rake and/or leaf blower. Call or log on to specific camping facility Web sites for details.

off. Guests are treated to a free breakfast bar on most Sundays from May to mid-September.

You may also rent a KOA-style "Kamping Kabin" or non-KOA-style cabin (no pets or smoking in cabins). One-room KOA cabins ($45 to $55 per night) have a double bed and set of bunks, small wall table and bench, air-conditioning, water access on site, and a porch swing. Deluxe one-room log cabins ($50 to $65 per night) sleep up to five (two adults and three children) with double bed and bunks, table, chairs, studio refrigerator, microwave, air-conditioning, and water access on site. All cabins have fire rings, picnic tables, and a charcoal grill. Bring your own blankets and sleeping bags.

Small or large RV park models (sleep two to seven, depending on the unit type) have bathrooms with shower; equipped kitchenettes with refrigerator, microwave, stove, coffeepot, toaster, glassware, dishes, cookware, and utensils; a raised barbecue grill; a picnic table; and a fire ring. TV and VCR in some units. Price: small $85 to $100 per night; large, $95 to $115.

Hershey Conewago Campground
1590 Hershey Road
(866) 246-1809, (717) 367-1179
www.hersheyconewago.com
Only 6 miles south of Hershey is this 26-acre campground (formerly Hershey KOA), with sites for tents and RVs along with rental log cabins overlooking a one-acre pond. All campsites come with picnic table, fire ring, and unlimited free hot showers at the bathhouse. Hookups with water, sewer, and 30 amp electric are available. Base rates (maximum two adults and two children) for tent are $24.00 no hookups to $27.50 with water and electric; for RV, $31.00 with water and electric, $34.50 for water/electric/sewer. Log Cabin ($49) has a double bed and two bunk beds, small table, porch with bench, picnic table, and a fire ring. Bring your own bedding and cooking gear. On-site facilities include a Laundromat; half-acre pond with carp, koi, and tadpoles; swimming pool;

18-hole minigolf; sand volleyball; horseshoes; and basketball/tennis court; large sand-based playground; arcade; and a country store with a data port for Internet access. Nightly children's movie.

Stay six days at Hershey Conewago and get the seventh day free. Discount tickets to Hersheypark are also available.

GETTYSBURG

Drummer Boy Camping Resort
1300 Hanover Road
(800) 293-2808, (717) 334-3277
www.drummerboycamping.com
A five-minute drive from the battlefield, this 90-acre property offers sites and facilities for tents and RVs of all sizes plus cabin and luxury cottage rentals.

Facilities include clean, modern restrooms, store, two Laundromats, gift shop, and snack bar; also available is high-speed wireless Internet access from an RV site (pay per use). Recreational amenities include a landscaped heated pool with waterslide and adult spa, whirlpool, minigolf, director-led planned activities, catch-and-release fishing and paddle boats in pond, playground, game room, nightly movies in mini-theater (June through September), volleyball, horseshoes, hiking trails, battlefield auto tour tape rentals, and bus tour arrangements.

Check out the ongoing schedule of special events such as themed dinners with entertainment, fishing contests, Thursday night bingo, Downtown Ghost Tour, quilting, ceramics, and scrap booking, Halloween weekends, and free historian-led downtown historical tours on Sunday mornings in summer. Nondenominational church services are held in the campground each Sunday between Memorial Day and Labor Day.

Pets are welcome (except in rental units).

Nightly campsite rates are based on two people, unless otherwise indicated. Rates range by time of week, season, and special events times. Sites with no hookup are priced from $27 to $40 per night, $168 to $244 weekly; with water and electric $31 to $44 nightly, $196 to $252 weekends; with water/electric/sewer, $35 to $48 nightly, $224 to $228 weekly. One- and two-room cabins (sleep four and six, respectively) include a double bed, twin bunks, electricity, dorm-size refrigerator, heating and air-conditioning, charcoal grill, picnic table, and water faucet (all cooking must be done outside). Price: $50 to $75 nightly, $335 to $420 weekly for one-room, $335 to $420 weekly; $65 to $85 daily, $440 to $525 weekly for two-room. Fully equipped log cottages, which sleep six with one queen-size bed in one room, two sets of bunks in a separate room, dining room table, bathroom, kitchenette (with dorm-size refrigerator, two-burner stove top, microwave oven, coffeemaker, dishes, pots, pans, and utensils), range from $110 to $135 daily, $765 to $875 weekly.

Drummer Boy offers a variety of special offers, including 10 percent discounts for AAA, AARP, and FMCA (Family Motor Coach Association) members and active military personnel. On Stars and Stripes Weekend in May, all firefighters, police officers, and active military with ID get 15 percent off.

The property also issues a "Frequent Camping Card" that offers campers who stay eight nights during one season $30 off a ninth night.

Gettysburg Campground
2030 Fairfield Road
(717) 335-3304
www.gettysburgcampground.com
Tent and RV sites along with rental cottages are found on this scenic site encompassing Marsh Creek (state-stocked for fishing), the western boundary of the battlefield, with a view of the South Mountains. Country store on site.

Recreational amenities include swimming pool, minigolf, game room, shuffleboard, playground, and horseshoes. Special events are held every weekend, such as Civil War–related activities, an Elvis tribute, and a classic car show.

Rates (which include tax) are for a family of four—two adults and two children under 18 years of age living at home. Tent sites (no hookups), $29.70 daily, $158.00 weekly; with water and electric $34.70 daily, $188.40 weekly; water/electric/sewer, $36.70 daily, $200.40 weekly ($4.00 additional per night for 50 amp).

On a designated weekend in April, police, fire, emergency, and military personnel with ID are invited to stay at Gettysburg Campground for one night free.

Rental cabins (sleeping facilities only) have one full-size bed and one set of bunk beds to sleep a total of four, small refrigerator, small table with two stools, outside picnic table, and fire ring ($45.78 to $52.32 nightly rate includes tax). Bring your own linens. Restrooms/showers/dishwashing station nearby.

Cottages ($100.28 to $109.00 daily) have full- or queen-size bed and two sets of bunks in separate room to sleep a total of six, full private bathroom with shower, fully equipped kitchenette, air-conditioning, heat, outside picnic table, and fire ring.

Gettysburg Campground has RV repair facilities on site.

Gettysburg KOA
20 Knox Road
(800) 562-1869 (reservations),
(717) 642-5713
www.attractionfinder.com/public/pa/gettysburgkoa
Gettysburg KOA offers accommodations for tents and RVs plus a wide range of KOA "Kamping Kabins," "Kottages," and "Kamping Lodges." Full hookup sites are available. Facilities include climate-controlled restrooms, coin-operated laundry, game room, store with gifts and souvenirs, heated pool (mid-May to Labor Day), minigolf, playground, nature trail, bike rentals, shuffleboard and horseshoes,

and "kamper kitchen" (stove, sink, and counter space for communal use). Guests at Gettysburg KOA can enjoy an all-you-can-eat pancake breakfast for $2.25 every weekend.

One-room Kabins sleep four with double bed and bunk; two-room has extra bunk bed to sleep six. Both types have air conditioners, heaters, picnic tables, fire ring with grill tops, and porch swing. Bring your own bedding, bath towels, and cooking and eating utensils. Deluxe Kottage sleeps five and comes with complete bathroom with shower, dining area with log table and chairs, kitchenette with appliances (refrigerator, stove top, coffeemaker, toaster, and microwave) and utensils, propane fireplace, air conditioner, porch swing, picnic table, and fire ring with grill top. Kamping Lodge sleeps six with many of the same amenities. No pets in Kottages or Lodges; $10 flat fee for pets in Kabins. Two-night minimum for Kottages and Lodges.

Rates per night are based on two adults and two children under 13. Tent (no hookup) is $20 to $39; with water and electric, $26 to $44; water/electric/sewer, $30 to $52. Kabins are $50 to $85; Kottages, $70 to $97; Lodges, $100 to $149.

Special events include period fashion shows, magic and music performances, wine-tasting parties, ghost stories around the fire, battle reenactments, fireworks, treasure hunts, a Haunted Halloween Trail, and a trick-or-treat parade. Self-guided auto tour of Gettysburg Battlefield on CD or cassette tape is for sale or rent at the campsite, or campers can take a free shuttle van to catch an air-conditioned bus for a two-hour battlefield tour led by a licensed guide.

Gettysburg KOA campers may purchase a package plan, which includes 20 percent savings on some local attractions and free use of the downtown trolley service. For all guests, a shuttle to and from town is available twice a day for $5.00 per person round trip (price includes the use of the downtown trolley service).

Granite Hill Campground
3340 Fairfield Road
(800) 642-8368, (717) 642-8749
www.granitehillcampground.com

This full-service 150-acre campground located 6 miles west of the battlefield has a variety of accommodation options, from tents to the largest motor homes, plus two-room rental cabins. Features include modern bathhouses and laundry, wireless Internet and cable TV access, and country store. Recreational amenities include swimming pool, 18-hole miniature golf course, tennis court, boating and fishing, playgrounds, paddle boat and kayak rentals, game room, free shuttle to Gettysburg and battlefield, and day camp for kids. There are lots of special events, including bingo, hayrides, dances, bonfires, ice-cream socials, themed dinners, and Halloween activities.

Space rates are based on two people and vary according to time of week and holiday periods. Base rate (without hookups) go from $24 to $31 daily, $143 weekly; with water and electric, $29 to $36 daily, $175 weekly; water/electric/sewer, $32 to $39 daily to $192 weekly. Two-room rental cabins sleep six in one double bed and two sets of bunks and provide fan, heater, picnic table, and outdoor grill (bring sleeping bags, camp stove, lantern, and cook kit). Rates based on two people range from $60 to $74 daily, $400 weekly.

Granite Hill Campground offers discounts off base rate to members of AAA

Since 1979, Granite Hill Campground has been the home of the Gettysburg Bluegrass Festival, held in May and August. Each festival features four full days of mainstage performances by some of the top musicians in the world, close-up programs with favorite artists, and workshops for all ages. For details, call the campground or visit www.gettysburgbluegrass.com.

and AARP. Get a "Frequent Camper Card" and you'll receive every eleventh night free.

You don't have to have a fishing license to enjoy a catch-and-release pond.

Round Top Campground
180 Knight Road
(717) 334-9565
www.roundtopcamp.com

Situated behind Little Round Top, this campground provides remote wooded hillside sites for tents, wide-open pull-throughs for large RVs, and fully furnished cottage rentals. The property provides clean restrooms, hot showers, a laundry room, store and gift shop, Internet access, and snack bar. An Olympic-size swimming pool, separate kiddie pool, sundeck, 18-hole minigolf, tennis, horseshoes, bocce, volleyball, basketball, shuffleboard, and scheduled weekend activities and entertainment such as bingo, dances, ice-cream socials, karaoke nights, and pancake breakfasts keep the family busy and happy. Leashed pets are welcome.

Rates (based on two people) are $18.00 for tent site (no hookups), $29.50 with water and electric, $31.50 with water/electric/sewer, $33.50 water/electric/sewer and cable, $35.50 all hookups plus 50 amp service. Add $2.00 to all rates on holidays.

Rustic cabins (sleep four, $50 per night) have double bed, crawl-in loft with twin mattresses, small table and chairs, heating and air-conditioning, overhead lights, outside water hookup, fire ring, and picnic table. Bring your own linens. Cottages and park models come with fully equipped kitchens, full bathroom, furnished dining and living areas, TV with VCR, separate sleeping areas (including linens), heat and air-conditioning, a porch, and an outdoor picnic table and fire ring. Cottages are $99 daily for four persons, $120 for six. Park models (four person) are $99. No pets in rentals.

HERSHEY/HUMMELSTOWN

Hershey Highmeadow Campground
1200 Matlack Road, Hummelstown
(800) HERSHEY, (717) 534–8999
www.hersheypa.com/accommodations/
hershey_highmeadow_campground

Part of the Hershey Resorts family and conveniently located only 1½ miles from Hersheypark (complimentary shuttle transportation is available in season), this 55-acre facility offers the entire gamut of camping accommodations, from tent sites to RV hookups to rustic and log cabins. Open all year, the property is fully operational from mid-April through October.

All sites feature picnic tables and grills. There's plenty to do here, with two swimming pools (open Memorial Day to Labor Day), kiddie wading pool, playground, game room, basketball and volleyball courts, campfire sing-alongs, and arts and crafts. Facilities include separate buildings with showers and restrooms, self-service laundry, country store, and gift shop.

Rates (based on two adults and two unmarried children under 21) vary according to season. Pets are permitted in campers only, not in tents, cabins, or tenting area. Basic (no hookup) tent sites range from $23.99 to $34.99; with partial hookup, $26.99 to $37.99; with full hookup, $34.99 to $41.99. Wheelchair-accessible restrooms and picnic tables are available upon request.

Rustic cabins (paneled with cement floor and no heat) sleep four with double and bunk beds, dresser, electric, camp refrigerator, microwave, breakfast bar, ceiling or wall fan, porch grill, and picnic table. Log cabins have wood floors and baseboard heat for year-round camping. Cabins have no indoor plumbing, but showers and restrooms are located nearby. Bring your own linens. A maximum of six people are permitted per cabin; cot rental is available at the office. No pets in cabins. Seasonal rates vary from $54.50 to $78.50 (included in this range is the $4.00 premium for log cabins).

As a guest at one of the Hershey Resort properties, guests may arrange for breakfast at Hersheypark (separate charge) with early admission. They are also entitled to Sweet Start privileges, allowing them to enter the park one hour prior to regular opening.

Hershey Highmeadow Campground guests have access to the private Hershey Country Club championship golf courses (golfing fees are additional) and receive free admission to Hershey Gardens (seasonally) and the Hershey Museum.

Discounted Hersheypark and Dutch Wonderland tickets are available at the campground.

INTERCOURSE

Beacon Hill Camping
Route 772 West (Newport Road)
(½ mile north of Route 340 intersection)
(717) 768-8775
www.beaconhillcamping.com
"Quiet Camping Suited to Adults" is the motto for this 50-site farming area facility for campers 16 years and over. In fact, quiet is the main selling point here—that plus the convenience of being in walking distance to everything the Village of Intercourse has to offer. No recreational amenities (except for the occasional ice-cream social in August), but there are full water, electric, and sewer hookups for $29.00 a day (50 amp service is available for an additional $3.00), pull-throughs, covered picnic shelter, modem access and WiFi, laundry facilities, and clean, heated showers. Some tent sites are available ($24). Camping cabins (rates are based on two persons a night, maximum occupancy four persons) come with air conditioners, small refrigerator, heater, rustic post-and-rail beds (bring sleeping bags), porch swing, picnic table, and park-style charcoal grill. Rates are $50 per night, seventh night free on weekly rental. Quiet pets on leashes are permitted in tents and campers; pets in cabins must be taken with you or crated.

LANCASTER

Old Mill Stream Camping Manor
2249 Route 30 East
(866) FUNatDW, (717) 299-2314
www.oldmillstreamcamping.com
Although this 15-acre year-round campground is within walking distance of Lancaster's outlet shopping, restaurants, and attractions, you'd never know it, situated as it is in a country setting beside a quiet stream. A range of accommodations will allow you to set up your tent or park your RV and enjoy the exact experience you want. For guest comfort and convenience, there are modern showers and restrooms, cable TV and modem access, game room, rental cars, two Laundromats, country store, playground, and nondenominational church service held on the grounds. Wheelchair-accessible facilities are available. Pets are permitted on leash. Site rental (up to four persons) without hookups is $27.00, $29.00 with water and electric, $36.00 with water/electric/sewer and cable TV (add $3.00 for 50 amp service). Ask about special midweek discounts.

PARADISE

Mill Bridge Village Campresort
101 South Ronks Road
(800) 645-2744, (717) 687-8181
www.millbridge.com
In the early 18th century, Herr's Grist Mill was where farmers came to grind their corn, purchase supplies, and catch up on the latest news. It was also a central stopover for travelers headed west. In 1844 the longest covered bridge in Lancaster County was built in this section of Paradise. Although the mill ceased operation in 1929, people still come from all over to visit these two registered historic landmarks, along with the shops and other attractions that are now known as Mill Bridge Village. Many of them set up their tents, hook up their RVs, or rent cabins at the village campgrounds.

Positively Primitive

There's a port-a-potty nearby, but that's it as far as the modern camping amenities go at the Mill Creek Camping Area in Lancaster County Central Park (1050 Rockford Road, Lancaster, PA 17602; 717–299–8215; www.co.lancaster.pa.us/parks). You need a camping permit ($16) to pitch a tent for up to four occupants. Add $2.00 for each extra person. Maximum stay at the Mill Creek Camping Area is 14 consecutive days, followed by a 14-day absence.

If you don't mind the rustic accommodations, the surroundings are beautiful and offer a range of outdoor activities for all ages. Located on the southern edge of Lancaster County along the Conestoga River, Central Park is a major recreational area with a swimming pool (admission is charged), skate park (free), basketball and tennis courts, softball and soccer fields, playgrounds, environmental center, and naturalist-led programs.

To get there from Lancaster City, take Duke Street south through the city to Chesapeake Street. Take a right onto Chesapeake Street; go 0.2 mile and turn left into the park.

For convenience, there's a country store, snack bar/Internet cafe, modern bathhouses with tiled showers (hot water), fire rings and picnic tables, and laundry area. Just for fun, there's a swimming pool, adult lounge with big-screen TV, game room, children's playground, fishing on the Pequea Creek, horseshoes, shuffleboard, basketball, free tours through the grist mill and covered bridge, crafts, scavenger hunts, hayrides, bingo, ice-cream socials, and movies.

Rates vary by season and, in spring and fall, time of week. Quoted rates are for a family of up to four people (mother, father, and children up to 17 years old). Tent site/pop-up with electric and water hookup, $25.00 to $36.50; trailer site with electric/water, $26.00 to $37.50; electric/water/sewer/cable $30.00 to $40.00. In spring and fall, stay two nights and get a third for free (Sunday through Thursday).

Resort cabin rentals include separate bedroom with queen-size bed, full bath with tub/shower, heat and air-conditioning, electric range, microwave, full-size refrigerator, coffeemaker, dishware, utensils, pots and pans, pillows, outdoor picnic table, and campfire ring. Bring your own bed linens and towels. No pets allowed in cabins. Depending on season and time of week, cabins rent for $75 to $115 (tax is additional).

RONKS

Flory's Cottages and Camping
99 North Ronks Road
(717) 687–6670
www.floryscamping.com
Surrounded by Amish farmland, this campground offers water, sewer, 30 or 50 amp electric, cable TV, and daily phone hookups. Rental cottages have one to three bedrooms and one or two baths to accommodate families and come with fully equipped kitchen, living room with cable TV, air-conditioning and heat, patio, and single parking space. Linens and towels are provided (if you have a big family, you might want to bring additional

kitchenware, linens, and towels). No pets are allowed in the cottages.

Facilities for the use of all campers include two clean bathhouses, laundry room with coin-operated washers and dryers, game room with pinball and snack machines, playground, and cookout area. There is no pool, but the owners suggest using one of the two community public pools (one in Lancaster, the other in Leola) located close by (there may be fees for swimming in these pools).

Camping rates are based on a family of four (two adults and two children ages 4 to 17) and vary by season. Sites with no hookup range from $24 to $27; with 30 amp electric/water/sewer, $27 to $31; with 50 amp electric/water/sewer, $29 to $33. (Air-conditioning/heating, phone, and TV hookups are additional.)

Cottage rates also vary seasonally. One bedroom (two people) with queen-size bed and twin sleeper goes from $79 to $119; two bedrooms (four people) with queen, double, and queen sleeper beds, $119 to $159; three bedrooms (six people) with two queen, one double, and one queen sleeper, $159 to $199. Park model and travel trailer accommodations are also available.

Stay seven days or more and get a 10 percent discount off campsite rates. If you rent a cabin, you get 10 percent for five or more days, 20 percent off for seven or more.

STRASBURG

Beaver Creek Farm Cabins
2 Little Beaver Road (1½ miles
southeast of Strasburg on Route 896)
(717) 687-7745
www.beavercreekfarmcabins.com
Just cabins here, set on 29 green acres.

Choose from large single model ($90 per day/$585 per week) with two bedrooms, kitchen and living room, combined tub and shower, and air-conditioning, or double cabin ($70 per day/$480 per week for half of the cabin), with one bedroom, kitchen, and bath (can be opened up to accommodate larger families). Cookouts in summer months. Recreational facilities include campfires, fishing, 18-hole mini-disc golf. Open all year; reservation by week only during mid-June, July, and August. No credit cards. No pets. No maid service. Coin-operated laundry on premises. Beaver Creek Farm Market and Bakery is located right across the street—dairy products, meats, vegetables, preserves, and baked goods (from scratch).

White Oak Campground
372 White Oak Road
(717) 687-6207
www.whiteoakcampground.com
Over 25 acres of grassy meadows and shady trees provide a setting for a relaxing camping experience, whether your choice of accommodation is a no-frills tent or a fully equipped RV. Camper conveniences include modern restrooms with free hot showers, general store, modem plug-in access, picnic table and fire ring at each site, playground area, arcade room, Enterprise Car Rental (717-442-0203) vehicle pickup and drop-off available at the campground, nondenominational church service, string-music jam sessions. No alcoholic beverages. Well-tended pets are welcome.

Rates for family of four (two adults and two children under 16) or less for campsite with no hookup is $22; with electric and water, $25; with electric/water/sewer, $28 (use of air-conditioning or electric heat is additional).

DINING DEUTSCH STYLE

Pennsylvania Dutch Country native and internationally renowned chef and cookbook author Betty Groff fondly recalls when her mother used to serve "French Goose" to her family. Like so many others in the area, Groff came from a farming family. So why the exotic entree? Actually, the dish was neither French nor made with any species of goose. It was pig stomach stuffed with a savory mixture of pork sausage, potatoes, and vegetables. But, says Groff, it was a delicacy in its own right.

Stuffed pig stomach is a good example of down-home Pennsylvania Dutch cooking because it clearly demonstrates the culinary creativity of this "waste not, want not" culture. Another is scrapple (also known as ponhaus or panhaas), a favorite breakfast food that was originally made from boiling and grinding the organs and meat scraps left over from butchering pigs (many home cooks and manufacturers now use pork butt), adding cornmeal, buckwheat, or oatmeal along with seasonings (salt, pepper, sometimes sage) to the meat, and molding it into loaf pans. After the mixture is cooled, it is sliced, fried in butter or bacon fat so it's crispy on the outside, and served plain or topped with golden table molasses or syrup.

Pork scraps (primarily from the head and neck) might also be mixed into a gela-

tin aspic and molded into a loaf to make a specialty known as souse or head cheese. The loaf is chilled before it is sliced for serving.

For farm families, a full pantry and smokehouse meant peace of mind between growing seasons. So in addition to eating their fill of the sun-warmed ears of corn at summer harvesttime, homemakers preserve a winter's worth of the plump kernels by pickling some for chowchow and other relishes, and baking and drying the rest to be reconstituted for soups, stews, casseroles, or fritters. Drying intensifies the sweetness of the corn and gives it a distinctive caramelized flavor.

During the fall apple harvest, just-picked fruits are eaten out of hand, sliced into pies, juiced into cider, smashed into sauces, stirred in huge steaming kettles into apple butter (*lattwaerrick*), and dried into schnitz. On many local Dutch-style restaurant menus, you'll see schnitz und knepp. Knepp are dumplings. This dried apple-and-dumpling dish is usually served with another Pennsylvania Dutch specialty, home-cured ham, a combination of sweet and salty that is characteristic of this type of cooking.

When spring brings dandelions into bloom, folks in this area break out the salad bowls to enjoy the young leaves, often lavishly cloaked in a warm bacon dressing, or they'll dip the flowers in a batter and deep-fry them (some say the taste is similar to fresh fried oysters).

Many fresh vegetables, potatoes, and noodles are served simply, accented only with a gloss of browned butter. Local cooks know that browning the butter gives it a richer, almost nutty taste. Aside from salt and pepper, a favorite flavoring for everything from chicken and corn soup to potpies and cakes is saffron. Pennsylvania

You don't have to grow and dry your own corn to enjoy its sweet and toasty flavor. Many Pennsylvania Dutch Country families use prepackaged John Cope's Dried Corn (www.copefoods.com), made by a family-owned company for more than a century in Rheems, Lancaster County.

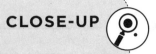

Dining in an Amish Home

To supplement their farm income, some Amish families will invite area visitors into their homes for a home-cooked dinner featuring local specialties. Most of these families prefer to take reservations through selected hotel, inn, and bed-and-breakfast owners, but one that you can contact directly is the Fisher Family Farm (4010 Old Philadelphia Pike [Route 340], Gordonville, PA 17532; 717–768–0733). To find Elam and Barbara Fisher's farm, take Route 30 East to the Route 340 exit, take a left at the red light, then continue about 1½ miles east of Intercourse; it's on the right, just past Zook's Stand and Cat Tail Road. The Fishers will schedule groups of 10 or more any day except Sunday. Singles, couples, and smaller groups can call to see if there might be a group scheduled; if so, they are welcome to join that group at the table. Dinner is served family style and often includes Barbara's baked chicken and/or ham, mashed potatoes and gravy, homemade bread, garden salad, pickled beets, and dessert of homemade ice cream or shoofly pie. The Fishers have no electricity. Donations are welcome (the average is usually around $13 per diner).

Big families mean big washloads for Amish households. PENNSYLVANIA DUTCH CONVENTION & VISITORS BUREAU

Many restaurants offering authentic Pennsylvania Dutch either serve smorgasbord or family style (pass the potatoes, please).

$	Under $10
$$	$10–$15
$$$	$16–$20
$$$$	$21–$25
$$$$$	$26–$30

Dutch homemakers prize the rich golden color and distinctive flavor that this spice lends to their recipes.

Many of the main dishes that are still so popular here were originated by homemakers who looked for tasty ways to stretch ingredients to feed large families. Any kind of meat—from chicken to pork to squirrel—can feed a crowd when it's cut into chunks, combined with a rich broth and chunks of carrot, potato, and/or other vegetables, topped with squares of freshly made noodle dough, and turned into a stove-top stew called bot boi, or potpie. Communal dinners at churches and firehouses often feature cream sauced chicken chunks served over just-pressed waffles. Mix paper-thin slices of dried beef with a cream sauce and serve over toast or home-fried or hash brown potatoes and you have frizzled beef, a breakfast staple.

If you're looking for lighter fare, there are plenty of contemporary restaurants in Pennsylvania Dutch Country. But if you're looking for a true taste of the area's German immigrant–based, hearty farm food tradition, leave the calorie counting for another meal and pass the browned butter.

Look for discount coupons for Pennsylvania Dutch family-style and smorgasbord meals at official area visitor centers (look on www.padutchcountry.com for addresses) or online at the individual restaurant Web sites.

AKRON

Akron Restaurant & Gift Shop $-$$
333 South Seventh Street (Route 272)
(717) 859-1181
Have your chicken in a potpie or over waffles at this more than 50-year-old family-owned a la carte dining spot. Fridays in winter, the menu features baked oyster pie; in summer, it's baked corn pie. Open for breakfast, lunch, and dinner weekdays and Saturday. Special children's menu offers complete dinners, including drink, vegetable, and dessert, for $1.75 to $2.00.

BIRD-IN-HAND

Amish Barn Restaurant $-$$
3029 Old Philadelphia Pike (Route 340, between Bird-in-Hand and Intercourse)
(717) 768-8886
www.amishbarnpa.com

Maundy Thursday, the Thursday before Easter, is also known as Green Thursday because it's the time when Pennsylvania Germans believe you should eat something green (preferably dandelion leaves) to guarantee good health. Some also believe that healing herbs gathered on Green Thursday yield the most powerful cures, so they pick a year's worth on this day.

Shrove Tuesday, the day before the beginning of Lent, is known as *Fastnacht,* designating it as the night before the fast begins. To use up all of the fat and eggs in the household in preparation for the fast, the Pennsylvania Dutch follow the German tradition of making doughnuts, or *fastnachts,* in square or round shapes. The fried treats are usually coated in regular or confectioner's sugar, or they may be split and smeared with jelly or golden molasses.

Saffron is generally acknowledged to be the most expensive spice in the world, so how did it come to have such a prominent place in the cooking of the down-to-earth, super-frugal Pennsylvania Dutch? The fact is that many of the German immigrants who came to Pennsylvania brought with them saffron crocus bulbs (the spice is the dried stigmas of the crocus flower) and planted them in their gardens. While saffron is not as widely grown in the area today, it is still readily available, even next to the cash register at some of the local convenience stores.

Breakfast, lunch, and dinner are served family-style or a la carte. Specialties include chicken bot boi (potpie), sauerkraut und speck (pork tenderloin slices over sauerkraut), Amish ham loaf, speck und bona (a slice of country ham over specially prepared green beans), chicken corn soup, and Lancaster County sausage. For dessert (or a filling breakfast), there's the restaurant's signature apple dumpling. All-you-can-eat family-style breakfast features sausage, scrapple, eggs, home fries, toast, buttermilk griddle cakes, and more. Open Sunday. There's a free petting zoo where kids can see and feed farm animals, including goats, pigs, turkeys, chickens, and a llama. Outdoor courtyard dining available, weather permitting. Restaurant is wheelchair accessible.

Bird-in-Hand Family Restaurant
& Smorgasbord $–$$
2760 Old Philadelphia Pike
(717) 768-8266
www.bird-in-hand.com
The third generation of the Smucker family continues to offer a breakfast, lunch, and dinner menu or smorgasbord dining with six help-yourself stations featuring homemade soups, salad bar, oven-fresh breads, hot entrees, and baked-on-the-spot desserts. The Noah's Ark–themed kids' buffet is just the right height. Selections include fried chicken, ham balls, baked fish, pork and sauerkraut, chicken potpie, baked ham, roast turkey, shepherd's pie, chowchow, pickled beets, and pickled egg. The dessert buffet displays homemade pies (apple, wet-bottom shoofly, seasonal pumpkin made from homegrown gourds), cakes (red velvet's a specialty), fruit crisp, cobblers, puddings, brownies, soft-serve ice cream, and flavored slushies. Closed Sunday.

Plain & Fancy Farm Restaurant $$$
3121 Old Philadelphia Pike (Route 340,
1 mile east of Bird-in-Hand)
(800) 669-3568, (717) 768-4400
www.plainandfancyfarm.com
One of the best known of the area's family-style restaurants, Plain & Fancy has been serving Pennsylvania Dutch specialties in a converted farm setting for more than 40 years. Come hungry, because it's an all-you-can-eat parade of courses that often include roast beef, fried chicken, mashed potatoes, chicken potpie, baked sausage, brown-buttered bowtie noodles, dried corn, homemade breads, sweet-and-sour relishes, shoofly pie, and apple dumplings. Open seven days. Children can eat for $6.95. Wheelchair accessible.

INTERCOURSE

Intercourse Village Restaurant $
9 Queen Road (Routes 340 and 772,
next to Best Western Hotel)
(717) 768-3636

Instead of drinking wine or water to cleanse the palate during and between rich courses, many Pennsylvania Dutch eat various sweet-and-sour (sugar-vinegar brined) relishes such as chowchow or pickled vegetables or rinds.

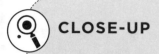

Food Fairs

Annual Rhubarb Festival: It's a riot of rhubarb every year when this vitamin C-packed veggie takes center stage at Kitchen Kettle Village (Route 340, Intercourse, PA 17534; 800–732–3538, 717–768–8261, www.kitchenkettle.com), on the third Friday and Saturday in May. There's a Rhubarb Race Car Derby; a baking contest to find the best rhubarb pie in Lancaster County; rhubarb cooking tips, demos, and tastings; jam making; children's game arcade; live entertainment; the Rhubarb Stroll parade, featuring musicians and costumed characters; and the crowning of the Rhubarb King and Queen.

Annual Shoofly Pie Bake-off and Eating Contest: Celebrity judges choose the best, and eager eaters vie to devour the most pies. This June event is held at the Rockvale Outlets (35 South Willowdale Drive, Lancaster, PA 17602; 717–293–9595; www.rockvalesquareoutlets.com).

National Apple Harvest Festival: Follow the aroma of the apple butter simmering away in huge kettles at this regional October event at the South Mountain Fairgrounds in Arendtsville, only 10 miles northwest of Gettysburg on Route 234. You can also get your orchard-fresh picks coated in candy, in pancakes, sauced, squeezed into cider (in an antique press), and just about any other way you like them. There are lots of apple-oriented activities, too, from bobbing and pie eating to syrup and jelly making, and all of it is overseen by Johnny Appleseed himself. Tour an orchard, watch scrapple being made, and sample other local foods such as funnel cakes, kettle corn, and open-pit beef. There are pony rides, puppet shows, and a petting zoo for the kids, hundreds of arts-and-crafts vendors, antique and classic cars, plus six stages of continuous live entertainment.

Fresh-from-the-oven pies are a Pennsylvania Dutch specialty. PENNSYLVANIA DUTCH CONVENTION AND VISITORS BUREAU

During the Civil War, Southerners gave the Pennsylvania Dutch the nickname "Sauerkraut Yankees," according to author William Woys Weaver, because the fermented cabbage dish was such an integral part of the cuisine of these this transplanted German population.

In Pennsylvania Dutch homes, pork and sauerkraut is the traditional New Year's Day good luck meal. Some say that the reason for the pork is that pigs root "forward," while chickens and turkeys scratch "backward." If you happen to be in the area, a number of firehouses feature this fortuitous fare at their New Year's day fund-raiser dinners.

All-you-can-eat lunch and dinner at bargain prices can be enjoyed here, one of the few places where you can order homemade pig stomach. For the less adventurous, there's also chicken potpie, chicken and waffles, beef stew, pork and sauerkraut, and ham and green beans. The dessert menu features shoofly pie, apple dumplings, and fritters topped with ice cream. Closed Sunday.

Stoltzfus Farm Restaurant $$
3716A East Newport Road
(717) 768-8156
Located 1 block east of Intercourse, this authentic Amish homestead farm (owner Amos Stoltzfus grew up here) serves family-style fare in all-you-can-eat portions. You can't get fresher meats because they come from the family's butcher shop, Stoltzfus Meats & Deli, located only ¼ mile away. Make sure you try some of the sausage (it's made fresh daily) and the special-recipe ham loaf. Open daily except Sunday from early April through November; closed December through March.

Stoltzfus Meats & Deli $
3614 East Newport Road
Cross Keys Village Center
(717) 768-7287
For a no-frills, belly-filling lunch or early dinner, order a sausage sandwich to eat in (there are a couple of tables) or to go.

LANCASTER

Lapp's Family Restaurant $-$$
2270 Lincoln Highway East
(717) 394-1606
www.lappsfamilyrestaurant.com
Hearty breakfast menu items at this Lancaster County landmark located across the street from Dutch Wonderland include signature baked oatmeal, creamed dried beef on toast, scrapple, sausage, eggs, and home fries (on weekends, there's an "all-you-care-to-eat" morning buffet for under $7.00). Lunch and dinner offerings include roast beef, smoked pork chops, roasted turkey with the trimmings, and chicken potpie. Menu items are available in regular-size portions for hearty appetites or smaller portions for lighter eaters. There's also a separate children's menu. Friday is seafood buffet night with an all-you-can-eat array of shrimp, crab legs, steamed clams, and more. Open Sunday, closed Monday. Lapp's also has a Deli & Bakery at 244 Granite Run Drive in Lancaster (717-581-5277).

A favorite Pennsylvania Dutch Country refresher is meadow tea, a flavorful brew made by boiling the dried leaves of one of a species of mintlike plants that grow wild in area meadows (many people also cultivate it in their gardens).

The Amish may be plain in their dress and demeanor, but when it comes to food, they're so creative that they can make even oatmeal into a delightfully different culinary creation. There are probably as many recipes for baked oatmeal as there are families and chefs that set a traditional Pennsylvania Dutch table. A number of upscale bed-and-breakfasts and inns have also developed their own signature stylings of this anything-but-plain dish. Some versions taste like a fresh-from-the-oven oatmeal cookie or cake, fragrant with cinnamon and vanilla, crunchy with nuts, and extra-chewy with soft, moist raisins. Others add apple or dried apricots, peaches, or cranberries. Some top it with milk or cream, some with whipped cream, others with nothing at all.

LITITZ

**Lititz Family Cupboard
Restaurant & Buffet $-$$**
**12 West Newport Road (just off Route
501 North)**
(717) 626-9102
Don't be deterred by a little bit of a wait if the locals have gotten here first. They know where to find really good home-style cooking at great prices. The breakfast and dinner buffets are both major bargains and give you ample opportunity to try lots of traditional Pennsylvania Dutch favorites. And if your mouth is watering for some stuffed pig stomach, you'll find it on the a la carte menu on Thursday. Closed Sunday.

RONKS

Miller's Smorgasbord $$$$
**2811 Lincoln Highway East (Route 30,
1 mile east of Route 896)**
(800) 669-3568, (717) 687-6621
www.millerssmorgasbord.com

For major social events such as barn raisings and weddings, women in the community create a "stack pie" by piling all of the sweet selections one on top of the other and slicing through from top to bottom for each serving.

It began as a truck stop in 1929 when Anna Miller began serving her homemade chicken and waffles to drivers while her husband serviced their rigs. Anna's specialty is still the star of the Sunday breakfast smorgasbord, which also features omelets, steak and eggs, creamed chipped beef, apple fritters, and grilled sticky buns. The dinner smorgasbord—available seven days a week—gives you a chance to try lots of Lancaster County classics. Special children's menu. Open seven days.

SMOKETOWN

Good N' Plenty Restaurant $-$$
Route 896
(between Routes 340 and 30)
(717) 394-7111
www.goodnplenty.com
Go to the restaurant's Web site before you visit for a $1.00 per meal discount coupon. Lots of bus groups dine here, but don't let that deter you from planning at least one meal at this former farmhouse, built in 1871 and opened for dining by Christ and Dolly Lapp in 1969. The Lapp family continues to operate the eatery, using original Pennsylvania Dutch recipes. Seating is family style (long communal tables), and so is the service. Don't be afraid to pass the platters, because the refills will continue until every appetite is satisfied. Open seven days.

OTHER AREA RESTAURANTS

In Pennsylvania Dutch Country, the Amish and Mennonites aren't the only ones who know how to make the most out of local ingredients. This diverse area has attracted stellar chefs, white-tablecloth restaurants, pubs, microbreweries, and tea and coffeehouses.

The pricing code designates the basic price of a dinner entree (unless otherwise stated) for one adult. Tax, gratuities, and alcoholic beverages are not included in this price. Many establishments have been designated nonsmoking, and those that do allow smoking are identified whenever possible. Most restaurants accept major credit cards. Those that do not are identified.

$	Under $15
$$	$15–$25
$$$	$26–$45
$$$$	$46–$60

ADAMSTOWN

Stoudt's Brewing Co. and Black Angus Restaurant & Brew Pub $-$$$
Route 272 North (1½ miles north of Pennsylvania Turnpike exit 286)
(717) 484-4386
www.stoudtsbeer.com
Aged, hand-cut steaks have been the mainstay of this Adamstown dining spot owned and operated by Ed and Carol Stoudt for more than 40 years. Prime New York sirloins ($19 to $35) and filet mignon ($26 to $33) are specialties. Other specialties are blackened prime rib flamed with Kentucky bourbon and finished with double cream sauce ($26) and a tower of two five-ounce grilled tenderloins with walnut-scented portobello and roasted potato cake ($32). The restaurant also features many seafood selections and a signature wild mushroom pie ($17).

For sandwiches, burgers, and more casual lunch and dinner fare, try Stoudt's Brew Pub. Tapas (country-style duck pâté, smoked trout, and smoked salmon), artisinal cheese plate, kielbasa, and German wursts go exceptionally well with the house Fat Dog Salmon.

In addition to a traditional pilsner and "Helles"-style golden lager, Stoudt Brewing Company is known for its fresh-brewed American Pale Ale and English-style Scarlet Lady Ale E.S.B. (Extra Special Bitter). Like fine wines, some big, bold beers require aging to attain their full flavors. The microbrewery's gourmet collection of bottle conditioned beers includes a Belgian abbey–style Triple Ale, Double India Pale Ale, and an English-style oatmeal- and Imperial-stout blend called Fat Dog. (Brewery tours are available on weekends.)

Both restaurant and brew pub are open seven days.

CASHTOWN

Historic Cashtown Inn $-$$
1325 Old Route 30
(800) 367-1797, (717) 334-9722
www.cashtowninn.com
Located 8 miles west of Gettysburg, this circa 1797 building was originally a stage-

If you know you're going to visit Pennsylvania Dutch Country on a specific day and have your heart set on dining at a particular establishment, make your reservations in advance, especially during fall and summer peak tourist times.

coach stop and became the headquarters for Confederate General A. P. Hill during the Gettysburg campaign. If you're going for lunch, try the popular Cashtown Crab Melt sandwich. For dinner, the specialties include the Seafood Trilogy (sea scallops, jumbo shrimp, and lump crabmeat in a mild Cajun cream sauce over baked puff pastry), pecan-crusted chicken with warm maple butter sauce, and orange wood-smoked salmon with sweet maple glaze.

Open Tuesday through Saturday for lunch and dinner, dinner only on Sunday.

EAST PETERSBURG

Haydn Zug's Restaurant   **$$**
1987 State Street (4 miles north
of Lancaster on Route 72)
(717) 569-8450
www.haydnzugs.com
The name pays homage to the colorful character who operated a general store on this site. The atmosphere is reminiscent of colonial times, with pewter table settings and the warm glow of candlelight. Specialties of the house include Norwegian Chicken (sautéed breasts with smoked salmon, capers, onion, tomato, and white wine), medallions of veal Vienna (with Roquefort and marsala sauce and mushrooms), and certified Angus beef filet mignon and New York strip. Desserts are decadent: Check out the Bananas Foster, Coca Mocha (available with or without alcohol), or Infinite Tasting Sampler (choose up to five tasting-sized specialties).

Lunch (prix fixe or a la carte) is served Monday through Saturday from 11:30 A.M. to 2:00 P.M., dinner from 4:30 to 9:00 P.M.

EPHRATA

Nav Jiwan Tea Room at
Ten Thousand Villages   **$**
240 North Reading Road
(Route 272 North), Suite 2
(717) 721-8400
www.tenthousandvillages.com

Located inside a shop that features handicrafts from artisans in third world countries (Ten Thousand Villages is a nonprofit program of the Mennonite Central Committee relief and development agency), Nav Jiwan Tea Room offers a soup-salad-sandwich lunch menu daily (kids' and vegetarian menus are available). Closed Sunday.

Every Friday evening, Nav Jiwan Tea Room presents a buffet dinner ($12.95) that explores a different country's cuisine with foods prepared in authentic style and served by volunteers. Recent menus have represented Egypt, Nepal, Nigeria, and El Salvador.

Restaurant at Doneckers   **$$–$$$**
333 North State Road
(717) 738-9501
www.doneckers.com
Regional ingredients are handled with respect and creativity by Culinary Institute of America–trained executive chef Craig Gable. The result is a seasonal menu that combines comfort classics with international accents. Recent examples have included wild mushroom cappuccino, roast duckling, and grilled dover sole. For a real culinary adventure, try the multi-course prix fixe ($65) chef's menu, which includes pairings with wines from the restaurant's extensive climate-controlled cellar. Open for lunch and dinner from 11:00 A.M. to 9:00 P.M. Monday through Thursday, until 10:00 P.M. Friday and Saturday. Closed on Sunday.

GETTYSBURG

Dobbin House Tavern   **$$**
89 Steinwehr Avenue
(Business Route 15 South)
(717) 334-2100
www.dobbinhouse.com
Built in 1776 by the Reverend Alexander Dobbin, this is Gettysburg's oldest building and was once a "station" on the Underground Railroad. It was also used as a hospital by both the North and South

CLOSE-UP

Dinner Theaters

Want some entertainment or education with your entree? Some comic or musical diversion with your dessert? Check out the area's year-round dinner theaters.

Dutch Apple Dinner Theatre
510 Centerville Road, Lancaster
(717) 898–1900
www.dutchapple.com
Talent from across the nation is recruited to perform in classic and contemporary musicals and children's theater productions. American-style buffet features salad bar, carved roast beef or ham, fish, chicken, home-made desserts, and locally made ice cream. Evening and twilight performances are $42.00 for adults, $22.00 for children ages 13 to 18, $18.00 for children 3 to 12 Sunday through Friday; matinees on selected Wednesdays, Thursdays, Saturdays, and Sundays, $44.00 for adults, $38.50 for children 18 and under. A limited number of "show only" seats (in the fourth and fifth levels of the theater) are available for each performance at $22 for adults, $16 for children.

Rainbow Dinner Theatre
Route 30 (3 miles east of Rockvale Outlets), Paradise
(800) 292–4301, (717) 687–4300
www.rainbowdinnertheatre.com
It is said that laughter is good for the digestion, and at the Rainbow Dinner Theatre the productions are all Broadway-caliber comedy all the time. Buffet dinner includes house favorites roast beef and stuffed chicken cutlets. Dessert is a selection of cakes, pies, and hand-dipped ice cream. Tuesday, Wednesday, Thursday, and selected Saturday matinees with meal cost $41 per person; Thursday evenings are $41, Friday and selected Sunday (the latter are twilight shows) $44, and Saturday $47.

after the Battle of Gettysburg (ask for a free tour). It's been restored to its original elegance, and the interior is done in authentic period antiques. Candlelight and costumed wait staff set the stage for 18th-century-style hospitality in one of six historic Alexander Dobbin Dining Rooms. Menu selections run the gamut from Colonial to continental. The "Compleat Dinner," which includes choice of main course, potato of the day, salad, baked-on-premise breads, and veggies, is usually a very good value. Entree selections are exten-sive, ranging from roast duck Adams County (with local apples and hard cider) to the Seafarers Feast (orange roughy, salmon, crab cake, shrimp, scallops, and lobster tail) and vegetarian dishes such as Vegetable Isabella. Children's menu is available.

The Springhouse Tavern, part of the Dobbin House Tavern complex, is an atmospheric fireplace-lit alehouse with a menu that includes casual bar food, char-broiled steaks and seafood, spit-roasted chicken, soups, salads, and sandwiches.

Farnsworth House Inn $-$$$
401 Baltimore Street
(717) 334-8838
www.farnsworthhouseinn.com

"Goober pea" (peanut) soup, pumpkin fritters, game pie (with turkey, pheasant, and
duck) and spoon bread are among the
Civil War–era specialties at this restored
(and said to be haunted) period dining
spot.

The original part of the house was built
in 1810, followed by the brick addition in
1833. It was a family residence during the
Battle of Gettysburg and still retains the
original walls, flooring, and rafters. Photographs by famed Civil War photographer
Mathew Brady hang in the dining room.
(Look for the bullet holes in the south
wall—the inn served as a sharpshooters'
post during the Civil War.)

In season, you can dine in the open-air
garden alongside a spring-fed stream. Children's menu is available. Extensive wine
(featuring local labels) and specialty drink
menus, too.

At the tavern, you can have your lunch
or dinner surrounded by props and uniforms that were used in the movie *Gettysburg*.

Both the restaurant and tavern are
open daily. Period entertainment is offered
most Friday and Saturday evenings from
May through November.

After dinner, descend the stone staircase to the 19th-century "Funeral Parlor,"
known as the Mourning Theatre, for an
hour of Gettysburg-centric ghost stories
told by costumed performers by the eerie
glow of candlelight. Admission is $7.00 per
person.

Gettysbrew Restaurant
and Brewery $-$$
248 Hunterstown Road
(717) 337-1001
www.gettysbrew.com

After the Battle of Gettysburg, the Mont-
fort Farm was one of the largest Confederate field hospitals, providing treatment
for over 1,300 soldiers. One of the Pennsylvania Dutch brick-end barns on the
property now houses the lively Gettysbrew Restaurant. Three copper-clad 525-
gallon tanks rising from the old dairy barn
into the restaurant are used to produce
five kinds of handcrafted ales and lagers,
ranging from the lightest Blonde (you can
add a fruity touch of raspberry, strawberry, peach, or other flavor for an extra
quarter) to Black Knight, made with rich,
deeply roasted malt. Sodas are handcrafted, too, right on the premises without
preservatives and with less sugar than
other commercially produced brands. Flavors include root beer, natural ginger ale,
green tea cola, and orange cream.

Ask for the Half Pint Brewery Tour and
you'll get a flight of all five Gettysbrew
beers for $10. The Soda Sampler brings a
half-pint of each fizzy flavor of own-make
soda for $4.00.

Dine in the restaurant or on the outdoor deck (weather permitting) on such
unusual appetizers as Texas Caviar (black
beans, jalapeño peppers, and spices,
served with bread sticks) and saganaki
(Greek kasseri cheese, baked in batter).
Sandwiches are served on piegga, a folded
focaccia bread with a hint of honey. The
Black Knight's Beef and Gettysbrew
Sausage Platter are made with the brewery's beers. Vegetarian options (including a
great three-cheese and vegetable lasagna)
are also available. Kids can order from their
own menu. Open daily; closed January and
February

Herr Tavern and Publick House $-$$$
900 Chambersburg Road
(800) 362-9849, (717) 334-4332
www.herrtavern.com

Thomas Sweeney built and opened the
tavern in 1815, but it's named after second
owner Fredrick Herr, who took over 13
years later. During the Battle of Gettysburg, the building was turned into the first
Confederate hospital. In 1978 current
owner Steven Wolf reopened the newly
renovated tavern as an eating and drinking destination.

"New American" cuisine adds new
twists to favorite traditions using the fresh-

est seasonal ingredients. Starters have included cool basil vichyssoise with lump crab and cucumber and jumbo Gulf shrimp served with golden margarita syrup and tri-colored salt; entrees have included roasted salmon with apricot–juniper berry glaze and lamb loin persillade. The restaurant also has an extensive international wine list.

Right across the parking lot is the Livery Lounge, a casual spot with a menu to match. Cue up or shoot some darts, then grab a burger, some wings, or a light entree.

Both the restaurant and the tavern are open Monday through Saturday for lunch and dinner, Sunday dinner only.

HERSHEY

Brian Kent's $$$
934 East Chocolate Avenue
(717) 533-3529
Eclectic dining featuring fresh seafood from around the world, beef, chicken, pork, and organic vegetables. Some examples from the seasonal menu have been tomato vodka chowder with clams, black bean goat cheese enchiladas, Jamaican jerk pork tenderloin with pineapple–mango salsa, and twin steak tournedos over potato pancake. This dinner-only spot is open Tuesday through Saturday.

The Circular Dining Room $$-$$$
The Hotel Hershey
100 Hotel Road
(717) 534-8800
With its classic chic ambience and views of The Hotel Hershey's formal gardens and reflecting pools, the Circular Dining Room is one of the area's most romantic restaurants. Many items have an intriguing chocolate twist, such as cocoa-seared scallops and filet and short rib duo served with red wine and chocolate sauce. Desserts feature—what else?—chocolate. A pianist performs on Friday and Saturday evenings and during Sunday brunch.

Dinner and Sunday brunch dress code at the Circular Dining Room requires jackets for gentlemen and appropriate attire for ladies. Breakfast and lunch are resort casual. Reservations are required for lunch, dinner, and Sunday brunch.

Around Halloween, the Circular Dining Room presents a live performance of *An Evening with Edgar Allan Poe* (one night only). For the Poe "appearance," a look-alike reads selections from the author's famous works.

The Forebay $$-$$$
Hershey Lodge
West Chocolate Avenue
and University Drive
(717) 520-5401
Relax in an intimate loft setting with a sig-

Concerned about how to keep Kosher while visiting the area's two major amusement parks? No problem! Just head for Central PA's Kosher Mart, which has locations at Dutch Wonderland (717-392-5111) and at Hersheypark (717-396-8991). You don't have to have a park admission to eat here; the Kosher Mart will issue you a special pass, and at the Dutch Wonderland location you can call in your order ahead and never even enter the park. Both locations are Shomer Shabbos, Glatt Kosher, and under the strict Orthodox supervision of Rabbi Shaya Sackett of Congregation Degel Israel. They use only pas ysrail bread, checked lettuce, Abeles & Hyman OU Glatt hot dogs, and OU Crown Heights David Elliott chicken. Both menus include several chicken specialties, including nuggets and wraps, falafel, dairy-free pizza, vegetarian beef 'n bean burrito, knishes, and fruit smoothies. Eat in or take out. Open during park hours except Friday night to Sunday morning. For more information, visit the Web site at www.ourkehilla.com.

nature chocolate martini, chocolate stout, or something more traditional. Follow that with blue cheese fondue, chocolate-seared divers scallops with vanilla-scented beurre blanc, Kona coffee–crusted American buffalo filet. Dessert, not surprisingly, is chocolate, chocolate, and more chocolate. Dress is resort casual. Children's menu is available. Smoking is permitted after 10:00 P.M., but no cigars or pipes are allowed.

The Fountain Café $–$$$
The Hotel Hershey
100 Hotel Road
(717) 534–8800

At lunchtime, unusual sandwich combinations such as smoked duck with arugula, brie and apple butter on a whole wheat wrap, and big-enough-for-sharing pizzas are the stars. In the evening, the menu goes to upscale offerings such as autumn-spiced sea scallops with pumpkin risotto; smoked Gouda cheese, bacon, and pea tendrils tossed with toasted hazelnut dressing; and sopressata-wrapped salmon with potato gnocci, pesto butter, and ratatouille. The "Death By Chocolate" martini is made with Stoli Vanilla, Godiva liqueur, chocolate sauce, and crème de cacao. Open Thursday through Monday. Outdoor seating is available in season.

Hershey Grill $$–$$$
Hershey Lodge
West Chocolate and University Drive
(717) 520–5656

If you think chocolate is addictive as a dessert, try one of executive chef Bill Justus's appetizers or entrees. Chocolate BBQ chicken wings have a spicy kick that you'll come to crave. Ditto for the chocolate chipotle demi-glace on the grilled rib eye steak. And the combination of semi-sweet chocolate chips combined with tomato and Pepper-Jack cheese crumbles on top of the grilled New York strip is a major wake-up call. For dessert, crack into a creamy chocolate crème brûlée. Open for lunch and dinner with outdoor seating available during summer months.

Hershey Pantry $–$$
801 East Chocolate Avenue
(717) 533–7505

Even the locals don't mind standing in line to get into this cute eatery with its everything-homemade menu. The lines move fast, so don't be deterred, or you'll miss out on one of the best breakfasts around. Favorites include French toast made from just-baked cinnamon bread or stuffed with cream cheese and oversized pancakes. That same cinnamon bread does lunch duty as the foundation for a popular turkey sandwich spiked with cranberry mayonnaise. Dinners range from signature crab cakes to Delmonico steak to apricot-glazed pork chops. The desserts are not to be missed—especially the chocolate cake with peanut butter icing, coconut cake, and cream pies (coconut, banana, and seasonal peach and strawberry varieties). Closed Sunday. No credit cards. Seating on the plant-filled, screened-in porch in season.

What If . . . of Hershey $$
845 East Chocolate Avenue
(717) 533–5858
www.whatifdining.com

What If . . . is a question that presents all kinds of possibilities. That's the thinking behind the eclectic cuisine that's created here. Favorites include arencini (Italian rice balls with peas, prosciutto, and homemade "red sauce"), European bean toss (Northern beans with tomato, basil, and garlic topped with portobello strips over field greens), and veal Frangelico (with walnuts, mango, and hazelnuts in a Frangelico brown sauce). Dessert can be as elegant as a silken crème brûlée or as homey as the oatmeal shortcake du jour served warm with vanilla ice cream. (A children's menu starts at $4.95.) The wine list features North American labels. Open Monday through Saturday for lunch and dinner, dinner only on Sunday.

INTERCOURSE

Kling House   **$**
Kitchen Kettle Village
Route 340 (10 minutes east of
Lancaster)
(800) 732-3538, (717) 768-2746
www.kitchenkettle.com/kling-house
Being located in the Kitchen Kettle Village
gives this restaurant easy access to all
kinds of made-on-the-premises relishes,
jams, and jellies, and all kinds of other
interesting accoutrements. The results?
How about corn relish in the ham and
Swiss Kling House omelet? Peach melba
pancakes layered with red raspberry
syrup? Or strawberry French toast topped
with strawberry rhubarb butter? For lunch
or dinner, try the signature Italian sausage
and clam soup or the cranberry chicken
salad sandwich. Closed Sunday.

LANCASTER

Fiorentino's
1411 Columbia Avenue
(717) 295-4964
See listing under Lititz. The Lancaster
location is open for lunch and dinner
Tuesday through Thursday from 11:00 A.M.
to 10:00 P.M., Friday and Saturday until
11:00 P.M., Sunday from 11:00 A.M. to 8:00
P.M. Closed on Monday.

House of Clarendon   **$–$$$**
201 West Walnut Street (corner of West
Walnut and Water Streets)
(717) 290-7800
www.houseofclarendon.com
At first glance, House of Clarendon looks
like a retail bakery, and it's an outstanding
one, where owner Julie Bashore, a master
confectioner with international credentials,
creates European-style sweets and elabo-
rate fondant-draped wedding cakes. But
just beyond the bakery display cases is a
separate English-style "parlour," a posh
setting for traditional high tea. The full
menu tea ($27.50) brings you seven

savory and seven sweet items, the mini
tea ($21.50) includes three savory and
four sweet. For savories, think hot English
sausage rolls, smoked cheese-filled vol au
vents, and seafood parcels with caviar.
Sweets might include banana split tartlets,
mini baked Alaska, and chocolate teacups
with mint ice-cream "tea." High tea reser-
vations are required. House of Clarendon
also offers a regular light luncheon menu
of croissant sandwiches, quiches, soups,
salads, and other items that change daily,
along with imported teas, cappuccino
drinks, and, of course, a variety of cookies,
pastries, and chocolates. Seating is avail-
able inside the cafe or, in season, at
umbrella-covered tables on the outdoor
deck. House of Clarendon is closed on
Sunday.

Lancaster Brewing Co. and
Walnut Street Grille   **$–$$**
302 North Plum Street
(corner of Walnut and Plum Streets)
(717) 391-6258
www.lancasterbrewing.com
Constructed in the 1880s, this structure
was a former tobacco, then scrap metal,
warehouse. Since 1995, it's been a brewery
and has gained a solid reputation for its
flagship Hop Hog (India Pale Ale), Milk
Stout (dark, sweet English-style ale),
Amish Four-Grain (made with oats, rye,
malted wheat, and hops), summery Strawberry Wheat, and German-style Gold Star
Pilsner. Lancaster Brewing also has an
impressive repertoire of seasonal bock,
lager, ale, and weizen (wheat) varieties.

You can sample Lancaster County
Brewing Co.'s beers at its Walnut Street
Grille, which serves soups (a specialty is
white chili, with chicken, cheese, and tor-
tilla chips), salads, and sandwiches (the
Brewer's Chicken is made with the company's Milk Stout). Dinner entrees include
shrimp scampi over linguine, Bangers &
Mash LBC (andouille sausages and garlic
mashed potatoes), and a vegetable grille.
Open seven days for lunch and dinner.

Once a backroom operation for innkeepers, beer brewing had become an established full-time craft for a number of English and Scottish immigrants in Lancaster by the late 1800s. For more than a century, Lancaster County produced 7 percent of all beer, ale, and lager in the United States, making it the brewing capital of Pennsylvania. In the 1840s, as an increasing number of Germans moved into the area, area aficionados turned their affection from English-style brews to German *lager bier.* At one time, there were so many German-style breweries that one local newspaper nicknamed Lancaster the "Munich of the United States."

Lemon Grass Thai Restaurant $-$$
2481 Lincoln Highway East
(across from Rockvale Outlets)
(717) 295-1621
www.thailemongrass.com

Hot or not, the choice is up to you. If you can't take the heat of some traditional Thai dishes, you'll still get lots of flavor from bouquets of fresh basil, mint, galanga, cilantro, kaffir lime leaves, and, of course, lemongrass. For adventurous palates there's Evil Jungle Princess, a spicy chicken-and-vegetable medley. The gentler Angel Breast is a spinach and shrimp-stuffed chicken breast in delicate orange sauce. Desserts include mango with sticky rice and homemade coconut ice cream. Extensive selection of vegetarian dishes, too. Open daily for lunch and dinner.

The Olde Greenfield Inn $$-$$$
595 Greenfield Road
(717) 393-0668
www.theoldegreenfieldinn.com

Book a table for two in the wine cellar at this 1780 stone farmhouse, or pick a perch in the balcony overlooking the lounge, where a pianist provides musical background to your meal on Friday and Saturday evenings. Weather permitting, you can relax over breakfast, lunch, dinner, or Sunday brunch alfresco on the enclosed brick patio.

Dinner fare includes such classics as prime rib, cut-to-order steaks, and jumbo crab cakes, along with a signature seafood-and-pasta combination and roasted halibut with Hollandaise sauce. Brunch ($6.00 to $16.00) is luxurious, with raspberry Chambord French toast, fresh banana pancakes, and Alaskan (smoked salmon) or Chesapeake (crab) eggs Benedict.

Children are welcomed with their own dinner menu, balloons, and coloring books and crayons.

The Pressroom $$-$$$
26-28 West King Street
(717) 399-5400
www.pressroomrestaurant.com

If the name doesn't clue you in, the newspaper-like menus and headline banners over the bar carry out the "pressroom" theme, which has been a favorite lunch and dinner spot for Lancaster locals since 1995. (Before that, the 1886 Victorian building had been Steinman Hardware store for nearly a century.) An open kitchen with exposed baking hearth adds a dynamic visual to the clubby mahogany decor, with its comfy booths and banquettes. In summer, there's seating in Steinman Park, under the shade of mature trees and with a 20-foot waterfall as your backdrop.

Sandwiches are named after old friends from the funny papers, such as the Blondie fried haddock and the Dagwood hot roast beef. The burgers and hearth-baked pizzas are popular, too. While the atmosphere remains casual at dinnertime, the menu gets fancier, offering seasonal selections that may include garlic and rosemary-encrusted rack of lamb, sweetbreads with wild mushrooms in a sherry shallot cream sauce, and prime rib (only on weekends). Open seven days.

Symposium Mediterranean Restaurant $-$$
125 South Centerville Road
(717) 391-7656
www.symposiumrestaurant.com

Sunny colors, warm woods, lots of windows, and huge skylights give Nick and Ruth Grigoriades' bistro and lounge a stay-awhile atmosphere. In spring and summer, the patio is open for dining, too. The lunch and dinner menus go well beyond Mediterranean, with dishes such as Tahini chicken (marinated 24 hours in yogurt), coconut duck breast (with a dark rum, coconut milk, and fried spinach sauce), nuts and berries pork (hazelnut encrusted medallions with blueberries, raspberries, and strawberries), and mango risotto and vanilla shrimp (with mango chutney and shrimp in a fresh vanilla bean cream sauce). But don't worry, you can also find such classics as moussaka and dolmades (stuffed grape leaves). A children's menu starts at $3.95.

The exhibition wood-burning oven turns out crispy pizzas, the gyros are authentic (you can get a gyro pizza, too), and you can have your burger with ground beef or ostrich.

Local performers provide live dinner music Thursday through Saturday evenings. Closed Sunday.

Tokyo Diner $-$$
1625 Manheim Pike (Route 72,
Chelsea Square Shopping Center)
(717) 569-4305

Watching a hibachi chef perform feats of balance and "magic" on his grill is worth the price of dinner alone. Sushi lovers will find happiness here, too, and there are plenty of other familiar and exotic options on the regular Japanese menu. Open seven days for lunch and dinner.

If you're looking for something a little more private and quiet than the high-spirited hibachi area, ask to be seated in the tatami room.

LEOLA

The Log Cabin $$-$$$
11 Lehoy Forest Drive (off Route 272,
6 miles northeast of Lancaster)
(717) 626-1181
www.logcabinrestaurant.com

Not what you'd expect in the middle of the forest (the Lehoy Forest), this former speakeasy (it was built during Prohibition) is a virtual gallery of 18th- to 20th-century art. Historical portraits by Lancaster County artists share wall space with Tibetan *thangkas*, a combination of painting and textile work, and the modern masters Matisse and Leger. Ask a staff member for a tour of the paintings and antiques, then allow the kitchen staff to show you their artistry. The fare tends to be upscale classic—filet mignon au poivre with brandy Dijon sauce, lobster tail, trout amandine, and lamb chops prepared on a chargrill. The wine list is extensive and international in scope. For a romantic rendezvous, ask for one of the cozy booths designed for two.

LITITZ

Fiorentino's Italian Restaurant & Bar $-$$
500 Airport Road
(inside Lancaster Airport)
(717) 569-6732
www.fiorentinos.com

Tucked away in the corner of this tiny airport is a surprising gem that turns out some excellent Italian specialties, including "Nanna's recipe" for pasta e fagioli, zesty pasta orietta (scallops, asparagus tips, and thinly sliced proscuitto sautéed in a spicy alfredo sauce and tossed with cavatappi [spiral pasta tubes]) and Risotto Kaleigh (chicken medallions and Gulf shrimp sautéed with tomatoes and shallots in a lemon and champagne sauce over risotto). Create your own pizzas, too. Private plane owners like to stop here for the budget-priced ($4.95 to $5.95) lunches. Opens at 7:00 A.M. daily. Dinner is served until 10:00

When it's time to take a coffee break, you could head for the local Starbucks (2208 Lincoln Highway East, Lancaster; 717-394-0932), or you could give the locals an opportunity to quench your caffeine cravings. A few you might want to try:

Aroma Borealis (52 North Queen Street, Lancaster; 717-509-9869; www.aromaborealis.net)

Das Cafe Haus (Main Street at the traffic light at 772 East and Route 340 East, Intercourse; 717-768-0098)

Merenda Zug's Espresso Bar (11 East Main Street, Centre Square, Strasburg; 717-687-8027)

Ragged Edge Coffeehouse (110 Chambersburg Street, Gettysburg; 717-334-4464)

Spill the Beans Cafe (43 East Main Street, Lititz; 717-627-7827)

Square One Coffee (145 North Duke Street, Lancaster; 717-392-3354)

P.M. Monday through Thursday, 11:00 P.M. Friday and Saturday, 8:00 P.M. Sunday.

General Sutter Inn $-$$$
14 East Main Street
(717) 626-2115
www.generalsutterinn.com

The inn actually is a trio of eating and drinking options, ranging from fine dining to casual cafe to Victorian-style bar and lounge. The original inn, the Zum Anchor (Sign of the Anchor), was built in 1764. More than 240 years later, it remains a hospitality landmark in Lititz. Well-thought-out presentations of game and fish are the hallmark of the 1764 Restaurant. Look for the Pennsylvania trout presentation of the day and interesting renditions of boar and rabbit sausages, buffalo tenderloin, and elk. Lunch selections (also served at the Sutter Cafe) can range from a simple ham and cheese sandwich, burger, or salad to Maine lobster and Maryland crab crepes.

Early diners can get a particularly good deal at the General Sutter Inn if they can get there between 5:00 and 5:45 P.M. The 1764 Restaurant offers a menu of Twilight Dinner Specials, including soup or salad, entree (perhaps poached filet of salmon in Bearnaise sauce or London broil

with sautéed mushrooms), and dessert for $12.95.

On Wednesdays, you can get dinner for two plus a bottle of merlot or pinot grigio from a special menu (talapia sauté putenesca or linguini carbonara, for example) for $32.

The Sutter Cafe (still also known as Zum Anchor) is a great breakfast spot, with offerings such as eggs Florentine and almond, amaretto, and raspberry French toast. Pearl's Bar and Tavern is the place for a glass of spirits and a light bite or appetizer. Breakfast and dinner are served daily, lunch Monday through Saturday, brunch on Sunday. In season, the Outdoor Patio serves lunch and light dinner fare.

Open for lunch and dinner. Children's menus ($2.49 to $9.49) are available at the restaurant and cafe.

Glassmyer's Restaurant $
23 North Broad Street
(717) 626-2345

Locals line up for breakfast and lunch at this old-fashioned soda fountain. Join them and be sure to eat your veggies—the green pepper, onion, and mushroom melange is one reason why the "melt" sandwiches here are so popular. Open Monday through Saturday from 6:30 A.M. to 2:00 P.M.

MANHEIM

Kreider Farms Restaurants $
Route 72 North
1461 Lancaster Road, Manheim
(717) 665-5039

Route 322 (across from Hershey
Medical Center), Hershey
(717) 533-8067

3101 Columbia Avenue, Lancaster
(717) 393-3410
www.kreiderfarms.com
Take a tour of the farm beginning with the "cow palace," a bovine dormitory so large "it could house the Titanic with room to spare," according to the Kreider family. You can also watch the cows ride on a "giant carousel" during the milking process, get a close-up glimpse of some big farm equipment, and pet and feed the calves. So where does all that fresh milk go? A good bit of it goes into the 27 flavors of ice cream that Kreider Farms makes. Along with the 1,500 dairy cows, the 3,000-acre property is also home to around 375,000 hens and two million chickens. When you have that many hens and cows working for you, you're bound to become known for breakfast, and Kreider Farms definitely is. A la carte three-egg omelets stuffed with meats, cheeses, and/or veggies go from $3.39 to $4.59. For really hearty appetites there's the Farmer's Dozen, consisting of four pancakes, three each eggs and bacon strips, one sausage patty, and home-fried potatoes for $5.49. At the Manheim location only, there's a Saturday and Sunday brunch buffet for under $8.00 for adults, children can eat for 59 cents per year of age.

Manheim also has a lunch buffet on Tuesday (under $9.00 for adults, children 59 cents per year of age) featuring fried chicken, fried and baked fish, roast beef, and turkey; the daily dinner buffet is under $15 for adults and 89 cents per year of age for children. For take-out rotisserie chickens by the piece or the meal, sandwiches, subs, pizza, and stromboli, this location has a Kreider Farms Express unit.

All three locations serve comfort food a la carte dinners. Open seven days.

MARIETTA

Josephine's Restaurant $$-$$$
324 West Market Street
(717) 426-2003
From private residence in 1792 to stagecoach stop in 1860 to tea room around the turn of the 20th century to a speakeasy during Prohibition, this log home has undergone a number of transformations throughout its history. Now it is a genteel dinner spot with a French-inspired menu and impressive wine list created by chef/sommelier/owner Daniel LeBoon. Pan-seared crab cakes are among LeBoon's specialties. Selections are seasonal but reflect the same innovation, such as veal tenderloin wrapped in apple-smoked bacon and pan-seared with a juniper berry crust, duck confit with spinach and dried cherries in a Chambord reduction, and short ribs in pomegranate–grapefruit reduction. Hand-whipped ice creams combine a whirlwind of flavors, such as Bing Cherry Swiss Chocolate Couverture Chambord. The wine list is diverse and thoughtful, too.

MOUNT JOY

Cameron Estate Inn & Restaurant $$-$$$
1855 Mansion Lane
(717) 492-0111
www.cameronestateinn.com
Two dining rooms, one illuminated by sunlight, the other by the crackling fire of a hearth, offer deluxe dining experiences in the circa 1805 summer mansion of Lincoln's first secretary of war. The food reflects the timeless surroundings with aristocratic selections such as bacon and Stilton terrine with rhubarb chutney and candied bacon, smoked salmon Napoleon layered with potato tuiles, and honey–tarragon game hen. Dinner is served Wednesday through Saturday, brunch

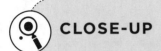

Bube's Brewery: A Complex Experience

From the outside Bube's Brewery (102 North Market Street; Mount Joy; 717-653-2056; www.bubesbrewery.com) looks like an abandoned factory. But inside, there's always so much going on in this block-long 19th-century brewery/restaurant complex that you could come back night after night and never have the same experience twice. Bavarian immigrant Alois Bube began his operation in 1876, when brewing German-style lager was big business in the Lancaster area. By the turn of the century, Bube had expanded his brewery several times and attached a Victorian hotel (the Central Hotel) to his building.

In fact, Bube's enterprise was so prosperous that when he died in 1908 at age 57, members of his family were able to live in the building until the 1960s (even though the brewery itself had ceased operating just prior to Prohibition in 1920). Fortunately, the family didn't feel the need to change a thing after Bube died, so the brewery/hotel remained intact—and it's a good thing, because there isn't another one like it in the country. Getting the complex up to modern speed—not to mention code—was something else altogether. The restoration began in 1968 and, according to hands-on owner Sam Allen, is an ongoing project. Although the original equipment is not used, Bube's Brewery once again produces its own premium German-style beers in the area that was once used as the icehouse.

Do-it-yourselfers can purchase a variety of malted grains, malt extracts, hops, and yeast as well as full startup kits at the brewery's Homebrew Shop.

Within the Bube's Brewery complex there are also four distinctly different eating and drinking establishments, which range from upscale fine dining to interactive dinner theater to tavern and *biergarten* casual. They are:

Alois: Encompassing the original bar and Victorian Hotel portion of the complex, each room has been individually decorated with hand stenciling and other painting techniques. The Alois Martini Bar, located in the "parlor," is a comfortable spot for predinner appetizers or casual dining ($4.00 to $10.75 for appetizers, $17.00 to $23.00 for a la carte entrees). In addition to over 100 different martinis and a selection of Bube's handcrafted brews, you can order wine by the glass or bottle, traditional cocktails, or alcohol-free versions of your favorites. If you go with the entire Alois Experience ($35 per person; reservations are strongly recommended), you'll have appetizers, cocktails, and a first course (examples are mango fritters or venison and blueberry sausage encroute) in the parlor, then move to one of the dining rooms for soup, salad, sorbet, entree, and dessert. Alois is open Wednesday through Sunday. Every Friday and Saturday and every other Sunday jazz musicians perform live. On select Saturday nights, Allen and his "house troupe" of actors and staff perform in original Murder Mysteries (call for schedule) that allow guests to sup while they solve ($35).

The Catacombs Restaurant: Forty-three feet underground, deep in the cellars of Bube's are stone-lined vaults where anything can happen. And it does. Some evenings, The Catacombs is an

Bube's Brewery has a multitude of personalities. BUBE'S BREWERY ARCHIVES

atmospheric restaurant with a gourmet-style menu that might include coquilles Catacombs and New York strip steak stuffed with jalapeño pepper ($17 to $28). Dinner is served seven nights. On most Sunday evenings, The Catacombs is transformed into the scene of a themed feast ($16 to $24), complete with imaginative menu, costumed characters, and appropriate entertainment. Most frequent is the Medieval Feast, but there are also Roman, Pirate, Halloween (October), and Christmas (December) versions.

The Biergarten Restaurant: Reminiscent of the neighborhood drinking "gardens" of Alois Bube's homeland, serving casual lunch (burgers, sandwiches, salads, and soups, $3.95 to $6.95) and dinner (steaks to Asian shrimp, $9.95 to $19.95).

The Bottling Works: Shares the same menu as the Beirgarten, but this restaurant/tavern is located inside the original bottling plant.

The visual arts are also well represented at Bube's, especially in the Brewery Gallery, with sculpture, painting, drawing, photography, and other media on display from noon to 9:00 P.M. weekdays and until 11:00 P.M. on Friday, Saturday, and Sunday; no admission charge.

Oh, yes, rumor has it that the brewery is haunted. If you want to become acquainted with these spirits of the nonliquid kind, take one of the guided ghost tours ($2.00 per person; call or check the Web site for schedules).

(entree prices range from $12 to $19) on Sunday. Vegetarian options are available.

PARADISE

Historic Revere Tavern   **$-$$**
3063 Lincoln Highway East
(U.S. Route 30)
(717) 687-8601
www.reveretavern.com
Once a popular stagecoach stop called Sign of the Spread Eagle, this 1740 inn has maintained its warm Colonial atmosphere, with original stone fireplaces and other historic trimmings. Steaks and seafood are the specialties here. If you've never tasted snapper soup, order it here. Or start your dinner with fried wild mushroom ravioli or clams Revere (topped with a mixture of bacon, spinach, cheddar cheese, and onions). Lunch is soups, salads, burgers, and sandwiches. Be sure to leave room for dessert, such as the signature tiramisu, peanut butter blitz (peanut butter mousse in a chocolate cookie crumb crust), chocolate bourbon pecan pie, or home-made cream puff filled with locally made Coleman's ice cream. Open seven days for dinner, Tuesday through Saturday for lunch. Children's menu.

STRASBURG

Iron Horse Inn Restaurant   **$-$$**
135 East Main Street
(866) 666-6362, (717) 687-6362
www.ironhorsepa.com
Back in the late 1800s, this building was known as The Hotel Strasburg and Conestoga Transportation Waiting Room. It's still a fun gathering spot for good food and spirits. The menu is eclectic, offering every kind of appetizer from escargots to crispy jumbo chicken wings. Beef is Black Angus from the filet mignon to the burgers. Salmon is Alaskan coho. In addition to nightly specials (Monday is prime rib night), Iron Horse features a different "Neighborhood Meal" every day except

Friday and Saturday. These home-style favorites include shepherd's pie and chicken and waffles. Open for lunch and dinner, closed Tuesday. Sunday brunch and children's menu. The wine list is extensive and features a number of Australian labels. Local brewers such as Stoudt's and Lancaster are represented on a beer list that includes a range of domestic and international selections.

VARIOUS LOCATIONS

Isaac's Restaurant & Deli   **$**
www.isaacsdeli.com
7 locations in Lancaster County
Downtown: 25 North Queen Street, (717) 394-4455 (in the heart of historic downtown in the Fulton Bank Building)
East: The Shoppes at Greenfield, (717) 393-6067 (right off Route 30)
North: Granite Run Square, (717) 560-7774 (off Route 30 and Route 283)
West: Sycamore Court, (717) 393-1199 (Centreville exit off Route 30 between Lancaster and York)
Ephrata: Cloister Shopping Center (on Route 272), (717) 733-7777
Lititz: 4 Trolley Run Road (just off Lititz Pike/Route 501), (717) 625-1181
Strasburg: Route 741 East (beside the Choo Choo Barn), (717) 687-7699
The pink flamingo logo will lead you to a tropical-themed spot where the sandwiches are named for birds and flowers. If you think a tribute to Pennsylvania's state bird, the ruffled grouse, is in order, you'll get a sandwich piled high with turkey breast, ham, and melted provolone. And don't let the dainty name of the Hummingbird fool you; it's a big beef, bacon, and melted cheese mouthful. Try a grilled soft pretzel roll sandwich. Isaac's also offers a variety of soups and salads (both the deli and the green varieties).
There's also an interesting "Isaac's World Cafe" menu that spotlights a different culture's cuisine each season. Items may be purchased a la carte, or get the "Complete Tour" (cup of soup, choice of

Dining on the Rails

For a taste of old-fashioned locomotive luxury, plan to have lunch or dinner on the painstakingly restored vintage Lee E. Brenner Dining Car at the Strasburg Rail Road (Route 741 East; Strasburg; 717-687-6486; www.thediningcar.net). It's a scenic ride on America's oldest steam railroad in the comfort of this mahogany-and-polished brass-appointed car with its custom-crafted tables and chairs. Lunch, which is served on all hourly trains from April through December, will take you all the way to Paradise with a menu of sandwiches priced from $9.25 for the Caboose (turkey or ham sandwich and cup of soup) to $10.75 for the Lee E. Brenner (sliced prime rib on a French roll with au jus and cole slaw) and desserts. Children's selections cost less than $3.00. Train ticket price is separate for lunch rides.

Dinner is by reservation only and may be Pennsylvania Dutch–style (salad, ham, turkey, and all the trimmings; apple cobbler or shoofly pie) or traditional (choice of prime rib, baked flounder, chicken cordon bleu, or vegetable platter). Children's choices are available. Price for the Pennsylvania Dutch dinner (selected dates from June through early September) is $39.45 for adults and $19.95 for children; traditional dinner (April through mid-December) is $41.95 for adults, $24.95 for children ages 2 to 11. Prices include dinner, train ride, entertainment (with traditional dinner shows), and applicable taxes.

The Strasburg Rail Road also hosts Murder Mystery Trains on selected dates from April to mid-November. Tickets (including dinner, entertainment, train fare, and taxes) cost $52.95 for adults, $35.95 for children ages 2 to 11.

If you'd rather buy a boxed lunch to take along for a picnic at Groff's Grove railroad stop, you can pick one up before you board at the Strasburg station's Sweet and Treat Shop (717-687-4252; www.thediningcar.net/sweetntreat.htm). A ham, turkey, or beef sandwich, cookie, and small juice drink cost $5.24 plus tax. No boxed lunches are permitted on the Lee E. Brenner Dining Car.

entrée, and dessert) for $11.95. A South American feast featured chicken tortilla soup, tequila lime shrimp skewers with lime vinaigrette, and dulce de leche sundae with caramel swirls.

THEATER ⓨ
AND NIGHTLIFE

It's not unusual to hear visitors to Pennsylvania Dutch Country complain that "nothing's open" after dark. While it's true that many of the museums and other popular attractions close at around 5:00 or 6:00 P.M., that doesn't mean the area rolls up its sidewalks and goes to sleep at dinnertime. The truth is that Lancaster County is actually a pretty lively place after dark. There are plenty of theaters offering everything from big Broadway-style musicals to avant-garde community and historic productions. Lancaster City and Hershey both have their own symphony orchestras. Lancaster also has its own opera company.

MUSIC

Hershey

Hersheypark Sports and Entertainment Complex
100 Hershey Park Drive
(717) 534-3911
www.hersheypa.com
Three distinctly different venues—Hersheypark Stadium, The Star Pavilion,

and Giant Center—present the biggest names in music and family entertainment and hometown and national athletic competitions. The address, box office phone number, and Web site are the same for all three venues.

Hersheypark Stadium/Arena
For outdoor events such as the annual Summer Concert Series, which hosts international big-name performers, the stadium can accommodate about 32,000 fans. These concerts generally start in May and continue until late September or early October. A state-of-the-art synthetic grass system also makes the stadium a major venue for the Pennsylvania Interscholastic Athletic Association football and soccer championships and the Big 33 Scholarship Program Football Classic. The stands can hold more than 16,000 sports fans.

The Star Pavilion
Located behind Hersheypark Stadium, The Star Pavilion provides a more intimate (8,000) outdoor venue for top-name concert performances, offering both stand and grass seating.

Giant Center
This year-round indoor venue is the home of the Hershey Bears professional hockey team (season is from mid-October to April) and hosts basketball games, ice shows, wrestling, in-the-round concerts, and other entertainment. The center has 12,500 seats for in-the-round concerts and 10,500 for hockey. It is wheelchair accessible. Interpreter services for concerts and show are available through the ADA coordinator (717-534-8958, TTY 717-534-8955) by request at least three weeks prior to the performance date. An FM loop assistive listening system is available

---

ℹ️ *Families with young children can get a free introduction to classical music and instruments at the Hershey Symphony Orchestra's annual "Young Person's Concert" held at the Hershey Theatre. In addition to a program selected specifically for young listeners, orchestra members interact with the audience and allow youngsters to hear, touch, and play a "petting zoo" of orchestra instruments.*

Free Summer Entertainment Series at Long's Park

On 13 summer weekends beginning in early June, Lancaster's Long's Park (located just off Route 30 on the Harrisburg Pike, across from Park City Center) hosts a free evening entertainment series featuring musical performers representing a range of genres. For more than four decades, the series has included an Independence Day concert by the Lancaster Symphony Orchestra and fireworks display. Also on the schedule is a Shakespeare in the Park production. All performances begin at 7:30 P.M. and are held rain or shine except in cases of "dangerously inclement weather."

Bring your own lawn chairs and blankets. Picnics are welcome, or purchase food from one of a variety of purveyors. No alcohol is permitted. Look for the current season's schedule at www.longspark.org or call (717) 295-7054.

through Guest Services (a credit card or driver's license deposit is required); neck loops and ear speakers are also available.

Hershey Symphony Orchestra
P.O. Box 93
Hershey, PA 17033
(717) 533-8449
www.hersheysymphony.org
Eighty accomplished musicians from around eastern and central Pennsylvania volunteer their time and talents to present concerts throughout the year, including four classical concerts at the Hershey Theatre, one of which is the free Family Discovery Concert. Programs cover a range of styles and periods, from classical to romantic, baroque to contemporary, symphonic to Broadway. The orchestra also promotes local musicians by inviting them to perform as guest soloists. Individual concert tickets are $15.00 for adults, $12.00 for seniors, and $5.00 for students 12 and older. Each year, the Hershey Symphony Orchestra also plays at a number of free events, including the Summer Pops series, throughout the Hershey area.

Lancaster

Chameleon Club
223 North Water Street
(717) 299-9684
www.chameleonclub.net
Since the late 1980s, the Chameleon Club has been presenting live original music from national touring artists and hot local bands in an intimate venue. Some of the major recording artists who have played here are Creed, Limp Bizkit, Soundgarden, and Weezer. (Ticket prices vary from around $6.00 to $20.00). On two other floors of the club are theme bars and Friday night dance parties with a resident DJ. Parking is available directly across the street at the city-operated Water Street garage.

Lancaster Opera Company
Fulton Opera House
12 North Prince Street
(717) 397-7425
www.atthefulton.org
One of the few nonprofit, all-volunteer opera companies in the country, this organization has an active performing membership of over 100. The company has its roots in the late 1940s, when husband and wife voice teachers Frederick and Dorothy Robinson moved their studios from Philadelphia to Lancaster. In 1951 a small group of their students created an opera workshop, rehearsing in the Robinsons' basement and performing at a local high school (and accompanied only by a piano) the following year. The group continued to grow and in 1960 performed for the first time at the Fulton, a production of *Madame Butterfly* with a full orchestra. Pricing for all box seats is $39. Other tickets range in price from $33 to $37 for adults, $15 for children age 17 and under. All seats in the Gallery (Section D) are $12. Students with current ID may purchase tickets (if available) for $9.00 at the box office a half hour prior to the curtain.

Each New Year's Eve, the Lancaster Symphony Orchestra performs at a celebration event at the American Music Theatre. Tickets are $55.

Lancaster Symphony Orchestra
44 North Queen Street,
Central Market Mall
(717) 291-6440
www.lancastersymphony.org
Since its 1947 debut at a local high school auditorium, the Lancaster Symphony Orchestra, led by Grammy-nominated music director and conductor Stephen Gunzenhauser, has grown into a major professional musical organization. Each year the orchestra presents 24 concerts at the Fulton Opera House and features international guest artists, guest conductors, and preconcert lectures. Ticket prices range from $19 to $52 for evening performances, $19 to $48 for matinees.

THEATER
Christiana

Freedom Chapel Dinner Theatre
15 North Bridge Street
(610) 593-7013
www.freedomchapeldinnertheatre.com
The building is historic (a former church built in 1858), and so is one of this theater's most popular productions, a reenactment of *The Christiana Trials of 1851,* based on a local incident that sparked the largest treason court case in America. Other shows on the year-round schedule range from Broadway hits to original plays. Tickets may be purchased with or without dinner (or lunch, in the case of matinees). Freedom Chapel Dinner Theatre is wheelchair accessible. Evening performances are Friday and Saturday beginning at 8:00 P.M. (arrive at 6:30 P.M. if dinner is included). Matinees are Tuesday, Wednesday, and Thursday beginning at 1:00 P.M. (arrive at 11:30 A.M. if lunch is included). Show-only tickets for both evening and matinee performances are $22 general admission, $20 for senior citizens; with lunch or dinner, $42 general admission, $40 for seniors. Tax and gratuity are not included.

Ephrata

Ephrata Area Community Theater
Brossman Complex
124 East Main Street
(717) 738-2228
www.lanccounty.com/ephrataact
Year-round live performances of full-stage original plays, children's shows, and concerts are done in a meticulously restored art deco theater located in downtown Ephrata. This is professional theater at

really affordable prices (between $8.00 and $12.00).

Ephrata Playhouse in the Park
320 Cocalico Street
(717) 733-7966
www.ephrataplayhouseinthepark.org
In the 1950s visiting Broadway producer John Cameron turned a former dance hall and roller rink dating to 1915 into the Legion Star Playhouse in Ephrata Community Park. As a nonprofit community theater under the auspices of the Ephrata Performing Arts Center (EPAC) since 1979, the Playhouse has remained a dynamic entertainment entity, staging six professional-quality productions per season (three musicals and a play in summer plus an additional musical in the fall and a final production in December) and giving talented local performers a venue in which to practice and hone their craft. Well known for its lavish Broadway musical productions, the theater also showcases original works and presents the Family Series of original and classic tales for children. The Playhouse is wheelchair accessible. Tickets for the May through mid-December Mainstage Series are $20.00; for the Family Series, $10.00 for adults, $5.00 for children 12 and under. Box office is open noon to 6:00 P.M. Monday through Friday, extended hours on show nights.

Fairfield/Gettysburg

Civil War Era Dinner Theater
The Historic Fairfield Inn 1757
15 West Main Street (Route 116 West), Fairfield
(888) 246-4432, (717) 642-5410
Year-round live dinner theater every Tuesday through Saturday at 7:00 P.M. (plus a Sunday matinee at 1:00 P.M.) features "Civil War–era" illusionist and storyteller "Professor Kerrigan," who performs feats of magic, tells of civilian life during that period, and relates some of the ghostly

Check out the photos on the Playhouse in the Park lobby wall and you'll find a resume from Robert DeNiro—he wasn't hired. There's also a well-circulated rumor that a young Philadelphia actor named Sylvester Stallone auditioned here (he didn't get a final call-back).

tales that continue to haunt this area. The show also includes a theatrical re-creation of a Civil War–era séance. Dinner is included for a ticket price of $39.95 for adults, $19.95 for children 12 and under.

Hershey

Hershey Theatre
15 East Caracas Avenue
(717) 534-3405
www.hersheytheatre.com
Touring Broadway shows, classical music and dance programs, and headline performers from around the world provide entertainment from September through April at this historic theater, which was built between 1929 and 1933 as part of town founder Milton S. Hershey's "Great Building Campaign." Tickets prices range between $20 and $65. The box office is open Monday through Friday, 10:00 A.M. to 5:00 P.M.; on performance days, 10:00 A.M. to curtain.

Be sure to give yourself plenty of time to admire the lobby, with its floor-to-ceiling tiles, polished Italian lava rock floor, and seamless 19-by-35-foot Oriental rug (originally purchased for $7,500). The walls and arches were fashioned from four different types of imported and domestic marble, and the ceiling is a work of art, with bas-relief images of wheat sheaves, beehives, swans, pastoral scenes, and chariots. A "canopy of gold" in the inner foyer was modeled after St. Mark's Cathedral in Venice, Italy. And, as you're walking to your seat on the main floor, think about the two

If you're interested in learning what goes on behind the scenes at a theater, a number of the local venues offer guided backstage tours for a separate ticket price.

years it took two German artisans to create its blue-and-gold pinpoint mosaic design.

Lancaster

American Music Theatre
2425 Lincoln Highway East
(800) 648–4102, (717) 397–7700
www.amtshows.com

Three original musical revues with professional performers and live orchestra plus more than 50 celebrity concerts presenting headliners from just about every genre of music, comedy, and dance make this venue a year-round favorite with both locals and tourists. Tickets for original productions are $35.00 for adults, $33.00 for seniors (55+), and $17.50 for children ages 3 to 17. (If you want to attend a performance of an original production during its two opening weeks, the prices are $30 for adults, $28 for seniors [55+], and $15 for children 3 to 17.) Prices for celebrity concerts are set individually. Thirty-minute backstage tours are available following 10:30 A.M. and 3:00 P.M. original productions for $3.50 per adult, $1.00 per child. You'll have a chance to meet some of the crew, get a close-up look at the sets, costumes, and props, plus learn about theater design, terminology, and how scenery changes can be accomplished so quickly and smoothly. Box office hours are Monday through Friday from 9:00 A.M. to 6:00 P.M., Saturday from 9:00 A.M. to 5:00 P.M. January through May. June to December, Monday through Saturday from 9:00 A.M. to 8:00 P.M., Sunday from noon to 4:00 P.M.; additional hours at show times.

Save money on tickets by taking advantage of American Music Theatre's Friday Family Night Rates for original productions. These special ticket rates are $25.00 for adults and senior citizens, $12.50 for children ages 3 to 17.

The Fulton Opera House
12 North Prince Street
(717) 397–7425
www.atthefulton.org

After more than a century and a half, the affectionately nicknamed "Grand Old Lady of Prince Street" and one of only eight theaters to be named a National Historic Landmark is more than alive and well; she's singing, dancing, and emoting with the energy of an ingénue. Home of Lancaster's professional regional theater (as well as its symphony orchestra and opera company), the Fulton presents a year-round schedule of major musicals, comedies, and dramas.

Called Fulton Hall (after the locally born inventor of the steamboat) when it first opened in 1852, this venue is considered to be the nation's oldest continuously operating theater. Among the show biz

The Fulton was built on the foundation of a pre–Revolutionary War jail (the exterior wall of the jail courtyard is now the back wall of the theater), where in 1763, a vigilante gang known as the Paxtang Boys massacred the last of the Conestoga Indians being held there for their protection. This horrible incident was the subject of one of the first plays ever written in America. It was called *A Dialogue Between Andrew Trueman and Thomas Zealot About the Killing of the Indians at Cannestogoe and Lancaster and The Paxton Boys, a Farce.*

All of the animal "stars" that appear in Sight & Sound productions live right on the theater complex grounds and are trained by its own animal husbandry staff of more than a dozen people. They also have access to 40 acres of pastureland near the complex. At last count, the resident animals numbered about 150 and included Vietnamese potbellied pigs, Angora goats, Barbados sheep, baby doll and Corriedale sheep, llamas, camels, Scottish Highlander and Jersey cattle, donkeys (full-size and miniature), goats, horses and ponies, dogs, cats, skunks, macaws, rabbits, chickens, doves, white pigeons, and Peking and Crescent ducks.

luminaries who trod its boards were Sarah Bernhardt, W. C. Fields, Al Jolson, and George M. Cohan.

Carefully restored Victorian on the outside, the Fulton is definitely up-to-date when it comes to production technology. Audiences with special needs also benefit from the additions of a sound system for the hearing impaired and a View-Via-Headphones system for the visually impaired. Wheelchair-accessible seating is available throughout the theater. Selected performances are ASL interpreted.

Tickets range from $25 to $45 for musicals (depending on day of week and section of theater), $19 to $39 for nonmusicals. Senior citizens' discounts are available.

Middle school, high school, and college students with ID may purchase tickets at the box office one hour before the curtain for $10 (one ticket per student). No advance reservations for this "student rush" program will be accepted.

Box office hours are Monday through Friday 10:00 A.M. to 5:00 P.M., Saturdays only during the run of a show, from noon to 4:00 P.M., and two hours before all performances. Hour-long historic tours of the Fulton Opera House are available Monday through Friday (except on "school day" performance days), weekends by appointment for groups of six or more, at 11:00 A.M. (weekends by appointment for groups of six or more) for $7.00 per person.

Ronks

Sight & Sound Theatres
300 Hartman Bridge Road (Route 896)
(717) 687-7800
www.sight-sound.com

Most months of the year, there's something big happening at this two-theater complex—big as in sets that rise up to 40 feet high, a cast of more than 50 professional performers, hundreds of costumes, live trained animals ranging from camels and horses to flight-trained birds, and elaborate special effects, including 3D video imaging, pyrotechnics, and lasers. Both the 2,000-seat Millennium Theatre and the 650-seat Living Waters Theatre (202 Hartman Bridge Road) mount epic theatrical interpretations of stories from the Bible. Productions have included *Noah—The Musical, Ruth,* and *Daniel—A Dream, A Den, A Deliverer.* Two perennial holiday favorites are the Easter spectacular *Behold the Lamb* and the *Miracle of Christmas,* which features flying angels, three camels, and an array of colorful special effects. Productions are definitely

Check out the wooden statue of inventor Robert Fulton in the lobby of the Fulton. It originally stood in front of the building. The statue currently adorning the exterior is a replica.

Lancaster's Sight & Sound Theatres present productions of epic proportion. PENNSYLVANIA DUTCH CONVENTION & VISITORS BUREAU

family-friendly but generally run about two to two and a half hours, so they may be a little long for very young children.

Sight & Sound Theatres, the largest faith-based live productions in America and sometimes referred to as "the Christian Broadway," was founded more than three decades ago by Lancaster County landscape painter Glenn Eshelman and his wife, Shirley. The Eshelmans' first "multimedia" production in the 1970s involved nothing more than a microphone, a record turntable, and a single slide projector. Both the Millennium and Living Waters theaters are wheelchair accessible. Sign language interpretation and hearing amplification system may be provided upon request. Specify any special needs when you make your reservation.

Depending on the particular show and day of the week (Saturday performance prices are higher), ticket prices for the Sight & Sound Theatres can range from $18 to $49 for adults and $12 to $49 for children. Box office hours are Monday through Saturday from 8:30 A.M. to 5:00 P.M. A 75-minute actor-guided behind-the-scenes-tour of the Millennium is available for $18 per adult, $12 per child.

HOMEGROWN
AND HOMEMADE

Everywhere you look you'll find evidence of the abundance of Pennsylvania Dutch Country. It's in the displays of homegrown fruits and vegetables piled high in crates and spilling seductively out of baskets at roadside stands that seem to sprout from the fertile soil on family farms on just about every back road. It's in the hand-lettered signs that beckon fast-food-jaded palates with the freshness of brown eggs gathered only a few hours ago, goat's milk, homemade root beer or birch beer, and pies with melt-in-your-mouth handmade crusts.

The abundance is as much artistic as it is agricultural. You can see it in the multicolored quilts, with their intricate patterns. It is in the masterfully crafted furnishings, toys, and decorative pieces that come from the barns and basements that have been converted into workshops.

Surprisingly, many of these home-based businesses are owned and operated by members of the Amish community, surprising because one of the basic tenets of Amish life has always been separation from the world outside the faith. But it all makes sense when you understand how this evolution "from plows to profits" (as professors Donald Kraybill and Steven M. Nolt described it in the subtitle of their 2004 book *Amish Enterprises*) occurred.

Although the number of Amish families has grown over the years, the amount of farmland that they can work and live on has actually shrunk as industrial, commercial, and residential construction has boomed all around their homesteads. Skyrocketing prices on any acreage that may be available further threatens the economic future of this independent society.

As a result, in some communities, upwards of 80 percent of Amish residents now work in factories and small businesses, according to Kraybill and Nolt. But that doesn't mean they have had to abandon their traditional belief system and lifestyle. Many members have combined generations-old skills with entrepreneurial strategies to enable them to develop their own cottage industries, ranging from small shops staffed only by family members to factories that offer employment opportunities to other members of the community. Some even hire non-Amish distributors to market their products to customers across the nation and around the world.

Statistics cited by Kraybill and Nolt demonstrate how adept the Amish are at nonagricultural pursuits. While the rate of failure for other American small businesses exceeds 50 percent, it is only 5 percent for those that are Amish-owned. Even more surprising is that 20 percent of Amish businesses are owned by women.

Due to religious considerations, most Amish- and Mennonite-owned businesses (both small and large) are closed on Sunday. Operations that are open on that day will be specified in the text.

In the world of Amish enterprise, you'll see certain names popping up over and over again, but it doesn't mean that only a few families hold the monopoly on retail operations. Among the Lancaster County Amish community, names such as Stoltzfus, King, Fisher, Beiler, and Lapp are pretty much as common as Smith and Jones are in the "English" (non-Amish) population.

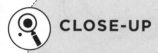

Humble Pies

Do you prefer your bottom to be wet or dry? If you're a shoofly pie connoisseur, you know that "wet bottom" means that there's a generous layer of sweet molasses filling under the crumb cake-like topping of this regional favorite. "Dry bottom" has a much thinner (sometimes almost barely there) layer of molasses filling, so it is more cake-like and less sweet throughout. Some bakers put chocolate in their shoofly pies, which tastes good but isn't quite the same. A dollop of whipped cream or scoop of vanilla ice cream on a warm slice can elevate this homey dessert to heavenly status.

Funny pie (sometimes called funny cake) is a shoofly derivation with a chocolate rather than molasses base.

Funeral pie is simply a raisin pie. Since the dried fruit was readily available and the recipe quick to prepare, this sweet was often served at the big meal following an Old Order Amish or Mennonite funeral or taken to the home of grieving families

Whoopie pie is not a pie at all. Rather, it is a sandwich-like creation consisting of two big cake-like cookies with a thick layer of fluffy icing in between. Traditionally, the cookies are chocolate—usually devil's food—and the icing is vanilla (the Ben & Jerry's ice cream flavor Makin' Whoopie Pie was inspired by this classic combo), but some adventurous types have come up with other flavor variations, including pumpkin and peanut butter. One Pennsylvania Dutch Country bakery makes these delights even more decadent with a dunk into more chocolate. Local cookbook author Betty Groff believes that the whoopie pie "cookie" cakes were originally made with leftover batter from cake baking. Some food authorities claim that they were first made in Maine. The origins of the name are shrouded in mystery, but the whoopies themselves can be found everywhere in the area, from big-time bakeries to the smallest roadside stands.

Chocolate cake, sweet fluffy cream—what else is there to say but "whoopie!" PENNSYLVANIA DUTCH CONVENTION & VISITORS BUREAU

BAKERY PRODUCTS

Just about every Pennsylvania Dutch–style bakery and restaurant has its own variation on the traditional sweet treat called shoofly pie. A sort of gooey, coffee cake with a layer of molasses and brown sugar on the bottom, this regionally renowned confection makes good use of ingredients that store well and never go out of season (unlike fruit). Most locals will tell you the name was derived from the fact that flies attracted to the sweet filling constantly had to be shooed away from pies cooling on windowsills and kitchen tables. (Another theory is that it took its name from Shoo Fly Molasses, a popular brand at the time of the pie's introduction at the 1876 Centennial Exposition in Philadelphia.)

Achenbach's Pastries, Inc.
375 East Main Street, Leola
(717) 656-6671
www.achenbachs.com

This particular incarnation of the business (located 10 miles east of Lancaster City on Route 23) has been turning out superior sweet stuff in Leola since 1954, but the family legacy goes all the way back to Great Depression days, when ancestor John Bender opened his first bakery in nearby Berks County. Three generations later, the signature pastry is still the Long John, a crispy-on-the-outside, creamy-on-the-inside deluxe doughnut creation that comes in vanilla, chocolate, or peanut butter. Other well-made local favorites baked here include whoopie pies (there's a chocolate chip variety and the extra-decadent chocolate-covered kind), shoofly pies, sticky buns, and apple fritters. Fancy cakes (which you can buy whole or by the slice) come in flavors such as lemon raspberry mousse and chocolate raspberry ganache.

Bird-in-Hand Bakery
2715 Old Philadelphia Pike (Route 340), Bird-in-Hand
(800) 524-3429, (717) 768-8273
www.bird-in-hand.com

The Smucker family still makes its wet-bottom shoofly pie (and lots of other home-style goodies) from Grandmom's recipe. Other stellar made-from-scratch attractions include whoopie pies, huge apple dumplings, pumpkin pies (the namesake ingredient is grown in the family's own patch), and old-fashioned red velvet cake. Aside from this main location, you can find the family's products at Bird-in-Hand Farmer's Market and Root's Market in Manheim.

Bird-in-Hand Bake Shop
542 Gibbons Road, Bird-in-Hand
(800) 340-8558, (717) 656-7947

Although this off-the-beaten-path bakery also specializes in wet-bottom shoofly pie and displays mastery in the art of making whoopies, Bird-in-Hand Bake Shop, owned by Erwin and Linda Miller since 1972, is a totally different operation than Bird-in-Hand Bakery. Take some of the soft, sweet potato rolls home for sandwiches. It's a little tricky to find, but if you head 1½ miles north of Route 340, turn right at the underpass (Beechdale Road), and take the long and winding road until you come to the second right-hand turn, Gibbons Road (next to the Little Red Schoolhouse), you can't miss it. They also serve up hand-dipped cones of Lancaster-made Coleman's ice cream.

Dutch Haven Shoo-fly Pie Bakery
2857A Lincoln Highway East
(U.S. Route 30), Ronks
(717) 687-0111

Shoofly pie was pretty much a well-kept

Funnel cakes, a regional specialty found in many farmers' markets, are made by pouring batter through a funnel into pans of hot fat to form large spirals, then deep frying them until they are crisp and golden. They are served immediately, often with a dusting of powdered sugar or a drizzle of honey or maple syrup. You can also find make-at-home batter mixes in many local shops.

Pennsylvania Dutch secret until this bakery started selling it to tourists in 1946 (does that make it a "pie"-oneer?) Anyway, Dutch Haven is still selling its signature wet-bottom classic from its bakery/restaurant (can't miss it; it's the place with the white windmill on its roof), and if you get a hankering when you go home, you can order more shipped to you by mail.

The Springerle House
15 East Main Street, Strasburg
(717) 687-8022
www.springerlehouse.com
Springerle, cookies imprinted with pictures in hand-carved molds, have been around for over a thousand years in Europe, and Heather Botchlet's family has been making them in Lancaster County for more than 100. Pennsylvania German immigrants, who first brought their intricately carved molds with them to the area around 1710, continued the tradition of making springerle, which they used as tokens of betrothal, to tell stories, and as a means of artistic expression. Botchlet, a fourth-generation springerle baker, makes her cookie molds, copied down to the last detail, from originals in German and Swiss museums. Her recipes follow European tradition as well.

From her shop, a restored 18th-century brick house just east of Strasburg Square (she also has a stand in the Lancaster Central Market), she sells hand-made springerle in lemon, orange, orange-vanilla, hazelnut, chocolate, almond, vanilla, and traditional anise flavors, some accented with edible gold paint. Botchlet also uses springerle molds to make hand-painted keepsake ornaments. Making springerle is a labor-intensive job, but if you want to try your hand at it, she has Swiss-cast molds for sale as well.

The Strasburg shop has a tea room, too, so you can sit, sip, and savor the springerle as well as other European-style cookies and treats Botchlet bakes.

CANDY

Regennas Candy Shop
120 West Lemon Street (rear), Lititz
(717) 626-2400
www.clearcandy.com
Not too many candy makers produce "clear toys" anymore, the transparent sugar sweets molded into miniature images of animals, people, and all kinds of other fun shapes. In original recipes that date all the way back to 1772, the candy

---

To find the bounty of Pennsylvania Dutch Country's farm stands and other home-based businesses, there are several prime back road routes you can follow. (Another bonus is the scenery, which consists primarily of farmland as far as the eye can see.) One is Route 897 South from Blue Ball to White Horse (Route 340). Continue west toward Intercourse, then take Route 772 north through Leola until you intersect with Route 272. Head north on 272 through Akron, Ephrata, Lititz, and Mount Joy to Marietta or south toward Willow Street.

Another is Route 23 beginning at Blue Ball, heading west through New Holland

and Leola to Marietta; or follow Route 322 northwest from Blue Ball to Ephrata. If you're a little more adventurous, just turn off any numbered route and meander.

Some of the stands along the back roads work on the honor box system. Products are marked with prices, so you'll know how much cash to leave in the box to pay for your order. (Free, detailed maps showing a variety of rural Lancaster County farm country routes can be picked up in most hotel lobbies.)

You also can find the wares of lots of local growers and crafters in one convenient place at one of the area's extensive, historic, and fun-to-shop farmers' markets.

was made with barley sugar, which was cheaper than imported sugarcane. That changed in 1818 when cane sugar became more readily available. C. Fred Regennas began making clear toys in 1894 and, with his sons Harry and Charles, opened a shop in Lititz in 1910. Now in its fifth generation, Regennas Candy Shop still uses the original clear toy recipe and hand pours the candy into more than 150 of the original molds. Available as a solid piece of hard candy or on a stick, the whimsical figures are made in amber, red, and green colors. For Easter and Christmas, special molds are used to make seasonal clear toys. One specialty is a clear toy Easter basket to fill with your favorite candy.

DAIRY PRODUCTS

Lancaster County produces more than 1.9 billion pounds of milk each year and where there's that much milk, there's bound to be some great ice cream and cheeses. Here are some of the best.

Boehringer's Drive-In
3160 North Reading Road (Route 272), Adamstown
(717) 484–4227
Nineteen flavors of superpremium stuff (17 percent butterfat) are made with real crushed vanilla bean, big chunks of strawberry, and lots of tender, loving care by third-generation ice-cream maker Sandra Schnader and her son Chris from treasured family recipes. Boehringer's has been a landmark since 1936. Distinctive flavors include real old-fashioned butter brickle, pineapple and lemon (ice cream, not sherbet), black raspberry, and chocolate almond Amaretto. Chris admits that his favorite is chocolate butter fudge (made with chocolate, fudge, and butterscotch). Outdoor picnic table seating is found along a peaceful creek. Boehringer's also serves burgers, fries, steaks, and hot dogs. Many people think the banana split is a meal in itself. Open March through September.

Talk about the odd couple! Are those bagels on display next to the ice cream counter? Yup, they're Lancaster Legal Bagels, to be exact (same owner as Coleman's), available at around nine varieties at a time.

Coleman's Ice Cream
2195-B Old Philadelphia Pike, Lancaster
(717) 394–8815
You can indulge in old-fashioned homemade ice cream in some pretty newfangled flavors, including cappuccino crunch and butter cashew (yes, there's also butter pecan for nut purists). Coleman's offers around 50 flavors in season and own-make sherbets as well. There's no room for seating inside, but you can settle in at one of the picnic tables outside and slurp your cup, cone, sundae, split, shake, or smoothie to your heart's content. Many of the area's top restaurants, bakeries, and other specialty shops hand-scoop Coleman's as well.

Greco's Italian Ices
& Homemade Ice Cream
49 North Broad Street, Lititz
(717) 625–1166
Don't miss this little hidden gem, tucked away beside a parking lot directly across from Wilbur Chocolate. Greco's own-make ice-cream repertoire includes around 40 flavors (if coconut is on the menu, get it), and the banana splits are hefty 32 ouncers.

Kreider Farms
1461 Lancaster Road (Route 72), Manheim
(717) 665–5039
www.kreiderfarms.com
Every day the 1,500 cows at Kreider Farms produce more than 12,000 gallons of milk, and some of that fresh moo juice goes into making the dairy's 32 flavors of small-batch ice cream. Chocoholics will have a field day with concoctions such as caramel-chocolate truffle, chocolate éclair

crunch, and mud pie with almonds. The dairy traces its history to 1935, when Noah W. and Mary R. Kreider started with 103 acres of land and a dozen dairy cows. As the Krieders' sons grew up and married, they bought adjoining farms, and in 1971, the family built a processing plant to bottle their own milk and make their own ice cream. Today, third-generation Ron Kreider is at the helm

Lapp Valley Farm
244 Mentzner Road (between Routes 23 and 340), New Holland
(717) 354-7988

You can watch the cows being milked on John Lapp's dairy farm, then cool off with a cone of homemade ice cream. Sixteen flavors include maple walnut and coconut. (You can also find Lapp's ice cream at Kitchen Kettle Village, 3529 Old Philadelphia Pike, Intercourse; 800-732-3538, 717-768-8261.)

Pine View Acres Dairy
2225 New Danville Pike, Lancaster
(717) 872-5486

In summer, you can choose from 25 varieties made from cream from the dairy's own herd. Nothing envelope-pushing flavor-wise here, just good ice cream. Outside picnic-table seating.

The Strasburg Country Store and Creamery
1 West Main Street, Strasburg
(717) 687-0766
www.strasburg.com

The waffles for the cones are homemade (you can smell them cooking for blocks around), and you can't top that with just any old ice cream. Theirs is pure, super-creamy (14½ percent butterfat), and made daily. Pick your pleasure at the marble soda fountain—a 600-pound souvenir of the 1890s complete with silver dispensers and huge glass cases. Try the black raspberry, caramel praline, Zagnut (like the candy bar), or chocolate (with locally made Wilbur chocolate melted down to its richly flavored essence). Pick your

favorite add-ins—granola bars, cookies, M&Ms, Reese's Pieces—and the staff will mix them into your ice cream right before your eyes. The ambience is authentic old-fashioned ice-cream parlor, with wrought iron tables and chairs, wide-plank hardwood floors, antique lighting, and tunes from a vintage nickelodeon.

Wakefield Dairy
125 Warfel Road, Peach Bottom
(717) 548-2179

You'll find Peach Bottom at the southern tip of Lancaster County, where Route 272 meets Route 222. And Peach Bottom is where you'll find Henry R. Lapp's artisan cheese making operation. Born on a dairy farm, Lapp is a relative newcomer to cheese crafting, but it's clear that he's serious about it. Working in a renovated 50-year-old tobacco farm (Lapp is Amish, so his equipment doesn't use conventional electricity), he uses the milk from his own Holstein herd to create his seven varieties of cheese, including cheddar, herbal jack, pepper jack, Colby, and Colby dill. He had a special cave constructed on his property to age his distinctively flavored and textured Bouche and Smethe. (There's a telephone booth outside, so you can call and order cheese.)

FARMERS' MARKETS

Bird-in-Hand Farmers' Market
Route 340 and Maple Avenue, Bird-in-Hand
(717) 393-9674
www.birdinhandfarmersmarket.com

Where else could you find everything from bakery products to lingerie in one location? Located on land that was once a duck farm, the market was opened in 1975 by Chris and Dolly Lapp. More than 30 local vendors gather here to offer a wide selection of edible, wearable, and decorative items, including homemade candy and fudge, smoked meats and cheeses, fresh produce, hand-dipped candles, hand-carved toys, spices, and leather products. Check out the Jake and Amos stand for more than 1,000 varieties of Lancaster County–grown jarred products, including pickled vegetables (a big specialty is chowchow), pickled red beet eggs, and all kinds of condiments, fruit spreads, and butters (look for sweet potato butter). Watch soft pretzels, funnel cakes, and fudge being made.

Open Wednesday through Saturday, July through October; Friday and Saturday in December, January, February, and March; Wednesday, Friday, and Saturday in April, May, June, and November.

Green Dragon Farmers' Market & Auction
955 North State Street, Ephrata
(717) 738-1117
www.greendragonmarket.com
No mythical beast, this dragon comes alive every Friday year-round with indoor and outdoor shopping featuring 400 local growers, merchants, and craftspeople in seven large market buildings and an array of smaller shops on 30 acres. It's easy to find; just look for the GREEN DRAGON sign on Route 272, north of Ephrata. It's also a popular place for locals and visitors to find just about everything that comes from Pennsylvania Dutch Country. (A must-try is the locally made Zerbe's potato chips.)

Lancaster Central Market
23 North Market Street (northwest corner of Penn Square), Lancaster
(717) 291-4723
America's oldest publicly owned, continuously operated farmers' market was founded in the 1730s, when residents Andrew and Ann Hamilton conveyed from their private Lancaster estate 120 square feet of land for the purpose of erecting a town market. Exactly when the first actual market house was built on this plot is not known, but references to it have been found in documents dating back as far as 1757.

The current market house dates to 1889 and was designed by Philadelphia architect James Warner in the Romanesque Revival style. Its distinctive 72-foot-high twin towers are covered in Spanish tile and topped off with terracotta finials. Every Tuesday, Friday, and Saturday more than 70 vendors (some whose family businesses have been "on market" since the early 1900s) sell Amish-made foods and crafts as part of an array of international goods reflecting cultures from around the world, including Europe, the Middle East, and the Caribbean. Among them you'll find Hodecker's bleached celery (a local specialty), cookies and ornaments from the Springerle House, natural hardwood smoked hams and bacon from S. Clyde Weaver, and fresh-picked fruits and ciders from Kauffman Fruit Farm, plus incredibly creamy sweets from the Pennsylvania Fudge Company.

Root's Country Market & Auction
705 Graystone Road, Manheim
(717) 898-7811
www.rootsmarket.com
Begun in 1925 as a poultry auction, Root's, which is open only on Tuesday, is the oldest single-family-run country market in Lancaster County. More than 200 stand holders (some of whom are second and third generations of family businesses) offer farm-fresh produce, meats, bakery items, flowers and plants, handmade crafts, and all manner of household items. Locally produced edibles include beef jerky from New Holland Meats, fruits and veggies from Keagy's, still-warm-from-the-oven sticky buns from Mary Jane's Bake Shoppe, and hand-twisted pretzels from Norm's Bakery.

Chowchow is another example of the thriftiness and ingenuity of Pennsylvania Dutch homemakers, who make this colorful relish by pickling vegetables from the September garden harvest. Cauliflower, beans, carrots, celery, lima beans, peppers, and often watermelon rind are pickled and jarred for year-round use.

FURNITURE AND OTHER WOODWORKING

Cherry Acres Furniture
23 East Main Street, Lititz
(7170 626-7557
www.cherryacres.com
Reclaimed lumber from sources that range from barn siding to house floors get a new lease on life in the hands of local artisans, who craft them it into original rustic-style furnishings made for today's lifestyles. In addition to stock items, which include everything from bars to bookcases to bedroom dressers, you can have a piece custom designed for your home. You'll also find a colorful collection of Talavera (hand-painted, glazed earthenware imported from Mexico) sinks and home decor accessories.

Woodworking and whoopie pies may seem to be an odd combination, but on some Amish and Mennonite farms, the men craft furniture, toys, and decorative items, and the women create their own specialties, which may include a variety of fruit and shoofly pies, cakes, jams, bread, and other edibles. You might also find quilts and other examples of the needlecraft for which Pennsylvania Dutch Country is so famous.

Creative Wood Carvings
346 North Belmont Road, Gordonville
(717) 768-3087
Earl R. Houck's motto is "I get high releasing beauty in wood." His inspiration is all around him in the form of birds, animals, insects, fish, frogs, and other creatures of nature. Houck, a craftsman born and raised in Amish country, carves realistic and whimsical sculptures in full size or miniature. He'll also take special orders. Look for the black bear climbing a sign post in front of the showroom.

E. G. Woodcraft/Glick's Food & Crafts
248A Monterey Road, Bird-in-Hand
(717) 656-1343
Located off route 772 1 mile east of Leola, this working Amish farm is home to Eli Glick and family. This is a great place to see all kinds of Pennsylvania Dutch crafts in the making, from cedar chests, hickory rockers, and tables to fruit, shoofly, and whoopie pies. Woodworking equipment is air powered (no electricity on this Amish farm), and baking is done in a huge old-time iron oven. Watch ice cream being made in a crank machine attached to a gas engine. Kids will love petting the goats, sheep, guinea pigs, and horses on the farm.

Fisher's Quality Furniture
3061 West Newport Road
(Route 772), Ronks
(717) 656-4423
The cherry and oak furniture in Levi Fisher's workshop is handcrafted close by this showroom. You'll find bedroom and dining room suites, corner cupboards, china cabinets, dry sinks, entertainment centers, dressers, tables, chairs, chests, and desks.

George's Woodcrafts, Inc.
9 Reichs Church Road, Marietta
(800) 799-1685, (717) 426-1004
www.georgeswood.com
Even the drawer bottoms and cabinet backs of these artisan home and office furnishings are made from solid hardwood: no skimping, no shortcuts. And each piece of furniture is signed by the craftsman who made it. From a one-man shop in 1971, George B. Martin has grown his operation to a crew of 10 woodcrafters. Ask for a tour and you can not only watch them work, but see where and how the walnut, oak, maple, and cherry wood is air and kiln dried. The wood is slow-dried (some take several years) to ensure stability. Sit in one of the rocking chairs (they recline) and check out George's Unique Museum, a personal collection of tractors, tools, a gas engine, and

many other relics that can give you a glimpse of how Amish families have worked for generations.

Lapp's Coach Shop
**3572 West Newport Road
(Route 772), Intercourse
(717) 768–8712 (call between 9:30 and
10:00 A.M. or leave message)
www.lappscoachshop.com**
Established in 1944 by John M. Lapp, who specialized in the restoration of antique carriages for museums and private collections, the workshop now produces an array of solid pine and oak furniture, solid cedar and cedar-lined chests, bent oak and hickory rockers, country classic pie and jelly safes, sleighs, rocking horses, and pedal carts. If you're looking for a sturdy children's wagon, this is the place to come. Lapp's carries as many as 20 different sizes and models.

Lapp's Furniture
**3017 Irishtown Road, Ronks
(717) 656–1426**
Custom rolltop desks are the specialty here, made with attention to such details as wooden ball-and-socket connections for smooth opening and closing. Solid North American hardwood construction is framed with mortise-and-tenon joints in the style of the Lancaster County barn builders. Raised panels on the front, sides, and back add to the beauty of the pieces, and dovetailed drawer joints are reminders of craftsmanship that is lost in large factories. Lapp's Furniture showroom is located between Routes 30 and 340, just off North Ronks Road; turn east on Irishtown Road and look for the sign about a mile on the left.

Lapp's Wooden Toys
**3006 Irishtown Road, Ronks
(717) 768–7234**
About as far from today's techno-toys as you can get, these simple, well-crafted playthings allow children to exercise their imaginations. Everything's produced in the adjoining woodshop. Note the fun details

on the furniture for 18-inch dolls—for example, the beds complete with mattress, quilt (after all, this is Amish country), and pillow. Young equine enthusiasts will love the horse barn, and tots with a taste for transportation will go for the trucks, trains, tractors, and wagons. Lapp's also does a twist on the popular marble roller toy, substituting tiny rolling chassis cars for the marbles.

Peaceful Valley Amish Furniture
**3347 Old Philadelphia Pike (¼ mile west
of Intercourse on Route 340), Ronks
(717) 768–0216**

**421 Hartman Bridge Road
(Route 896), Strasburg
(717) 687–8336**
Both locations have a nice selection of oak and pine furniture crafted by Amish and Mennonite artisans. Glider rocking chairs are a specialty, but there are all kinds of other items, from cabinets, chests, desks, and tables to birdhouses, rocking horses, and charming ornamental wishing wells.

JAMS, JELLIES, AND RELISHES

Intercourse Canning Company
**3612 East Newport Road
P.O. Box 541
Intercourse, PA 17534
(717) 768–0156
www.intercoursecanning.com**
Proprietor Susan Adams and her staff refer to the preserved and jarred locally grown products as "Amish hors d'oeuvres." Wooden shelves and hand-woven baskets overflow with all manner of pickled vegetables, including dilled brussel sprouts, asparagus, baby carrots, and corn, as well as red beet eggs and chow-chow. Other distinctive Pennsylvania Dutch items include apple, peach, pear, and pumpkin butters; peanut butter "cream" (with marshmallow); and a variety of other spreads, sauces, and sweet-and-savory sides. The store carries its own

CLOSE-UP

Seven Sweets & Sours Festival

According to Pennsylvania Dutch tradition, every dinner should be accompanied by seven "sweets and sours," referring to any of the wide assortment of pickled vegetables, relishes, jellies, jams, fruit butters, spiced fruits, and other preserved produce that make use of the bounty of the area's farms. Among the sweets and sours, you'll often also find schmierkase—a soft, spreadable cheese very much like cottage cheese—a favorite when paired with apple butter and spread on bread.

Every year on the third weekend of September, Kitchen Kettle Village hosts a festival celebrating this tradition. There are untold numbers of tastings, pumpkin painting, cookie decorating, local artists making scarecrows, live music, and other harvesttime-oriented events.

Farm families still preserve and pickle an assortment of "sweets and sours." PENNSYLVANIA DUTCH CONVENTION & VISITORS BUREAU

proprietary label products and an assortment of Jake & Amos items. They'll be happy to let you taste before you buy. (A second Intercourse Canning Company store is located at Tanger Outlet Center, 626 Stanley K. Tanger Boulevard, Route 30, Lancaster; 717–396–9520. The Tanger location is open on Sunday.)

Kitchen Kettle Village
3529 Old Philadelphia Pike, Intercourse
(800) 732-3538, (717) 768-8261
www.kitchenkettle.com
They're still "putting up" the jams, jellies, and relishes just like founder Pat Burnley and her late husband, Bob, did more than 50 years ago, and you can watch a lot of the action. You'll find 72 original recipes for old-time regional specialties such as apple butter, pickled beets, chowchow, carrot jam, and peanut butter schmier (like nut fudge with a hint of brown sugar), as well as an array of new-fangled nibbles, including Vidalia onion relish, zesty salsa, and jalapeño jam.

MEATS

New Holland Meats, Inc.
Outlet Store: 1016 West Main Street, Blue Ball
(888) 644-5375
www.newhollandmeats.com
The meat market itself was first established on the farm of co-owner Frank Ludwig in 1927. In 1946 the growing business moved to this location in Blue Ball ½ mile west of the Routes 23/322 intersection. Fast-forward to the early 1980s, when current owner David R. Horst developed a signature recipe for Hickory Smoked Beef Jerky. A specialty of the house, the jerky is now available in Smokey BBQ and Teriyaki (created by David's wife, Sharon) as well. (The store is closed Saturday and Sunday.) The Horsts also sell their other Pennsylvania Dutch Country–style specialty meats, including scrapple, sweet bologna, fresh sausage, sugar-cured bacon, and filled or unfilled pig stomach. Look for New Holland Meats (including jerkys) on Tuesdays at Root's Country Market & Auction in Manheim and Fridays at Green Dragon Farmers' Market in Ephrata (see descriptions under "Farmers' Markets" heading in this chapter).

S. Clyde Weaver Smoked Meats & Cheese
1655-B Lititz Pike (Lancaster Shopping Center, at Routes 501/30 junction), Lancaster
(717) 392-5244
www.sclydeweaver.com
Now in its third generation, this company, founded by S. Clyde and Emma Weaver in 1920, is particularly well known for its all-natural hardwood-smoked, no-water-added hams. Great bacon and bologna, too.

Seltzer's Smokehouse Meats
230 North College Street, Palmyra
(800) 282-6336, (717) 838-6336
The smoked bologna named after Lebanon County may have been invented by German immigrants farmers, but it's unlike any European sausage you've ever tasted. Henry Seltzer, a butcher in Palmyra (an area right outside the town that would later be known as Hershey) developed his own signature recipe in 1902, using lean beef and a secret blend of spices and seasonings. Not-so-secret is the slow smoking process, in 30-foot-tall all-wood buildings over hand-tended hardwood flames. Third-generation president Craig Seltzer continues to make his family's Lebanon bologna the same exact way. And every week, the company sells 100,000 pounds of its deeply smoky, savory specialty. No plant tours are offered, but you can see the process on video in the retail outlet store. While you're there, be sure to sample all five varieties of Seltzer's Lebanon Bologna.

Stoltzfus Meats & Deli
3614 Old Philadelphia Pike
Cross Keys Village Center, Intercourse
(800) 34-SMOKE
www.stoltzfusmeats.com
Begun by Amos Stoltzfus in 1958, this shop, now operated by his sons, is best known for its old-fashioned sweet bologna as well as such smoked specialties as ring bologna, hams, bacon, sausage, and turkey. This is a good place

CLOSE-UP

Pennsylvania Pottery

Two forms of pottery that are particularly identified with Pennsylvania Dutch Country are salt-glazed stoneware and redware. The technique of salt glazing, used in Germany for over 500 years, got its name from the process of introducing salt into the kiln at above 2000° Fahrenheit so it forms a sodium vapor. The vapor is carried throughout the oven by the flames and sticks to the clay of the baking pottery, forming a random coating. The practice was pretty much abandoned in the late 1800s, when the industrial revolution brought more advanced and consistent glazing technologies. The unique beauty achieved by salt glazing makes the stoneware much prized today.

Redware, which also traces its origins to Germany, is made by applying a glaze to the pottery before it is placed in the kiln. A lower oven temperature of just under 2000° Fahrenheit allows the glaze to melt evenly, making it possible for the artisan to have better control over color and decoration.

German potters generally used one of three methods to form their pieces. The first is throwing, which requires the use of a traditional potter's wheel. The second is slip casting, which is done by pouring liquid clay (called slip) into plaster molds to form a fine, thin wall. The third method is hand building. All of these methods continue to be used by today's potters.

Decorations are created by slip trailing (painting with liquid clay), brushing (creating a textured surface while the pottery clay is still wet), and sgrafitto (carving into the clay).

to try out such Pennsylvania Dutch favorites as scrapple and dried beef (usually combined with creamed sauce and served over toast as creamed chipped beef or frizzled beef, a popular farm breakfast item).

POTTERY

Eldreth Pottery
Production: 902 Hart Road, Oxford
(717) 529–6241
Showroom: 246 North Decatur Street
(Route 896), Strasburg
(717) 687–8445
www.eldrethpottery.com
Masterful examples of gray and blue salt-glazed stoneware are as functional as they are beautiful. All of the pottery is made in

Oxford, about 23 miles south of the Strasburg showroom. At the showroom, you'll find everything from baking and serving dishes to champagne buckets and storage crocks (some with wooden lids). There's also some wonderful redware in vibrant colors and patterns that run the gamut from flora to fauna in dinnerware and serving pieces, whimsical sculptures and wreaths, and other practical and decorative items. In addition to the first-quality, limited editions and one-of-a-kind pieces, you'll find a good selection of production seconds, many of which are slightly flawed but priced often appreciably lower. If you're into folk art, take a look at the collectible Santas and other sculptures designed from carvings by owner David Eldreth.

You can learn to do the "twist" from the pros at Sturgis Pretzel House in Lititz. PENNSYLVANIA DUTCH CONVENTION & VISITORS BUREAU

Pots by de Perrot
201 South Locust Street, Lititz
(717) 627–6789
www.potsbydeperrot.com
Steve and Shirley de Perrot create decorative and functional stoneware pottery and tile art in a variety of styles and glazes. The couple crafts a range of items from tile tables, mirrors, and trivets to stoneware baking dishes, platters, and birdbaths. The Perrots' gallery is open Wednesday through Saturday.

Village Pottery
Route 340, east of Lancaster
(next to The Old Country Store)
P.O. Box 419
Intercourse, PA 17534
(800) 390–8436, (717) 768–7171
www.villagepottery.cc
A diverse collection of functional and decorative collections and pieces handmade by skilled artisans can be found here. Look for original redware designs by Ned Foltz, fanciful face mugs by Brooke Gehman,

wheel-thrown stoneware miniatures slip trailed with a cobalt stain–dipped calligraphy pen, nature sculptures by Margaret L. Hudson, and crystalline-glazed porcelain by Tim Martin.

PRETZELS

Hammond Pretzel Bakery
716 South West End Avenue, Lancaster
(717) 392–7532
www.hammondpretzels.com
One of the first pretzel bakers in Lancaster, William Hammond passed his craft to his children, who passed it to the next generation. His grandson opened this bakery in the 1930s, and it's still owned and operated by members of the family. Look through the window that faces the parking lot before you go in any weekday between 7:00 A.M. and 3:00 P.M. (and Saturday in November and December) to see the crew mixing, kneading, cutting, rolling, twisting, and baking in the soapstone

In Philadelphia, they like them soft and chewy; in Pennsylvania Dutch Country, the most prized pretzels are hard, crisp, and crunchy. Bakers make the twisting look easy, but if you've ever tried it yourself, you know that turning out batch after batch of perfect pretzels with speed and precision takes a lot of practice.

The first pretzel bakery in America was founded in 1861 by Lititz bread baker Julius Sturgis. Legend has it that Sturgis got the recipe 11 years prior from a hobo who had given it to him to thank the baker for providing him with a meal. Sturgis Pretzel House is still baking from that original recipe, and, though the majority of the manufacturing has been automated, they'll show you how it's done and let you twist one of your very own (219 East Main Street/Route 772, Lititz; 717-626-4354; www.sturgispretzel.com).

hearth oven. Whether you like your pretzels heavily or not at all salted, golden brown or deep rich mahogany-colored, or even made with oat bran, you'll want to stock up at the on-site store.

Immergut Hand-Rolled Soft Pretzels
3537 Old Philadelphia Pike, Intercourse
(717) 768-0657
Watch the bakers as they work, then enjoy a twisted treat (regular or whole wheat) with a cold glass of hand-squeezed lemonade.

Intercourse Pretzel Factory
3614 Old Philadelphia Pike, Intercourse
(717) 768-3432
This working factory only makes about 100 pounds of pretzels (approximately 1,800 twists) per day, so you may want to call if you're set on seeing some live baking. Factory hours are scheduled for Tuesday through Sunday from Easter through Columbus Day (also Monday in July and

August) from 9:00 A.M. to 3:00 P.M., Saturday only the rest of the time. (Dough can be temperamental when the humidity's high, so sometimes the schedule gets pushed off.) Twist one of your own during the 10-minute tour. Interesting flavors include herb, cheese, and brown butter. For something a little more decadent, try a big chocolate- or molasses-caramel crunch–covered pretzel. Soft and stuffed pretzels are also made daily.

Martin's Pretzels
1229 Diamond Street, Akron
(717) 859-1272
www.martinspretzels.com
Two rolls, a quick twist, and a pinch. Pretzel making is still a totally hands-on business at Martin's. Conservative Mennonite-owned and -staffed, the production room rings with hymns sung by the traditionally garbed workers who roll, twist, and pinch an average of 12 sourdough pretzels apiece every minute, just as they have been doing for more than 60 years. That may sound pretty fast, but when you compare it with the average of 245 pretzels per minute that can be extruded by machines, it makes you wonder how an operation like this can survive in this day and age. The reason is that Martin's makes a very distinctively light (supposedly the finished pretzel weighs less than the flour that went into it) and deeply flavorful product that has a very

Steve de Perrot's tile art can also be seen in a special alcove at the Lititz Public Library (651 Kissel Hill Road, Lititz; 717-626-2255; www.lititzlibrary .org). Individual tiles are purchased by individuals who want to honor a friend, loved one, or other memorable person.

loyal fan base all over the country. Many people taste the pretzels at New York City's green markets, where fans buy them by the bushel. But if you want to see them made, you have to come to Akron (drive down Route 22 to Route 222 South to Akron, turn left at the square, and go about a mile; the bakery will be on the left). You can see (and hear) most of the process through the large lunchroom window. Twisting generally commences at 6:00 A.M., and visitors are advised to get there anytime between 8:00 A.M. and 3:00 P.M. for prime viewing.

QUILTS AND OTHER NEEDLECRAFT

As John A. Hostetler explains in his book *Amish Society*, "the Amish did not invent the quilting tradition or quilted bedcovers." In fact, it is believed that they learned the art of quilt making from Quakers and others already living in Pennsylvania at the time of their arrival. But there is definitely good reason why their talent and skill have made Lancaster County the "Quilt Capital of the World."

Quilts are an expression of Amish life, from the intricate patterns and stitches that symbolize members' relationships with the church and their community, to the clever frugality of using bits and pieces of fabric to create a useful household item, to the focus on family that is at the core of every part of the Amish homemaker's life.

Quilts are made of two outer fabric layers sandwiching a filling of batting material. The stitches go through all three layers and hold them together. According to Phyllis Pellman Good, co-owner of the Old Country Store and People's Place Quilt Museum, Amish women used to base their fees for making quilts on the number of yards of thread they used. Highly skilled quilters will use somewhere between 12 and 14 small, even stitches per inch. Quilting stitches are often done on treadle-powered (nonelectric) sewing machines. Appliqué stitches, which are much finer

If you want to buy your quilts where many locals do, go to one of the "mud sales," the annual auctions/sales held at various companies during the months of February and March. For details about mud sales, see the Shopping chapter.

and should be hidden, are generally sewn by hand.

Traditional Amish pattern designs are generally made up of various combinations of squares and rectangles, with such visually evocative names as Diamond in the Square, Sunshine and Shadow, Log Cabin, Bars, Double Wedding Ring, Irish Chain, and Bear's Paw.

Women in the community often get together to work on quilts at gatherings called sewing circles or quilting bees. These get-togethers also give these hard-working women a chance to relax and socialize.

As you travel through Pennsylvania Dutch Country, you will see quilts that reflect the Plain colors of Amish clothing and others that incorporate a myriad of brights, pastels, and print fabrics. In Amish households, only traditional colors are permissible. But just because a quilt isn't "Plain" doesn't mean it is not authentic. Amish women do use other colors and prints to make quilts to sell to tourists and others outside of their community.

Bird-in-Hand Country Store
2679-B Old Philadelphia Pike,
Bird-in-Hand
(717) 393-5321
www.bihcs.com
Since 1991, Marc and Kim Hondares have been selling Amish- and Mennonite-made quilts. In addition to having a variety of patterns in stock, they accept custom orders and carry a large assortment of fabrics (wool, cottons, silks, flannels, homespuns, and batiks, to name a few) as well as sewing notions for do-it-your-selfers.

The Quilting Heritage of Lancaster County

Since the 1800s, quilting has been an essential part of the family, social, and, eventually, economic life of the Pennsylvania Dutch Amish and Mennonite communities. In fact, fine quilting is so closely identified with this area that it has two museums dedicated to the art and craft.

The Lancaster Quilt & Textile Museum (37 Market Street, adjacent to the Central Market and the Heritage Center, Lancaster; 717-299-6440; www.textile museum.com) is the newest of these institutions, opened in 2004 in a 1912 Beaux Arts building in downtown Lancaster, and has one of the world's largest collections of 19th- and 20th-century Amish quilts indigenous to this region. The foundation for the museum is a permanent exhibition of the internationally renowned collection of 82 Amish quilts that had been the pride and joy of Esprit women's sportswear founder Doug Tompkins and had been displayed in the company's San Francisco headquarters during the 1970s and '80s. (The U.S. Postal Service used items from this collection for its 2002 quilt stamp series.) Lancaster's Heritage Center Museum borrowed the money to buy the quilts for $1 million in 2002. Other interactive exhibitions will focus on Amish history and the quilt-making process. Hours are Tuesday through Sunday, 10:00 A.M. to 5:00 P.M. Admission is $6.00 for adults, $4.00 for children over six and students with valid ID. The museum gift shop has do-it-yourself kits, including embroidery, quilting, rug hooking, and folk art dolls, for begin-

Country Lane Quilts
221 South Groffdale Road
(1 mile south of Route 23), Leola
(717) 656-8476
www.countrylanequilts.com
The way Katie Stoltzfus tells it, she had just laundered one of her handmade quilts and hung it on the line to dry when a passing feed salesman suggested that she might want to try selling them at a friend's nearby furniture store. Although that deal fell through, another store agreed to carry her quilts. One spring, when she had made too many for the store to handle, she decided to sell the excess from her home parlor. Her business grew so large that it now takes up its own addition to the Stoltzfus home and employs between 40 and 50 local women who do the hand quilting from their homes.

The Old Country Store
3510 Old Philadelphia Pike
P.O. Box 419
Intercourse, PA 17534
(800) 828-8218, (717) 768-7101
www.theoldcountrystore.com
The Old Country Store stocks thousands of craft items, including an extensive collection of quilts, made by more than 300 local Amish and Mennonite artisans. There are also lots of different fabrics and fabric packs for needlecraft novices and pros,

ner and advanced crafters; hard-to-find quilting publications; 1-inch-scale framed miniature quilts; tin quilt templates; and hand-cut paper quilt designs.

The People's Place Quilt Museum, located on the second floor of the Old Country Store (3510 Old Philadelphia Pike, Intercourse; 800-828-8218; www.ppquiltmuseum.com), is owned by local historians Phyllis Pellman and Merle Good. The majority of this collection of antique Amish and Mennonite quilts predates the 1940s. This is also a prime stop for traveling quilt exhibitions. In addition to framed antique quilt reproductions, handmade on a 1-inch scale and created with antique fabrics, the museum shop carries unique quilt block collage brooches, unusual art books, pillows made from hand-dyed cotton fabrics, and other one-of-a-kind folk objects and art pieces. Open Monday through Saturday, 9:00 A.M. to 5:00 P.M.; no admission charge.

Handmade quilts from Pennsylvania Dutch Country become heirlooms treasured by families around the world. PENNSYLVANIA DUTCH CONVENTION & VISITORS BUREAU

traditional handmade faceless Amish dolls, and "Bunsfords," a menagerie of cuties made from corn husks. Make sure you take the time to tour the quilt museum upstairs. The Country Store is part of The People's Place complex, a center for information, education, films, and exhibits on Amish and Mennonite culture.

Esh's Quilts and Crafts
3829 Old Philadelphia Pike, Gordonville
(717) 768-8435
www.eshhandmadequilts.com
Even if you miss the sign on the side of the road, the colorful handmade quilts hanging on the porch should catch your attention. Jacob and Anna Esh have run

their craft business from their farm 1 mile east of Intercourse on Route 340 since 1980. The Esh family also offers a nice selection of handmade cedar chests and other items for the home.

Family Farm Quilts
3511 West Newport Road
(Route 772), Ronks
(717) 768-8375
www.familyfarmquilts.com
Here you'll find Amish- and Mennonite-made quilts, wallhangings, and other fabric crafts including dolls (the "washcloth" dolls are especially cute), Log Cabin quilt pattern placemats and coasters, quillows, hot pads, spice pads, and potholders.

Amish children like to play with dolls, just like other youngsters, but often you'll see rag dolls in Lancaster County without any faces. Not everyone (not even every Amish person) agrees on the reasons why. One of the most common explanations is based on the same religious belief that prohibits Amish individuals from being photographed. However, some Amish dolls with faces sewn or drawn on date to the early 1900s. That seems to support a second theory that most rag dolls before the 1900s, regardless of their cultural origin, were faceless.

The original Raggedy Ann doll, for example, discovered by cartoonist Johnny Gruelle's daughter, Marcella, and subsequently the title character of a series of famous stories he wrote in the early 20th century, did not have a face. Gruelle drew the now familiar features on the homemade plaything that had originally belonged to his mother.

Lapp's Quilts & Crafts
206 North Star Road, Ronks

Handmade quilts and other decorative items are for sale in the basement of this Amish farmhouse. Take Route 30 from Lancaster to Route 896 South to North Star Road East; it's the first farm on your right after the schoolhouse.

Riehl's Quilts & Crafts
247 East Eby Road, Leola
(717) 656-0697
www.lancastersource.com/riehlsquilts

More than 200 locally crafted quilts from crib to king size are on display at this Amish dairy farm. Take Route 340 to Route 772 West. Turn right onto Stumptown Road, then right onto Eby Road.

Smucker's Quilts
117 North Groffdale Road
(right off of Route 23), New Holland
(717) 656-8730

Rachel Smucker, with assistance from her

In big shops and on out-of-the-way farms, you'll see signs offering "quillows" for sale. This ingenious creation is actually a combination of a pillow and a lap quilt (the quilt provides the stuffing for the pillow).

mother-in-law, opened her original quilt shop in a small storage barn on her family's dairy farm more than 15 years ago. Business was so good that she now sells her quilts from the basement of her farmhouse. At any given time, Rachel has hundreds of quilts, quillows, quilted lap throws, spice mats, and other fabric arts in stock. She chooses the colors and orders the fabrics, then sends the pieces out to the 40 or so Amish and Mennonite women who have become part of her cottage industry network.

Sylvia Petershiem Quilts and Crafts
2544 Old Philadelphia Pike,
Bird-in-Hand
(717) 392-6404

Another home basement shop with more than 200 locally crafted quilts, or choose your own color and pattern combination for a one-of-a-kind creation.

Witmer Quilt Shop
1070 West Main Street (on Route 23),
New Holland
(717) 656-9526

Emma Witmer's mother opened this shop with her homemade quilts more than 30 years ago, and Emma continues the tradition with her own original designs in the two bedrooms she has converted into a showroom. There's nothing formal as far as display goes—just two beds piled high with beautifully patterned examples of Amish and Mennonite artistry (Emma employs more than 100 local ladies to do the stitching, cutting, tracing, and piecing). She also sells restored antique quilts.

MISCELLANEOUS HANDMADE ITEMS

Cramer's Dried Flower Farm Store
116 Trail Road North, Elizabethtown
(717) 367-9494
Up until 1993, Cramer's Posie Patch farm was an almost exclusively wholesale operation. Now the farm store is open to the general public to use in decorating or crafting. Don't expect a slick store; it's just an old weathered packing barn tucked back on a country road amid 25 acres of flower fields and herb gardens. Buy the homegrown flowers in big colorful bunches (no dyes are used; all of the botanicals are dried with forced hot air to retain their natural hues), arrangements, or finished or unfinished wreaths or swags. Stock up, even if the car's already full. Cramer's will ship your selections home to you for a 20 percent charge. (You'll find the farm about 4 miles north of Route 283—Rheems/Elizabethtown exit; follow Cloverleaf Road north from the exit where the road makes a sharp right turn, then continue straight ahead onto Greentree Road. Stay on Greentree until it ends at Elizabethtown Road, turn right on Elizabethtown Road to Trail Road. The farm is on the left-hand side of Trail Road, ¼ mile down.)

The Old Candle Barn
3551 Old Philadelphia Pike
P.O. Box 10
Intercourse, PA 17534
(717) 768-8926
www.oldcandlebarn.com
Visit the candle factory Monday through Friday from 8:00 A.M. to 4:00 P.M. and watch local artisans dip and pour the old-fashioned way. This company has been making its candles this way for more than 35 years. Inside the shop, you'll find a variety of scents, from Berry Festival to Hazelnut Coffee and from Banana Nut Bread to Honeydew Melon.

WINE

Mount Hope Estate and Winery
Route 72 (north of Manheim at exit 20/266 of the Pennsylvania Turnpike)
(717) 665-7021, ext. 129
www.parenfaire.com

Mount Hope Wine Gallery (Retail Shop)
3174 Old Philadelphia Pike, Bird-in-Hand
(717) 768-7194
From mid-August through mid-October, this 87-acre Manheim winery is home to the Pennsylvania Renaissance Faire. Its 200-year-old Victorian mansion is also the setting for theatrical performances rang-

Just as the Amish and Mennonites came to Lancaster County after fleeing religious persecution in their native countries, so have a number of people from the Hmong tribe of Vietnam and Laos. Many of the Hmong who came as refugees at the end of the Vietnam War were sponsored by local Mennonite families, who helped them adapt to the American way of life.

Also like the immigrants from hundreds of years ago, many of the Hmong women are skilled in needlework. Their specialty is in reverse appliqué and cross-stitch, both of which are applicable to quilt making. As a result, numerous Hmong women now sew quilts in commercial shops and home-based businesses, many of which are owned and operated by the Amish and Mennonites.

CLOSE-UP

Hex Signs

Although the Plain folks (that is, the Old Order Amish and Mennonites) of Pennsylvania Dutch Country kept their home decorating decidedly low-key, the same could not necessarily be said of the Lutherans and other Reformed groups whose worldly tastes earned them the title "Fancy." When they came to this area more than three centuries ago, many "Fancy" farmers hand painted on the exterior walls of their barns reproductions of the mythical bird, floral, and other geometric designs that had traditionally been drawn on birth and marriage certificates, family Bibles, quilts, and some furniture in their European homelands. Misunderstanding the German word for *six* (*sechs*), their neighbors began to call the designs "hex" patterns.

Each of the symbols in the barn signs, now commonly known as hex signs, had a precise meaning or "legend." The sun wheel, for instance, stood for warmth and fertility; a cluster of oak leaves and acorns meant strength, health, and long life, like the mighty oak tree; tulips represented faith, and birds called *distelfinks* (goldfinches) symbolized good luck. Newlyweds often had a "Haus Segen" (house blessing) pattern on their new homes. Blue was considered to be a color of protection, green was symbolic of growing things, and brown stood for Mother Earth.

You can see many of these traditional designs—and purchase silk-screened hex signs for your home or garden—at Will Char, The Hex Place (3056 U.S. Route 30 East, Paradise; 717–687–8329; www.hex signs.com). The silk-screening process was pioneered by Jacob Zook, an 11th-generation Pennsylvania Dutchman living in Paradise in the early 1940s. The hex signs that bear his name are still hand silk-screened by local crafters.

ing from *Beowulf* and Shakespeare to Edgar Allan Poe and Charles Dickens. But there doesn't have to be a special event to make a trip to this winery (or its Bird-in-Hand retail store) worthwhile. Come any day for a free tasting (bring a picnic lunch if you wish) of Mount Hope's "Royal Series" cabernet sauvignon, chardonnay, Riesling, or merlot. Try one of the "Euro hybrids," such as Seyval blanc or Vidal blanc, or savor the sweetness of ice wine (a late harvest wine made from Vidal grapes frozen on the vine). May wine,

scented with the herb woodruff, is one of a "Specialty Series," as is Pennsylvania Dutch spiced apple. Other orchard and berry patch favorites include peach, cherry, strawberry, blackberry, blueberry, and raspberry.

Nissley Vineyards & Winery Estate
140 Vintage Drive, Bainbridge
(800) 522-2387, (717) 426-3514
www.nissleywine.com
Set on 300 acres, this family-owned winery has been producing estate-bottled

selections including Vidal blanc, vignoles, Chambourcin, and cabernet franc since 1978. Signature Naughty Marietta (named for the nearby town) is a light-bodied semidry red and Candlelight a delicate rose in the white zinfandel style. On the sweeter side, there are a number of selections, including traditional white Niagara and pale red Concord, as well as other fruit wines made from black raspberries, cherries, and apples.

Pick up a free self-guided tasting tour pamphlet inside. (To find the winery, take Route 30 to Columbia, exit at Route 441, and drive north for 8 miles. Turn right on Wickersham Road, and continue 1½ miles, following signs at intersections.) Open seven days.

SHOPPING ⊕

Nowhere is Pennsylvania Dutch Country's juxtaposition of old and new, plain and fancy, frugal and lavish more apparent than in its range of retail options, from out-in-the-woods rustic markets to hole-in-the-wall, one-of-a-kind, mom-and-pop boutiques; from tiny workshops, studios, and galleries of artists whose names you've yet to learn to as-far-as-the-eye-can-see stretches of name brands in huge outlet malls. Antiques and collectibles? Adamstown (www.antiques capital.com) has so many markets, shops, showcase malls, and centers that they virtually overflow into neighboring towns. A number are situated in and around the town of Denver, just a few miles north of Adamstown on Route 272.

ANTIQUES
Adamstown

This town isn't known as the "Antiques Capital of America" for nothing. Get off the Pennsylvania Turnpike (I–76) at exit 286 and you can find anything from mementos of early America to preserved pieces of Europe's past within a few miles along Routes 272 and 222.

The history of Adamstown antiquing goes back to the early 1960s, when a well-known Lebanon County dealer named Charles Wiek initiated a series of Sunday morning outdoor flea markets in a favorite picnic spot known as Shupp's Grove. Close to a major highway, it became a convenient place for sellers from the surrounding counties—and soon a number of surrounding states—to set up temporary shop each weekend during the warm weather seasons.

Sometime in the mid-'60s, Terry Heilman, manager of a nearby operation called Renningers Farmers Market, decided to give dealers the opportunity to extend their selling season into fall and winter by offering them indoor space in his building. Many of the dealers liked the idea that they could now conduct business on even the most miserable rainy days and that they did not have to take the time and trouble to pack up all of their merchandise and haul it off come closing time.

By the time spring rolled around, many of the merchants decided to stay at Renningers year-round. In fact, there were so many that Renningers Farmers Market changed its name to Renningers Antiques Market.

A few years later, another now familiar name entered the Adamstown antique arena when Black Angus Steakhouse owner Ed Stoudt opened a market in the basement of his restaurant. The venture was so successful that Stoudt soon constructed a separate new building to house his antiques enterprise.

As growing numbers of aficionados became aware of Adamstown's abundance of antiques, it became clear to dealers that their Sunday-only schedule had to change. However, for many of these individuals, selling antiques was only a part-time job, and they couldn't spare any additional hours to operate their booths. Those who were full-time pros couldn't be confined to a full-time selling schedule either because they had to be out and around finding and buying merchandise. To solve the time problem, some dealers decided to cooperate by taking turns covering the markets where they had their booths.

Today, some of the area's antiques shops and markets are still weekend-only operations, while others are also open for several days—and some even every day—during the week. During Antique Extravaganza weekends (the last full weekends in April, June, and September), many antique dealers extend their days and hours.

Antiques and collectibles abound in Adamstown. PENNSYLVANIA DUTCH CONVENTION & VISITORS BUREAU

In the Adamstown area, you'll find everything from individual dealers who specialize in particular items or eras to co-op enterprises where a number of dealers operate their own booths in a single location. Some co-ops call themselves "showcase shops" because the dealers in them display their offerings in glass cases. An example is the Antique Showcase at the Black Horse, 2180 Reading Road (Pennsylvania Turnpike exit 286 and Route 272), Denver (717-335-3300; www.black horselodge.com/antiques.asp), with 300 showcases, open seven days a week year-round.

The Country French Connection
2887 North Reading Road
(717) 484-0200
www.countryfrenchantiques.com
If you're looking for an 18th- or 19th-century French armoire, farm dining table, or bedroom suite, this shop set in a barn that's an antique itself (built in 1790) should be on your list. To accessorize, you can also find French pottery, copper cookware, and other accessories. Open seven days from 10:00 A.M. to 4:00 P.M.

Shupp's Grove
Pennsylvania Turnpike to exit 286,
right onto Route 272 North,
then right on Route 897 South
(1 mile to Grove on the left)
(717) 484-4115
www.shuppsgrove.com
The original and still a major player, this outdoor market has evolved from a warm-weather-only, solely-on-Sunday operation to three seasons (late April through October), two days a week (Saturday and Sunday from 7:00 A.M. to 5:00 P.M.). Each

Three times during its operating season, Shupp's Grove hosts special "Extravaganza" weekends, during which they allow early buyers who pay a gate fee of $5.00 to come in and shop on Friday from 3:00 to 7:00 P.M.

week highlights—but is never limited to—a particular theme, such as vintage kitchen and cast iron, garden and architecture, retro '60s and '70s, and science fiction. Nice to know for specialty item collectors who may want to plan a trip to coincide with a certain theme.

Denver

German Trading Post
2152 North Reading Road
(intersection of Route 272 and
Pennsylvania Turnpike exit 286)
(717) 336-8447
www.germantradingpost.com
You'll find all kinds of antiques and collectibles, including glassware, postcards, furniture, jewelry, linens, musical instruments, primitives, pottery, ceramics, and silver. Open on Saturday and Monday, 10:00 A.M. to 5:00 P.M., Sunday, 8:00 A.M. to 5:00 P.M. Live auctions of just about anything you can imagine are also held on Monday from 2:00 P.M. until the evening hours; if it's furniture you're after, be there at 7:00 P.M.

Oley Valley Architectural Antiques
2453 North Reading Road
(Route 272, ½ mile off exit 286
of the Pennsylvania Turnpike)
(717) 335-3585
www.oleyvalley.com
In business since 1973 and in its present 18,000-square-foot facility across the street from Renningers Antique Market since 1997, Oley Valley features more than 1,000 pieces representing Gothic, English, French, and Victorian architecture and furniture. Its selections of reclaimed stained,

beveled, and leaded glass windows; fireplace mantels (Victorian, Formal, Period, Country) in a variety of sizes from small to extra large; and antique bars (front and back wall units) are particularly impressive. Open weekdays (closed Tuesday and Wednesday) from 10:00 A.M. to 5:00 P.M., Saturday and Sunday from 10:00 A.M. to 6:00 P.M.

Renningers Antiques Market
2500 North Reading Road
(Route 272, ½ mile off exit 286
of the Pennsylvania Turnpike)
(717) 336-2177
www.renningers.com
Another of the originals, Renningers indoor antiques and collectibles market, which began in the early 1960s, is still open year-round and only on Sunday (7:30 A.M. to 4:00 P.M.). Every week, more than 375 dealers come together to make this a must-stop for collectors. During the spring, summer, and fall up to 400 additional sellers set up shop outdoors (sunrise to 4:00 P.M.).

Gettysburg

The Horse Soldier
777 Baltimore Street
(717) 334-0347
www.horsesoldier.com
A family-owned and -operated enterprise since 1971, this shop is packed with military antiques dating from the American Revolution to World War I, with particular emphasis on the American Civil War. There's an extensive collection of relics excavated from the Gettysburg Battlefield as well as firearms, edged weapons, 19th-century civilian and military portraits, documents, currency, bottles, soldiers' letters, and instruments from musical to medical. The Horse Soldier unconditionally guarantees everything it sells and offers appraisal and research services. Open six days (closed Wednesday) from 9:00 A.M. to 5:00 P.M. (hours extend until 7:00 P.M. in summer).

Shopping at Stoudtburg

What began as an antiques market in the basement of Julius Stoudt's restaurant in the early 1960s has evolved into a virtual shopping empire collectively called Stoudtburg. Under this Stoudtburg banner, and all within easy walking distance of one another, you'll find a multibuilding Sunday-only antiques mall, a six-day-a-week antique shop, a renowned microbrewery, the original Black Angus Restaurant (now with a brew pub), and an artisan bread bakery. At **Stoudt's Black Angus Antiques Mall** (Route 272, 2 miles north of Pennsylvania Turnpike exit 286 on the left-hand side of the road; 717-484-4386; www.stoudtsbeer.com), which bills itself as "The Antique Capital's Largest Under-Roof Antiques Mall," more than 500 dealers gather every Sunday year-round from 7:30 A.M to 5:00 P.M. Specialties include fine furniture, lighting fixtures, estate jewelry, china, and antique toys. The mall is also open Saturday on the last weekends of April, June, and September during the town-wide Antique Extravaganza. For six-day-a-week shopping (closed Wednesday) year-round there's **The Clock Tower Antique Center** (717-484-2757) with over 100 glass showcases. Open weekdays (except Wednesday) and Saturday from 10:00 A.M. to 5:00 P.M., Sunday from 7:00 A.M. to 4:00 P.M.

The Shops of Stoudtburg Village (717-484-4389) is a European-style designed community where shopkeepers live on the second floor above their first-floor businesses. So far, the village is home to close to about a dozen or so shops, but it continually grows. **Blumen Geschaft** (7 Market Plaza; 717-484-2100),

one of the colorful and eclectic residents, intermingles antiques with dried floral arrangements and handcrafted cloth and wood decorative items. Open daily (except Tuesday and Wednesday) from 10:00 A.M. to 5:00 P.M. **Kerschner's Antiques** (8 Market Plaza; 717-484-0505, 717-484-0421) has estate and vintage jewelry; original-design watercolor greeting cards; player piano, nickelodeon, and carousel music CDs and tapes; and a lovely music box museum. Open Friday, Saturday, and Sunday from 10:00 A.M. to 5:00 P.M., weekdays by chance.

Sisters' Gallery (17 Market Plaza; 717-484-0858; www.sistersgallery-stoudtburg.com) is owned by artists Mary Stoudt and Jean Cocuzza, who, though they are indeed siblings, have very distinctive visions and styles and work in very different media. Mary Stoudt specializes in textiles, particularly in contemporary quilts and "techno-Dutch" collages, using her own quilting technique that involves layering disparate types of fabric, paper, plastic, slides, and other often highly unusual materials. She also creates "poetry necklaces," decoratively stitched and beaded pouches with bits of poetry or a quote tucked inside. Jean is a painter in oil, watercolor, and pastel who soaks in her experiences and surroundings that range from urban architecture to nature's countryside and expresses them in subtle shades of color and light. Contributing their own singular talents to the venture are the sisters' daughters and a group of artist friends. Open Friday, Saturday, and Sunday from 10:00 A.M. to 5:00 P.M.

Five times a year, between and including Memorial Day and Labor Day weekends, Renningers Antiques Market hosts Special Sunday Events that attract almost twice the number of dealers from all over the country as its regular weekly market. The market's annual February Mid-Winter Classic (indoors, of course) is another huge event, featuring more than 300 antiques and collectibles dealers from around the world.

The Inkwell Autograph Gallery
529 Baltimore Street
(717) 337-2220
www.inkwellgallery.com
Interested in getting Abe Lincoln's "John Hancock"? How about a scribble from the probably platinum pen of professional socialite Paris Hilton? Or a written Roosevelt remembrance—your choice of Theodore or Franklin? Signature seekers will find a who's who of the notable and notorious, domestic and international, past and present. The Civil War offerings are particularly extensive, representing both North and South (Jefferson Davis was listed last time I looked). Also impressive are the availability of autographs from U.S. presidents and first ladies, luminaries from all realms of the arts and sciences, and sports figures and other historic or otherwise renowned figures. Established in 1995, the Inkwell offers a 100 percent guarantee that its autographs are authentic (most of the signed books for sale are obtained in person by the gallery owner, according to the company). Just about all of the signatures are museum-quality framed for preservation and display. In addition to selling autographs, the Inkwell buys single pieces to entire collections. Open weekdays (except Wednesday) and Saturday from 10:00 A.M. to 6:00 P.M., Sunday (during tourist season) from noon to 5:00 P.M.

Lord Nelson's Gallery
27½ Chambersburg Street
(800) 664-9797
www.lordnelsons.com
No Battle of Gettysburg antiques at this shop located in the James Gettys Hotel building, ½ block from Lincoln Square; instead Lord Nelson's (named after a beloved pet, not the Battle of Trafalgar admiral) specializes in art from the French and Indian War period. Original paintings, sculpture, prints, and posters by today's premier artists depict the lives, times, and trials of the Native Americans of the Eastern Woodland and the frontiersmen of the 18th century. There's also a large section of the shop devoted to wildlife, nostalgia, and handcrafted art, gifts, and accessories. Open Monday to Thursday and Saturday from 9:30 A.M. to 6:00 P.M., Friday until 8:00 P.M., and Sunday from noon to 4:00 P.M. Call for seasonal extended hours.

17 On the Square
17 Lincoln Square
(717) 339-0017
www.17onthesquare.com
Antiques, apples, and art share space and center stage in a 19th-century building, offering an unusual and interesting shopping experience in the heart of Gettysburg. The antiques showroom includes displays and cases of anything and everything from advertising to 19th- and 20th-century art, American and Chinese furniture to flow blue, Limoges, and RS Prussia china, from militaria to Orientalia. Another building tenant, The House of Time, features antique watches and clocks (including parts and repair). In season, the Farm Market sells locally grown apples and other fruit and, year-round, a good assortment of Pennsylvania-made gourmet items and specialty foods, including

honeys, jams and jellies, syrups, vinegars, mustards, soup mixes, and relishes. Also Pennsylvania-made are the vintages from Seven Valleys Vineyard, which you can taste and purchase at vintners' Fred and Lynn Hunter's shop. Once a vineyard for other wineries, Seven Valleys has been producing its own wines since 1994. Call for hours.

The Union Drummer Boy
13 Baltimore Street
(just off Lincoln Square)
(717) 334-2350
www.uniondb.com
Gleaming glass cases display a museum's worth of antiques and artifacts (everything 100 percent guaranteed for authenticity) gleaned from more than 20 Civil War and military shows around the country. Some of the items have been excavated from the Gettysburg Battlefield, others have been passed down through generations. Since these dealers purchase entire collections as well as single items, the inventory is diverse and includes artillery, uniforms, letters and documents, flags, autographs, medical instruments, historical prints, and sculptures. The experts here also will appraise pieces from the period that are brought to the gallery. Open seven days a week from 10:00 A.M. to 5:00 P.M.

Hershey

Crossroads Antique Mall
825 Cocoa Ave
(intersection of Routes 743 and 322)
(717) 520-1600
www.crossroadsantiquemall.com
Collectors will like this co-op because of the dozens of dealers and variety of antiques and collectibles, including rustic furniture, primitives, pottery, china, porcelain, glass, dolls, and toys. If you're interested in items with a local connection, this is also a good place to browse. (Every month, the mall features cases filled with

17 on the Square creates and sells Civil War wearables and accessories, including uniforms and civilian clothing for men and women, a good find for reenactors and living historians. It also sells period clothing on consignment for a flat 20 percent fee.

merchandise representing selected themes such as milk bottles or holiday-oriented, patriotic, or Hershey Centennial items.) The mall's setting, inside Hershey's largest parabolic arch barn, is also a draw for architectural enthusiasts. It was originally on one of the many local farm properties purchased by chocolate entrepreneur Milton S. Hershey to provide a consistent supply of fresh milk for his products and to serve as a hands-on farming skills training facility for students of the school he and his wife had founded. Open Thursday to Monday (closed Tuesday and Wednesday) from 10:00 A.M. to 5:30 P.M. In June, July, and August the mall is open every day.

Ziegler's Antique Mall
2975 Elizabethtown Road
(Route 743 South)
(7170 533-1662
www.zieglersantiques.com
You actually get three different kinds of shops in one here. First is Ziegler's in the Country, a 100-dealer co-op with merchandise that covers the antiques gamut. Personal Passions sells French Country home accessories, from furniture to floral arrangements, lamps to wall hangings. Neoclassic Courtyard imports lawn and

If you're in town the second week of October during the AACA Eastern National Antique & Classic Car Show, Crossroads Antique Mall dealers feature car-related collectibles. Hours of operation are extended until 7:00 P.M.

garden statuary from around the world. The mall is open Thursday to Monday from 9:00 A.M. to 5:00 P.M.

Hummelstown

Olde Factory Antiques & Crafts
139 South Hanover Street
(717) 566-5685
www.oldefactory.com
Consider it an aerobic workout to take in all three floors (over 24,000 square feet total) and 200 booths of antiques, collectibles, and crafts from furniture to glassware, American Girl dresses to teddy bears. Whether you're a rare book collector or just a voracious reader, don't miss Tarmans Books on the second floor. Between its own inventory of antique titles and that of two other bookdealers in the Olde Factory, Tarmans estimates that you'll find a total of about 10,000 volumes. Olde Factory Antiques has a wheelchair-accessible elevator. Hours are Monday to Saturday from 10:00 A.M. to 6:00 P.M., Sunday from noon to 5:00 P.M.

Lititz

A Colorful Past
33 East Main Street
(717) 627-7278
www.acolorfulpast.net
Antique furniture, vintage collectibles, and estate jewelry are specialties, but I think the real draw here is the made-to-order stained glass and blown glass art. Most unusual are the stained-glass fireplace screens, crafted in vibrant florals and other natural themes. You'll also find a good selection of lamps, windows, suncatchers, and ornaments. Handblown "Van Glow" ornaments and suncatchers blend swirls of color inspired by Vincent Van Gogh's *Starry Night*. Open January 1 through June 1 on Monday and Tuesday by appointment, Wednesday to Saturday from 10:00 A.M. to 5:00 P.M.; rest of the

year open Monday to Saturday from 10:00 A.M. to 5:00 P.M.

Heritage Map Museum
P.O. Box 412
Lititz, PA 17543
(717) 626-8858
www.carto.com
The word *museum* is not meant to be misleading. For 10 years, until May 2003, the world-class Heritage Map Museum, displaying the collection of 15th- to 19th-century maps of James E. Hess, made Lititz a must-stop destination for many teachers, genealogists, and history buffs as well as collectors. Hess and his rare and wonderful collection are still here, only now in a more intimate gallery setting, where, by appointment only (call for address), members of the public are welcome to view and purchase originals and the highest resolution archival prints (using archival inks and canvas) available anywhere in the world. This extensive cartographic collection spans time and the globe, including every state and every country.

The 1754 Checkerboard House Gift & Antique Shop
312 East 28th Division Highway (Route 322)
(866) 627-5212, (717) 627-5212
www.checkerboardhouse.com
With its dark and light sandstone patterned exterior (it took seven years to cut the stone and build the house), this distinctive Georgian-style structure is hard to miss. Once known as the Spotted House, it was an inn during the Revolutionary War, and, yes, it is said that George Washington slept here. Instead of having a retail atmosphere, the shop is set up to resemble a home where all of the antique furnishings and accessories (including the glassware, quilts, candles, linens, and floral arrangements) just happen to be for sale. Take note of the beautiful wood floors, trim work, doors, and windows—they're all original. Open Monday to Friday from 10:00 A.M. to 5:30 P.M., Saturday until 4:00 P.M.

Strasburg

Strasburg Antique Market
207 Georgetown Road
(717) 687-5624
A restored tobacco warehouse provides a fitting setting for 70 antiques dealers. You'll find a range of merchandise and time periods represented here, including 19th-century furniture, ceramics, metalwork, silver, pottery, glass, primitives, toys and games, jewelry, ephemera, dolls, books, sewing items, and prints. Open every day but Tuesday from 10:00 A.M to 5:00 P.M.

ART

Gettysburg

Gallon Historical Art
9 Steinwehr Avenue
(717) 334-0430
www.gallon.com
Dale Gallon has been a leading name in Civil War art for more than 20 years, publishing four limited edition prints per year, each of these scrupulously researched and executed, signed and numbered works eagerly sought by multitudes of art collectors and Civil War buffs. Though born in California (he is a graduate of the Art Center College of Design in Los Angeles and taught art at the University of California–Long Beach), Gallon's fascination with the Battle of Gettysburg drew him to the town in 1984, where he set up his home, studio, and walk-in gallery. To date, he has produced over 100 paintings. Call for hours.

Just Jennifer Gallery
33 York Street
(717) 338-9099
www.justjennifergallery.com
More than 40 fine artists are represented here, working in genres that range from traditional landscapes and wildlife to contemporary realism. Harley-Davidson devo-

Dale Gallon is such a stickler for historic accuracy that he employs a staff historian to research every detail. This historian writes a comprehensive essay that accompanies each print. In addition, Gallon identifies important people and landmarks on the upper and lower borders of each print.

tees can find works by David Uhl and Scott Jacobs. Other interesting offerings from artisans around the country include glass ornaments and suncatchers, bronze sculpture, hand-painted ceramics and pottery, and Native American sterling silver jewelry with turquoise and other stones. Check the schedule for featured artist appearances. Open Monday to Saturday from noon to 7:00 P.M., Sunday, noon to 5:00 P.M.

Lititz

Gypsy Hill Gallery
47 East Main Street
(717) 626-8141
www.gypsyhillgallery.com
More than 70 artists and craftspeople are represented at this Lititz gallery, with hundreds of works spanning a multitude of media, from oils and watercolors to mixed media, wood, fiber, pottery, glass, and metal. Styles range from classic to contemporary. Open Monday to Saturday, 10:00 A.M. to 6:00 P.M., Tuesday to Saturday January 1 to March 31.

BASKETS

Paradise

Basketville
3361 Lincoln Highway East
(717) 442-9444
www.basketville.com
If you can't come up with a trillion things

If these aren't enough baskets to hold your Pennsylvania Dutch–bought goodies, there are many more where they came from. PENNSYLVANIA DUTCH CONVENTION & VISITORS BUREAU

to do with woven wood, don't worry, this company has done it for you. Based in Putney, Vermont, Basketville has designed carriers in every form for just about every function, from toting picnics and pies to displaying fruits and flowers. You'll find scores of hardwood, willow, and rattan in designs that range from Shaker to Nantucket, with scores of company originals in between. Besides the baskets, the store has a large collection of wicker and rattan furniture as well as silk and dried flowers (custom arrangements are a specialty). Open year-round seven days a week. Opening time is at 9:00 A.M., but closing time can vary from 5:00 P.M. in winter to between 7:00 and 9:00 P.M. during summer.

BOOKS

Lancaster

The Book Haven
2022 Marietta Avenue
(717) 393–0920

The Book Haven has three floors, 100 categories, and over 75,000 books in stock. Specialties include Pennsylvania and local history, children's illustrated, and Early American imprints. Browsers are treated with respect and patience, so you have plenty of time to find the books that fit your particular interest. Open Monday to Friday from 10:00 A.M. to 5:00 P.M., except for Wednesday, when it's open to 9:00 P.M., and Saturday to 4:00 P.M.

Comic Store Station Square
2828 McGovern Avenue
(Station Square Shopping Center)
(717) 397-8737
www.comicstorepa.com
Comprehensive selection of new comic books, some hard-to-find editions from independent publishers, others from the big guys like Marvel, DC, Image, and Dark Horse. Big backstock, too. Major finds such as "Superman #2" issue from fall 1939 for $1,400. Open Monday to Friday from 9:00 A.M to 8:30 P.M., Saturday from 10:00 A.M. to 8:00 P.M., Sunday noon to 5:00 P.M.

CLOTHING
Lititz

The Tiger's Eye
49 East Main Street
(717) 627-2244
www.tigerseyelititz.com
Nadine Buch Poling had worked as an accessories buyer for a large regional department store for 30 years when, in 1995, a downsizing within the company left her looking for other options. Using her skill and experience, she decided to open a small shop where she could sell jewelry, handbags, scarves, one small line of shoes, and a limited line of clothing. In 1996 she opened The Tiger's Eye, named after one of her favorite gemstones. Three years later, she moved into her current shop, more than four times the size of the original, and now she represents over 400 vendors of fashion-forward and art-to-wear fashions. Some examples are Staley/Gretzinger clothing designs using silkscreen, hand-painted block prints, hand-dyed fabric, and fabric appliqué techniques; linens and blends for body types from petite through "generous 3" from Flax; hand-knit, homespun sweaters from Amy Brill; versatile, easy-care Pleats by Babette microfiber wardrobe separates; and appliquéd jackets and coats

Clothing and shoe purchases are not taxable in Pennsylvania.

from Beppa. Open Monday to Saturday from 10:00 A.M. to 5:00 P.M. (Thursday until 7:00 P.M.).

GIFTS AND COLLECTIBLES
Lancaster

Sam's Steins & Collectibles
2207 Lincoln Highway East (Route 30)
(717) 394-6404
www.samssteins.com
You name the beer, Sam's has the steins, more than 900 different ones in stock. Some are seriously artistic, others (such as the Budweiser frog, Corona parrot, and Foster's kangaroo) are just plain fun. Other breweriana available at this shop includes die-cast beer trucks, beer neons, coasters, glasses, bottle openers, trays, tap handles, tin signs, and posters. Open Monday to Saturday from 10:00 A.M. to 6:00 P.M., also Sunday from October to the end of December (call for hours).

Lititz

The Barking Lamb
49 North Broad Street
(717) 627-1077
www.thebarkinglamb.com
The emphasis of this collection of one-of-a-kind creations from around the world is fun. Take Glamkats, posable soft sculptures made from luxe fabrics with Lucite eyes, golden whiskers, and beaded mouths; or Ne'Owa home ornaments, made by painting on the inside of mouth-blown glass (each is signed by the artist). Windstone Editions are whimsical dragon and gargoyle candle lamps; Takara Breezy Singers are professionally carved birds that move

and sing (songs are provided by the Cornell Lab of Ornithology) with the aid of motion-activated photo sensors. And right out of Scandinavian mythology are Arensbak Trolls from 5 Art Studio, a family-owned company that had its start in 1959 when Danish immigrant Ken Arensbak made his first troll out of acorns, pinecones, nuts, seeds, and an old gnarled tree stump. Each signed piece is still made by hand by Arensbak family members on "Troll Mountain" in Cosby, Tennessee. The Barking Lamb is open Monday, Wednesday, Thursday, Friday, and Saturday from 10:00 A.M. to 5:00 P.M.

The North Star of Lititz
53 North Broad Street
(Route 501 North)
(717) 625-1945
www.thenorthstaroflititz.com
Handblown glass in a rainbow of colors and dazzling array of intricate designs are fashioned into jewelry, Christmas ornaments, lamps, bottles, and other home decor items. Whimsical and fashion pieces are priced from inexpensive to serious collector level. Open Tuesday to Saturday from 10:00 A.M. to 5:00 P.M.

Mount Joy

Wilton Armetale Factory Store
Plumb and Square Streets
(1 block south of Route 230)
(717) 653-4444
www.armetale.com
Armetele metal is a food-safe alloy cast from a mold made of natural sand using a technique perfected long before the American Revolution. The resulting gift-, cooking-, and dinnerware are virtually indestructible and go from stovetop, oven, grill, or freezer to table without chipping, denting, or breaking. The pieces are striking, with the class of silver and the warmth of pewter, and can be used with virtually any style of table setting. At the factory store, set in an old end-of-the-

19th-century tobacco leaf-drying barn, you can save up to 60 percent off the prices that you would find in upscale department stores and specialty shops. Some are seconds, closeouts, and discontinued items, and the inventory changes weekly. Open Monday to Saturday from 9:30 A.M. to 5:30 P.M.; in November and December, the store is also open on Sunday from noon to 5:00 P.M.

HOME ACCESSORIES
Bird-in-Hand

Bird-in-Hand Iron Works
3109 Old Philadelphia Pike (Route 340)
(717) 768-8101
www.birdinhandiron.com
On display at this 1,800-square-foot shop are thousands of items from over 200 vendors who work in cast iron, wrought iron, tin, pewter, and cast aluminum. Nearly all of the inventory here is American-made, more than 25 percent of it made by local crafters. Items for home and garden include hooks and brackets in a range of shapes and sizes, iron lamps and shades, chandeliers and candelabras, towel bars and bootscrapers, plant poles and flag holders, sconces and candle stands, switch plate covers, and more than 60 different weathervanes in stock (plus another 60 available on order). Many of the metal items are hand-forged, one-of-a-kind pieces, and hundreds of new seasonal metal works are added each year. Open Monday to Saturday, January and February from 10:00 A.M. to 4:00 P.M., March through June until 5:00 P.M., July and August 9:30 A.M. to 5:30 P.M., September through December 10:00 A.M. to 5:00 P.M.

Columbia

Susquehanna Glass
731 Avenue H
(800) 592-3646, (717) 684-2155
www.theglassfactory.com

In addition to offering discount prices on glassware, crystal, dinnerware, and flatware from manufacturers such as Lenox, Gorham, Reed & Barton, Wedgwood, and Fiestaware, this is a working glassware- and crystal-decorating operation that's been around since 1910. That's when Albert Roye put a glass-cutting wheel in a small shed behind his house. Artisans here still use traditional methods to decorate glass and crystal. Using a stone wheel, they can hand cut patterns and monograms. For sand etching, they use masks and sand to etch detailed designs.

There are some minimum quantities and a one-time setup charge for sand etching and color screening. Hand cutting requires no minimum quantity or setup charges. Open Monday to Saturday from 9:00 A.M. to 5:00 P.M.

Ephrata

Ten Thousand Villages
240 North Reading Road (Route 272)
(717) 721-8400
www.tenthousandvillages.com
When your home looks good, you feel good. And when you can do some good at the same time, what could be better. Ten Thousand Villages is a nonprofit program of the Mennonite Central Committee (MCC) relief and development agency of Mennonite and Brethern in Christ churches in North America that has been working to fight poverty around the world since 1946. In this shop, the MCC sells exquisite crafts handmade by third world adult artisans who would otherwise be unemployed or underemployed, providing vital fair income for food, education, health care, and housing for them and their families. More than 30 countries are represented. The wide selection of crafts includes pottery, jewelry, baskets, toys, crèches, hand-loomed textiles, and musical instruments.

Check out the Oriental Rug Room for hand-knotted Persians, Bokharas, and tribal rugs.

Take your drinking glasses that may have chips on their rims or feet to Susquehanna Glass. The artisans will repair them for a nominal fee.

Open Monday to Thursday and Saturday from 9:00 A.M. to 5:00 P.M., Friday until 9:00 P.M.

Lancaster

The Clay Distelfink
2246 Old Philadelphia Pike
(717) 399-1994
www.claydistelfink.com
The *distelfink,* the Pennsylvania Dutch name for the goldfinch, is considered to be a symbol of good luck. Artist Marilyn Stoltzfus incorporates the distelfink as well as many other images that the Pennsylvania Dutch relate to good fortune into designs for her handcrafted redware plates, made in the style of German pottery of the 1600s to 1800s. Using the sgraffito method (strategically scratching a top color to reveal a second color underneath), Stoltzfus incorporates flowers and other symbols into one-of-a-kind wedding, anniversary, and baby plates. Each piece is individually designed and personalized to reflect the history of the recipient and his or her family. Open by appointment.

Lancaster Pottery & Glass
2335 Lincoln Highway East
(866) 231-7789
www.800padutch.com/z/lancaster pottery.htm
For the sake of accuracy, this shop should probably be called "Lancaster Pottery, Glass, Banners, Candles, Collectibles, Kitchen Gadgets, and Amish Wagons," but that's probably too much of a mouthful. The decorative home and garden banner selection, in particular, is very, very big, with over 500 style choices. The candles

are locally hand-poured, and collectibles run the gamut from Anheuser-Busch steins to Mary's Moo Moos. Speedway Express wagons for riding, gardening, farming, and construction are handmade by a local Amish family from hardwood with heavy-gauge steel framework. Open Monday to Saturday from 9:00 A.M. to 9:00 P.M., Sunday from 9:00 A.M. to 6:00 P.M.

New Holland

Kauffman's Hardware and Country Wares
201–215 East Main Street
(717) 354-4606

Built in 1779, this landmark redbrick structure has been a town hall, post office, tavern house, general store, money-lending house, private school, and fire company headquarters. The basement housed the town jail. In 1946 the Kauffman family turned it into a full-service hardware store, which is still is today. Displayed on its three floors are a number of antiques, artifacts, and historical documents for viewing and all kinds of country-style housewares and gifts, such as wooden wagons, clothes trees, boot scrapers, hanging pot racks, floor and table lights, locally made wrought iron courting candles, stoneware, oven and table ware, paintings and plaques, books, cards, sunbonnets and, straw hats. Open daily (except Sunday), Monday through Wednesday from 6:30 A.M. to 5:30 P.M., Thursday and Friday until 8:00 P.M., and Saturday until 5:00 P.M.

Ronks

The Outhouse
2853 Lincoln Highway
(800) 346-7678, (717) 687-9580
www.outhousepa.com

This is a goofy kind of place with a wild sense of humor (much of it good-natured potty humor without using potty mouth) and lines of merchandise (funny signs, doormats, T-shirts) to prove it. But The Outhouse, located at the Village of Dutch Delights, has a serious line of expertly crafted weathervanes, wind cups, and cupolas that make a stop there more than worthwhile. Generally open Monday to Thursday from 9:00 A.M. to 6:00 P.M., Friday until 8:00 P.M., and Saturday until 7:00 P.M.; winter hours may vary, so call before visiting.

FURNITURE
Lititz

The Shaker Shoppe
616 Owl Hill Road
(717) 626-9461
www.shakershoppe.com

Simplicity and made-to-last craftsmanship are the hallmarks of the products created by the Shakers. Their admiration of this style is what led Tom and Sue Rossman to open this showroom for wood furnishings, including chairs, tables, hutches, entertainment centers, armoires, bookcases, and beds, that use Shaker techniques such as hand dovetailing, mortise and tenons, and hand planing. Paint and stain colors are chosen for warmth and to accentuate the wood's natural grain. Final finishes are hand-rubbed to achieve an antique-like patina. Smaller accessory items such as hanging mirrors, clocks, wall shelves, sconces and cupboards are also available. The Rossmans accept custom orders. Hours are Tuesday and Wednesday from noon to 5:00 P.M., Thursday and Friday until 8:00 P.M., Saturday from 10:00 A.M. to 3:00 P.M. (other hours by appointment).

JEWELRY
Lancaster

j a sharp Custom Jeweler
334 North Queen Street
(215) 295-9661
www.jasharp.com

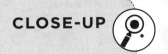

Mud Sales

They might smile politely if you should happen to ask, "Do you sell mud here?" But believe me, they've heard that joke many, many times before. However, it's only natural to wonder why these major community events held in the late winter and early spring in local firehouses all over the county are called "mud sales." The reason, quite simply, is that these dazzlingly diverse sales/auctions, held annually since the 1960s to raise funds for the volunteer local fire companies, take place when the ground is beginning to thaw and is often muddy. If you're going to be in the area during that period, bring a pair of mud-proof boots, check out the schedule at www.padutchcountry.com (or call 800–PADUTCH), and head out to at least one of them.

Held at community fire stations, mud sales attract both local farmers and visitors from far and wide with big bargains on everything from used and handmade furniture, quilts, building materials, live-stock, buggies and carriages, farming and garden supplies . . . you name it, it's probably there. Most of the time, you'll find more Amish and Mennonite than "English" buyers and sellers here. The bidding is fast and furious at simultaneous auctions of everything from horses and mules, farm tools and bathtubs, to groceries and aluminum siding. Mud sale auctions are also among the best places to bid on locally crafted quilts, from the most basic utilitarian designs to the most elaborate. There is usually a great selection of home-baked fruit and shoofly pies and other local treats for sale as well. Mud sales start early (often at 8:00 or 8:30 A.M.), and they start on time. Parking can be a little tricky in some of the smaller towns, too, so stake out your place as early as you can. It will be worth it. There's no place where you'll get more of the authentic flavor of Pennsylvania Dutch Country than at a mud sale.

With action all around you and everything from livestock to living room furniture on sale, it's hard to know where to head first at a mud sale. PENNSYLVANIA DUTCH CONVENTION & VISITORS BUREAU

Since this is Gettysburg, Boyds has created a special commemorative collection of bears representing Union and Confederate soldiers and their wives. All four are dressed in uniforms and outfits that were designed by a noted historian to be authentic miniature re-creations of original garments worn during that era.

Jude Sharp has been designing custom gold, silver, and platinum jewelry since 1970. A graduate of Tyler College of Art with a BFA in metal, she has also completed courses in stone setting, repairs, platinum techniques, and hand engraving taught by the Gemological Institute of America. Choose from Sharp's wide collection of original designs, or she'll sit down with you to sketch out something completely different. If you want stones in your piece, Sharp can get them, or she can use stones from jewelry that you already own.

Open Tuesday to Saturday from 11:00 A.M. to 5:30 P.M., first Friday of each month until 8:00 P.M.

TEDDY BEARS AND DOLLS
Gettysburg

Boyds Bear Country
75 Cunningham Road
(866) 367-8338, (717) 630-2600
www.boydsbearcountry.com
This famous maker of cuddly critters says it has created "The World's Most Humongous Teddy Bear Store," and with a collection that covers three floors and encompasses more than 70,000 cuddly

Aimee & Daria's periodically offer doll-making classes, no experience necessary. Participants must be four years old and accompanied by an adult. Fee includes all necessary materials and tools.

critters, that's probably not an exaggeration. In this big old barn (literally) of a showroom, you'll see scads of stuffed softies posing in a variety of tableaux representing the seasons, working on the farm, and celebrating their all-American patriotism as well as Easter, Halloween, Christmas, and other kid-favorite holidays all year long. Creative types can make and dress their own bear or simply adopt a cute cub straight from the "nursery." The bears also have lots of fuzzy friends, including hares, tabbies, moose, and mice, to complete the scenes and take-home collections. Weekends are filled with live music by traditional country music bands, solo artists, or local school ensembles. There are plenty of eateries with whimsical names and a range of menu options from fruits and smoothies to full-size meals. Open daily from 10:00 A.M. to 6:00 P.M.

Lititz

The Teddy Bear Emporium
51 North Broad Street
(717) 626–TEDI
www.teddybearemp.com
Look for Bart the Bear sitting on his usual bench right outside this shop located across the street from Wilbur Chocolate. Inside are all of the top names in teddies, both stuffed and carved. Among them are Steiff, Gund, Mary Meyer, Boyds, North American Bear, World of Bear Miniatures, Bearington, Russ Berrie, Artist Bears, and Real Fur Bears. Make-your-own at home with a Teddies To Go kit. Open Tuesday to Saturday from 10:00 A.M. to 5:00 P.M.

Ronks

Aimee & Daria's Doll Outlet
2682 Lincoln Highway East
(717) 687–8118
www.800padutch.com/z/aimee&daria
.htm
It began more than a decade ago when

mother and daughter Aimee and Brenda Sheaffer decided to sell their personal doll collections to raise money for children in need. Expanded now to three buildings, the shop now has more than 5,000 dolls in stock, as well as clothes (they specialize in outfits for American Girl dolls), furniture, and other accessories. Just about every size and price range are here, representing just about every major company. If you have a broken doll, check out the spare parts room.

FACTORY OUTLETS

Shoppers come by the busloads to take advantage of the bargains at the many brand-name factory outlet stores and malls throughout Pennsylvania Dutch Country. Unless otherwise specified, the outlet complexes listed here include a range of merchandise, from fashion to home furnishings, jewelry to gourmet food, luggage to electronics.

Gettysburg

Gettysburg Village Factory Stores
1863 Gettysburg Village Drive
(800) 868-7553, (717) 337-9705
www.gettysburgvillage.com
Located at the intersection of Route 15 and Baltimore Pike (State Road 97), this 260,000-square-foot center features more than 70 stores, a hotel, a food court, and a nine-screen movie theater. A 240,000-square-foot addition is on the drawing boards, according to Philadelphia-based development company AMC Delancey Group. Stroller and wheelchair rentals are available. The stores are open Monday to Saturday from 10:00 A.M. to 9:00 P.M., Sunday from 10:00 A.M. to 6:00 P.M. in summer; Sunday to Thursday from 10:00 A.M. to 6:00 P.M., Friday and Saturday in winter (January–March) from 10:00 A.M. to 9:00 P.M. Call for holiday hours.

Give your feet a rest and let the Rockvale Outlets' shuttle transport you through this 75-acre sea of shops. ROCKVALE OUTLETS

Hershey

The Outlets at Hershey
46 Outlet Square
(717) 520-1236
www.theoutletsathershey.com
You'll find savings of between 30 and 70 percent off regular retail at 60 stores located right next to Hersheypark. (For additional savings, stop by the management office and pick up a free Preferred Shopper Card and a listing of monthly discounts from participating merchants, or print out a card at www.outletsathershey .com/PreferredShopper.html.) Shopping hours are generally Monday to Saturday from 9:30 A.M. to 9:00 P.M., Sunday from 11:00 A.M. to 5:00 P.M., except in winter (January 3–February 28), when the hours change to Monday to Friday 9:30 A.M. to 6:00 P.M. and Sunday 11:00 A.M. to 5:00 P.M.

Lancaster

Rockvale Outlets
35 South Willowdale Drive
(intersection of Routes 30 and 896)
(717) 293-9595
www.rockvalesquareoutlets.com
With 120 stores covering 76 acres, it's no wonder that this center operates a courtesy shuttle to get shoppers from one end to the other. (It runs from April through December, 11:00 A.M. to 6:00 P.M. Wednesday to Sunday, noon to 6:00 P.M. Sunday.) The center is open Monday to Saturday from 9:30 A.M. to 9:00 P.M., Sunday from 10:00 A.M. to 6:00 P.M. Wheelchair loaners are available. Be sure to visit the information center to pick up your Rockvale Rewards Club membership card, which can entitle you to even deeper discounts. Money-saving Senior Citizens Priority Club Cards are also available.

Tanger Outlets
311 Stanley K. Tanger Boulevard
(800) 408-3477, (717) 392-7260
www.tangeroutlet.com

Tanger rhymes with *hanger,* and you'll find plenty of them in the many designer outlets that are among the 60 name-brand outlet stores here. You can expect to save between 20 and 40 percent below retail. AAA members can get an exclusive savings book with an additional 15 to 20 percent discount from participating merchants by coming to the Tanger Outlet Center Management Office. The outlets are open year-round (holiday hours may vary) Monday to Saturday from 9:00 A.M. to 9:00 P.M., Sunday from 10:00 A.M. to 6:00 P.M.

MULTIPLE-SHOP CENTERS

Ephrata

Doneckers
100, 318-409 North State Street
(717) 738-9500
www.doneckers.com
The huge multidepartment personal and home fashion center simply known as The Store actually originated as a mail-order business operated by C. Paul Donecker and his son Bill in 1949. About eight years later, the Doneckers purchased an old tobacco warehouse, and this became their first furniture and dry goods showroom. As the years went on, the entire family became involved in the business, including Bill's mother, wife, and sister, and in 1961 they converted three second-floor apartments at the rear of the building into a dress shop. Subsequent expansions added thousands of square feet and a number of shops: The Carriage Room for better dresses, The Loft for ladies' traditional sportswear, Young World for children, and The Men's Store. In 1989 the family turned a former shoe factory into The Artworks at Doneckers (717-738-9503), a showcase for working artists and art from around the world, with four floors of studios and specialty shops. The Christopher Radko Christmas Gallery (717-738-9607) offers Pennsylvania's largest selection of the

famous artist's mouth-blown, hand-painted ornaments as well as other Radko-designed fashion and home items. The Fine Furniture Galleries (717–738–9610), which occupies four floors and 48,000 square feet, displays upscale furniture along with accessories and bed linens. Doneckers also has its own team of interior designers.

The Store and The Fine Furniture Galleries are open Monday, Tuesday, and Thursday from 10:00 A.M. to 8:00 P.M., Friday from 10:00 A.M. to 9:00 P.M., Saturday from 10:00 A.M. to 5:00 P.M.

The Christopher Radko Christmas Gallery (717–738–9607) is open Monday, Tuesday, and Thursday from 10:00 A.M. to 5:00 P.M., Friday from 10:00 A.M. to 9:00 P.M., Saturday from 10:00 A.M. to 5:00 P.M.

The Artworks at Doneckers is open daily (closed Wednesday and Sunday) from 10:00 A.M. to 5:00 P.M.

Intercourse

Kitchen Kettle Village
3529 Old Philadephia Pike
(800) 732–3538, (717) 768–8261
www.kitchenkettle.com

Born and raised in Lancaster County, Pat Burnley had learned the art and science of canning foods at her mother's side. After college, she married a city boy, who moved back to the area with her. After buying about a half dozen secret recipes from a lady who was retiring from the jelly-making business, they decided to start their own operation in the garage of their home in 1954. With three young children, the Burnleys' venture was a risky one, but today that Jam & Relish Kitchen is the centerpiece of a complex of 32 shops, restaurants (one of these, The Kling House, is actually in Pat's childhood home), and lodging accommodations. Pat is now semiretired (but still active as the official taste tester and hostess), and the three children have become active partners in the family business. There's never a dull moment now, especially during the Village's four annual festivals—the Rhubarb Festival (always the third Friday and Saturday in May), the Berry Festival (the third Friday and Saturday in June), the Seven Sweets and Sours Festival (the third Friday and Saturday in September), and Holly Days (selected Saturdays in November and December). The Village also hosts a "Guest Chef Cooking Series" at various times during the year. Even when there's not a designated special event going on, there's always a banjo band, petting zoo, and two horse-drawn wagons giving guests rides. The Village is wheelchair accessible and is open year-round from 9:00 A.M. to 5:00 P.M.

Among the other shops are Tin-'N'-Treasures (717–768–0681), which features windowsill lights, decorative switchplates, lamps, and rustic barn stars. Lupe's Baby Boutique (717–768–7146), another Village resident, features hand-loomed buntings, blankets, sweaters, christening garments, and custom-made dresses in exclusive, hand-detailed designs. Cloverfields Bags

BB's Grocery (581 Camargo Road, Quarryville) isn't a tourist site; it's a real working Amish-run grocery store (no electricity is used; gas generators power freezers) frequented by locals looking for bargains. Operated by Ben Beiler (the "BB" in the name), this store is anything but fancy. Some of the cans may be dented and boxes are scrunched a bit; some dates are close to expiration. But shoppers don't mind at all because the prices are so low. In keeping with Amish custom, there's no electric lighting in this store, so it closes at sundown. Open Tuesday, Wednesday, Friday, and Saturday from 8:00 A.M. to 4:00 P.M.

> *On the last Wednesday of each month at 11:00 A.M., Park City offers Club Noggin, a free educational program for preschool children. Kids get to move, sing, play, and make a project to take home.*

(717–333–BAGS) are locally handcrafted and signed fabric handbags, totes, and garment bags. At Deerskin Leather (800–732–3538, ext. 2780), you may witness the tooling of belt leather and choose from a wide selection of coats, totes, hats, backpacks, wallets, and handbags. You might also see Phil or Stephanie Garnett do a pot throwing demonstration at their Garnett Pottery (717–768–7199) shop. And it's hard to decide whether to follow the sounds of the popping at Pappy's Kettle Corn (717–572–4906) for a sweet and salty treat or follow your nose to Pepper Lane Fudge and Sweets (866–PLFUDGE), where Deb, the master fudge maker, has been stirring up her preservative-free family recipe (its pedigree goes back to the 1830s) for more than 20 years.

Lancaster

Park City Center
142 Park City Center (Route 30)
(717) 393-3851
Over 170 stores and restaurants are here. The mall is anchored by retail giants Sears, JCPenney, Bon Ton, Boscov's, and Kohl's. Wheelchairs are available. Open Monday to Saturday from 10:00 A.M. to 9:30 P.M., Sunday from noon to 6:00 P.M.

MISCELLANEOUS
Leola

Zimmerman Marketplace
254 East Main Street
(717) 656-8290
www.zimmermanmarketplace.com
Pennsylvania Dutch Country is known for its plethora of produce, and Zimmerman has plenty of it; but it's neither sweet nor juicy, nor was it grown in any orchard or berry patch. The fruit and veggies may look delicious, but they're fake, made of durable compressed polyfoam, then airbrushed and detailed to give them a realistic, sun-ripened look. Even more fun are the pies, cakes, and doughnuts as well as eggs that look like the hen just laid them. Zimmerman also offers pie racks and food servers to help you create colorful displays. Open Monday, Tuesday, Wednesday, and Friday from 10:00 A.M. to 5:30 P.M., Thursday until 6:00 P.M., Saturday until 2:00 P.M.

Lititz

The Pilot Shop at Airways
Lancaster Airport, 520 Airport Road
(800) 247-8294, (717) 569-5341
www.flyairways.com
This "aviation superstore" sells all kinds of pilot supplies, from aircraft parts to headsets and GPS, charts and maps, simulators, and software, at discounted prices. For aficionados there are extensive collections of airline collectibles, radio-controlled models, aircraft replicas, toys, and kites. The Pilot Shop is located 3.3 miles off Route 30 on Route 501 North (Lititz Pike). Turn on Airport Road at the sign; it's in the last building on the left, the largest hangar. Open from 8:00 A.M. to 7:00 P.M. Monday to Friday, 8:00 A.M. to 5:00 P.M. Saturday and Sunday.

ATTRACTIONS

If you have the time and energy, Pennsylvania Dutch Country has enough attractions to keep you busy from when the roosters wake up until the cows come home. Discover everything from the homes of presidents to the headquarters of wartime officers, peaceful family farms to one of the most infamous battlefields in history, mysterious underground caverns to sky-kissing coasters. Follow a cocoa bean on an exotic journey and a pretzel through its own twists and turns. Delve into old cultures and new scientific innovations. Ride a buggy across a covered bridge or a railroad train to Paradise.

Although rates are subject to change, we use the following pricing code to indicate the adult admission charge for each attraction. Keep in mind that many attractions have special discounted rates for youngsters and for seniors. Some also offer money-saving combination or package prices with other nearby attractions.

$	Under $5
$$	$5–$10
$$$	$11–$15
$$$$	$16–$20
$$$$$	$21–$25
$$$$$$	$26 and above

VISITOR INFORMATION CENTERS

Ephrata Visitors Center
77 Park Avenue, Suite 1, Ephrata
(717) 738–9010
www.ephrata-area.org
Ephrata is the hub of northeastern Lancaster County and the geographic heart of all of the attractions for the area encompassing the county and nearby Hershey. Year-round hours of operation are Monday to Friday from 8:30 A.M. to 4:30 P.M.

Gettysburg Convention and Visitors Bureau
102 Carlisle Street, Gettysburg
(800) 337–5015, (717) 334–6274
www.gettysbg.com
Very conveniently located just 1 block north of Lincoln Square, this center is stocked with free maps and brochures. You can also get assistance with last-minute motel and restaurant reservations and pick up brochures and maps for self-guided tours of the Downtown Historic District (walking), Scenic Valley (36-mile, two-hour driving), and Conewago (40-mile meander through the eastern half of Adams County). Open Monday to Friday from 8:30 A.M. to 5:00 P.M.

The Lancaster Chamber of Commerce Downtown Visitors Information Center
100 South Queen Street, Lancaster
(717) 397–3531
www.lancaster-chamber.com
The Lancaster Chamber of Commerce Downtown Visitors Information Center offers information on downtown Lancaster, area attractions, lodging, and other member businesses and organizations. Open Monday to Friday 8:30 A.M. to 5:00 P.M.; from April through December, it is also open on Saturday from 9:00 A.M. to 3:00 P.M. and Sunday from 10:00 A.M. until 2:00 P.M.

Lititz Springs Park Welcome Center
18 North Broad Street, Lititz
(717) 626–8981
www.lititzspringspark.org
Although the original railroad passenger depot, designed by famed architect Frank

Many attractions offer admission price discount coupons available from their individual Web sites.

Sundays Are Fun Days in Pennsylvania Dutch Country

Often people hesitate to extend their Pennsylvania Dutch Country visits to include a Sunday stay because they've heard that "everything's closed" and there's nothing to do. While it is true that Amish farm stands and workshops are closed on their worship day, there are still all kinds of things, from amusement parks to zoos, that remain open. Many Amish-oriented (not Amish-operated) attractions are open on Sunday, and you can even get yourself some authentic chow-

chow and shoofly pie. Sunday is also a great time to explore the town of Gettysburg, with its rich history and Civil War battlefield. Or immerse yourself in the sweet experiences of Hershey, Chocolatetown U.S.A. Each attraction that is open on Sunday will specify hours for that day. For more "open Sunday" sites, look in the chapters Homegrown and Homemade; Parks, Recreation, and Golf; and Shopping.

Furness and built in 1884, was demolished in the mid-1950s, the Victorian Gothic replica that has sat at the northwest corner of Lititz Springs Park only since 1999 retains the long-ago charm of this tiny borough. Open Monday to Saturday from 10:00 A.M. to 4:00 P.M.

**Pennsylvania Dutch Country
Visitors Center
501 Greenfield Road
(just off Route 30), Lancaster
(800) PA-DUTCH, (717) 299-8901
www.padutchcountry.com**
Find out where to go and what's going on from a friendly staff of consultants who are also happy to map out the quickest or most scenic route. There's also a free short film and wall-to-wall brochures and other informative materials. Open November 1 to May 24, Monday to Saturday from 8:30 A.M. to 5:00 P.M., Sunday from 9:00

A.M. to 5:00 P.M.; May 25 to October 31, Monday to Saturday from 8:00 A.M. to 6:00 P.M., Sunday from 9:00 A.M. to 5:00 P.M.; Easter, 10:00 A.M. to 5:00 P.M.; Memorial Day, July 4, Labor Day, and Columbus Day weekends, Friday and Saturday from 8:00 A.M. to 7:00 P.M., Sunday from 8:00 A.M. to 6:00 P.M. Closed Thanksgiving Day, Christmas Day, and New Years Day.

**Susquehanna Heritage Tourist
and Information Center
445 Linden Street, Columbia
(717) 684-5249
www.parivertowns.com**
This is the place to come for in-depth information on the river towns of Columbia, Marietta, and Wrightstown. Open Monday to Friday from 9:00 A.M. to 4:30 P.M., Saturday from 9:00 A.M. to 4:00 P.M., Sunday from noon to 3:00 P.M.

AMUSEMENT PARKS

Hershey

Hersheypark $$$$$
300 Park Boulevard
(800) HERSHEY
www.hersheypa.com

This is big coaster country. There are 10 to be exact, including Storm Runner, a high-speeder that launches from 0 to 72 miles per hour in two seconds, 18 stories straight up. Great Bear is a looping, inverted steel coaster that lifts you 90 feet off the ground. And the Sooperdooper-looper—well, the name alone says it all. Six water rides include Canyon Rapids white-water adventure through five acres of canyon walls and waterfalls; the aerial Roller Soaker, which allows viewers to squirt riders and vice versa; and Tidal Force, one of the highest splashdowns around a Tiny Timbers flume for the little ones. The 36-inch-tall and under crowd has more than 20 rides to call their own. All told, Hersheypark has more than 60 rides and attractions covering 110 acres. Carousel fans should take note of the circa 1919 all-wood model with Wurlitzer organ. At the Aquatheatre, Atlantic bottle-nosed dolphins and California sea lions put on a splashy spectacular. There's all kinds of strolling and theatrical entertainment and personal appearances by the bigger-than-life Hershey Characters.

Hersheypark is open every day (including Sunday) in June, July, and August, as well as selected days in April (Springtime in the Park—free admission, pay as you ride), September, October (Hersheypark in the Dark—free admission, pay as you ride, and trick-or-treat), and December (Christmas Candylane—free admission, pay as you ride, more than a million lights, Santa and his reindeer). Regular admission is discounted for children ages three through eight (ages two and under free) and for seniors 55 and up. Specially priced combination ticket with Dutch Wonderland is also available.

Arrive at Hersheypark later in the afternoon (times vary according to park closing times) and get a discounted sunset rate. Or you can use those evening hours as a free "preview" when you purchase a regular admission for the next day.

If you are planning to visit Hersheypark two days in a row, ask about the discounted consecutive day admission. If you're planning to visit multiple times in the same summer season (but not on two or three consecutive days), there are also money-saving two- or three-day Flex Tickets.

Lancaster

Dutch Wonderland $$$$$
2249 Route 30 East
(866) FUNatDW (386–2839)
www.dutchwonderland.com

At some amusement parks, little kids can feel somewhat left out when they're too big for the "baby rides" and too small for everything else. But Dutch Wonderland actually caters to children ages 10 and under with a number of just-the-right-size rides, including two roller coasters and two water adventures. There's a friendly dragon named Duke, who invites young ones to splash around in his tropical

Visit Dutch Wonderland three hours before park closing and get a special twilight rate. Or use those three hours as a free "preview" when you purchase a regular admission for the next day. If you're planning to visit the park more than once during a single summer season, think about purchasing a money-saving two-day Flex Ticket. If you are planning to visit Dutch Wonderland two days in a row, ask about the discounted consecutive day admission.

CLOSE-UP

Multiple Attraction Discount Passes

Special "passport" tickets can save you money on visits to multiple attractions in Lancaster County. The Trail of History Museum Multi-Pass can save a family of four more than 50 percent and an individual more than 25 percent over regular individual admission rates to four of the area's most-visited museums: the Railroad Museum of Pennsylvania, Ephrata Cloister, Landis Valley Museum, and Cornwall Iron Furnace (located in nearby Lebanon County). Cost of the Trail of History pass is $44.95 for a family of four or $19.95 for an individual. These passes may be purchased at the Pennsylvania Dutch Convention and Visitors Bureau (501 Greenfield Road, Lancaster) or at any of the four participating museums.

There's also a Dutch Country Pass ($24.95 for adults and $14.95 for children ages 6 through 12) that offers a selection of activities. Participating attractions are Mill Bridge Village, National Watch and Clock Museum, North Museum of Natural History and Science, Railroad Museum of Pennsylvania, Amish Barn Buggy Ride, Amish F/X Theatre, Laserdome, and National Christmas Center. As a bonus, the pass comes with additional discount coupons for everything from outlet and specialty store shopping to theater, dining, and minigolf. You can purchase this pass at the Pennsylvania Dutch Convention and Visitors Bureau or at any of the participating attractions.

Getting around Gettysburg can be easier (no ticket lines) and more economical with a package plan from the Gettysburg Tour Center (778 Baltimore Street, Gettysburg; 717–334–6296; www.gettys

---

island–themed lagoon with its water-spilling coconuts, shooting geysers, bubblers, spray nozzles and jets, spinning water wheel, and large tipping bucket. Parents and guardians have it made in the shade of palm trees and thatched umbrellas.

Dutch Wonderland opened in 1963 with only 18 acres and four rides. Now the 48-acre park offers over 30 different rides, shows (including *Bubba Bear and the Badland Band,* an animated country music concert; a high-theatrical high-dive show built around the fairytale character of the Frog Prince; and the Middle Earth Theater, where kids can star as knights, elf princesses, goblins, animals, and wizards in their own show) and attractions for all

ages. Kids can dodge asteroids in space, take a parachute "jump," zoom down a double-splash flume, and lots more. In 2001 Hershey Entertainment & Resorts purchased Dutch Wonderland and has been expanding the property while maintaining its distinctive Pennsylvania Dutch character.

Dutch Wonderland is open for summer (including Sunday) from the end of April until the end of September. It is also open on selected weekends in October, November, and December for special seasonal events, such as Fall Farm Festival (all rides plus farming- and harvest-themed activities, such as cow milking and scarecrow-making contests, hayrides, and special entertainment), Happy Haunt-

Period-dressed guides await guests at Lancaster's Landis Valley Museum. PENNSYLVANIA DUTCH CONVENTION & VISITORS BUREAU

burgbattlefieldtours.com) that can save you money on many of the attractions you want to see. Included with every package plan is free unlimited use of the Gettysburg Town Trolley, which stops at most of the popular attractions and travels to many of the downtown area's hotels, motels, and campgrounds. Packages range from $30.95 ($20.95 for children ages 4 to 11) for four attractions to $49.95 ($30.95 for children) for battlefield bus tour plus seven attractions.

ings (themed rides and attractions, trick-or-treating, magic shows, face and pumpkin painting, games, and costume parade), and Winter Wonderland (thousands of lights and displays, games, entertainment, decorating cookies, Santa, special holiday gift shopping area for kids; admission is free, selected rides are pay-as-you-go).

Regular-season discounted admissions for children under age six (age two and under are free) and seniors (60+). Special discounted tickets packages combining tickets to Dutch Wonderland with other area attractions include the Wonder Pass (with Wonderland Mini-Golf), Wonder Rail Pass (including Wonderland Mini-Golf and an all-day pass at Strasburg Rail Road), and combination ticket with Hersheypark.

ANIMALS

Gettysburg

Land of Little Horses $$
125 Glenwood Drive
(717) 334-7259
www.landoflittlehorses.com
Argentinean breeders began the quest to produce the perfectly proportioned miniature horses over 140 years ago. The result was the 26-inch-tall Falabella, brought to Gettysburg from their South American birthplace over 30 years ago. You can meet some of these minis during Close Encounters time at this farm, learn about their history, and ask questions. You can also see them perform in an Old

West-themed show in the indoor arena. More than just horses, this farm is home to llama, fallow deer, miniature donkeys and cows, sheep, exotic birds, and racing pigs. Hay rides and pony rides are available for an additional $2.00 each. Open daily (including Sunday) from April through November; depending on month and day of week, opening hours may vary from 10:00 A.M. to noon. Closing time throughout the season is 5:00 P.M.

ZooAmerica:
North American Wildlife Park   **$$**
100 West Hersheypark Drive
(717) 534-3900
www.zooamerica.com
Located just across a walking bridge from Hersheypark is this 11-acre walk-through zoo, where over 200 animals, representing 75 species native to the five regions of North America, live in naturalistic habitats. In the frigid North Woods, representing an evergreen forest stretching from Newfoundland across Canada into Alaska, you'll see tundra swans, gray wolves, snowy owls, peregrine falcons, and porcupines. The Eastern Woodlands, with its four-season cycle of moderate climate, is home to red-tailed hawks, white-tailed deer, black bears, bobcats, several species of owls, river otters, and wild turkeys. Wildlife in Big Sky Country, from the grasslands to the snowcapped peaks of the Rocky Mountains, provides environments for golden eagles, bison, mountain lions, American elk, blacktail prairie dogs, turkey vultures, and black-billed magpies.

And the intense heat of the Cactus Community of the Arizona Sonoran Desert is a haven to a wild mix of creatures, including roadrunners, ringtails, tarantulas, coatis, scorpions, spiny lizards, desert tortoises, gila monsters, and vampire bats. Snakes are also among the stars of The Grassy Waters of the Florida Everglades, along with armadillos, alligators, American crocodiles, box and softshell turtles, and tree frogs.

ZooAmerica is open year-round. Hours are generally 9:00 or 10:00 A.M. to 5:00 P.M. at the earliest, 9:00 P.M. at the latest (depending on the month and day). Open Sunday. Reduced admission for juniors three to eight (kids under three get in free) and seniors 55 and older. Picnic facilities are available year-round, and prepared food services are open on a seasonal basis.

Lancaster

That Fish Place/That Pet Place
237 Centerville Road
(800) 733-3829
www.thatpetplace.com
This huge pet store could just as easily have been listed in the Shopping chapter, but the size and scope of its fishy, finny, feathery, and furry stock also make it a great rainy day family stop as well as an animal lover's paradise any day. In more than 800 aquariums, you'll see over 500 species of fresh- and saltwater fish and invertebrates and 120 varieties of live plants. Another room is home to snakes, reptiles, chameleons, hamsters, rats, ferrets, frogs, gerbils, guinea pigs, iguanas, rabbits, and hedgehogs. Parakeets, finches, lovebirds, cockatiels, and other winged wonders make the aviary a flurry of color and song. And you're free to reach in and stroke a starfish, handle a horseshoe crab, and interact with a ray in the 2,000-gallon Marineland Touch Tank. Store hours are Monday to Saturday from 9:00 A.M. to 9:00 P.M., Sunday from 10:00 A.M. to 6:00 P.M. Admission is free.

Same-day admission to ZooAmerica is included in the Hersheypark one-price admission plan during the regular summer season when entered from within Hersheypark. Separate admission to the wildlife park ($8.00 ages 9 to 54 and $7.00 ages 3 to 8 and 55 and up) is available year-round at the entrance on Route 743.

Who says there's no such thing as a free ride? Not Lancaster City's Red Rose Transit Authority (RRTA), which offers just that on the first Friday evening (5:00 to 9:00 P.M.) of each month to make it easier and more convenient for locals and tourists to enjoy the festivities downtown. That's when more than 35 shops, boutiques, museums, galleries, and eateries extend their hours. Some of the museums and galleries also hold exhibit openings and artist receptions on First Fridays. Look for posters and rainbow-colored windsocks at participating locations. For more information, call (717) 391-9534, or check the Web site at www.cityof lancasterpa.com.

ART

Gettysburg

Coster Avenue Mural
Coster Avenue
(717) 334-1124, ext. 431
Unless you know this 80-foot mural commemorating a little discussed "Fight at the Brickyard" during the Battle of Gettysburg is here, you'll probably miss it because it's tucked away on a dead-end street in a northeast suburb of the city. The painting, first dedicated in 1988 and restored in 2001, came to be in this location because this small strip of land (about an acre or two), now owned by the National Park Service, marks the spot where the Union Brigade of the Eleventh Corps fought two Confederate brigades on July 1. The street is named for Colonel Charles Coster, leader of the Eleventh.

FACTORY TOURS

Hershey

Hershey's Chocolate World
800 Park Boulevard
(717) 534-4900
www.hersheys.com/chocolateworld
You can't actually tour the Hershey factory, but you can learn about the chocolate-making process on a fun-filled ride narrated by a comely trio of crooning cows (milk is an integral ingredient in making the company's signature sweets) and their bull buddy, Hef. Hershey recently reinvented this ride to the tune of $5 million.

Your adventure concludes with a sweet surprise. (If that just whets your appetite for chocolate, you'll find the Hershey Company's Official Visitor Center and a store that's stocked to overflowing with confectionery creations conveniently located in the same building.) An average of about three million visitors per year take the simulated chocolate-making tour, making Hershey's Chocolate World the nation's most popular corporate attraction, according to the company. The ride is free and offered seven days, year-round.

Hershey's Factory Works
Become an "official" member of the Hershey Factory work crew (complete with "employee" photo ID and hat) and take your place on the production line, where you'll operate the "Kiss Works" machine. Can you keep up with the conveyor belt? That's part of the job, too, as you pluck and package these one-bite wonders.

Hershey's Really Big 3D Show $
The "really big" part is not an editorial comment; it's the name of this 30-minute, three-dimensional animated musical extravaganza starring the Hershey Product Characters.

The theater is really big, too, a 250-seater. The interactive production begins as a chocolate history lesson; but, let's face it, with giant candy bars in the lead roles, how serious can it be? Admission discounts are available for children and seniors.

Hershey Trolley Works $$
(717) 533-3000

Take a tour through Chocolate Town as singing conductors provide a musical and historical background. Reduced fares for children. This seasonal tour departs rain or shine from the Chocolate World main entrance; tokens must be purchased prior to boarding. (Seating is limited, so if you really want to ride, purchase your tokens as early as possible on the day of your visit.)

Lancaster

A.R.T. Research Enterprises $$$
3050 Industry Drive
(717) 290-1303

Not a museum or a gallery, this is a working fine art foundry, the largest on the East Coast. Here is one of the few places left where you can see the ancient *cire perdue,* or lost wax, method of casting metal sculpture. In addition to creating new sculptures, the artists here restore historic statues (if you're lucky, they may be working on one during your visit) that are on display all over the world. While you're there, be sure to take a stroll through the sculpture garden. Open Monday to Friday for tours by reservation only. Reduced rates for seniors and students; children under nine years of age are free.

Lititz

Sturgis Pretzel House $
219 East Main Street (Route 772)
(717) 626-4354
www.sturgispretzel.com

Local legend has it that bread baker Julius

Sturgis was given a pretzel recipe in 1850 as a thank-you gift from a hobo to whom he had given a meal. Eleven years later, he baked his last loaf and switched his entire operation to pretzel baking, making his the first commercial pretzel bakery in America. In 1971 owners Clyde and Barbara Tshudy (Clyde learned the trade from Julius Sturgis' son Lewis) automated the bakery, installing the first commercial pretzel machine that could extrude 245 hard pretzels a minute, or a total of five tons per day. (According to company information, the fastest human twister can shape only 40 pretzels a minute by hand.) Visitors are welcome to tour the plant, still located in the original house, built in 1784 from stones dug from the streets of Lititz, where Sturgis began his bakery. You'll get a hands-on twisting lesson (and a certificate to commemorate it) and lots of samples to taste. In addition to the traditional salted and unsalted varieties, Sturgis is constantly experimenting with new seasoning and spice combinations—jalapeño anyone? Perhaps Maryland crab? Cappuccino orange? You never know, and that's part of the fun. Open Monday to Saturday from 9:00 A.M. to 5:00 P.M.

FILMS AND HISTORIC PRODUCTIONS

Gettysburg

Gettysburg Battle Theatre $$
571 Steinwehr Avenue
(717) 334-6100

Next to the field where Confederate general George Pickett led his troops on the brutal and bloody charge that has since born his name, this multimedia theater presents a half-hour film covering the three-day Battle of Gettysburg and the immediate period leading up to it. You can also view a battlefield diorama composed of 25,000 hand-painted miniature soldiers. Open Sunday to Thursday from 9:00 A.M. to 5:00 P.M., Friday and Saturday to 9:00 P.M. Closed December through February.

At the A. Lincoln Theater (additional $$ charge) located on the site, presidential scholar and portrayer Jim Getty stars in a one-man live production of *Mr. Lincoln Returns.* Call for performance days and times; reservations are recommended. During the course of the "visit," America's 16th president recalls stories of his youth and of his later personal and political life.

Intercourse

The Amish Experience F/X Theater $$
3121 Old Philadelphia Pike (Route 340)
(717) 768–3600, ext. 10
www.amishexperience.com
Located at the Plain & Fancy Farm restaurant and shopping complex, The Amish Experience F/X Theater presents a multimedia production, *Jacob's Choice,* that tells the story of the Old Order Amish culture and lifestyle from the perspective of one young man and his family. At the age when he must decide whether to join the Amish church of his ancestors or go out and seek a life in the world outside of his home and culture, Jacob Fisher examines the history of his community and faith from his immigrant ancestors' flight from religious persecution in Europe in the 1700s to the present. Five specially designed projection surfaces with three-dimensional imagery bring the characters and action to life. Open seven days April through June (8:30 A.M. to 5:00 P.M., Sunday 10:30 A.M. to 5:00 P.M.) and July through October (Monday to Saturday 8:30 A.M. to 8:00 P.M., Sunday 10:30 A.M. to 5:00 P.M.); November and December (10:00 A.M. to 5:00 P.M., Sunday from 11:00 A.M.) and weekends only in January through March (10:00 A.M. to 5:00 P.M., Sunday from 11:00 A.M.). Shows are every hour on the hour. Discounts are available for children ages 4 to 12.

Lancaster

Mennonite Information Center and
Biblical Tabernacle Reproduction
2209 Millstream Road
(717) 299–0954
www.mennoniteinfoctr.com
Anyone interested in authentic information on the Mennonite and Amish faiths and cultures should be sure to visit this information center (located east of Lancaster, along Route 30, beside the Tanger Outlet Center and across from Dutch Wonderland).

You can get some of the basics by watching the free documentary *Postcards from a Heritage of Faith.* For a more in-depth exploration of the religious and social history and traditions of the Old Order community, there is also a 30-minute, three-screen production entitled *Who Are the Amish?* ($). This is a fully equipped information center with maps, brochures, and guides highlighting Amish and Mennonite-related sites. You'll also find a good selection of books on everything from Anabaptist theology to Pennsylvania Dutch cooking.

Also on the site is the Biblical Tabernacle ($$, reduced admission for senior citizens 60 and older and children), a full-size, detailed reproduction of Moses' Tabernacle in the Wilderness designed from biblical descriptions in the book of Exodus. As you walk through the tabernacle, a guide will outline the history that is depicted.

Hire a local Mennonite tour guide ($$$$$ for two hours) to ride along in your

---

If you plan to also visit the Amish Experience F/X Theater (see details under the Films and Historic Productions heading in this chapter) and/or take an Amish Farmlands Tour (see details in the Tours chapter), you can save on combination tickets. Call for details.

Children must be at least 10 years old and 58 inches tall to drive a go-kart, or they can ride free as a passenger with a licensed driver. To operate a bumper boat alone, they must be at least 44 inches tall. Batters must be nine years old or belong to a league that pitches to them.

car for an off-the-beaten-path experience that can be tailored to any interest. Your guide can tell you about Amish farm life as you wander along back roads with views of fields, orchards, water wheels, and windmills. Visit some of the area's covered bridges, historic mills, and farm- and home-based shops that only the locals know.

The center is open all year every day except Sunday from 8:00 A.M. to 5:00 P.M. from April 1 to October 31, November to December from 8:30 A.M. to 4:30 P.M., and January through February from 10:00 A.M. to 3:00 P.M.

FUN AND GAMES

Hershey

Adventure Sports in Hershey   **$-$$**
3010 Elizabethtown Road
(717) 533-7479
www.adventurehershey.com
All sports activities for all ages are here, including 18-hole fantasy concept miniature golf, bumper boats, professional indoor/outdoor hardball and softball batting cages (lighted for night fun), an 1,100-

 On selected Saturdays, Laserdome presents silent film masterpieces, such as Metropolis, The Cabinet of Dr. Caligari, The General, *and* The Phantom of the Opera, *in its Planetarium Theater with live original musical score for $5.00 per person.*

foot go-kart track, a video arcade with more than 60 games, including Daytona racing and linked games for competitive action, a 36-tee lighted-for-night driving range (lessons with a PGA golf pro are available by appointment), black-lighted air hockey, and Skee-Ball. There's an ice-cream parlor and picnic area for between-game snacking. This facility is wheelchair accessible. No credit cards.

Open seven days, April to October. Hours are 10:00 A.M. to 10:00 P.M. from Memorial Day through Labor Day; call for off-season hours.

Wonderland Mini-Golf   **$$**
Dutch Wonderland
2249 Lincoln Highway East
(866) FUNatDW (386-2839)
www.dutchwonderland.com/mini-golf/
Just a short walk from Dutch Wonderland is this 18-hole miniature golf course where kids three and under play for free (they get a special child-safe plastic club). Open every day mid-June through August, selected days in May and September, from 2:00 P.M. to 9:00 P.M. or 10:00 P.M., depending on time of year. Air-conditioned on-premise Par 3 Ice Cream Parlor & Cafe serves hand-dipped ice cream, sundaes, shakes, and pizza.

Manheim

Laserdome   **$$$**
2050 Auction Road
(717) 492-0002
www.laserdome.com
Multilevel Lasertron is fast and furious in this 6,000-square-foot arena. There are light shows and laser concerts, too, ranging from rock to pop to hip hop. Open September through May, Tuesday through Thursday 5:00 A.M. to 10:00 P.M., Friday 5:00 P.M. to 1:00 A.M., Saturday noon to 1:00 A.M., Sunday noon to 10:00 P.M. June through August, Sunday and Tuesday through Thursday noon to 10:00 P.M.; Friday and Saturday noon to 1:00 A.M.

Strasburg

The Village Greens Miniature Golf **$$**
Route 741 West
(717) 687-6933
www.villagegreens.com
Two courses make minigolfing a challenge for a range of ages and skill levels. The Orange course is the more traditional of the two with a covered bridge, cave, and tobacco shed to keep things interesting. If you want to go for the Gold, be ready for a number of natural waterways and other holes, traps, and jumps in a mature wooded hillside setting. Both courses on the 13-acre property are elaborately landscaped with shrubbery and flowers (thousands of yellow daffodils in summer, colorful annuals in midsummer, foliage in fall). A snack bar with outdoor patio and inside air-conditioned seating serves milkshakes, hand-dipped ice cream, and sandwiches. Regular season is late March, April and October, Monday through Thursday from 10:00 A.M. to 4:00 P.M., Friday and Saturday until 9:00 P.M., Sunday noon to 5:00 P.M. May, June 1 through 9, and September 5 through 30, Monday through Thursday 10:00 A.M. to 8:00 P.M., Friday and Saturday until 10:00 P.M., Sunday noon to 8:00 P.M. June 10 through September 4, Monday through Thursday 10:00 A.M. to 10:00 P.M., Friday and Saturday 10:00 A.M. to 11:00 P.M., Sunday noon until 10:00 P.M. Discounted rates for senior citizens and children. Special events include October 31 "Trick or Treat Nite," with free golf for ages 18 and under (accompanied by adult), and Christmas Spectacular, a stroll-through display of 100,000 lights over 10 acres, live music, Santa, and free hot chocolate on December weekend evenings ($$, reduced rates for children and seniors, youngsters under three are free; benefits the Schreiber Pediatric Rehabilitation Center).

HISTORIC HOMES AND GARDENS

Columbia

Wright's Ferry Mansion **$$**
38 South Second Street
(Second and Cherry Streets)
(717) 684-4325
English Quaker Susanna Wright, one of the early settlers of this Susquehanna River region, was the first inhabitant of this stone house, built in 1738. The early-18th-century Philadelphia-made furniture reflects the simplicity and elegance of her life. At the same time, artistic accessories such as English ceramics, needlework, metals, and glass show her wide-ranging tastes. A strong believer in self-sufficiency, Wright used her extensive knowledge and skills to encourage industry, provide medical and legal assistance to community members, and support the literary arts. Open May through October, Tuesday, Wednesday, Friday, and Saturday from 10:00 A.M. to 3:00 P.M.

Ephrata

Ephrata Cloister **$$**
632 West Main Street (Route 322
West near intersection with Route 272)
(717) 733-6600
www.ephratacloister.com
No one lives in the nine 18th-century medieval-looking buildings that remain on this 24-acre complex anymore. But once this was a thriving community that somehow harmoniously combined asceticism and celibacy with family, art, and industry. One of America's first religious communities, Ephrata Cloister was founded in 1732,

Every Tuesday is Senior Day at The Village Greens Miniature Golf, offering further reductions on both courses to players 60 and over.

Residents of Ephrata Cloister lived ascetic lives, yet produced art of great and lasting beauty.
PENNSYLVANIA DUTCH CONVENTION & VISITORS BUREAU

when Protestant religious reformer Conrad Beissel, an immigrant from Germany, and a group of his followers, called Brothers and Sisters, settled here to practice a theology based on Anabaptism, ascetic living, and celibacy. Support for their community came from a combination of their own limited industry (a paper mill, printing office, and book bindery) and the assistance of a group of married couples and families from the region.

Aside from their publishing business, the Brothers and Sisters of Ephrata Cloister were known for producing memorable a cappella music and the elaborate, artistic Germanic calligraphy called *Frakturschriften* (also known as fraktur). Between the 1740s and '50s, the Cloister had a high of nearly 80 celibate members and around 200 supporting family members. However, after Beissel's death in 1768, the community went into a decline, until

the last of the celibate Brothers and Sisters died in 1813. The married family members of the congregation formed the German Seventh Day Baptist Church, and a number of its poorer members moved into the Cloister buildings.

Today, visitors can tour the Cloister to get a sense of how this unique community lived, worshipped, and worked. A good place to begin is at the visitor center where a self-guided exhibit and 15-minute orientation video provide background. Then you can take a guided tour of the Sisters' House (called The Saron) and the Meetinghouse (Saal)—both of these buildings are only open for guided tours. There are also seven other historic buildings that you can view on your own. (The entire tour is about 2 city blocks in length.)

Ephrata Cloister is open daily year-round. Hours are Monday to Saturday from 9:00 A.M. to 5:00 P.M., Sunday noon to 5:00 P.M. The site is open Memorial Day, July 4, and Labor Day. Special events and educational programs are scheduled at selected times, and there is a picnic grove on the grounds. Seniors and AAA members are eligible for discounted admissions. Visitors with special needs should call in advance for assistance (some of the buildings have some limits for wheelchair accessibility). Interpretive brochures are available in German, French, and Spanish. A German-speaking guide is available on a limited schedule.

Gettysburg

Cyclorama Center Museum
Gettysburg National Military Park
97 Taneytown Road
(717) 334-1124
www.nps.gov/gett
This building, adjacent to the visitor center, houses a giant 360-degree painting that depicts the climactic moment in Pickett's Charge. It will be closed for restorations until 2007 or 2008.

Eisenhower National Historic Site $$
97 Taneytown Road
(717) 338-9114
www.nps.gov/eise/home.htm
Thirty-fourth president Dwight D. Eisenhower purchased a 189-acre farm adjacent to the Gettysburg Battlefield and with a view of South Mountain in 1950 to serve as a weekend retreat and site to meet with world leaders. It was the only home the Eisenhowers ever owned. Among the historical figures who visited him here were Soviet premier Nikita Khrushchev, French president Charles de Gaulle, Prime Minister Winston Churchill, and Governor Ronald Reagan. Eisenhower maintained the farm even after he and his wife, Mamie, retired here in 1961. Mamie Eisenhower continued to live here for about 10 years after the former president died in 1969. The house and grounds, including putting green, skeet range, and outbuildings, are open for

Kids ages 7 through 12 visiting the Eisenhower National Historic Site can become members of the Junior Secret Service (with authentic badge and certificate) by picking up a special "training manual" at the visitor center and fulfilling such assignments as using binoculars to locate suspicious persons and objects and reporting to the Agent-in-Charge on the radio using code names and correct procedures.

self-guided tours daily (including Sunday) from 9:00 A.M. to 4:00 P.M.

Due to a lack of on-site parking and space limitations in the Eisenhower home, access to the property is available only via shuttle bus that departs from the Gettysburg National Military Park Visitor Center (1 mile south of Gettysburg on U.S. Business 15, Steinwehr Avenue). Price of the shuttle is included in the admission fee; discounted admission prices for teens (ages 13 to 16) and children (6 to 12). Throughout the summer and in spring and fall, as staff permits, the site offers 20-minute ranger-led "Exploring Eisenhower" walks and discussions of various Eisenhower-related topics pertaining to his military career, presidency, hobbies, the cold war, civil rights, and his relationships with world leaders and Presidents Kennedy and Johnson. Summer "Hike with Ike" guided walking tours of downtown Gettysburg, with an emphasis on Eisenhower's life in the community, are also available. Special events are scheduled during various weekends throughout the year. They include Fifties Weekend, revisiting popular culture and cold war tensions of the times; World War II Weekend; with a living history encampment; and An Eisenhower Christmas, displaying original decorations and cards.

Electric Map $
Gettysburg National Military Park
97 Taneytown Road
(717) 334-1124
www.nps.gov/gett

Evergreen Cemetery (799 Baltimore Street, Gettysburg; 717-334-4121; www.evergreencemetery.org) is the third and final resting place for Jennie Wade. This monument, erected in 1900, is a much-visited site. By executive order, the American flag flies at the grave 24 hours a day. Also at the cemetery is the Gettys- burg Civil War Women's Memorial, a 7- foot bronze statue of a six-months' preg- nant Elizabeth Thorn, who buried the first 91 soldiers from the Battle of Gettysburg in Evergreen Cemetery. Sculpted by Ron Tunison, the memorial is located 50 feet southwest of the cemetery gatehouse.

Located in the visitor center, this 30- minute audiovisual presentation gives a briefing of the three-day conflict on a giant relief map of the battlefield. It pro- vides an excellent orientation for any bat- tlefield tour. Children under six are admitted free. Before you leave the build- ing, also check out the George Rosensteel Collection of original artifacts, uniforms, and weapons of the Civil War.

Gettysburg National Cemetery
Gettysburg National Military Park
**97 Taneytown Road
(Pennsylvania Route 134)
(717) 334-1124, ext. 431
www.nps.gov/gett/gncem.htm**
President Abraham Lincoln dedicated this National Cemetery on November 19, 1863, with what would become one of the most famous speeches in the history of Amer- ica. It is the resting place for more than 7,000 American soldiers and dependents, more than half from the Civil War and the rest from subsequent conflicts through Vietnam. The Gettysburg National Ceme- tery is open year-round from dawn to sunset. There is no charge for admission.

Jennie Wade House Museum $$
**548 Baltimore Street
(717) 334-4100
www.jennie-wade-house.com**
On July 3, 1863, 20-year-old Mary Virginia Wade (nicknamed "Ginny," which was mis- spelled "Jennie" in the newspaper account of her death) was baking bread for Union soldiers in her sister's house at the north- west edge of Cemetery Ridge when a stray bullet penetrated two wooden doors and instantly struck her dead, making her the only civilian killed during the Battle of Gettysburg. (Historians specify that other civilians died after the battle as a direct result of it, including children who would discover unexploded artillery shells or loaded muskets in the surrounding fields, but Wade is the only one who died during the course of it.) The house has been pre- served and is furnished from cellar to attic just as it was on Jennie Wade's last day. Open seven days from 9:00 A.M. to 9:00 P.M. June through August, to 7:00 P.M. April through May and September through October, and to 5:00 P.M. the rest of the year.

Schriver House Museum $$
**309 Baltimore Street
(717) 337-2800
www.schriverhouse.com**
George Washington Schriver, his wife, Het- tie, and their young daughters, Mollie and Sadie, were just settling into their newly built home on Baltimore Avenue when the Civil War broke out in 1861. In the cellar they planned to open a saloon and in another building just behind the house, a two-lane, 10-pin bowling alley. George soon joined the Union cavalry and headed off to the fighting, leaving his wife and children behind. On a July morning in 1863, cannon sent Hettie fleeing, with her own two children and the daughter of a neigh-

boring family, to her parents' farm 3 miles south of the home. Unfortunately, that farm was situated between Big and Little Round Top, right in the heart of the battle.

Although the next three days were harrowing, Hettie, her parents, and the children survived. When she returned to the house on Baltimore Street, a neighbor told her that a number of Confederate soldiers had set up a sharpshooters' nest in her garret. At least two of these snipers had been killed there. George Washington Schriver came home five months after the Battle of Gettysburg but returned to the cavalry, was taken prisoner, and died in Andersonville, Georgia, in August 1864.

Restoration has returned the Schriver home to its original appearance. Visitors can tour all four floors, from the cellar saloon to the sharpshooters' garret, as guides in period dress tell the story of how the war came home to one Gettysburg family. Open April through November, Monday to Saturday from 10:00 A.M. to 5:00 P.M., Sunday noon to 5:00 P.M.; December, February, and March, Saturday and Sunday from noon to 5:00 P.M.; closed in January. Admission discounts for seniors and children.

Hershey

Hershey Gardens   **$$**
170 Hotel Road
(717) 534-3493
www.hersheygardens.org
When chocolatier and philanthropist Milton Hershey was asked to sponsor a

national rosarium in Washington, D.C., he said yes . . . and no. He did decide to plant a "nice garden of roses" for the public to enjoy, only it wouldn't be in the nation's capital—it would be in his eponymous hometown. Hershey opened his first garden—consisting of three and a half acres of roses—in 1937. By 1942 Hershey Gardens had bloomed into its present size of 23 acres.

In addition to the original rose garden, which is made up of more than 7,000 plants in 275 varieties, this bountiful botanical oasis features seasonal displays, unusual trees, a Children's Garden, and the Butterfly House.

The one-and-a-half-acre Children's Garden is actually 30 different themed displays that use color and design to help children learn their ABCs, colors, counting, and math.

In the Butterfly House, 300 species native to North America flutter freely among flowers and plants as you observe their beauty and behaviors. Staff and volunteer "flight attendants" explain the life cycle, from egg to caterpillar to cocoon and finally to full-fledged butterfly.

Hershey Gardens is open daily from mid-April through May from 9:00 A.M. to 5:00 P.M.; June through August, from 9:00 A.M. to 6:00 P.M.; and October until 5:00 P.M. The Butterfly House is open daily from late May through mid-September, weather permitting, and closes at 6:00 P.M. Basic Hershey Gardens admission includes the Butterfly House. Special prices for seniors and youngsters ages 2 to 15, children under 2 are free.

June through August is primetime for the roses as well as rhododendrons, azaleas, peonies, and other flowering perennials, herbs, and shrubs. But spring and early fall bring their own beautiful blooms. April to May is tulip time (30,000 of them), along with other flowering bulbs, cherries and plums, magnolias, dogwoods, and crabapples. In September and October, leaf peepers can take in the autumn array of colors, as well as the chrysanthemums and late-blooming roses, annuals, and ornamental grasses.

 CLOSE-UP

Gettysburg National Military Park

One of the bloodiest battles of the American Civil War, the three-day Battle of Gettysburg, which raged from July 1 through 3, 1863, is often referred to as the turning point of the war. The "Angle," a small patch of earth on Cemetery Ridge, is considered the high watermark of the Confederacy because it was the site of the greatest military advancement made by the Confederate Army during the course of the entire war. It was also the site where the Union Army repulsed Pickett's Charge, the last major Confederate offensive to be launched on northern soil. At the end of this major clash between the Union's Army of the Potomac and the Army of Northern Virginia, more than 51,000 soldiers were killed, wounded, captured, or missing.

Much care has been taken to preserve and restore as much of the battlefield as possible. Gettysburg National Military Park (97 Taneytown Road, Gettysburg; 717-334-1123; www.nps.gov/gett) incorporates nearly 6,000 acres, with 26 miles of paved park roads and over 1,400 monuments, markers, and memorials. At the summit of Oak Hill, surrounded by guns that marked Confederate artillery positions, is the Eternal Light Peace Memorial, dedicated on July 3, 1938, during the 75th anniversary commemoration of the battle

by former Union and Confederate soldiers. President Franklin Delano Roosevelt was the guest speaker for the unveiling of this 47½-foot monument (the dark stone base is made of Maine granite and the lighter colored shaft of Alabama Rockwood limestone).

If you would like to take a self-guided tour of the battlefield, pick up a free copy of the Gettysburg National Military Park brochure at the visitor center. The brochure has a map of the park that coincides with park tour route signs and wayside exhibits. Audio programs are available at specified stops. Plan on at least two hours for this tour. Self-guided audiocassette tours (between $10 and $15) are also available for purchase at the Gettysburg Convention and Visitors Bureau (102 Carlisle Street, Gettysburg; 800-337-5015, 717-334-6274; www .gettysbg.com). Information about bus tours of the battlefield may be found at the bureau as well.

From mid-June to mid-August, Gettysburg park rangers offer a range of guided walks and tours of the battlefield, all free. Among the topics explored are the battle day by day, major sites such as Little Round Top and Cemetery Hill, and battlefield monuments. A three-hour battlefield hike is offered once a week, and

Lancaster

The Amish Farm and House $$
2395 Route 30 East
(717) 394-6185
www.amishfarmandhouse.com

This 25-acre property has been a true working farm since it was deeded from William Penn in 1715. Many buildings from the early 19th century have been preserved, including an 1803 stone bank tobacco barn and an 1805 farmhouse, home to genera-

Monuments mark the spots where battles raged on the now peaceful fields of Gettysburg. PAUL WITT, COMPLIMENTS OF GETTYSBURG CVB

evening campfire programs at the park amphitheater (Auto Tour Stop 6) are given nightly. Listings are available at www.nps.gov/gett/events.htm. Living history reenactments are held throughout the year and are listed on the same Web site.

You may also choose to tour in your own vehicle in the company of a licensed battlefield guide ($40 covers one to six people). To earn their licensing from the National Park Service, these self-employed individuals must demonstrate their knowledge through comprehensive testing (for more details, visit www.gettysburgtourguides.org). Tours generally last about two hours, can be customized to your special needs and interests, and are arranged from the visitor center on a first come, first served basis beginning at 8:00 A.M. each day. During the summer months, there are free ranger-led programs and special walks.

Gettysburg National Military Park is open year-round, and there is no fee for entrance to the park, National Cemetery, or park buildings. Park grounds and roads are open daily from 6:00 A.M. to 10:00 P.M. The visitor center is open September through May from 8:00 A.M. to 5:00 P.M. and June through August until 6:00 P.M.

tions of Old Amish families and furnished in their traditional style. Take a guided tour of the house, then you're on your own to visit the limekiln, springhouse, corn and straw barns, summer kitchen, bake oven, smokehouse, outhouse, millhouse, chicken house,

waterwheel, and pumps. Visit the blacksmith in his shop as he crafts horseshoes and other wrought iron items. Other on-site demos between April and October include quilt making and wood carving. Buggy rides are also available during those months. The Early American Museum displays Indian relics, antique farm equipment, Amish transportation, and a Conestoga wagon. Goats, sheep, cows, and chickens live in the barns and meadows. Playground and picnic areas are available. Special annual events include spring Sheep Shearing Days, fall evening Kerosene Lamp Tours, and the mid-July to mid-October Corn Maze to explore. Special discount rates for seniors (60+) and children ages 5 to 11. Open daily January through March and November through December from 8:30 A.M. to 4:00 P.M., April through May and September through October from 8:30 A.M. to 5:00 P.M., and June through August until 6:00 P.M.

---

i *Next door to the Demuth House is the tobacco shop founded by the family in 1770s. It is the oldest tobacco shop in the nation and the second oldest business in Lancaster. Demuth Tobacco Shop remains in operation.*

Charles Demuth House and Garden
120 East King Street (rear)
(717) 299-9940
www.demuth.org

Master watercolorist Charles Demuth (1883–1935) created almost all of his works in the second-floor studio of this 18th-century home, his residence for most of his life. Demuth was born on North Lime Street in Lancaster and moved to King Street at the age of seven. Though in frail health, Demuth completed more than 1,000 works during his lifetime; many of these paintings hang in major museums throughout the world. His works reflect a diversity of inspiration sources, from his mother's Victorian garden (it still blooms from April through November) to the fruits and vegetables on display at the local farmers' markets to the architecture of the rooftops, steeples, smokestacks,

and grain elevators in the city and on surrounding farms. A tour of the home reveals much about Demuth's personal life and family history. His studio has also been re-created, and an on-site gallery offers several rotating exhibitions each year along with the museum's permanent collection of Demuth's art. No admission (donations encouraged). Open Tuesday to Saturday from 10:00 A.M. to 4:00 P.M., Sunday 1:00 to 4:00 P.M. Closed January.

James Buchanan's Wheatland $
1120 Marietta Avenue
(717) 392–8721
www.wheatland.org

Named for the surrounding wheat fields, this 1828 Federal-style mansion was the home and private retreat of America's 15th president for 20 years (1848–1868), including the tempestuous time of his term (1857–1861) as the nation teetered on the edge of civil war. It was in this house that Buchanan organized his presidential campaign quarters and, later, family members held his funeral. At the time of Buchanan's ownership, the property totaled more than 22 acres; today the foundation that bears his name retains a little over four, including the home and three outbuildings: a carriage house that now serves as the museum's visitor center, a smokehouse/icehouse, and a privy. Period landscaped gardens on the property include herbs and vegetables grown during that period. Guided tours of the Victorian era–furnished mansion depicting the life of America's only bachelor president begin with a video in the Carriage House. Christmas Candlelight Tours of the mansion and grounds are available in December. Open from 10:00 A.M. to 4:00 P.M. daily (including Sunday) from April through October and Friday to Monday in November. Call for December days and hours. Discounted admissions for seniors, students (ages 12 and up, including college students with valid ID), children (ages 6 to 11), and AAA members; children under 6 admitted free.

Wheatland is the preserved home of America's 15th president, James Buchanan. PENNSYLVANIA DUTCH CONVENTION & VISITORS BUREAU

Rock Ford Plantation   **$$**
881 Rockford Road (in Lancaster County Central Park)
(717) 392–7223
www.rockfordplantation.org
Irish-born Edward Hand came to Lancaster to practice medicine in 1774 after training at Dublin's Trinity College and serving as surgeon's mate in service to his home country. Soon after, he joined the Continental Army and led troops at Boston, Long Island, White Plains, and Trenton, earning the title of adjutant general in 1781. After the war, Hand returned to Lancaster, where he held various political offices in the Congress, State General Assembly, and as Burgess of Lancaster. Rock Ford, a brick Georgian mansion set along the wooded banks of the Conestoga River 1 mile south of the city, is where Hand spent the last eight years of his life. (The name Rock Ford is said to have derived from the fact that there were no bridges that crossed the Conestoga near the home, so anyone who wanted to get across would have to ford the river by walking on rock outcroppings.)

Recognized as the most intact building predating 1800 in Lancaster County, the Rock Ford mansion retains not only its original floors and rails, but also detailing such as shutters, cupboards, paneling, and window panes. Costumed interpreters explain the details of everyday life on the property through furnishings and artifacts from Hand's own estate inventory. Open

In the 18th century, the word plantation *was used to describe any farm under cultivation.*

hearth cooking demonstrations, hands-on activities, and special events add color and perspective to the experience. Open April through October, Thursday to Sunday from 11:00 A.M. to 3:00 P.M. Ticket prices are reduced for seniors and children under the age of 12.

Willow Street

Hans Herr House and Museum $
1849 Hans Herr Drive
(717) 464-4438
www.hansherr.org

Built in 1719 by bishop Christian Herr, this medieval Germanic-style residence was home to the area's first Mennonite settlers and is the oldest still-standing Mennonite meetinghouse in America, as well as the oldest building in Lancaster County. It is believed that Christian's parents, Hans (also a bishop) and Elizabeth, lived there and it is definitely known that several generations of Christian's family did. The

home is now part of a museum complex that includes two other Pennsylvania German farmhouses (the 1890s Victorian-style Shaub House, which is now the Visitor Center, and the Georgian-style 1852 Huber House), both of which were built by relatives of Christian Herr. All of the buildings and grounds have been restored to reflect the styles, daily lifestyles and faith of these early Mennonite settlers between the years 1719 and 1750.

In addition to the houses, the museum also includes three exhibit buildings, a working blacksmith shop, outdoor bake oven, and smoke house. Open Monday through Saturday from 9:00 A.M. to 4:00 P.M. April through November. Admission discounts are available for youngsters ages 7 through 12; children younger than 7 are free.

Although the main exhibit buildings are fully wheelchair accessible, the restored 1719 House is not.

Each year, the Hans Herr House and Museum hosts three major festivals. Her-

Cooking and crafting demos are part of the historical experience at Willow Street's Hans Herr House and Museum. PENNSYLVANIA DUTCH CONVENTION & VISITORS BUREAU

itage Day, held the first Saturday in August, offers a glimpse of 18th- to 20th-century farm life through demonstrations of plowing with oxen, hay making, threshing, gardening, hearth cooking, and other chores and crafts. Snitz Fest, held the first Saturday in October, is a celebration of the apple, a food staple for the early Pennsylvania Dutch. You'll see apples being pressed into cider and cut and dried to make snitz, sample 18th-century recipes, take a wagon ride to see the historic varieties of apple trees (and do a taste-testing of the fruit), and observe harvesttime activities such as threshing and corn shucking. Christmas Candlelight tours, offered on the first Friday and Saturday in December, include a holiday wagon ride, hearth cooking, caroling around a bonfire, hot cider and pretzels, storytelling frontiersmen and trappers, and special exhibits and the reading of the biblical Christmas story in German.

MUSEUMS

Bird-in-Hand

The Americana Museum of Bird-in-Hand   **$**
2707 Old Philadelphia Pike
(717) 391–9780
www.bird-in-hand.com/americana museum
The tiny village of Bird-in-Hand has been a center of commerce and craft since its early days, a fact that locals George and Pat Desmond wanted to document. For more than 30 years, the pair accumulated an extensive collection of items and artifacts from the late 19th and early 20th centuries that represent the life and commerce of this area. From these, they have assembled replicas of 12 different businesses from a century ago, including a tea parlor, country general store, and shops ranging from barber to blacksmith, wheelwright to woodworker, apothecary to millinery.

For children ages 4 to 10 and their parents, Hans Herr House and Museum offers an annual interactive program called "Mama (or Papa) and Me." Event activities in past years have included butter churning, spinning and weaving, frontier life skills, and colonial period toys and games. Reservations are suggested.

Be sure to check out the mural painted by local artist Wayne Fettro. On selected days, crafters conduct live demos on rug hooking, carving, and decorative iron working. These demonstrations are free of charge. Tours of this museum are self-guided. If you would like to broaden your view, ask about the Victorian Carriage Rides through the village and surrounding farmlands that are available on selected days for an additional fee. The museum is open Tuesday to Saturday from April through November (winter tours are by request only).

Weavertown One-Room School   **$**
Route 340 (1 mile east of Bird-in-Hand)
(717) 768–4424
www.weavertownoneroomschool.com
Throughout Pennsylvania Dutch farm country you'll see a number of little one-room schools that are still attended by Amish students (formal education for these youngsters goes up to eighth grade, after which they take their places on their

If Christian Herr built and owned the house, why is the site called the Hans Herr House? Actually, the house in which the Herr family lived is referred to as the "1719 House" or "Christian Herr House." It is the entire museum complex that bears the elder Herr's name in deference to his position as family patriarch and prominent member of the community.

> *Amish schoolteachers are usually unmarried and only a few years older than the eighth-grade pupils in the classroom. They usually have no education beyond the eighth grade. Also, Amish children generally receive no homework because they have a full schedule of chores to do when they return home in the afternoon.*

farms or begin working in their family businesses). All of the grades gather together for their lessons in the one room. The Weavertown school, built in 1877 and a typical example of the educational facilities of its time, still held classes up until 1969. Its original blackboards, wooden desks, and potbellied stove were left intact, and 30 lifelike audio-animatronic characters were added to demonstrate actual classroom activities of the time as conducted by a teacher and her pupils. Open weekends in March and November from 10:00 A.M. to 5:00 P.M.; daily April 1 through May 28 and September 5 through October 29 from 10:00 A.M. to 5:00 P.M.; daily Memorial Day through Labor Day from 9:00 A.M. to 5:00 P.M.

Columbia

National Watch and Clock Museum $$
514 Poplar Street
(717) 684-8261
www.nawcc.org
Time may fly, but it does leave some astonishing tracking devices behind to remind us of the ingenuity and creativity of artisans who used timepieces as their media. Horology is the art and design of making clocks, and you'll see more than 12,000 examples from around the world in what is widely recognized as the largest and most comprehensive horological collection in North America. Trace the history of timekeeping from the early sundials to modern atomic and radio-controlled

clocks and watches, tools, and other related items. In addition to an array of 19th-century pieces, the museum features early English tallcase clocks and Asian and other European devises.

Tours are self-guided. Wheelchair accessible. Open January through March, Tuesday to Saturday from 10:00 A.M. to 4:00 P.M., closed Sunday and Monday; April through December, Tuesday through Saturday 10:00 A.M. to 5:00 P.M., Sunday noon to 4:00 P.M.

Cornwall

Cornwall Iron Furnace $
Rexmont and Boyd Streets
(717) 272-9711
www.phmc.state.pa.us
This attraction is actually located in nearby Lebanon County, but it is included here for two reasons, first because it is an interesting and educational site well worth a visit; second, because it is a participant in the "Trail of History Museum Multi-Pass" program. A reminder of America's early industrial age, this complex (in operation from 1742 to 1883) includes a completely preserved stone furnace, steam-powered air-blast machinery, and several related mid-19th-century buildings, all of which were involved in the production of pig iron and domestic products. During the American Revolution, the furnace cast cannon barrels as well. Guided tours and exhibits in the visitor center explain the workings and history of the furnace. Open Tuesday to Saturday from 9:00 A.M. to 5:00 P.M., Sunday from noon to 5:00 P.M.

Gettysburg

American Civil War Museum $$
297 Steinwehr Avenue
(717) 334-6245
www.e-gettysburg.com
Haunting voices and sounds of battle give life to the 200 life-size figures that depict

more than 30 scenes from the Civil War. Jennie Wade, the only civilian to die during the Battle of Gettysburg, tells her story as she bakes bread in the last moments of her life; John Brown walks to the gallows; slaves use the Underground Railroad to escape to freedom. Through this multisensory presentation, you will follow the course of political, economic, and social events that exploded as the Civil War. In the Battleroom Auditorium, a digitally enhanced multimedia presentation re-creates the Battle of Gettysburg, followed by a reading of the Gettysburg Address by an animated Abraham Lincoln. The American Civil War Museum (formerly known as the National Civil War Wax Museum) is wheelchair accessible and offers discounts on youth and children's admission. It is open seven days year-round, from 9:00 A.M. to 9:00 P.M. in summer and 9:00 A.M. to 5:00 P.M. the remainder of the year.

Explore & More:
A Hands-on Museum for Children $$
20 East High Street
(717) 337-9151
www.exploreandmore.org

This real 1860s house-turned-playhouse for the three-to-eight-year-old crowd offers all kinds of age- and developmental skill-appropriate activities. There's a pretend Civil War–era general store; an art studio, where kids can create their own masterpieces with paint, feathers, pipe cleaners, glitter, glue, and sculpture dough; and a "hard hat" area, where they can hoist heavy loads with pulleys and watch the inner workings of gears; find out how far a whisper will travel; stand inside a bubble; experiment with magnets and visit the mice, frogs, hermit crabs, and other petite creatures. The museum is located right behind the Adams County Library. Special discounts for adult admissions. Open October to mid-April on Monday, Tuesday, Thursday, Friday, and Saturday from 10:00 A.M. to 5:00 P.M., Sunday noon to 5:00 P.M.; mid-April through September, Monday to Saturday from 10:00 A.M. to 5:00 P.M. Closed Sunday.

From April to December, the American Civil War Museum presents free living history encampments adjacent to the National Park Service Visitor Center (97 Taneytown Road, Gettysburg).

General Lee's Headquarters Museum $
401 Buford Avenue
(717) 334-3141
www.civilwarheadquarters.com

Less than 30 years after this stone house was built, in 1834, General Robert E. Lee made it his personal base of operation during the Battle of Gettysburg because of its location near the battle lines and its thick walls that offered protection from artillery shells. At the time of the war, the home, which was believed to be a duplex, was owned by statesman Thaddeus Stevens and was the dwelling of Mrs. Mary Thompson, known by the residents of Gettysburg simply as the Widow Thompson. She had the eastern side of the building, Lee took the west. It is reported that Mrs. Thompson was impressed with General Lee's gentlemanly behavior but horrified by the lack of same displayed by some of his attendants, who committed robbery and acts of destruction while they occupied the house. Since 1922 the house has operated as a museum, exhibiting artifacts and relics discovered in the battlefield. Youths ages 15 and under are admitted free as are residents of Adams County. Open mid-March through November (including Sunday) from 9:00 A.M. to 5:00 P.M., with extended hours in summer.

Hall of Presidents
and First Ladies Museum $$
789 Baltimore Street
(717) 334-5717

The presidents (actually, life-size wax replicas of them) speak their minds, and the First Ladies model inaugural gowns reproduced down to the last detail from the real things in the Smithsonian Collection. In the "Eisenhowers at Gettysburg" exhibit, you can see how the First Family lived on their farm just outside town. Open seven days in summer from 9:00 A.M. to 5:00 P.M., rest of year until 7:00 P.M.

Lincoln Train Museum $$
425 Steinwehr Avenue
(717) 334-5678
A 15-minute simulated "ride" lets you accompany President Lincoln from Washington to Gettysburg for the dedication of the National Military Cemetery. Model and military railroad displays feature more than 1,000 operating trains plus dioramas depicting the role of the railroad during the Civil War. Open daily (including Sunday) mid-March to July and August to mid-November from 9:00 A.M. to 5:00 P.M., July to August until 9:00 P.M.

Soldiers' National Museum $$
777 Baltimore Street
(717) 334-4890
During the Battle of Gettysburg, this building served as the headquarters for Union general O. O. Howard, and afterward, until 1877, it was the National Soldier's Orphan Homestead. During the 1950s and '60s, it was a museum of the Civil War, and there is still a large collection of artifacts and memorabilia from that era, including a life-size narrated Confederate encampment and detailed dioramas of 10 major conflicts of the war. In addition, the museum features displays of numerous military items from the days of Columbus to Desert Storm. Open seven days year-round. Summer hours are 9:00 A.M. to 9:00 P.M., to 5:00 P.M. the rest of the year.

Hershey

AACA (American Antique
Automobile Club) Museum $$
161 Museum Drive
(717) 566-7100
www.aacamuseum.org
Auto aficionados can travel through time and space, experiencing the evolution of

design and the fickleness of fashion, as the main exhibit, "From Sea to Shining Sea," spans the history of American cars from the early to late 20th century, from New York to San Francisco. More than 90 historic cars, from Henry Ford's Model T to the epitome of road royalty as exemplified by Packard, Pierce, Lincoln, and Cord, are on display in exhibition areas that cover close to 70,000 square feet and three levels. In addition to the museum's permanent collection, special exhibitions on specific makes and models are featured throughout the year. Reduced admission prices for seniors and children. Open Labor Day through Memorial Day on Wednesday to Sunday from 9:00 A.M. to 5:00 P.M.; Memorial Day through Labor Day daily from 9:00 A.M. to 5:00 P.M.

Hershey Museum $$
170 West Hersheypark Drive
(717) 534-3439
www.hersheymuseum.org

It started in 1933, when Milton Hershey bought a collection of Native American objects, including clothing, pottery, baskets, rugs, and tools, to display in the town he had built.

He expanded its size and scope when he acquired a collection of Pennsylvania German furniture, folk art, textiles, and household items that would show how this industrious immigrant community lived, worked, and raised their children in the years between 1800 and 1850. From the volunteer fire company Hershey created with more than 30 of his neighbors in 1905 is the original hook-and-ladder wagon, plus an assortment of other firefighting gear from the 18th through 20th centuries. Later additions to the museum include a section devoted to exhibits, original working machinery, and memorabilia that tell the story of the man, the company, and the town named Hershey. Another is a display entitled "Victorian America: The Middle Class at Home, 1875 to 1900." There are

a number of hands-on exhibits to keep the kids interested and entertained. Open seven days a week, Labor Day through Memorial Day, from 10:00 A.M. to 5:00 P.M., Memorial Day through Labor Day until 6:00 P.M. Seniors 65 and older and children ages 3 to 15 receive discounts on admission; children under 3 are free.

Milton Hershey School & Founders Hall Visitors Center
U.S. Route 322/Governor Road
(717) 520-2000
www.mhs-pa.org

Never able to have any children of their own, Milton and Catherine Hershey turned the residence and property (called The Homestead) where he had been born into a home and school for orphaned boys. From an initial enrollment of four boys in 1910, the Milton Hershey School (MHS) has grown into the largest residential prekindergarten through grade 12 school in the United States, providing more than 1,300 boys and girls each year with education, housing, food, medical and psychological health care, recreation opportunities, and clothing with no financial obligations to their families. The school's nationwide alumni base is more than 8,000. Members of the public are welcome to learn more about the school through a 20-minute video and a host available to answer questions seven days a week year-round (10:00 A.M. to 3:00 P.M., closed on school holidays) at the visitor center located in Founders Hall, the main administration building of Milton Hershey School. In the original Homestead part of the campus—in fact, in the room where Milton Hershey was born—is the Milton and Catherine Hershey Exhibit. This free, open-to-the-public tribute to the Hersheys features a pictorial and written history of their lives, as well as an extensive collection of personal items. The Homestead is open Monday to Friday from 8:00 A.M. to 4:30 P.M.

Intercourse

Amish Country Homestead   **$$**
The Amish Experience
Route 340
(717) 768–8400, ext. 210
www.amishexperience.com
Situated in the Plain & Fancy restaurant
and shops complex between the dining
room and F/X Theater is the Old Amish
homestead. Inside are nine rooms on two
floors, furnished to suit the Plain lifestyle
down to the pantry stocked with home-
canned vegetables and the traditional
clothing. Guides interpret the day-to-day
lives of today's Amish and their traditions
and practices, including how and why
Sunday worship services are held in the
home rather than in a church. Open seven
days year-round; hours vary.

*If you plan to visit the Amish Country
Homestead and/or take an Amish
Farmlands Tour (see details in the
Tours chapter), you can save on
combination tickets. Call for details.*

The People's Place Quilt Museum
3510 Old Philadelphia Pike (Route 340)
(800) 828–8218, ext. 231,
(717) 768–7101, ext. 231
www.ppquiltmuseum.com
A good portion of the quilts on perma-
nent display in this museum are pre-1940
creations made by Amish and Mennonite
women. However, each year also brings
new exhibits of antique and contemporary
works from around the world. Educational
features show you the skill and artistry
that go into the making of a quilt. This
museum has a particularly interesting
shop filled with one-of-a-kind folk objects
and art pieces, many handmade by arti-
sans across the country. Items include pil-
lows made of hand-dyed cotton fabrics,
bentwood reproduction doll buggies,
rusty tin and tea-dyed ornaments, carved

farm animals, and folk art birds and dolls.
For a unique gift or keepsake, there are
framed antique quilt reproductions, and a
selection of quilt block collage brooches.
This free museum is open Monday to Sat-
urday from 9:00 A.M. to 5:00 P.M.; closed
Sunday.

Lancaster

Hands-on House,
Children's Museum of Lancaster   **$$**
721 Landis Valley Road
(717) 569–KIDS
www.handsonhouse.org
Interactive exhibits and programs geared
to children from ages 2 to 10 make this a
great family spot. Kids can star in their
own adventures against the scenery of the
"Mostly Make-Believe Exhibit" and discover
how Lancaster County farmers grow food
at another called "E-I-E-I-Know." "Rainbow's End" offers ample opportunity for
two- and three-dimensional design and
color creativity, and "Marty's Machine
Shop" provides hands-on experience with
gears, wheels, and pulleys. The museum is
wheelchair accessible. Open Labor Day to
Memorial Day, Tuesday to Thursday from
11:00 A.M. to 4:00 P.M., Friday and Saturday
from 10:00 A.M. to 5:00 P.M., and Sunday
from noon until 5:00 P.M.; Memorial Day to
Labor Day, Monday to Thursday and Saturday from 10:00 A.M. to 5:00 P.M., Friday
from 10:00 A.M. to 8:00 P.M., and Sunday
from noon to 5:00 P.M.

Lancaster County Museum   **$$**
2249 Route 30 East
(717) 393–3679
www.discoverlancaster.com
Unless you're in the right place at the
right time, you may never see a real
Amish barn raising. But through the won-
der of hydraulics and animatronics, you
can see one re-created right here along
with more than 30 other life-size scenes
of local, cultural, and historical significance
dating from the 1600s to the present day.
Over 160 figures re-create the lives and

times of Lancaster County's early Native Americans, the area's first Amish and Mennonite settlers, and those who fought in the Revolutionary and Civil Wars. Take the interactive presidential quiz and find out if you're a history whiz. Discounted admission rates are offered to seniors (60+) and children (ages 5 to 11). The museum is open daily January 2 to April 30 and September 7 to November 20 from 9:00 A.M. to 4:00 P.M.; May 1 to Labor Day 9:00 A.M. to 6:00 P.M., and November 21 to December 31, Monday to Thursday 9:00 A.M. to 4:00 P.M. and until 6:00 P.M. Friday, Saturday, and Sunday.

Lancaster Cultural History Museum $$
13 West King Street
(717) 299-6440
www.culturalhistorymuseum.com

Form and function, detail and design—the furnishings, everyday items, and art of a period can tell you a great deal about its people and their lives. This museum explores the cultural history of Lancaster County through interpreted exhibits and displays of 300 years of fine to folk art, furniture, children's toys, fraktur, textiles, and other artifacts collected from area homes and passed down through generations. Located on Penn Square in the heart of downtown Lancaster, the museum is housed in two historic buildings, the former City Hall of Lancaster and the Masonic Lodge No. 43, both built in the 1790s. Open year-round from 10:00 A.M. to 5:00 P.M. Tuesday to Saturday and from noon until 5:00 P.M. on Sunday. Admission discounts are available for children ages six and over and students with valid ID; children under six are free. Discounted joint admissions with the Lancaster Quilt and Textile Museum are also offered.

Lancaster Museum of Art
135 North Lime Street
(717) 394-3497
www.lancastermuseumart.com

Contemporary regional artists are well represented in the permanent collection of this 4,000-square-foot facility that is a focal point for Lancaster County visual art exhibition and education. Throughout the year, 16 additional traveling or temporary shows feature the works of regional, national, and international artists in a variety of media, including children's art and juried and contemporary crafts. The Grubb Mansion, in which the museum is located, is a Greek Revival town house, built around 1845, for a town iron master whose family patronized some of the most important artists of the Greater Philadelphia area. Open Monday to Saturday from 10:00 A.M. to 4:00 P.M., Sunday from noon to 4:00 P.M. Admission is free.

Lancaster Newspaper Newseum
28 South Queen Street
(717) 291-8600

Start reading the historic headlines in the sidewalk-facing windows, and you can't help but get hooked. Take a self-guided tour of newspaper equipment, printing and production methods (from the invention of the Egyptian alphabet to the publication of the first American newspaper to today's use of video terminal displays and fiber optics), and the evolution of journal-

In August, the Lancaster Art Museum presents a festival called Art in the Park at Musser Park, located at the rear of the building on the corners of North Lime, East Chestnut, and North Shippen Streets, in downtown Lancaster. More than 1,000 families participate in this annual event, which allows youngsters to create hands-on projects such as sculptures, jewelry, masks, and paintings. There's even a special "toddler tent" for young artists under age four. Art in the Park is a free event.

ism, over more than 200 years. This exhibit, sponsored by Lancaster Newspapers, Inc., publishers of the *Intelligencer Journal* and *Lancaster New Era* and *Sunday News,* is free and open 24 hours a day, seven days a week.

Lancaster Quilt and Textile Museum $$
37 North Market Street
(717) 397–2970
www.lancasterheritage.com

The centerpiece of the permanent exhibition here is the Esprit Collection, 82 quilts crafted in Lancaster County between the late 19th and early 20th centuries that were collected by Esprit Corporation founder Doug Tomkins and displayed at the company's San Francisco headquarters for a number of years. In 2004 the collection made its hometown debut in its own museum in the grand Beaux Arts Lancaster Trust Company building, which had been a local downtown landmark since 1912.

In addition to the Esprit collection, which rotates through exhibition cycles every six to eight months, the museum features a range of other 18th- to 20th-century Amish quilts, decorative needlework art, and household items made in the Pennsylvania Dutch region. The museum is open year-round Tuesday to Saturday from 10:00 A.M. to 5:00 P.M., Sunday from noon to 5:00 P.M. Rates are reduced for children and students with valid ID; children under six are free. Discounted joint rates with the Lancaster Cultural History Museum are available.

Landis Valley Farm and Museum $$
2451 Kissel Hill Road (just off Route 272/Oregon Pike)
(717) 569–0401
www.landisvalleymuseum.org

Just 2 miles north of downtown Lancaster is the largest living history village of Pennsylvania Dutch life. Using two dozen original and re-created buildings with more than 24 exhibits; period landscaping; over 100,000 early farm, trade, and household objects; live heritage breed animals; and a population of costumed guides and artisans, Landis Valley authentically re-creates Pennsylvania German village and farm life as it was between the mid-18th and 19th centuries. A 12-minute orientation film provides background. It's never the same place twice because, like any village, Landis Valley changes with the seasons, and a stroll around the 100-acre property constantly reveals new colors, scents, sights, and sounds. There's also always something different on the monthly schedule of special performances, craft demonstrations, and living history programs. Landis Valley Farm and Museum is open daily from 9:00 A.M. to 5:00 P.M. Monday to Saturday and from noon to 5:00 P.M. on Sunday. Reduced admission rates for seniors and youths (ages 6 to 17) and AAA members; children under 6 are free. Wheelchairs are available. Food is available for purchase during summer months, and a picnic grove is open all year.

Annual special events include seasonal demonstrations of hearth cooking, weaving, horse-drawn plowing, and other farm activities. At the Herb and Garden Faire, held the Friday and Saturday of Mother's Day weekend, heirloom vegetables and ornamental plants are for sale; and on the third weekend in July, Landis Valley becomes a Civil War village, with hundreds of military and civilian encampments, reenactors, and seminars.

North Museum of Natural History
and Science $$
400 College Avenue
(717) 291–3941
www.northmuseum.org

Wonders of earth and not of the earth, from depths underneath our feet to the farthest points beyond our reach . . . at least for now. Two floors of permanent and rotating exhibits display and explain fossils, minerals, rare shells, and other natural remainders of eons past when dinosaurs were the masters of the terrain. Study the creatures of the earth that have disappeared into extinction and others that have survived, including hands-on encounters with live turtles, snakes, salamanders, and exotic insects. Artifact collections explore the lives of the Native Americans. Illuminate your intellect with discoveries about light in the Fluorescent Room. One of the museum's most popular attractions is its planetarium, the largest in central Pennsylvania, equipped with "All-Sky" and video technology to bring the study of constellations, planets, galaxies, and nebulae more down to earth. An unusual gift shop features fossils for sale at a range of prices to appeal to both beginning and advanced collectors.

The museum is closed most Mondays, open Tuesday to Saturday from 10:00 A.M. to 5:00 P.M. and Sunday from noon until 5:00 P.M.; extended hours the first and third Friday of each month until mid-December from 10:00 A.M. to 8:30 P.M. Planetarium programs are shown every Tuesday to Sunday in summer; Friday, Saturday, and Sunday the rest of the year. Reduced admission for seniors (65+) and juniors (ages 3 to 12). Discount for combined admission for museum and planetarium.

Lititz

Wilbur Chocolate Candy Americana Museum and Factory Store
48 North Broad Street
(888) 294–5287, (717) 626–3249,
(717) 626–3540
www.wilburbuds.com
The factory upstairs is off-limits to tourists because of strict government safety, health, and insurance regulations. But you can learn a lot about chocolate making in the museum and watch all kinds of treats such as marshmallows, almond bark, peanut butter meltaways, heavenly hash, mint drizzle, and almond butter crunch being made on a smaller scale through the window of the special "Candy Kitchen."

Unlike most museums, this one makes you hungry. The smell of chocolate haunts you as you watch a video that follows the history of this favored flavor from its

ancient beginnings. It follows you everywhere as you peruse more than 1,000 varieties of antique and vintage candy molds, tins, boxes, and equipment, as well as the lovely collection of more than 150 hand-painted antique porcelain chocolate pots from Europe and the Orient.

Wilbur, now owned by international giant Cargill, has specialized in making premium chocolate and cocoa products since 1884. Although started in Philadelphia, the company eventually constructed a five-story building in Lititz for manufacturing in 1913. In 1905 Lawrence Wilbur, a third-generation member of the founding family, developed a machine to individually foil-wrap the company's signature candy, the Wilbur Bud, which had been introduced in 1893. Today, Wilbur Chocolate Company continues to produce over 150 million pounds of chocolate and confectionery products each year for confectioners, dairies, bakers, and candy makers across the nation. An old-fashioned candy store at the museum also sells specialty candies, fudge and chocolate dipped items. The tour is free and so is the Wilbur Bud sample. Open 10:00 A.M. to 5:00 P.M. Monday to Saturday; closed Sunday.

Paradise

National Christmas Center   **$$**
3427 Lincoln Highway East
(717) 442–7950
www.nationalchristmascenter.com
Don't wait for December to experience the joys of Christmas. This themed museum celebrates the holidays eight months a year. Take a self-guided tour through life-size exhibits depicting a colorfully animated—and always busy—Santa's workshop; TudorTowne, a fantastical Old World English village, where over 125 costumed animal characters play out 16 different animated scenes; and Toyland, with its 30-foot diameter accessorized model train circling a giant Christmas tree. Take a walk around the

world and learn the seasonal traditions of Russia, Germany, the Netherlands, Scandinavia, England, Italy, and Scotland. See how the Nativity has been depicted in art by various cultures at different times in history. And visit Christmases past to see how the first tree in Lancaster County would have been decorated in the early 1820s, images of holiday-cheerful shop windows, and hundreds of historic items from Grandma's glass ornaments to cookie cutters. Tours are self-guided, and the museum is wheelchair accessible. The Christmas season begins in May with weekends-only openings, then expands to seven days from June through December from 10:00 A.M. to 6:00 P.M. Santa and his helpers rest from January through April. Discount rate for children ages 3 to 12.

Ronks

Mascot Roller Mills
Stumptown Road and Newport Road
(Route 772) (southeast of Leola)
(717) 656-7616
www.resslermill.com
Grain mills were once the heart and soul of many rural American towns and villages. Not only were they the place where local farmers came to process, buy, and sell wheat and corn, they were also centers for community news exchange and social interaction. Unfortunately, many mills that were so integral to the history of rural America did not survive the ravages of time, fire, floods, and modernization. Mascot Roller Mills is one that not only has survived but also still actually functions, grinding corn for neighboring Amish

---

The name "Mascot" was suggested for the mill and surrounding village by the wife of William Ressler's son Jacob after a little dog that the couple saw in a Broadway stage show while on their honeymoon.

---

families. Although this water-powered mill was originally built in the 1730s, the major part of its history can be traced from 1850 to 1977, when three generations of the William Ressler family owned and operated it. Next to the mill is the home where the family lived, preserved in its mid-19th-century appearance and furnishings. Guides are on hand when the mills are open during the months of May through October (Monday through Saturday from 9:00 A.M. to 4:00 P.M.). Admission is free.

Mill Bridge Village $
101 South Ronks Road
(800) 645-2744, (717) 687-8181
www.millbridge.com
On a land grant from William Penn, John Herr built a water-driven gristmill in 1738. This mill became the centerpiece of a settlement that is now a tourist attraction. In addition to touring the working mill, visitors can walk or take a buggy ride through one of the country's last surviving double-arched covered bridges (at 180 feet long, it's also the longest of its kind in the county), watch a 30-minute film on Amish history and culture, see antique farm equipment and old-fashioned beeswax ornaments, and dip their own candles. Open seven days a week from 9:00 A.M. to 4:00 P.M.; closed December 1 through March 31. Wheelchair accessible. Reduced admission for children ages 6 to 10.

Strasburg

The Amish Village $$
Route 896 (2 miles north of Strasburg)
(717) 687-8511
www.800padutch.com/avillage.html
Your guide will explain the workings of an Old Amish farm as you tour the authentically furnished 1840 home, operating waterwheel and windmill, and outbuildings, including blacksmith shop, one-room schoolhouse, and operating smokehouse. Visit the pigs, horses, goats, miniature mules, peacocks, and other animals in the

barn. Wheelchair accessible. Open spring, summer, and fall, Monday to Saturday from 9:00 A.M. to 5:00 P.M., Sunday from 10:00 A.M. to 5:00 P.M. Reduced admission rates for children ages 12 and under; 5 and under are free.

NATURAL WONDERS
Hummelstown

Indian Echo Caverns $$
368 Middletown Road
(717) 566-8131
www.indianechocaverns.com
Only 3 miles west of Hershey (off U.S. Route 322 and Interstate 283 at the Hummelstown/Middletown exits) is this reminder that the earth's beauty is more than skin-deep. Deep below the surface are caverns that were naturally made by water flowing over 440-million-year-old limestone. It is believed that the Susquehannock Indian tribe that once lived in this area used the caverns as refuge during harsh weather. French fur trappers later wrote about these natural phenomena during the late 17th and early 18th centuries. In 1929 an entrepreneur named John Bieber made the inside pathways visitor-safe and opened up many of the underground "rooms" that had been blocked by large mineral deposits.

Today, those pathways still carry visitors deep into the underground world of lakes, stalactites, and stalagmites for a 45-minute guided walk that follows the path of our Native American and European ancestors and explains the geology and history of the formations and cavern rooms. Before you leave the site, stop in at Gem Mill Junction, where you can pan for gemstones, and chunks of amethyst, jasper, calcite, agate, and many more specimens in flowing chutes of water like the prospectors did hundreds of years ago. If you like, you can have one of the stones turned into a necklace.

Indian Echo Caverns are open Memorial Day to Labor Day from 9:00 A.M. to 6:00 P.M., 10:00 A.M. to 4:00 P.M. the remainder of the year. Hearing-impaired guests may pick up a written tour guide. With its numerous stairs and narrow passageways, this attraction makes maneuvering wheelchairs extremely difficult. Special discount admission prices are available for seniors and children ages 3 to 11; children 2 and under are free. Gem Mill Junction is a seasonal attraction, open seven days a week between Memorial Day and Labor Day.

Even in the hottest part of summer, the temperature in the caverns is a constant 52° Fahrenheit, so you may want to bring along a sweater or light jacket.

Ronks

Cherry-Crest Farm $$$
150 Cherry Hill Road
(717) 687-6843
www.cherrycrestfarm.com
Outdoor "agritainment" is the name of the game from July through October at this working farm that features all kinds of family-friendly activities plus pick-your-own produce. The main attraction, though, is definitely The Amazing Maize Maze, a five-acre labyrinth carved from the cornfields to deliberately discombobulate erstwhile explorers. Blunder your way along more than 2½ miles of paths, bridges, and tunnel slides to music spun by the "Maze Master." Each year's maze is different, designed according to the whim and wisdom of former Disney Broadway producer and co-owner Don Frantz.

Mid-September to late October is Harvest Fest time, when the popcorn is ready to pick right off the stalk (the whole ear is microwavable) and the fields remain open past dark on selected weekends for Flashlight Maze fun (usual hours are 10:00 A.M. to 5:00 P.M.). Bring your own flashlight, and stop into the gift shop for glow necklaces and bracelets to further illuminate your

Getting lost is half the fun at the Cherry-Crest Farm "Amazing Maize Maze." PENNSYLVANIA DUTCH CONVENTION & VISITORS BUREAU

view (and yourself). Flashlight Maze hours are from 6:30 to 11:00 P.M., with last entrance into the maze at 9:30. Special lower admission rates are charged, and bonfire and wagon ride are included.

Your daily Cherry-Crest Farm admission includes the maze plus farm tours with animal petting and education center (baby chick hatchery, under-glass beehive, cow milking, and interactive displays); wagon ride; hay jump tent, tunnel, and chute slide; obstacle course; singing chicken show; pumpkin slinging; and pedal carts. Fall brings 27 different varieties of mums and pick-your-own pumpkins, chili peppers, sunflowers, and, of course, popcorn. Discounted admission rates for children ages 3 through 11; under 3 are free. If you plan to visit the nearby Strasburg Rail Road as well as Cherry-Crest Farm, ask about money-saving combination tickets.

RAILROADS

Gettysburg

Pioneer Lines Scenic Railway $$$
106 North Washington Street
(717) 334-6932
www.gettysburgrail.com
It's no longer the Gettysburg & Harrisburg Railroad as it was in 1884 (although the passenger benches are the originals), but the trains are still running from the downtown area's Washington Street depot. A basic ticket will buy you a one-hour, 16-mile rail tour of the area where the first day of the Civil War battle was fought and farther to check out more of the historic sites and rural scenery of Adams County. Trains run on selected days (including Sunday) from May through October, with a couple of special holiday excursions in November and December. For an additional fee (and with a 48-hour reservation), you can arrange to have a "conductor's bagged lunch" (sandwich,

chips, applesauce, cookies, and beverage) waiting for you. Seasonal murder mystery dinner trains (three hours with a catered country-style dinner) and narrated ghost trains (one hour) are also available.

Middletown

Middletown & Hummelstown
Railroad   **$$**
136 Brown Street
(717) 944–4435, ext. 0
www.mhrailroad.com
Located only a little over 8 miles south of Hershey, the M & H Railroad first took to the track in 1890 and operated as part of the Reading Railroad until 1976. Today visitors can follow the towpath of the historic Union Canal along the Swatara Creek on an 11-mile, 90-minute round-trip ride in a 1920s vintage Lackawanna & Western coach or 1955 General Electric diesel locomotive. At the station, you can see a collection of old-time equipment, including streetcars, a snowsweeper, a trolley freight car, a steam locomotive, and a wooden boxcar with link-and-pin couplers. From Middletown, you'll depart from the 1891 freight station for Indian Echo Caverns Platform in Hummelstown. Have your camera out for a breathtaking shot while you're rolling across a bridge 35 feet above the Swatara. You'll have time to visit the caverns if you wish and then take the return trip along with an accordionist or banjo player, who will lead a sing-a-

long of classic railroad songs. The M & H Railroad schedules trips to Indian Echo Caverns on selected days (including Sunday) from late May through October. The trains are wheelchair accessible. Reduced fares for seniors and children ages 3 to 11. Combination tickets with cavern tour are not discounted, but they do eliminate the wait in line for a tour ticket at the Hummelstown station.

Strasburg

Choo Choo Barn—Traintown, USA $$
Route 741 East
(800) 450–2920, (717) 687–7911
www.choochoobarn.com
More minis! What began as a small setup in the basement of the home of the George Groff family in the early 1960s has grown to more than 1,700 square feet of hand-built scenes and buildings featuring over 150 animated figures and vehicles. Look closely and you'll see all kinds of familiar local sights—from an operating quarry to a lively community baseball game, an Amish barn raising to a three-ring circus, and a Memorial Day parade to the rides at Dutch Wonderland—all painstakingly rendered and hand-painted in miniature. And, of course, there are the tiny trains, 22 operating models. Serious aficionados will want to know that the majority of these trains are O gauge, but there are some HO gauge and one N gauge on display as well. Reduced admis-

Throughout the year, the Middletown & Hummelstown Railroad offers special-event trains, including murder mystery, dinner theater, and "Moonlite Dinner with Sinatra Sounds"; fall foliage and pumpkin patch rides; Santa rides and "Polar Bear Express" nighttime trains to the North Pole, with cookies and milk and story-telling; Civil War reenactments; "Hobo

Campfire Express" (train ride plus chili and open-fire marshmallow roasting in the woods) and "Hobo Sack Lunch" trains; and, in July, the "Children's Miracle Network Train Robbery," where kids can use water pistols (no supersoakers, please) to defend their fellow passengers and their possessions.

sion for children 5 to 12 years old; under 5 free. Open seven days a week mid-March through December 31 from 10:00 A.M. to 5:00 P.M. (Monday and Friday tend to be the least crowded days of the week, so, if you can, it's a good idea to schedule your visit then.) On Fridays in December, hours are extended to 8:00 P.M., and the admission charge is waived for each person who donates a canned food item for distribution to the needy.

Choo Choo Barn is closed January through mid-March. Strasburg Train Shop, Thomas' Trackside Station, and Railroad Books & Videos are open daily year-round from 10:00 A.M. to 5:00 P.M.

Model railroaders will probably also like to visit the site's Shops of Traintown, including the Strasburg Train Shop (717-687-0464), for buying and selling used trains and for finding more than 1,000 books and videos on railroading, train prints, postcards, and clothing. Thomas' Trackside Station (800-450-2920, 717-687-7911) is an officially licensed Thomas & Friends store.

National Toy Train Museum $
300 Paradise Lane
(717) 687-8976
www.traincollectors.org/toytrain.html
They're small but powerful and so much fun to watch, especially here at the national headquarters of the Train Collectors Association. Five operating layouts (standard tinplate trains from the 1920s and '30s, O gauge items from the 1940s to the present, S gauge highlighting American Flyer trains from the 1950s, G gauge modern trains for indoor and outdoor display, and HO gauges) made up of hundreds of models span more than two centuries. Continuously running videos range from the educational to the comic. Got a question? Find the answer in the Toy Train Reference Library, which has catalogs, magazines, and books on the subject that go back to 1900. Open weekends in April, November, and December and daily May through October from 10:00 A.M. to 5:00 P.M. Discount on admis-

sion for senior citizens (age 65+), children ages 6 to 12; under 6 free. Special family rates (two adults and three or more children or one adult and four or more children).

Railroad Museum of Pennsylvania $$
Route 741, east of Strasburg
(717) 687-8628
rrmuseumpa.org
Railroading history continues right across the street from the train station at this museum with its world-class collection of more than 100 historical locomotives, from steam to electric, and railroad cars. There are also exhibits of railroad art and artifacts spanning 1825 to the present. For some background, it's a good idea to start with the orientation video. But don't worry, this isn't one of those look-but-don't-touch kind of museums. You can sit in the engineer's seat; walk through a private car, caboose, and early-20th-century depot; take a look at the underside of a 62-ton steam locomotive; and try some of the hands-on activities. Check out the station board in the lobby to find out what's happening. Open November through March, Tuesday to Saturday from 9:00 A.M. to 5:00 P.M., Sunday from noon to 5:00 P.M.; April through October, Monday to Saturday from 9:00 A.M. to 5:00 P.M., Sunday from noon to 5:00 P.M. Admission discounts for seniors over 60 and children to age 17. Wheelchairs are available, and special access considerations should be discussed in advance by calling the museum.

Strasburg Rail Road $$-$$$
Route 741, east of Strasburg
(717) 687-7522
www.strasburgrailroad.com
Andrew Jackson was president of the United States in 1832 when the Strasburg Rail Road was first incorporated by a special act of the Pennsylvania Legislature. When the first train ran is not quite clear, but an early timetable has runs scheduled as of December 1851. Originally, the 4½-mile straight track was used for passenger and freight transportation until around the

Relive railroad glory days in Strasburg. PENNSYLVANIA DUTCH CONVENTION & VISITORS BUREAU

turn of the 20th century, when a streetcar line between Lancaster and Strasburg siphoned away most of the riders. After the end of World War II, the freight business declined as a result of highway improvements. Instead of letting the railroad disappear into history, Lancaster industrialist and rail fan Henry K. Long and a group of investors restored the original track and began acquiring vintage locomotives and passenger cars from across North America.

From late May through most of November, selected dates in December, and around the Easter holidays, America's oldest short-line railroad's coal-burning steam engine once again puffs its way from the circa 1915 East Strasburg Station through miles of Pennsylvania Dutch farmland to Paradise, a scenic 45-minute rail

ride, as a narrator gives historic perspective. Passenger cars have been restored to their original Victorian charm, and depending on your preference—and pocketbook— you can ride regular coach (heated with potbellied stoves in winter) or upgrade to an open air, deluxe lounge (with solid cherry interiors and stained-glass accents), or dining car. If you're really feeling flush, you can go first class all the way in one of the rich and roomy parlor cars. Pack a picnic lunch (or buy one at the station) for the stop-off at pretty Groff's Grove. Fares vary by selected accommodation, and reductions are available for children. Call for weekday and Sunday schedules.

Other station activities that you can enjoy at a la carte or special package prices include a noontime "behind the scenes" guided tour of the mechanical

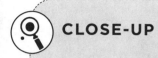
Covered Bridges of Lancaster County

From the 1820s to 1900, there were about 1,500 covered bridges built in Pennsylvania. Today, 219 of these bridges remain in 40 of the state's 67 counties. Lancaster County has 28 of them. Although romantics have dubbed these sheltered structures "kissing bridges," the actual reason covers were built over them was to protect the construction from weather damage.

It is on record that the longest covered bridge in the world was built in Lancaster County—across the Susquehanna River between Columbia and Wrightsville, a distance of 5,960 feet—but, sadly, it was destroyed by ice and high water in 1832. The longest double-arched covered bridge in Lancaster County is the 180-foot Herr's Mill Covered Bridge over the Pequea Creek.

The Pennsylvania Dutch Convention and Visitors Bureau publishes a map pinpointing all of the remaining covered bridges throughout the county. For a free copy of this map, call (800) PA-DUTCH, or log onto www.padutchcountry.com/covered_bridge.

You can also print out six different driving tours focusing on the bridges of central, south-central, northwestern (this area is divided into two separate tours), northeastern, and southeastern Lancaster County from the Pennsylvania Dutch Convention and Visitors Bureau Web site at www.padutchcountry.com/covered_bridge.

You can really appreciate the architecture of Lancaster County's covered bridges when you ride through on a bicycle. PENNSYLVANIA DUTCH CONVENTION & VISITORS BUREAU

shop where trains are built and refurbished, and a self-guided tour of the President's Car, a "mansion on wheels" that was used to transport railroad tycoons and dignitaries. Climb the Switch Tower, built in 1835, for an unparalleled view of the action of the train yard and the quiet of the countryside. Junior engineers can propel their own circa 1930s hand cars and ride on "The Cagney," a miniature steam engine made in the 1900s for carnivals and amusement parks. (Ask about the money-saving all-day passes that allow for unlimited rides and tours and combination multiday ticket packages with Dutch Wonderland, Strasburg Railroad, and the Amazing Maize Maze at Cherry-Crest Farm.)

Special-event train rides include a "Day Out with Thomas the Tank Engine" (a full-size operating steam locomotive pulled by Thomas with special guest Sir Topham Hat), Veterans Day "Trains & Troops," with military reenactors representing all eras, and holiday Easter Bunny and Santa Paradise Express Trains.

TOURS

By buggy or bus, bicycle seat or balloon basket, horse or four-wheeled horsepower—or your own two feet—a great way to discover Pennsylvania Dutch Country is on a tour. Join up with a group or strike out on your own. You could pay for the services of a guide to lead the way and interpret the sights along your route, or you could stop at the local visitor center (Pennsylvania Dutch Convention and Visitors Bureau, 501 Greenfield Road at Route 30, Lancaster; 800–PA–DUTCH, 717–299–8901; www.padutchcountry.com) or the Gettysburg Convention and Visitors Bureau Information Center (102 Carlisle Street, Gettysburg; 800–337–5015, 717–334–6274; www.gettysburgcvb.org) to get a variety of free self-guided maps and printed tours of historic areas. Themes range from religion to slavery and from covered bridges to farm markets.

SELF-GUIDED THEME TOURS
Gettysburg

Greystone's American History Store
461 Baltimore Street
(717) 338–0631
Greystone's has an excellent two-hour Gettysburg Battlefield Self-Guided Auto Tour available on cassette ($8.75) or CD ($14.04). Open from 10:00 A.M. to 8:00 P.M. daily.

i *For some pretour background, Greystone's has several thousand book titles (the entire first floor is all Civil War volumes; the second offers a selection covering time periods from ancient to modern). History-related films are also available.*

Gettysburg Expedition Guide by TravelBrains
Available at the Gettysburg National Park Service Visitors Center
(888) 458–6475
www.travelbrains.com
Everything you need to go it on your own. Included is a CD-ROM, a driving tour (tape or CD), and a 56-page full-color guidebook filled with detailed maps, photographs, and trivia. The package costs $29.95.

Lancaster County and Gettysburg

Auto Tape Tours
P.O. Box 227
Allendale, NJ 07401
(201) 236–1666
www.autotapetours.com
Pop these 90-minute tapes with narration, music, and sound effects into your car's tape or CD player and get directions and background on the sights you want to see. There's one for Amish Country and a separate one for the Gettysburg Battlefield. Cost: $12.95 plus $2.00 shipping and handling per cassette tape, $15.95 plus $3.00 postage and handling for CD.

BUS/MOTOR COACH TOURS

Amish Neighbors Tours/All About Tours
29 North Decatur Street (Route 896), Strasburg
(717) 687–8650, (717) 560–7421
www.amishneighborstours.com
Three options for guided tours of the Amish farmlands and Hershey, with lots of interesting stops along the way. Weekdays and Saturdays, the three-hour Amish

Farmlands Tour (9:00 A.M. to noon and 1:00 to 4:00 P.M.; $24 for adults, $19 for children age 3 to 11) offers a firsthand glimpse of the way the Amish live and work. On Sunday mornings, you can take a five-hour journey to Hershey (9:00 A.M. to 2:00 P.M.; $31 for adults, $26 for children age 3 to 11) or a two-hour "Just Passin' Through" farmlands tour (3:00 to 5:00 P.M., $22/$17).

HOT AIR BALLOONS

Ephrata

Adventures Aloft
24 East Main Street
(800) 747-1380, (717) 733-3777,
(717) 738-0585 (voice mail; press 1)
www.adventuresaloft.biz
Float along at treetop level or several thousand feet above the ground; wherever the wind takes you, that's where you'll go on this airborne tour over Central Lancaster County. Adventures Aloft has been offering these high-flying adventures since 1983. The flight itself usually lasts about an hour, depending on wind and weather conditions, but allot yourself between three and five hours for the entire experience, from preflight balloon inflation to landing ceremony and morning breakfast. (For safety's sake, flights may be postponed or canceled for the day if weather conditions are not favorable.) Launch sites also vary according to each day's wind conditions.

Depending on the weights of the passengers, pilot, and propane tanks, and the temperature of the day, one balloon can carry between three and five passengers in addition to the pilot. Your pilot will relate a brief history of ballooning and award you with a postflight certificate and commemorative balloon pin or other keepsake memento. A traditional postflight toast is also included.

Breakfast at a local restaurant is included with Adventures Aloft morning

flights booked for Monday through Saturday; a continental breakfast is included on Sunday and holiday flights. Round-trip transportation is included for passengers; family and friends may follow in their own cars. Flights are $175 per person.

United States Hot Air Balloon Team
Corporate address: 490 Hopewell Road
St. Peters
(800) 76-FLY-US, (610) 469-0782
www.ushotairballoon.com
This company's Pennsylvania Dutch Country flights take off from Lancaster Host Resort (2300 Lincoln Highway East/Route 30, Lancaster). There are several options available, ranging from a one-hour Amish farm country adventure to a three-day package that includes ballooning, posh overnight accommodations, gourmet-style meals, and three champagne toasts.

The one-hour "Heart of the Pennsylvania Dutch Country" flight ($179 per person) takes you on a 6- to 10-mile journey (depending on the winds) over scenic fields and farms. Early morning (6:00 A.M.) and dusk (6:30 P.M.) flight times are offered. Allot a total of two and a half hours for the entire experience. Postflight champagne toast in keepsake glass and a commemorative certificate are included. The Three-Day Pennsylvania Tour ($750

In keeping with a centuries-old tradition, balloonists usually drink a post-flight champagne toast. According to Adventures Aloft, this tradition began in the late 1700s, when early French balloonists would frighten farmers by landing in their fields. To avoid finding themselves on the sharp end of a pitchfork, the balloonists began offering farmers champagne upon their descent as a demonstration of goodwill.

per person) begins with a flight above the Lancaster farmlands. Next day, you'll float above the Susquehanna River, with a bird's-eye view of its rolling green hillsides and tiny towns. The third day you'll ascend from the lawn of the luxurious Hotel Hershey in neighboring Dauphin County and view the colorful planned landscape of the town that chocolate built.

GHOST TOURS

Civil War soldiers and other-century civilians are said to roam the streets and buildings of the towns of Lancaster County and Gettysburg. The many reasons why these permanent residents can't seem to rest in peace make for colorful legend and lore that are related with relish by tour guides (many in period dress) as you gingerly make your way along the sleeping (maybe . . . maybe not) street. As they regale you with tales of old, you can decide for yourself how many are based in actual history and how many are probable products of fertile local imaginations.

Gettysburg

Ghostly Images of Gettysburg
Gettysburg Tour Center
778 Baltimore Street
(717) 334–6296
www.gettysburgbattlefieldtours.com/
ghost_main.htm

Ghostly Images offers walking and bus tours that invite you to visit some of the "liveliest" currently occupied ghostly abodes. During the 90-minute Jennie Wade "Fright-seeing" Tour, history buffs and their guides hoof the haunts of a 5-block area, culminating with a visit to the Jennie Wade House, where the only civilian to die during the Battle of Gettysburg met her tragic end. You'll hear about the spirit of Wade herself, which is said to still inhabit the house, and learn of the experiences of a local psychic who says she has encountered more than 10 other souls here. Available nightly starting in late March through mid-November and the last two Fridays and Saturdays in November; tickets cost $7.00.

Every Friday starting late March through mid-November, guides give walkers the ghostly scoop on this 90-minute Mystical Mystery Tour ($7.00) as they relate local tales of the unexplainable that have been passed along for centuries. For the first part of the 90-minute Orphan Tour ($7.00), available every Friday and Saturday in April, May, and June, the guided group takes a spooky stroll on Steinwehr Street, ending with a visit inside the "haunted orphanage," where, after the battle, orphans of Union soldiers were housed under the cruel custodianship of Rose Carmichael. Her misdeeds are well documented and told through the stories of individuals who lived, visited, and worked in the building. The two-hour Haunted Bus Tour travels the darkened countryside in search of—and inside of—a haunted destination ($19.95). Midnight in a Haunted House and Midnight in an Orphanage, both $11, make sure you're in the right place at the right time when the clock chimes 12. Supernatural Supper (first and third Saturday of each month from April through early November) includes a buffet dinner, ghost stories, and a visit to the Jennie Wade House. Ticket price is $20.95. Spirits of the Tavern Tour (last Saturday of every month from end of April through October) takes you on a haunted pub crawl (drinks are extra) to locations

where terrifying tales are on tap ($19.95).
Arrive for all tours 15 minutes prior to
scheduled departure time.

Original Ghosts of Gettysburg Tour
**271 Baltimore Street
(717) 337-0445
www.ghostsofgettysburg.com**
Former National Park Ranger/historian-
turned-author Mark Nesbitt, author of the
Ghosts of Gettysburg book series, stories
from which have been featured on the
History Channel, A&E, the Travel Channel,
and *Unsolved Mysteries,* offered his first
candlelight walking tour of what he
believes "may very well be, acre for acre,
the most haunted place in America," in
1994. Nesbitt's company offers a variety
of walking tours that range from one and
a quarter hours to an hour and fifty minutes. Bus and train tours are also available.
The hour-and-15-minute Baltimore Street
Tour ($7.00 for adults; children 7 and
under free) covers about ¾ mile and takes
in the County Courthouse, which held
scores of wounded soldiers (and may now
be home to their spirits), and the church
"where so many amputations occurred
they had to drill holes in the floor to let
the blood run out and where a spectral
undertaker continues to walk to the
nearby cemetery . . . removed decades
ago." The hour-and-50-minute Carlisle
Street Tour ($7.50; children 7 and under
are free) covers about 1¼ miles, taking you
to a building "where a modern elevator
took two unsuspecting passengers down
for a vision of hell on earth—a Civil War
hospital, the structure where young
actresses see 'The General' materialize in a
vacant seat to admire their performances,"
and the place where "three wings of a
defeated Union Army and their pursuers
all came together to provide the focal
point for intense emotional energy and
produce continuing, bizarre poltergeist
activity."

The ¾-mile Steinwehr Avenue Tour,
offered from July through November
($7.00 for adults; children 7 and under are

free), goes to the Gettysburg National
Cemetery, a modern hotel "where disem-
bodied, phantom arms appear in the dead
of night to awaken unsuspecting tourists,"
and the fields where Pickett's men charged
and died. Tickets must be purchased at
least 30 minutes prior to tour time, and
directions to the meeting place will be
given. The ¾-mile Seminary Ridge Tour
($7.00 for adults; free for children 7 and
under) visits ghostly gathering places as
Robert E. Lee's headquarters and the
buildings of the Lutheran Theological Seminary, used as hospitals and temporary
resting places for the dead during the war
and the scenes of "unexplainable activity"
since. Tickets should be purchased at least
30 minutes prior to tour time, where you'll
also be given directions to the tour meeting place. On Saturday at 7:00 P.M., Original
Ghost Tours of Gettysburg offers a 90-
minute Bus Tour ($17 for adults, $15 for
children age 5 to 10; youngsters under 5
not admitted), which features battle-
related houses, farms, and burial sites that
have been the subject of sightings (and
hearings) for years. Reservations are
required for this tour. The Gettysburg
Ghost Train Tour, in partnership with Pioneer Rail Lines, takes visitors through portions of the battlefield, including Oak
Ridge, "where the phantom messenger still
rides," as guides spin tales of legendary
ghost trains and passengers who long ago
disembarked but never really departed.
(Reservations for this tour should be made
directly through Pioneer Rail Lines, 106
North Washington Street, Gettysburg;
717-334-6932; www.gettysburgrail.com.)
Train tours are available on selected Fridays from May through October.

If you're interested in learning more about modern ghost hunting, Rick Fisher also conducts Haunted Workshops, teaching the use of paranormal investigation techniques and equipment ($42). The five-hour workshops, offered in September and October, include a ghost tour of Marietta. For an even more in-depth experience, ask about his Paranormal Workshop and Overnight Investigation ($42, limit of 15 participants) at the Railroad House Bed & Breakfast. Each spring, Fisher also hosts the Pennsylvania Paranormal Conference, an all-day event featuring presentations by nationally recognized speakers, at a local site.

**Sleepy Hollow of Gettysburg
Candlelight Ghost Tours
65 Steinwehr Avenue
(717) 337-9322
www.sleepyhollowofgettysburg.com**
Tour owner and operator Cindy Codori Shultz is the sixth-generation granddaughter of Nicholas Codori, whose farm was the site of Pickett's Charge during the Battle of Gettysburg. Without canned scripts or predetermined routes, the 10 different period–costumed guides are free to weave in their own research and personal experiences to bring fresh information and "spirit" to each outing. Walks travel within a 3- to 5-block radius around the historic area, last about one hour, and depart nightly at 8:30 and 9:00 P.M. just about year-round. Price is $6.00 per person; children under 7 are free as are guests using wheelchairs. All tours take place rain or shine.

From late November through the end of December (except for Christmas Eve or Day), the company trades "cannons for Cratchits and soldiers for Scrooge," switching to the holiday festive A Carol by Candlelight Yuletide Tour, complete with a hot chocolate nightcap. There's also a New Year's Eve Walk. Ghosts of the Gettysburg Battlefield may join you on the company's Seminary Ridge Tour, which begins at the steps of Robert E. Lee's headquarters (Buford Avenue, Route 30 West) and focuses on the site of the primary Confederate position west of Gettysburg for the final two days of the battle.

Marietta

**Ghosts of Marietta Walking Tour
Departure point: basement of the
Railroad House Bed & Breakfast, corner
of West Front and South Perry Streets
Tour company phone: (717) 426-4141
http://home.supernet.com/~rfisher/
pghs.html**
As founder of the Paranormal Society of Pennsylvania, Rick Fisher "investigates reported hauntings, strange creatures, UFOs, mysterious places, and unexplained phenomena" and has made numerous print and broadcast media appearances, including the Travel Channel's Ghostly Gettysburg and Supernatural Destinations. At 8:00 on Friday and Saturday evenings from April through November, Fisher leads a one-hour walking tour of the Susquehanna River town of Marietta. The Railroad House Bed & Breakfast is more than just the departure point of the tour; it is said to be a center of paranormal activity. But it's not the only one. Cost: $12 per person; reservations are required.

Strasburg

**Ghosts of Lancaster County
Mrs. Penn's Shoppe
2 West Main Street (at the light
at the corner of Routes 896 and 741)
(717) 687-6687
www.ghosttour.com**
Evening candlelight tours are conducted

of the town once known as Hell's Hole (in reference to some of the more rough-around-the-edges wagon drivers who used to frequent the local tavern and inn). Hear of haunted mansions, secret doings in the cemetery, and other scary stuff. Tickets are sold on a first come, first served basis. First tour of the evening begins at 7:30 P.M., another begins at 8:00 P.M., and they continue on the half hour until 9:00 P.M. as each time slot fills up. Tours last approximately one hour and ten minutes and are scheduled on Friday and Saturday in April and May, Tuesday to Saturday in June and July, every evening in August, Friday and Saturday in September, every evening in October, and selected dates in November. Price is $13.00 per adult, $7.00 for children age 5 to 12.

STEP-ON TOURS

The Mennonite Information Center
2209 Millstream Road, Lancaster
(800) 858–8320
http://mennoniteinfoctr.tripod.com/id4.html
Discover the back roads and the back story from the perspective of a local Mennonite or Amish-Mennonite guide, who will ride along with you in your car. These aren't your typical tourist route excursions; your guide will customize your route and experience according to your interests. Because your guide is a part of the community, he or she will be able to suggest visits to places you would probably miss on your own and may even be able to arrange for a "not usually open to

Step-on tours allow you to pick up your guide at the designated tour center and away you go in your own vehicle. You drive, while your guide points out sites (and sights) of interest and offers interesting background information.

tourists" visit to a friend's farm, home, or home-based business.

The center is open all year every day except Sunday from 8:00 A.M. to 5:00 P.M. from April 1 to October 31; November to December from 8:30 A.M. to 4:30 P.M.; and January through February from 10:00 A.M. to 3:00 P.M. Tours are a minimum of two hours but may be extended. Rates are $36 per vehicle with 1 to 7 persons ($12 for each additional hour) and $40 for a vehicle with 7 to 14 persons ($14 for each additional hour).

Old Order Amish Tours
63 East Brook Road
(Route 896 North), Ronks
(717) 299–6535
Because this is a private tour, the places you visit can be customized to suit your interests. A particularly popular stop is the Old Order Amish working farm and home (the owners are friends of the guide). During your two-hour (or longer) farmland foray, you can visit Amish woodworking and quilt shops, a bookstore, and the home of a woman who bakes traditional Dutch goodies. Tours are available six days a week (no Sundays) and cost $40 for two people. Call to make arrangements at least a day or two ahead of your visit.

Unless tips are already included in the price of a tour or if the company has a specific "no tipping" policy (ask or read the fine print on your ticket), guides and drivers appreciate a monetary thank-you.

For up to a half-day tour at least $1.00 or $2.00 per person for the guide is generally appropriate, double that for a full-day tour. Same for the bus driver.

CLOSE-UP

Buggy Rides

It may seem odd to outsiders to line up at a traffic light behind a horse-drawn buggy, but for the Amish and their Lancaster County neighbors, it's part of daily life. For tourists who want to know how it feels to take travel Amish-style there are a number of companies in Lancaster County that offer rides.

Most companies stick primarily to the scenic back roads and may include as part of your tour a stop at an Amish farm or two—you don't get out, but you can purchase crafts, baked goods and other items. If the prospect of a sales pitch (however charming) makes you uncomfortable, choose a company that offers private rides. Since you and your group will be the only riders, you may request that the driver skip the shopping stop. Whether you stop at an Amish farm or are just passing through, remember to refrain from snapping photos of the people who live there unless you ask first. The Amish church prohibits its members from appearing in photographs.

Some operators use the closed-sided buggies often used by Amish families. Others offer the option of riding in an Amish "market wagon" which has sides that roll up. For larger families and groups, you can also find operators that offer rides in larger open wagons.

According to the owners of Aaron & Jessica's Buggy Rides in Bird-in-Hand, buggy horses are usually either American standardbred or American saddlebred. Wagons are usually pulled by draft horses.

Old Order Amish don't generally own buggy rides, but some companies are owned by individuals and families who, while they are no longer practicing mem-

WALKING TOUR

Lancaster

Historic Lancaster Walking Tour
100 South Queen Street
(717) 392-1776
A brief film presentation lays the groundwork for your 90-minute return to a time when Lancaster City was known as Hickorytown. Every day from April through October (November through March by reservation), interpreters in colonial garb lead tours down cobbled streets to more visit more than 50 locations, including historic homes, courtyards, churchyards, and gardens. These tours were initiated during the Bicentennial in July 1976. They were so popular, they became permanent parts of the Lancaster experience. Prices are $7.00, $6.00 for senior citizens and groups of 10 or more. Tour times are Monday, Wednesday, Thursday, Sunday, and holidays 1:00 P.M.; Tuesday, Friday, and Saturday 10:00 A.M. and 1:00 P.M.

BUGGY RIDES

Bird-in-Hand

Aaron and Jessica's Buggy Rides
3121A Old Philadelphia Pike
(717) 768-8828
www.amishbuggyrides.com
Owned by a family with Mennonite and

Riding along country roads in a horse-drawn buggy is a highly anticipated part of many visitors' Pennsylvania Dutch Country experience. PENNSYLVANIA DUTCH CONVENTION & VISITORS BUREAU

bers of the Old Order community, were brought up with and are quite knowledgeable about its tenets and traditions. Others may be members of the Mennonite or Brethren churches. Ditto for the drivers. Feel free to ask respectful questions. Tips are welcome, unless otherwise specified.

Look for discount coupons on buggy rides on the companies' Web sites; at the visitor centers, hotels, motels and inns; and in local publications such as the *Amish News* (a publication for tourists, not by and for the Amish community). Some operators offer rides on Sunday.

Brethren roots, this company offers four different tour routes (each one covering about 3½ miles in about a half hour) on private roads that run through noncommercial working Amish farms. This is a good tour for seeing some real, non-touristy authentically Amish places such as a buggy factory, grocery store, shoe store, blacksmith, and horse dealer (different stops are offered on various routes) as well as the expected one-room schools, farm stands, and quilt and furniture shops. It's also a good choice if you have brought any pets along—they may ride with you. Aaron & Jessica's prefers to use Amish open-sided market wagons because they offer riders a broader view of the country-side. A larger market wagon made in 1886 is available for larger groups. Rides are wheelchair accessible.

This is an all-weather operation (if there's enough snow, you can take a sleigh ride). Hours are Monday through Saturday from 8:00 A.M. to sunset, Sunday from 10:00 A.M. to 5:00 P.M. April through November; Monday to Saturday from 10:00 A.M. to 4:30 P.M. from December through March. Rides are given on a first come, first served basis, but same-day reservations are available if you make them in person. Prices are $10.00 for adults, $5.00 for children ages 12 and under, and free for children under 2.

Abe's Buggy rides
2596 Old Philadelphia Pike (Route 340)
(717) 392-1794
www.abesbuggyrides.com
One of the employees here is a former missionary who lived in Guatemala for 20 years, so Spanish speakers can ask their questions—and have them answered—in their native tongue. Abe's, in business since 1968, uses original closed-sided Amish family-style buggies for its 2-mile (approximately 25-minute) tours. Among the sights you'll see is a 1770 water-powered mill and a 1749 Quaker meetinghouse. Drivers are either Amish-born, Amish-Mennonite, or have Amish family members. You may request a private ride or share with others. There's an on-site petting zoo and a blacksmith who comes to shoe the horses one day a week (call if you want to find out if he's working the day of your ride). Abe's is open from 9:00 A.M. to dusk Monday to Friday, Saturday until 6:00 P.M. in summer; Monday to Saturday from 10:00 A.M. to 3:00 P.M. in winter. Abe's is closed on Sunday and may close on rainy or extremely cold and windy days. No reservations are necessary, but they are accepted. Prices are $10.00 for adults, $5.00 for children age 3 to 12, free for children 2 and under.

Ronks

Ed's Buggy Rides
253 Hartman Bridge Road (Route 896)
(717) 687-0360
www.edsbuggyrides.com
No coupons are needed to get the price of $8.00 for adults, $4.00 for children on this 3-mile (minimum one-hour) tour of the countryside. For some background, you can begin by watching a free 45-minute video about the Amish culture. This family-owned operation uses both open- and closed-sided Amish family carriages and larger open Amish spring wagons for its private road and back road farmland rides. Ed's has an arrangement with a working Amish farm along its route that allows its buggies to park and for visitors to get off and visit the resident family's craft shop. Open daily, including Sunday, from 9:00 A.M. to at least sunset.

Strasburg

AAA Buggy Rides
312 Paradise Lane
(717) 391-9500
www.aaabuggyrides.com
Travel more than 3 miles (about 25 minutes) along the back roads of Paradise Valley in an Amish family carriage or open horse-drawn wagon any day—including Sunday—the weather allows. The Amish farm stop is optional and extended rides are available. Located right down the street from the Strasburg Railroad, this operator also has a small petting zoo on the property. Buggy ride prices are $10.00 for adults, $5.00 for children 12 and under; children under 2 ride free.

GETTYSBURG BATTLEFIELD TOURS

Association of Licensed Battlefield Guides
97 Taneytown Road
(877) 438-8929, (717) 334-1124, ext. 477
At the front desk of the National Park Service visitor center, you can hire a licensed battlefield guide to join you in your car for a private two-hour tour of the Gettysburg Battlefield. Tours are arranged on a first come, first served basis beginning at 8:00 A.M. each day. Your tour may be customized to suit any particular areas of interest. Price for a step-on tour for up to 6 people is $40, $60 for 7 to 15 people.

The designation "licensed battlefield guide" can be used only by individuals who have been tested and licensed by the National Park Service.

If you are planning to include other Gettysburg attractions on your travel itinerary, check out some of the battlefield-plus packages available from Gettysburg Tour Center. These can save you money on admissions to up to seven of the area's most popular sites and include free unlimited use of the Gettysburg Town Trolley, which stops at most of the popular attractions and travels to many of the area's hotels, motels, and campgrounds.

Gettysbike Tours
240 Steinwehr Avenue
(717) 752-7752
www.gettysbike.com
Licensed battlefield guides lead two-hour bicycle tours of the Gettysburg Battlefield (bike rental is included in the $30 per person price). From mid-April to mid-October, you can take a Sunset Battlefield Tour that begins at about 6:00 P.M. If you don't need the historical narrative, you can hire an escort (it's a big battlefield out there, and it's easy to lose your way on a bike) to tour the battlefield with you ($20 per person fee includes bike rental). Either way, this operator provides a trailer with first-aid supplies, rain-proof ponchos, and a place to safely stow personal possessions such as purses and camera for an unencumbered ride. Reservations are encouraged for any bike tour.

Gettysburg Battlefield Bus Tours
Gettysburg Tour Center
778 Baltimore Street
(717) 334-6296
www.gettysburgbattlefieldtours.com
This operator offers two types of two-hour-long tours—one type led by a licensed battlefield guide ($23.95 for adults, $14.90 for children), the other with a "dramatized audio" narrative and special effects soundtrack ($19.95 for adults, $12.35 for children). Both tours are available daily year-round. In season, the dramatized audio version travels on an open-air double-decker bus. Tickets are available at many Gettysburg area accommodations including bed-and-breakfasts, hotels and motels, inns, and campgrounds.

Gettysburg Carriage Company -
Shady Glen Farm
Corporate address: 830 Hilltown Road,
Biglerville, PA 17307
(717) 337-3400
Half-hour horse-drawn carriage rides travel Gettysburg historic areas or back roads ($35.00 for one to three people, $10.00 for each additional adult, $5.00 per child) are offered Monday to Saturday from April through the end of December. Other choices include a one-and-a-quarter-hour battlefield ride ($75 per couple) or a three-hour Picnic Ride in the Country out to the Cashtown area with a stop midway for an alfresco lunch ($150 per couple with catered picnic lunch; wine is also available). Tours leave from locales in the town of Gettysburg.

HORSEBACK BATTLEFIELD TOURS

Hickory Hollow Farm
219 Crooked Creek Road, Gettysburg
(717) 334-0349
www.hickoryhollowfarm.com
Riders from age eight and up can get a very different perspective on history from the saddle as a licensed battlefield guide relates the events of the three-day conflict on this now peaceful site. Cost is $50 per

Gettysbike is a little difficult to see from Steinwehr Avenue, so look for Flex & Flanigan's souvenir shop; the tour operation is right behind it.

hour (maximum six riders), with a two-hour minimum and six-hour maximum. Helmets are required for riders 16 years of age or younger. One- to four-hour scenic rides without the historic narrative of a licensed battlefield guide are also available ($40 for one hour, $35 per hour for two to four hours for a maximum of 10 riders). To get to Hickory Hollow Farm from downtown Gettysburg (the intersection of Routes 97 and 30), take Route 30 West for 4 miles, then turn right on Crooked Creek Road. Approximately ½ mile from Route 30 is the farm.

PARKS, RECREATION, AND GOLF ♣

GOLF COURSES

Denver

Hawk Valley Golf Club
1309 Crestview Drive
(800) 522-HAWK, (717) 445-5445
www.golfthehawk.com
Built on former farmland, this 18-hole, par 72, public Lancaster County course rolls along 125 acres, past stands of mature trees and seven ponds. Anyone who has played a course designed by William Gordon will recognize the architect's complex green designs and will be anticipating the extra challenges (Hawk Valley has more than 50 strategic traps) that are his signature. The club house and pro shop are situated in a converted bank barn, and a spring house, located next to the old stone farm house, is now home to the 19th Hole snack stop. Hawk Valley is located 3 miles from exit 286 of the Pennsylvania Turnpike. Greens fees are $20 ($25 with cart) Monday through Friday; $45 (walk or ride) Saturday and Sunday before 11:00 A.M., $30 from 11:00 A.M. to 3:00 P.M. After 3:00 P.M. on weekends, greens fee is $18 ($25 with cart). Private lessons are available.

Gettysburg

The Links at Gettysburg
601 Mason Dixon Road
(717) 359-8000
www.thelinksatgettysburg.com
Lakes (more than 10) and creeks on just about every hole and red rock cliffs make this meandering Blue Mountain public 18-hole, par 72 course a visual delight as well as a technical challenge. Located about 6 miles from the Gettysburg Battlefield, the Lindsay Bruce Ervin–designed Links at Gettysburg is open year-round.

Individual lessons and group clinics are available at the Nike School. One popular package ($80) includes one hour of private instruction with video analysis, a free sleeve of Nike golf balls, an instruction manual, and discounts on Links golf equipment and apparel. All of the instruction takes place on a practice area with natural turf driving range and elevated tees, a chipping green, a practice bunker, and two bent grass putting greens. A pro shop on the premises offers equipment, clothing, and other accessories.

In-season (April 1 to November 1) greens fees are $80.00 for 18 holes, cart, and one token (worth $7.00) for range balls; twilight (after 2:00 P.M.) fees are $50.00. Off-season (November 1–April 1) fees are $50.

Hershey

Hershey Country Club
1000 East Derry Road
(800) HERSHEY, (717) 533-2360
www.hersheygolf.com
Guests staying at any of the Hershey Resort properties (the Hotel Hershey, Hershey Lodge, and Hershey Highmeadow Campground) have access to all four golf courses (a total of 63 holes) at the country club, including the championship East and West Courses. Two other golfing facil-

---

Taxes are additional on greens fees, unless otherwise specified. 　ℹ️ ities, the 18-hole Parkview and 9-hole Spring Creek Golf Courses, are open to the public as well. If golfing is a family affair for you, keep in mind that Spring Creek was designed with children and teens in mind.

Founded by Milton Hershey in 1930, the country cub has hosted many links legends including Henry Picard, Byron Nelson, Sam Snead, Arnold Palmer, and Jack Nicklaus. Golfing great Ben Hogan was the Hershey Country Club resident pro from 1941 to 1951.

The par 73 West Course, designed by Maurice McCarthy, offers a sweeping view of the town of Hershey and play on the front lawn of High Point Mansion, Milton Hershey's estate. George Fazio designed the par 71 East Course, which features three man-made lakes and more than 100 bunkers. The East Course is the home of the Reese's Cup Classic PGA tournament.

Greens fees for the two Country Club courses are $99 (including cart). PGA-certified instruction is available, and there is a pro shop (717-533-2464) on the premises.

Parkview, another highly regarded course that has hosted its share of celebs, was also designed by Maurice McCarthy. Built in 1929, its natural hilly terrain and water-play-providing stream give this par 71 18-hole challenge some distinctive twists. Parkview also has its own pro shop (717-534-3450). Greens fees include cart rental. If you live within a 50-mile radius of

Parkview, weekday greens fees are $29.00 before 3:00 P.M., $22.50 after 3:00 P.M. on weekdays. Players from outside the 50-mile radius pay $50. On weekends, everyone pays $41.50 before 2:00 P.M., $25.50 after.

Nine-hole, par 33 Spring Creek Golf Course (450 East Chocolate Avenue, Hershey; 717-533-2847) features a skill-honing water challenge. Weekday greens fees are $13.00 to walk, $21.50 with cart rental; on weekends $13.00 to walk, $24.50 with cart.

Lancaster

Lancaster Host Resort
2300 Lincoln Highway East (Route 30)
(800) 233-0121, (717) 299-5500
www.lancasterhost.com
Although the resort is situated right on one of Lancaster's busiest traffic arteries, the view from this 18-hole, par 71 championship golf course, surrounded by three working Amish farms, is purely rural. Gentle terrain allows for easy walking, water from several on-course lakes for challenging play. Refreshments are available at Mulligan's on the tenth green.

Many of the game's most illustrious names, including Arnold Palmer, Jack Nicklaus, and Sam Snead, have taken on this challenge over the course's more than four-decade history. It has also been the site of the Philadelphia PGA and numerous other PGA events. There's plenty of room—enough for up to 20 golfers—on the driving range's practice facility. You don't even have to quit when the sun goes down; there's a night-lit putting green. Private and group instruction, video analysis with golf lesson, and junior golf clinics are available. The resort also offers all-inclusive golf-and-stay packages. Greens fees vary; call for specifics.

Overlook Golf Course
2040 Lititz Pike (Route 501)
(717) 290-7180
www.overlookgolfcourse.com

Like Augusta National Golf Course, The Links at Gettysburg has its own "Amen Corner," beginning at the 13th hole with its large lake on the left, river to the right, and undulating green surface. A river runs through—or, more precisely to the left of—the entire 14th hole; greenside bunkers on the right require precision play. To reach the green on hole 15, you have to avoid a large trap with water running down the left side of the hole and trees to the right.

Not a particularly difficult course (look out for the pond between the tee and the green on hole five), but a lovely one with well-manicured greens and narrow fairways. The course has a pro shop (717–569–9551). On weekdays, greens fees are $21 ($34 with cart rental); after 1:00 P.M. $16 ($29 with cart), senior (60+) and junior (17 and under) $17 ($25); twilight (after 6:00 P.M.) $11 ($20). Call for nine-hole rates. Weekend greens fees are $26 ($39 with cart), senior $23 ($31), and junior $17 ($30) after noon. After 3:00 P.M. fees are $19 ($32 with cart rental). Professional instruction is available for adults and juniors.

Willow Valley Resort
2416 Willow Street Pike
(800) 444–1714
www.willowvalley.com
If you're up for a round but limited on time, you can play this nine-hole, par 33 public course in two hours or less. Left your clubs at home? No problem; you can rent a set for $9.00 and a pull cart to transport them for an additional $3.00 (power cart rental is $7.00 per person). Greens fees Monday through Friday are $11, weekends and holidays $13. On weekends, seniors can play for $9.00. After 6:00 P.M., the twilight rate of $6.00 kicks in.

Manheim

Tree Top Golf Course
1624 Creek Road
(717) 665–6262
www.treetopgolf.com
Play 18 holes (par 65) by day any time of year and on selected nights June through October. Built in 1974, this family-owned and -operated public course is set in the quiet of the countryside. Ride and pull carts are available and the course has a pro shop (717–665–2420) and snack shop. Greens fees are $13 weekdays, $17 weekend walking and $23 weekdays, $27 weekend riding. After 1:00 P.M. fees are $11.00

walking, $14.50 riding weekdays; $19.50 walking, $23.00 riding weekends. Call for nine-hole rates.

Millersville

Crossgates Golf Club
1 Crossland Pass
(717) 872–4500
www.crossgatesgolf.com
None of your clubs will feel neglected on this challenging 18-hole, par 72 public course located a few minutes from downtown Lancaster. The Conestoga River and gentle hills add to the serenity of the surroundings. For practice, Crossgates also has a driving range and putting greens. A pro shop, private or group lessons, and Celi's Clubhouse (717–872–2628), an open-to-the-public family restaurant and lounge, round out the amenities at this facility. Pull and power carts are available. Weekday greens fees are $25.00 ($39.90 with power cart) until 1:00 P.M. On weekends and holidays greens fees are $29.50 ($43.50 with cart) until 1:00 P.M. Crossgates offers special "Matinee" (after 2:00 P.M.) and "Twilight" (after 4:00 P.M.) deals on greens fees on both weekdays and weekends. Monday through Friday, there's also an "Early Bird" (6:30 to 7:52 A.M.) special that includes cart rental, and discounted rates for seniors, ladies, and juniors on selected days. Call or visit the club's Web site for nine-hole game rates.

Mount Joy

Groff's Farm Golf Club
650 Pinkerton Road
(717) 653–2048, ext. 2
www.groffsfarmgolfclub.com
Designed in the traditional Scottish links style, this scenic 18-hole, par 71 championship course follows the unique contours of this former farm terrain, with rolling hills, quick greens, open fairways, and distinctive holes that can be played from

numerous tees to challenge golfers of all levels. Because it's tucked away in the rural area of Mount Joy, Groff's can be a little tricky to find, but the streets are well marked. From Lancaster, take Route 283 West to Route 230 West (Main Street), turn left onto Marietta Avenue, and then left onto Pinkerton Road; the golf course is 1 mile ahead on the left.

Groff's also has a driving range (open seven days) with 50 individual hitting areas and a putting green for short-game sharpening. Individual or group lessons, clinics, rules interpretations, and club fittings are offered by professionals from both the PGA and LPGA. EZ Go golf carts and men's and ladies' locker rooms and showers are available, and there is a pro shop on the premises.

If you want to take a break and watch your favorite sport on TV, the on-premise Gimmie's Sports Bar has several you can view while you're munching on "secret-sauced" wings, nachos, crab dip, big burgers, or other sandwiches. The fully stocked bar offers on-tap beverages and Gimmie's hosts karaoke, live acoustic music, and DJs in the evenings.

Weekday greens fees for 18 holes are $21 walking, $31 with cart; $24 (including cart) for seniors 60+; and $15 for juniors (under 18) walking. To ride in a cart, young golfers must be accompanied by an adult. Weekend fees are $27 walking, $40 riding; $21 walking, $34 riding after 1:00 P.M. Twilight fees (after 4:00 P.M.) all seven days are $14 walk, $22 to ride.

Quarryville

Tanglewood Manor Golf Club
653 Scotland Road
(800) 942-2444, ext. 715,
(717) 786-2500, ext. 1
www.twgolf.com
Fairways lined with mature trees, stone bridges, water views (and hazards), elevated tees, and fast greens make this 18-hole, par 72 course located in southern Lancaster County a favorite of golf-loving locals and tourists. PGA professionals are on hand for lessons and a fully stocked pro shop for equipment and supplies. You can book your tee times up to two weeks in advance.

At the Golf Learning Center (717-786-2500, ext. 2) 50 lighted tee stations (many are covered for rain or shine use), target, putting, and chipping greens, and a practice bunker give you lots of practice and skill-sharpening opportunities. The Gallery Grille (717-786-2500, ext. 3) will keep you fueled up for play with extensive breakfast, lunch, and dinner offerings.

Greens fees are $40 (including cart) weekdays before 2:00 P.M., $26 after 2:00 P.M. On weekends and holidays before 2:00 P.M., fees are $50 (including cart), $36 after 2:00 P.M. Seniors and juniors play for $26 Monday through Friday. Ask about off-season and twilight discounts.

PARKS

Lancaster County Parks and Recreation operates six regional parks and two recreational trails, a total of a little more than 2,000 acres, all of which are open to non-residents.

Lancaster City

Lancaster County Central Park
Chesapeake Street
Named for its central location on the southern edge of Lancaster City, this 544-acre park is the largest of the county's parks. (From the city, take Duke Street south until you come to Chesapeake Street. Take a right onto Chesapeake Street; go 0.2 mile and turn left into the park.) You could spend an entire day—or even more—here, visiting the Garden of the Five Senses, the public skate park and the swimming pool.

Garden of the Five Senses

Perched on a hill overlooking the Conestoga River, with woods on the south side and grass expanses on the north, the Garden of the Five Senses is a flower-filled oasis that offers a relaxing place to sit, stroll, or play year-round. How keen is your sense of smell? Find out by taking a sniff of the "mystery scents" at various points along the garden's paved walkway. Listen to the musical sounds of the waterfall, fountain, and stream. Interpretive signs in English and in Braille offer insights as to the workings of the five senses in both humans and animals. Strollers and wheelchairs are welcome.

Skate Park

Open from sunrise to sunset year-round, this park has a variety of skating terrain and challenging features, including a nearly 200-foot-long snake run; three bowls ranging from 4- to 10-feet deep; and a 16-foot-wide, 25-foot-long full pipe, the only one of its kind in the United States.

Swimming Pool
1050 Rockford Road
(717) 299-8215

From the shallow wading area to the 6-foot deep end, this 15,255-square-foot pool is a great place to cool off on hot summer days. A tubular slide and numerous fountains are splashy additions. There's plenty of room around the pool for sunbathing and there's a basketball court and playground for working up a sweat. Refreshments are available at a concession stand in the complex. Open every day from early June through late August (11:30 A.M. to 7:00 P.M. Monday through Saturday; 12:30 to 7:00 P.M. on Sunday). It is also open on selected pre-season weekends in May and June and in September post-season. Daily admission rates are $5.00 for adults, $4.00 for youths ages 4 through 17, free for children under 4 years. From 4:00 P.M. to closing, admission is $3.00.

Park in the lot right off of Eshelman Mill Road, south of the Lancaster County Central Park skate park. Wheelchair access is available from this lot. Another small lot on Davis Drive also offers parking for those in wheelchairs. ℹ️

Other Lancaster County Parks

BETWEEN COLUMBIA AND MARIETTA

Chickies Rock Park
(717) 299-8215, (717) 299-8220

Derived from the Native American word *Chiquesalunga*, which means "place of the crayfish," Chickies Rock Park is located between the boroughs of Columbia and Marietta. From Lancaster take Route 30 West 10 miles to the Columbia/Route 441 exit; turn right at the end of the exit onto Route 441 North. Go 1 mile to the parking area on the left. A walking trail to the overlook begins here.

Lancaster County's second largest regional park spans more than 422 acres and offers a multitude of recreational amenities, including volleyball courts; playgrounds; hiking, horseback riding, cross-country skiing, and mountain biking trails; sledding slopes; a boat launch; stream fishing areas (Donegal Creek is managed as a fly-fishing-only area for trout); and picnic areas. Access to Donegal Creek and Chiques Creek are available from the east side of Route 441. Rising 200 feet above

Lancaster County Central Park was once home to the Susquehannock tribe of Native Americans. There is a Susquehannock burial site in the park along Golf Road that is marked with a plaque. Some tribal artifacts are also on display in the park's Environmental Center. ℹ️

the Susquehanna River is the park's namesake Chickies Rock, a quartzite cliff with views that make the hike up well worthwhile. Throughout the park, you'll also see the remnants of several historic iron furnaces, canal walls, and a local trolley line.

EASTERN LANCASTER COUNTY

Money Rocks Park

If you've never gotten an up-close-and-personal glimpse of Pennsylvania's state wildflower and bird (the mountain laurel and ruffled grouse, respectively), here's your chance. Located in eastern Lancaster County, this more than 300-acre woodland park is set in a former mining and logging area in the Welsh Mountains (home of the second most continuous forest remaining in Lancaster County). The name, Money Rocks, comes from the legend that farmers in the Pequea Valley once hid cash among the rocky boulders that are a major physical feature of the park. The rocky ridge overlooks some beautiful scenery. In winter, take in the view from Cockscomb, another outcropping of rocks a little farther along the ridge. Money Rocks Park offers excellent hiking, cross-country skiing, sledding, rock climbing, mountain biking, and horse trails. From New Holland, take Route 23 East to Route 322 East. Turn right and follow Route 322 East for 4 miles to Narvon Road. Take a right onto Narvon Road and follow for 1 mile. The parking lot is on the right, across from Alexander Drive.

To fish in Pennsylvania, all individuals age 16 and over need a current state fishing license signed in ink and displayed on a hat or outer garment. Licenses are not needed on Fish for Free days. Visit the Pennsylvania Fish and Boat Commission Web site (www.fish.state.pa.us) or call (717) 705-7800 for more information.

NEAR LITITZ

Speedwell Forge Park

Located just north of Lititz, this 415-acre park is not developed for recreation, except for a hiking trail and small parking area (along Speedwell Forge Road and Oak Lane). It does offer a wonderland of wildlife, thriving in a range of habitats from wooded wetland to an undisturbed meadow along the Hammer Creek. From mid-April until late-May, the flowers are in riotous bloom, including colorful showy orchids, nodding trillium, perfoliate bellwort, and other unusual species. From Lititz, follow Route 501 North 5 miles to Brickerville. Turn left on to Route 322 West for 200 yards and turn left onto Long Lane. Follow Long Lane for 1½ miles. When the road ends, turn left onto Speedwell Forge Road. Follow ½ mile; cross a small bridge and turn right into the parking lot.

SOUTHEASTERN LANCASTER COUNTY

Theodore A. Parker III Natural Area

Named after a renowned local ornithologist, this virtually undisturbed 90 acres in a quiet valley in southeastern Lancaster County features a hiking trail that runs parallel to a burbling stream. In addition to the wild flora, there is also an abundance of animal life to observe, including deer, raccoon, opossum, and a variety of birds. The waters teem with brown and brook trout and fishing is permitted during authorized seasons. From Quarryville follow Route 222 South for 3 miles. Go past Solanco High School and turn left onto Blackburn Road. Follow Blackburn Road 3 miles and turn left onto Wesley Road. Follow Wesley Road across a small bridge and turn left into the parking area.

WEST LAMPETER TOWNSHIP

D. F. Buchmiller Park

Known for its expansive open lawn areas and arboretum-type plantings, this 79-acre park in West Lampeter Township has six tennis courts, a playground, a ballfield, and a disc golf course. From Lancaster, take Prince Street (Route 222/272) south, cross the Conestoga River and continue 1 mile. The park entrance is just past the tennis courts on the right.

Other Public Parks

ELIZABETHTOWN

Elizabethtown Community Park
600 South Hanover Street
(717) 367–1700
A lovely local favorite, Community Park features basketball courts, an amphitheater, a baseball field, a children's "fun fort," and other playground equipment.

LANCASTER

Long's Park
Intersection of Harrisburg Pike
and the Route 30 Bypass
(717) 295–7054
www.longspark.org
Situated just northwest of Lancaster City, this 71-acre park has a three-acre spring-fed lake, petting zoo, children's playgrounds, tennis courts, a fitness trail, and a snack bar. In addition to providing a recreational environment for locals and visitors, Long's Park also hosts a number of special events, including a free summer-long entertainment series and a major arts and crafts festival.

STATE PARKS AND PRESERVES

Lancaster County Parks and Recreation
Rail-Trails
(717) 299–8215
Once a major railroading hub, Lancaster County has reclaimed a number of former rail line sites and adapted them for public recreation. One example is the 5-mile Conewago Recreation Trail, which follows Conewago Creek between Route 230 and the Lebanon County line, northwest of Elizabethtown. Lancaster Junction Recre-

ation Trail was reclaimed from a little more than 2-mile stretch along the former Reading-Columbia rail line between the hamlet of Lancaster Junction and Route 283. (From Lancaster, follow Route 283 West for 7 miles and get off at the Spooky Nook Road exit. Turn right onto Spooky Nook Road and right again onto Champ Road. Follow Champ Road for about ½ mile to the trail entrance at the road's end.) The northern half of this trail borders Chickies Creek. Both the Conewago Recreation Trail and Lancaster Junction Trail pass through some of the county's most scenic farm- and woodlands. Both also have well-graded, level surfaces that are excellent for hiking, jogging, horseback riding, and cross-country skiing.

Middle Creek Wildlife Management Area
P.O. Box 110
Kleinfeltersville, PA 17039
(717) 733–1512
www.pgc.state.pa.us
Considered by many naturalists to be one of the best places for bird-watchers, photographers, and hikers, this 5,000-acre area, owned by the Pennsylvania Game Commission, has a 400-acre shallow water lake that provides prime nesting space for Canada geese (a large flock remains in the area year-round). In November and again from late February through late March, large flocks of tundra swans migrate through this area as well.

Middle Creek has about 9 miles of developed trails for walking (hiking trails are open year-round, dawn to dusk), or you may prefer to take a self-guided driving tour (March through mid-September). Stop in at the visitor center for informa-

To catch the creatures of the Middle Creek Wildlife Management Area at their most active, come just after dawn or around dusk. To avoid disturbing the wildlife, remember to stay on the roads and developed trails or in your car.

tion and to check out the "please touch" wildlife and environmental displays. Throughout the year, various family-oriented educational programs are available for free. The visitor center is open from March 1 to November 30 from 8:00 A.M. to 4:00 P.M. Tuesday through Saturday, and from noon to 5:00 P.M. on Sunday.

Fishing (including shoreline and ice fishing) is permitted in specified areas, as are hunting and trapping during legally prescribed seasons. Boats propelled by paddles and oars are allowed from mid-May through mid-September. Four picnic areas offer tables, toilets, and drinking water.

To get to Middle Creek, take I–76 West to exit 21. Take Route 272 (North Reading Road) north for 3 miles (pass Renningers). At the light, turn left onto Route 897. Go 14 miles to Kleinfeltersville. Take the first left after the stop sign and go 2 miles to visitor center entrance.

Shenk's Ferry Wildflower Preserve
Holtwood Environmental Preserve Office
9 New Village Road, Holtwood
(800) 354–8383
www.pplprojectearth.com

More than 73 species of spring wildflowers are in bloom in this 50-acre wooded glen from mid-March until the end of May. The Virginia bluebells are particularly breathtaking in April. From Lancaster, take new Danville Pike to Conestoga, veer left onto River Corner Road at the post office. After 1.3 miles you will come to River Road. Go straight across River Road to Shenk's Ferry Road. Turn left at Green Hill Road. Follow this road through the tunnel and bear left 200 feet past the tunnel. The trailhead is located next to Grubb Run.

At the Shenk's Ferry Web site, you'll find a listing of the flowers and the specific month each one blooms.

Susquehannock State Park
1880 Park Drive, Drumore
(717) 432–5011

Situated on a wooded plateau above the Susquehanna River, this 224-acre park features 380-foot-high cliffs that offer panoramic views. Most dramatic is the view from Hawk Point Overlook, from where you can see numerous islands, including Mt. Johnson Island (to the left of the overlook), the world's first bald eagle sanctuary. There's an optical viewer for eagle-, hawk-, osprey-, and vulture-spotting. The easiest way to get to there is via the 0.55-mile Overlook Trail.

Five miles of hiking trails offer natural wonders that change with the seasons, such as Virginia bluebells in late April and early May, massive blooms of rhododendron in late June and early July, and riots of various summer wildflowers, native holly, and paw paw trees. Shaded picnic areas are available throughout the park.

Before embarking on your hike, stop at the park office and pick up a copy of *A Field Guide to the Natural History of Susquehannock State Park*. The park office is not always open, so your best bet is to send for a copy of the guide in advance. There is no charge.

Tucquan Glen Nature Preserve

The Lancaster County Conservancy (717–392–7891, www.lancasterconservancy.org) protects more than 2,900 acres of land for ecosystem preservation and public recreation. Without a doubt, the best known and most impressive is the 336-acre Tucquan Glen Nature Preserve in Marctic Township. From Lancaster City, take PA Route 272 South (Willow Street Pike/Lancaster Pike), toward Willow Street. Continue south on PA Route 272 to Smithville. Turn right on Pensy Road (just past Frey's Evergreen Plantation on the left and before the large stone arch railroad bridge over the highway). Follow Pensy Road for approximately 4 miles, then at Martic Forge turn left onto River Road. Follow River Road for approximately 3 miles. There are three well marked parking areas; the first two are on the left and the third is on the right a short distance after the second lot. The main parking lot is on River Road.

Preserving nature's beauty is a priority in Lancaster County. PENNSYLVANIA DUTCH CONVENTION & VISITORS BUREAU

Virtually unspoiled, this area features a more than 2-mile trail of moderate difficulty and maximum visual reward in the form of expansive blooms of rhododendron in early summer, a forest canopy with 40 species of trees, some reaching heights of 80 feet or more, sparkling waterfalls, and an array of wildlife. The Tucquan Creek and its tributary Clark Run are so clean and clear that they are listed as Pennsylvania Wild and Scenic Rivers. A rhododendron and hemlock canopied trail follows Tucquan Creek from River Road to the Susquehanna River.

SPECTATOR SPORTS

Buck Motorsports Park
900 Lancaster Pike, Quarryville
(10 miles south of Lancaster on Route 272)
(800) 344-7855, (717) 859-4244; track (day of event only) (717) 284-2139
www.buckmotorsports.com

For more than 30 years, "the Buck" has been offering weekend motorsports excitement in Lancaster County. From the

If the kids need to let off a little steam before a Barnstormers' game or between innings, there's a play area at Clipper Magazine Stadium complete with inflatables, a rock-climbing wall, and other fun stuff located down the third base line.

May season-opener to the early October finale, there's something for every fan, from stock cars to hot rods to big rigs. On the schedule are plenty of truck and tractor pulls and demolition derbies for those who like their action non-stop. Pit area visits (for autographs and photo ops) are welcome. Admission varies with events, but generally ranges from about $12.00 to $15.00 for adults, $6.00 to $8.00 for children ages 5 through 12, and free for children under 5. Events start at 7:00 P.M., gates open at 5:00 P.M. Parking and camping on the grounds are both free.

Hershey Bears Hockey Club
Giant Center
950 West Hersheypark Drive
Hershey box office (717) 534–3911;
team office (717) 534–3380
www.hersheypa.com
Originally named the "Hershey B'ars," this team joined the American Hockey League (AHL) in 1938 and have won the coveted Calder Cup multiple times. During their regular season, which runs from October through April, tickets for seats at the 100 level cost $21; $15 at the 200 level.

Parking is free at the Clipper Magazine Stadium Lot (access via Clay Street, off of Prince Street). But even if this lot is full, you can also park free at Armstrong/Liberty (both are best accessed via Clay or Liberty Streets off of Prince Street; a pedestrian walkway connects these lots to the stadium lot) and at the Lancaster General Hospital Parking Garage (in the employee parking garage between North Queen and Duke Streets, accessed by entering on North Queen Street, across from the YMCA).

Lancaster Barnstormers
Clipper Magazine Stadium
650 North Prince Street, Lancaster
(717) 509–HITS
www.lancasterbarnstormers.com
This new professional minor league (Atlantic League) baseball team played its first game in May 2005. The $23 million Clipper Magazine Stadium, which can accommodate 6,500 fans, is new, too. Regular season (70 home games, 70 away) goes from April through September. Adult tickets are $5.00, reserved field box seats are $7.50; and reserved dugout box seats (limited availability), $9.00. General admission for children under 5 or those ages 12 and under who come in sports uniforms is free (a complimentary ticket must still be obtained through the ticket office prior to admission to the stadium). Students (ages 5 to 12) and seniors (65+) are eligible for discounted $3.00 admission. Limited numbers of lawn seats are available for purchase on the day of game at the ticket office beginning at 4:00 P.M. for evening games and 9:00 A.M. for afternoon games. Call in advance for wheelchair seating accommodations. Stadium gates open an hour prior to game time Monday through Thursday and an hour and a half prior to first pitch on weekends.

WATER SPORTS AND RECREATION

Shank's Mare Outfitters
2092 Long Level Road, Wrightsville
(877) 554–5080, (717) 252–1616
www.shanksmare.com
Rent a kayak (single models are $20 for up to two hours, $27 for two to four hours; doubles for $23 up to two hours, $27 for two to four hours) and take a leisurely paddle down the scenic Susque-

hanna River. Sit-on-top kayaks are also available for novices. Classes for every level from sit-on-top kayak beginner to more advanced cockpit kayak lessons are available. Some of Shank's Mare Outfitters' classes and adventures require preregistration and prepayment. Check the Web site for details.

Shank's Mare also offers a schedule of adventures (equipment rental is additional and fees vary according to activity). The annual schedule may include a Parent & Kids Rendezvous, Sunday Brunch Rendezvous, Full Moon Paddle Night, Sunrise

If you want to paddle the Susquehanna River Trail on your own schedule—and in your own canoe or kayak—you can purchase a waterproof map for $15 at the PA Dutch Country Visitors Center, 501 Greenfield Road (off of Route 30); Lancaster, PA 17601. Call (800) PA-DUTCH or (717) 299-8901 or visit www.padutch country.com for more information.

Paddle Rendezvous, and Fall Foliage Paddle Night Rendezvous.

ANNUAL EVENTS

Pennsylvania Dutch Country is all about tradition, so it's no surprise that numerous annual events held here have their roots in decades, generations, and even centuries past. This is just a sampling of don't miss celebrations and commemorations that keep the history and spirit of this area so fresh and alive. Many more are highlighted in other chapters of this book.

JANUARY

Annual Sauerkraut Dinner
Upper Leacock Township War Memorial
50 West Main Street (Route 23), Leola
(717) 656-9881
www.uppleacockfire.com
Throughout the year, many of the volunteer fire companies in Pennsylvania Dutch Country's towns and villages raise funds to support their operations with community breakfasts. Some have chicken dinners (or variations such as chicken and waffles, chicken potpie or chicken corn soup) and ox or pig roasts. Pork and sauerkraut is a special New Years Day "good luck" tradition. Call for prices.

FEBRUARY

Mud Sale Season Kick-off
Strasburg Fire Company
46 Main Street, Strasburg
(717) 687-7232
Strasburg Fire Company launches the mud sale season every year on the last Saturday of February with an all-day whirlwind of auctions and sales of everything from livestock to quilts, farm equipment to home furnishings (many made by local crafters), and lots and lots of homemade Pennsylvania Dutch foods. Mud sales, named for the sometimes messy outdoor settings that result from the late

winter, early spring thaws, are major fundraisers for the area's volunteer fire companies and attract many local buyers and sellers. The sales continue at various firehouses every month through late September. Admission is free.

Open Hearth Cooking
Landis Valley Museum
2451 Kissel Hill Road, Lancaster
(717) 569-0401
www.landisvalleymuseum.org
Kids really warm up to interactive activities, especially ones that taste good. This cooking lesson is designed for children ages 8 to 16. Space is limited to 10 participants, so sign up early. Cost is $20 per person.

MARCH

Charter Day
Pennsylvania Dutch Country
Welcome Center
500 Greenfield Road at Route 30,
Lancaster
(800) 723-8824, (717) 299-8901
www.padutch.com
Various state museums such as the Landis Valley Museum, Ephrata Cloister, and Railroad Museum of Pennsylvania offer free admission to the public on different days throughout the month of March. Check out the Web site or call to find specific days.

APRIL

History Meets the Arts
Gettysburg/Adams County Area
Chamber of Commerce
18 Carlisle Street, Gettysburg
(717) 334-8151
www.gettysburg-chamber.org
More than 75 nationally renowned artists,

sculptors, and artisans representing all periods of American history, including the Colonial era, the French and Indian War, the American Revolution, the American Civil War, the American West, and World Wars I and II, appear at participating galleries and other places of business throughout Gettysburg for this three-day event. Various genres such as aviation, wildlife, Native American, and Harley-Davidson art are also highlighted.

19th-Century Artisans' Fair
Rupp House History Center
451 Baltimore Street, Gettysburg
(717) 334-0772, (717) 334-7292
www.friendsofgettysburg.org
A part of the annual Gettysburg History Meets the Arts celebration, this event gives you an opportunity to practice Victorian dancing; learn about basket and fabric weaving and quilt making, and take home 19th-century recipes. Free admission.

MAY

Herb and Garden Faire
Landis Valley Museum
2451 Kissel Hill Road, Lancaster
(717) 569-0401
www.landisvalleymuseum.org
If you're interested in heirloom plants, this is one of the East Coast's largest sale of hard-to-find varieties of herbs, vegetables, and ornamentals. More than 90 vendors also offer garden equipment and outdoor arts and crafts during the two-day event. Museum admission is required: $9.00 for

adults, $7.00 for seniors, $6.00 for children ages 6 to 17, under 6 free.

Sertoma Chicken Barbecue
Long's Park, Harrisburg Pike (Route 30, across from Park City Mall), Lancaster
(717) 295-7054
www.lancastersertomabbq.com
Listed in the *Guinness Book of World Records* as the largest one-day chicken barbecue, this event is always held on the third Saturday of May. Every year since 1953, the Sertoma Club of Lancaster cooks and sells an average of more than 30,000 complete chicken dinners (they hit the million mark in 2003) on barbecue pits set up in Long's Park. Eat in the park, where there is also live music and other entertainment, or pick up dinner-to-go in one of the drive-through lines.

Pay in advance $7.00 per dinner or $8.00 the day of the event (10:00 A.M. to 6:00 P.M.). Profits go to the upkeep and improvement of Long's Park and to support community activities that assist speech- and hearing-impaired children.

JUNE

Intercourse Heritage Days
Intercourse Community Park
Route 340, Intercourse
(717) 768-8585
www.intercourseheritagedays.com
Who knew a small town could offer such big fun? Activities during the course of the three-day event include an old-time spelling bee (for young and veteran spellers); a volleyball tournament featuring

Since the 1980s, Landis Valley Museum's Heirloom Seed Project has focused on preserving seeds from plants that had historical significance for Pennsylvania Germans from 1750 to 1940. "Unlike hybrid plants, gardeners can save seeds from heirloom varieties with the assurance that the fruit from each new generation of plants will bear fruit that is similar to the fruit from the past seasons," according to the project's Web site.

local teams; kid stuff, such as wagon rides, inflatable jumper, petting zoo, and playground; and games from yesterday, including horseshoes and quoits. Come for the pancake and sausage breakfast in the park (prepared by the Intercourse Fire Department), and stay for the evening Taste of Intercourse Food Showcase, featuring local heritage displays, an antique car show, Pennsylvania Dutch Food Showcase, the Covered Dish Social (everyone brings a favorite prepared dish to share), and the Ice Cream Social. Visit the Heritage Displays, where artisans are at work creating quilts, wood carvings, candle dipping, and homemade ice cream. Take a self-guided Heritage Bike Tour of the village's historic sites (free map is available), or just admire the display of four-wheeled wonders at the Classic Car Show. There's also live musical entertainment and a grand fireworks display. Free admission.

Pedal to Preserve
Lancaster Farmland Trust
128 East Marion Street, Lancaster
(717) 293-0707
www.savelancasterfarms.org
Put your mettle to the pedal and support Lancaster County farmland preservation efforts. This Lancaster Farmland Trust

Register fund-raiser offers three riding events covering 6, 20, or 50 miles. Collect pledges if you wish, but it's not a prerequisite for participation. All riders must wear helmets and closed-toe shoes for safety purposes. Cost is $20 for preregistration (includes a "Pedal to Preserve" T-shirt), $30 day of event. Children ages 12 and under are free.

JULY

Fourth of July Celebration
in Lititz Springs Park
Center of Lititz, 7 miles north of
Lancaster on Route 501, Lititz
(717) 626–8981
www.shoplititz.com
For close to 190 years, the village of Lititz has commemorated Independence Day in grand style. The celebration really begins the Saturday prior to July 4 with a 6:30 P.M. grand parade through the streets followed by free live entertainment at the park's band shell. That Sunday beginning at 2:00 P.M., a free Family Day in Lititz Park offers fun and games, including duck races, bingo, a pie-eating contest, candy scramble, cake walk, and live entertainment. On July 4, Lititz Park is the scene of more merriment with festivities that include a baby parade, illumination of 7,000 candles along Lititz Springs Creek, a Queen of Candles pageant, all kinds of live entertainment, and a high-tech fireworks display. Advance tickets for the July 4 day of activities are $8.00 for adults and $4.00 for children ages 2 to 10; children under 2 years are free. Adult tickets are $10 at the gate. (Bring lawn chairs and blankets for viewing the fireworks show and other entertainment.)

Garden Ganza
Maytown Historical Society
4 West High Street, Maytown
(717) 426–1526
Tiny Maytown, in the northwest corner of Lancaster County, has many hidden surprises. You can find them during the gar-

CLOSE-UP

Annual Celtic Fling & Highland Games

Mount Hope Estate & Winery
Route 72 and Pennsylvania Turnpike exit
20, Manheim
(717) 665–7021
www.parenfaire.com

Hundreds of traditional musicians, dancers, crafters, Scottish clans, Irish societies, and athletes from all over North America and Europe celebrate Celtic traditions and heritage during this two-day event. Among the featured attractions are athletic competitions, with both men and women vying in such "heavy" events categories as the tossing of the caber (an 18-foot tree trunk weighing up to 150 pounds); "weight for distance" throwing of a 28- or 56-pound ball on a chain; "hammer throw" (16- and 22-pound lead hammers); and the clachneart, or "stone of strength" (like today's shot put, but with stones weighing 20 pounds or more). These games are sanctioned by the Mid-Atlantic Scottish Athletics Association.

There's also a fencing tournament for épée (dueling sword) wielders in a range of age groups and a number of sanctioned dance contests, include the Celtic Fling Feis (pronounced "fesh"), featuring 800 children and young adults competing in jigs, reels, and other categories, and the Scottish Highland Dancing Competition.

Watch demonstrations by bagpipers, sheep-herding border collies, and crafters such as weavers, spinners, and glassblowers. Shop for imported and handmade Celtic merchandise and crafts in more than 150 shops and tents (if you don't have a kilt, here's the place to get one). Taste Scottish, Irish, and Welsh specialties such as scones, briodies, pastries, soda bread, shepherd's pie, pasties (meat pies), and cockaleekie soup, as well as free samplings of Scotch and Irish whiskey.

The festival culminates in a traditional Ceilidh (pronounced "KAY-lee"), a grand finale of music and dance.

The Celtic Fling & Highland Games are held on a Saturday and Sunday in late June, from 11:00 A.M. until 7:30 P.M. Admission to the festival is $21.95 for adults and $8.95 for children ages 5 to 11. Two-day admission at the front gate is $35 for adults and $15 for children ages 5 to 11. Located in northern Lancaster County on the grounds of the Pennsylvania Renaissance Faire, the Fling is on Route 72, ½ mile south of Pennsylvania Turnpike exit 266, 14 miles east of Hershey, and 15 miles north of Lancaster. Advance discount tickets are available at the Web site's "Virtual Box Office."

den tour sponsored by the town's historical society. Tucked away behind buildings ranging from early log structures to 19th-century homes made from locally produced bricks are some of the most picturesque backyards, gardens, and

ponds you can imagine. Tours are held rain or shine and cost $6.00 in advance, $8.00 on event day. While you're in Maytown, check out the art, craft, and garden show in the historic center square. (Admission to the show is free.)

Gettysburg Civil War Battle Reenactment
The Gettysburg Anniversary Committee
P.O. Box 3482
Gettysburg, PA 17325
(717) 338-1525
www.gettysburgreenactment.com

Authentically costumed reenactors take you back to the three days that changed the course of the Civil War. All events are held at the Reenactment Site on Table Rock Road in Gettysburg (from downtown, take Business 15 North—Carlisle Street—to Boyd's School Road; make a left and then a right on Table Rock Road to the parking area).

Demonstrations include medical and veterinary techniques and equipment, daily life in the 1860s, signal corps, a Civil War wedding, fashions, music, and live mortar fire competitions. Learn about Civil War spies and the generals Meade, Longstreet, Hill, Custer, Stuart, Pickett, and others, along with their troops in action.

General admission tickets admit you to the reenactment site, all activities, and demonstrations. You may stand or bring your own lawn chair. For the best views, you might want to pay the extra for grandstand admission, which reserves space for you on the bleachers at the "50 yard line" of the battlefield. Space on the bleachers does not mean specific seats, so you will have to come early to secure a really prime viewing location. To secure a grandstand seat, you must first purchase a general admission ticket, then add an extra $8.00 per person per day.

General admission for adults is $20 for one day, $35 for two days, and $48 for all three days. For children age 6 to 12, the cost is $10, $18, and $24. There is no general admission charge for children under 6, but the $8.00 grandstand charge will be applied if you want bleacher seats. Tickets purchased at the gate will be priced higher.

Kutztown Pennsylvania German Festival
Kutztown Fairgrounds
144-205 White Oak Street
(off Route 222 North), Kutztown
(888) 674-6136
www.kutztownfestival.com

Do you want to see (and perhaps buy) Pennsylvania Dutch quilts and wallhangings? There are generally over 2,500 of them, many handcrafted by local Mennonite women, at this annual fair's sale and auction. The 24 winners of the big quilting competition will also be auctioned off on the second Saturday of the nine-day festival. Do-it-yourself quilters will find all kinds of hard-to-get supplies. Never sewed a stitch? Watch the demonstrations, then create your own square and sign it. It will be added to the Festival Quilt.

Five stages feature live continuous entertainment such as square dancing, a comedy show, and bands every day. Each year there is a reenactment of a Mennonite wedding and other scenes from daily 19th-century life. Seminars on Pennsylvania Dutch traditions, dialect, and other areas of interest are also held.

More than 200 artisans and folk artists show their skills and sell their wares. You'll find fine examples of blacksmithing, weaving, woodcarving, metalworking, paper cutting, stained glass, toys, tinning, tole painting (painted designs on surfaces such as metal), broom making, and other crafts of Pennsylvania Dutch Country's earlier eras.

For children, there are animals for petting, plus puppet shows, sing-alongs, story

These annual Gettysburg battle reenactments are extremely well attended, so if you want to get a seat with a good view, plan to arrive at least two hours before the first battles begin. To avoid the outgoing traffic, hang around after the battles to relax, shop at Sutlers' Row (authors, artists, and other vendors), and eat at one of the on-site food vendors.

times, magic, craft areas, pony rides, hay maze, the tractor-pulled "Hex Express" train fashioned from 55-gallon drums, and a 19th-century carousel.

If you've ever said you were so hungry you could eat an ox, now's the chance to prove it. A 1,200-pound ox is spit-roasted over a bed of coals and sliced for platters and sandwiches. Sample other local specialties such as shoofly pie and potpie at the all-you-can-eat family supper. You can also follow your nose to the vendors selling bread just baked in an 18th-century oven or frying up fresh batches of funnel cake. Fair hours are 9:00 A.M. to 6:00 P.M.; parking is free. Adult admission is $10.00 per day (or $18.00 for an all-week pass), $9.00 for senior citizens; children 12 and under are free.

AUGUST

Art in the Park
Musser Park, North Lime and East
Chestnut Streets (behind the Lancaster
Museum of Art), Lancaster
(717) 394-3497
www.lmapa.org
Free hands-on projects for children and their families spark creativity and an appreciation of the arts. In past years, projects have included jewelry making, sunshades, and mural painting. More than 1,000 generally participate each year. There's a Children's Art Gallery and special Toddler Tent for youngsters under the age of four. Activities go from 10:00 A.M. to 2:00 P.M.

AUGUST TO OCTOBER

Pennsylvania Renaissance Faire
Mount Hope Estate and Winery
Route 72 and Pennsylvania Turnpike,
exit 20, Manheim
(717) 665-7021, ext. 231
www.parenfaire.com
It's the Ren again . . . the Renaissance era, that is, in the 35-acre Shire, when royalty

comes out to mix with the rest of us and hundreds of costumed characters from peasants and pirates to merchants and musicians interact and entertain. The pageantry begins in early August and continues for 12 weekends (plus Labor Day Monday) through late October, with days of jesting and jousting, tournaments and troubadours, and street performers who swallow swords and fire. Check out the gigantic chess board with its human pawns and rooks and knights. At the Ren Faire, it really does seem as if all the world's a stage—actually it's 12 stages, including a three-story replica of Shakespeare's Globe Theatre and a towering four-story Royal Reviewing Pavilion. With 90 shows a day on the schedule—ranging from the bawdy to the Bard—you can't possibly catch them during a single visit. Dozens of "Olde World" artisans produce period crafts such as Elizabethan pottery, herbal potpourris, leather goods, jewelry, blown glass, and all kinds of other useful and decorative items. The "Royal Kitchens" turn out a variety of portable edibles, from hearty steak-upon-a-stick and giant turkey legs to lighter fresh fruit–filled crepes.

Purchase tickets in advance over the Web site's "Virtual Box Office," and you can get substantial savings on adult tickets—$19.95 advance, $24.95 at the gate (adults who come in period costume get a $2.00 discount); for children ages 5 to 11 advance admission is $8.00, $9.95 at the

---

For one evening a week from early August to early September, Mount Hope Mansion, home of the Pennsylvania Renaissance Faire, transforms into a comedy club for "Friday Knights at the Improv." This inside evening venue allows the Ren actors to step out of their 16th-century costumes and roles, trading épées and swords for razor-sharp wit. Shows are at 7:00 P.M. Tickets for adults (18 and over) are $20.

Look for discount coupons on Renaissance Faire food vendor fare on the event's Web site.

gate. Special Web pricing for a Two-Day Pass (valid for any two Faire Days of the season) is $36 for adults, $15 for children. A Season Pass (valid each day of the Faire plus includes a special cast picnic) for adults is $80, $35 for children. There's also a Royal Pass option ($150 adults, no children's pricing), which includes one ticket to Friday Knight at the Improv, one season pass to the Faire and two complimentary individual guest passes, a royal parking pass, and admission to the cast picnic. Rides or games are not included in any admission ticket or packages. Prices for these activities range from $1.00 to $3.00.

Gettysburg Bluegrass Festival
Granite Hill Campground
3340 Fairfield Road, Gettysburg
(717) 642-8749
www.gettysburgbluegrass.com
Many of the country's premier pickers, puckers, strummers, and singers converge in Gettysburg every year for this major outdoor event that made its debut in 1979. The Main Stage showcases 40 hours of music over the four days of the festival. On the separate Workshop Stage, skilled musicians conduct learning sessions in a more intimate setting. There's also a Gettysburg Bluegrass Academy for Kids, which offers budding young talent (kindergarten through grade 12) instruc-

All musical and workshop events at the Gettysburg Bluegrass Festival have lawn seating only, so bring your own folding chair if you want to get as close to the stage as possible. If you prefer a blanket or lounge chair, you will be required to sit near the back or sides of the seating area.

tion on all six primary bluegrass instruments. Kids must bring their own instruments. Early tuition is $35; after the early registration deadline, applicants pay $40 for any remaining spaces.

The Granite Hill Campground festival site is located 6 miles west of Gettysburg on Pennsylvania Route 116. For adults, one-day tickets are priced at $25 in advance, $30 for Thursday; $30/$35 for Friday, $38/$45 for Saturday, $20/$25 for Sunday. A four-day full festival ticket is $100 in advance, $115 at the gate; three-days is $86/$100, and two days $58/$70. Senior citizens age 65+ receive a $5.00 discount off the gate price, children ages 12 to 16 are admitted at half the gate price (available for purchase at the gate only), and children under 12 with parent get in free. Cash only is accepted at the gate. Major credit cards are welcome for advance purchases.

SEPTEMBER

Eisenhower World War II Weekend
Eisenhower National Historic Site
97 Taneytown Road, Gettysburg
(717) 338-9114
www.nps.gov/eise/home
Each year on the third weekend of September, more than 100 World War II Allied and German soldier reenactors set up a living history encampment complete with dozens of original tanks and military vehicles at the Eisenhower NHS in Gettysburg. Well-versed volunteers present programs on World War II medical services, weapons and equipment, communications, military vehicles, and the life of the common GI. They also conduct a mock Air Force bombing mission briefing, and featured guest speakers, all veterans of World War II, speak about their own experiences during wartime. Hours for the two-day event are Saturday from 9:00 A.M. to 4:30 P.M. and Sunday to 4:00 P.M. Admission to the Eisenhower National Historic Site is by shuttle bus from the National Park Service Visitor Center on Taneytown

Road. On-site parking for cars only is available in a farm field accessible off Emmitsburg Road, Business Route 15. Entrance fees are $7.00 for adults, $4.00 for children ages 13 to 16, $3.00 for children ages 6 through 12.

Ephrata Fair
Ephrata Farmers Day Association
19 South State Street, Ephrata
(717) 733-4451
www.ephratafair.org
Pennsylvania's largest street fair traces its roots all the way back to 1919, when local businessmen sponsored a celebration to honor World War I veterans. Over the years, this event generated revenues for the purchase of the town park. Bigger and better than ever (both Main and State Streets are closed for its duration to provide room for all of the booth, exhibits, rides, and vendors), the five-day fair attracts tens of thousands of locals and visitors to this tuck-away town. On the annual agenda are multiple parades (including one for babies and another for bigger kiddies), 4-H and FFA (Future Farmers of America) livestock auctions, an antique tractor pull, tug-of-war, a beauty pageant, and competitions in art, vegetable growing, needlecraft, scarecrow making, homemade wine, and, most popular of all, baking (first place winners in this contest are offered at a bake sale). A separate Tent City (accessible by shuttle bus) holds animal exhibits and is the site of the famous "pig chase." A giant midway has a host of rides and games ("All You Can Ride" special savings of $1.00 off the regular $14.00 price are available with a coupon you can get from the Ephrata Fair Office).

Long's Park Art and Craft Festival
Harrisburg Pike, across from Park City Mall, Lancaster
(717) 295-7054
www.longspark.org
Four days and more than 200 exhibitors make this juried show one of the top events of its kind in the country. Look for

Wednesday is Senior Citizens' Day at the Ephrata Fair, with entertainment in the Bingo Tent, free coffee, tea, and cookies at the Fair Office, and reduced prices on other food at participating vendors from 10:00 A.M. to 2:00 P.M. Pick up a complimentary qualifying badge at the Fair Office.

jewelry, paintings, apparel, ceramics, sculpture, and all kinds of contemporary crafts from artisans from around the world. Sample local restaurant fare and enjoy live entertainment. Advance tickets are $9.00 for a one-day pass or $12.00 for a multiday pass.

OCTOBER

Antique Car Show
Hersheypark and Giant
Center Parking Lots
100 West Hersheypark Drive, Hershey
(717) 534-1910
www.aaca.org
The Eastern Division of the Antique Automobile Club of America (AACA) National Fall Meet is held every year here for three days during the first full week in October. One of the largest antique automobile shows and flea markets in the United States, it features over 9,000 flea market spaces, over 1,000 car corral spaces, and approximately 1,500 show cars on 300 acres of parking lot and surrounding area. Junior auto aficionados (age 15 and under) display their collections of model cars, trucks, planes, boats, artwork, junior-made crafts, and other collectibles. Free admission (daytime parking is $8.00).

Bridge Bust
Veteran's Memorial Bridge, Columbia
(717) 684-5249
www.parivertowns.com/bridgebust.htm
Take a leisurely stroll across the mile-long Veteran's Memorial Bridge that spans the Susquehanna River from Columbia to

Wrightsville. Lining the bridge are more than 250 vendors of all kinds of arts, crafts, foods, and maybe even some antiques. You never know what you're going to find in terms of merchandise, but the 1-mile walk is healthy exercise and the view more than worth the $1.00 price of admission. The event begins at 8:00 A.M. and ends at 4:00 P.M.

Chocolate Walk
Various locations throughout Lititz
(717) 627-2463
www.shoplititz.com

Buy an official button and punch card ($10 in advance, $15 day of event) at the Lititz Welcome Center/Train Station or other participating location and feel free to partake of the sweet sensations dreamed up by candy makers and pastry chefs at more than 20 tasting sites throughout Lititz (the aromas emanating from the Wilbur Chocolate Factory in the center of Lititz only make the experience even more delicious). The chocolate begins to flow at 10:00 A.M., and the treats keep coming until 4:00 P.M. (Button sales are limited to about 1,750.) Funds raised from this event are donated to the Lititz Public Library, Schreiber Pediatric Center, and local Kiwanis-sponsored youth activities.

National Apple Harvest Festival
South Mountain Fairgrounds
(10 miles northwest of Gettysburg on Pennsylvania Route 234), Arendtsville
(717) 677-9413
www.appleharvest.com

Adams County is apple country, so, it stands to reason that the first two weekends in October should be the time to celebrate the sweet harvest. An annual event for more than four decades, this festival honors the orchards with plenty of apple products in just about every form, including pressed (into cider), sauced, candied, frittered, and made into pancakes and syrup. Hot apple butter bubbles in kettles. You can bob for apples, enter a pie-eating contest (or buy a fresh-baked pie at an auction that benefits St. Jude's Children's

Hospital), see apples turned into art, visit the orchards where they grow, and meet Johnny Appleseed himself. Since no one can live on apples alone, vendors also sell freshly made scrapple, chicken and pork barbecue, pit beef, locally made sausage, and the ever-fragrant funnel cakes. The festival goes from 8:00 A.M. to 6:00 P.M., rain or shine. General admission is $7.00, $6.00 for senior citizens, and free for kids age 12 and under. Admission includes parking and shuttle service, plus all entertainment and exhibits.

Whoopie Pie Festival
Hershey Farm Restaurant and Inn
Route 896 (1½ miles south of Route 30), Strasburg
(717) 687-8635
www.whoopiepiefestival.com,
www.hersheyfarm.com

Take two moist rounds of cake and squoosh them together with lots of fluffy white icing—that's the handheld treat called a whoopie pie. Although New England claims to be its birthplace, the whoopie has become such an integral part of the Pennsylvania Dutch Country food tradition that Hershey Farm launched this annual event in 2005 to celebrate the sweet. Bring the kids for an active agenda of races, treasure hunts, eating contests, pony and hayrides, face painting, and a taste of the world's biggest whoopie. Free admission.

NOVEMBER

Anniversary of Lincoln's Gettysburg Address and Annual Luminaria
Gettysburg National Military Park
97 Taneytown Road, Gettysburg
(717) 334-1124, ext. 422 or 431
www.nps.gov/gett

This free commemorative event begins with a wreath-laying ceremony at the Soldiers National Monument in Gettysburg National Military Park at 10:00 A.M. Remarks by a prominent keynote speaker follow, and James Getty, who has been

Poe-pourri

Tea with Poe
The Hotel Hershey Fountain Lobby
Hotel Road, Hershey
(717) 534-8800
www.hersheypa.com
Nothing could be better at chasing the chills than a bracing cup of hot tea, especially when master of the macabre Edgar Allan Poe returns from the afterlife for a special Halloween holiday reading of some of his scariest stories. Advance reservations and prepayment for this October event are required. Tickets for adults (includes full English tea) are $43; children three to eight are $23, and two and younger are free.

Edgar Allan Poe Forevermore
Mount Hope Estate and Winery
Route 72 and Pennsylvania Turnpike exit 20, Manheim
(717) 665-7021
www.parenfaire.com
Poe returns to Pennsylvania Dutch Country for his annual November haunting of the Victorian Mount Hope Mansion. Each year, he meets up with a new set of equally historic (and equally dead) cohorts, such as P. T. Barnum, Lord Byron, and Mary Shelley, to find adventure and a convenient forum for the telling of his most famous frightening fables. Friday, Saturday, and Sunday adult tickets are $18.95, midweek evening adult tickets are $14.95 (no special children's price for these performances).

portraying Abraham Lincoln here since 1978, recites the 16th president's famous address. Thousands of Civil War reenactors participate in this event.

DECEMBER

Bird-in-Hand Holiday Celebration
Events at various venues townwide
(717) 768-8266
All dressed up for the holidays, the village of Bird-in-Hand welcomes families for holiday fun every weekend in December with a variety of free events, including Christmas cookie decorating, ornament crafting, and other make-and-take projects. There

are also "Jingle Rides" (hayrides on sleigh bell–adorned tractors), caroling, and other live entertainment. All events are free.

Ephrata Cloister Lantern Tours
632 West Main Street, Ephrata
(717) 733-6600
www.ephratacloister.org
Junior high and high school students portray the residents of this unique religious community to give a glimpse of how they may have lived in the 1700s. Reservations are required for these special post-Christmas evening (6:00 to 9:00 P.M.) tours. Tickets for adults are $7.00, senior citizens $6.50, children ages 6 to 17 $5.00. Children under 6 are free.

DAY TRIPS

What do motorcycles and merlot, potato chips and paper have in common? They're all made in York County, Pennsylvania, situated about 30 minutes west of Lancaster (and the same distance east of Gettysburg). If you have an insatiable appetite to find out how your favorite products are produced, York—aka "The Factory Tour Capital of the World"—is a day-trip destination you won't want to miss. Insatiable appetites for potato chips and pretzels are also welcome, particularly in York County's second-largest town, Hanover, a munchies' manufacturing mecca that has been nicknamed "The Snack Food Capital of the World." The destination for your second day-trip option is the Brandywine Valley, tucked into the southeastern corner of Pennsylvania, a little over 60 miles from Lancaster, and named for the Brandywine River that runs through that area of Chester County. The designation "Brandywine Valley" also encompasses adjacent parts of Delaware, but for the purposes of this day trip, we will be focusing on the towns of Chadds Ford, Kennett Square, and West Chester on the Pennsylvania side.

YORK COUNTY

Named after the city in England, York, Pennsylvania, has a special place in American history. From September 30, 1777, to June 27, 1778, the Continental Congress,

---

While the Continental Congress was based in York, it proclaimed the first "national day of Thanksgiving" on Thursday, December 18, 1777, to celebrate the victory of American troops at the Battle of Saratoga, New York.

---

having sought refuge in York Town when the British occupied Philadelphia, drafted the Articles of Confederation (the nation's first constitution and the first document containing a reference to the United States of America) in the town's courthouse. During those nine months, York served as the nation's first capital.

York County had its beginnings in the early 1680s, when William Penn and his family purchased the Susquehanna River and the land "lying on the west side of said river to the setting of the sun . . . " from the area's Native American tribes, members of the Five Nations. In 1722 a tract of land around 6 miles wide and 15 miles long was named Sprigettsbury Manor (Sprigett Penn was William's grandson), and in 1729 the first authorized settlement was built on Kruetz Creek in the area now known as York County.

The town of York was laid out on the banks of Codorus Creek in 1741, with lots offered to applicants who would pay annual rents of seven shillings a year and promise to erect "a substantial dwelling of 16 feet square at least . . . within the space of one year."

Everyone knows about the Battle of Gettysburg, but York was actually the first part of Pennsylvania invaded by Confederate soldiers during the Civil War. On June 30, Confederate troops took over the town of York, planning to cross the Susquehanna River at Wrightsville into Columbia, Lancaster County, and onward to Harrisburg and Pennsylvania. Although the local militia was half-trained and fortifications were scarce, the townspeople halted the Confederate advance by setting fire to the Wrightsville–Columbia Bridge, one of the longest covered bridges in the world. (When the fire spread into the town itself, both residents and military invaders took up buckets to fight the flames.) Historians conjecture that if the Southern troops had been able to successfully cross the bridge, the Battle of Gettysburg, considered the turning point of the war, might never have been fought.

During World War II, York took the spotlight again, this time for formulating a 14-point program to achieve maximum productivity from its local resources by combining and sharing personnel, equipment, and community facilities. Dubbed the "York Plan," this program was so effective at ramping up and streamlining production of vital war materials that it was emulated by other towns throughout the nation.

Although its production capabilities still keep the county in the national spotlight, it would be totally incorrect to assume that York is all work and no play. The fact is that York County has 22 golf courses and more than 4,000 acres of county and state parks offering opportunities for skiing, hiking, biking, boating, fishing, birdwatching, and other outdoor recreation (visit www.yorkpa.org for details).

York is also home to America's oldest fair, an annual event since 1765. The York Fair still attracts about 700,000 attendees every year with its giant midway, headline country music performers, livestock and agricultural exhibits, food, and all kinds of family fun. For more information, call (717) 848-2596, or visit the Web site at www.yorkfair.com.

Factory Tours

Family Heir-Loom Weavers
775 Meadowview Drive, Red Lion
(717) 246-2431
www.familyheirloomweavers.com
A restored log house is the perfect setting for this "homespun" family-owned and -operated business. The Kline family weavers specialize in ingrain (flat, woven, and reversible) wool carpets in designs from the 1700s through the 1920s, Jacquard woven 19th-century coverlets,

placemats, and table runners, and authentic fabric for Civil War reenactors. The company's products are featured in many of the nation's historic properties and in period films including *Cold Mountain.* Artisans weave carpets using original techniques, then bind them and apply fringe or hand-seam pieces together to room size. Hour-long free tours are available Monday to Friday from 8:00 A.M. to 4:00 P.M.; call for reservations. Visitors must be at least eight years old.

It takes 1 ton of Glatfelter paper to make about 12,000 decks of playing cards.

Glatfelter
228 South Main Street, Spring Grove
(717) 225-4711
www.glatfelter.com
Founded in 1864 by Philip H. Glatfelter, this company is one of the world's leading manufacturers of specialty papers for a variety of purposes, from publishing to postage to playing cards. Free, two-hour guided tours begin in the company's wood yard and chip mill, then follow production as it transforms pulp into paper. Each year more than 25 billion stamps are produced in the United States on Glatfelter paper.

Tours are available October 1 to May 1 (high heat and humidity levels prohibit tours in summer) on Tuesday and Thursday from 9:00 A.M. to 1:00 P.M.; reservations are required. No cameras are permitted.

Harley-Davidson Vehicle Operations
1425 Eden Road, York
(877) 883-1450
www.harley-davidson.com
Free guided tours of this largest Harley-Davidson manufacturing facility are offered Monday to Friday from 9:00 A.M. to 2:00 P.M. at regular intervals on a first come, first served basis. (During the summer, from early June to mid-August, Saturday tours are also available from 10:00

Artisans still weave rugs on old-fashioned looms in York County. YORK COUNTY CONVENTION & VISITORS BUREAU

A.M. to 1:00 P.M.) This 1.5 million-square-foot manufacturing plant, which was established in 1973, employs 3,200 (about half of the company's total workforce), working round-the-clock assembling Touring and Softail models, some factory-custom motorcycles, and replacement parts. A film and exhibits at the Vaughn L. Beals Tour Center introduce you to Harley-Davidson's history and the workings of its York facility. On the factory floor, you'll visit various areas where parts

are formed, welded, machined, polished, and assembled, then move on to where the finished motorcycles are roll-tested prior to crating. (Want to find out how cool you'd feel in the saddle of a Harley? Take a seat on one of the touring models!) Visitors must wear closed-toe shoes and be ready to show a government-issued photo ID. The factory also has a gift shop with Harley-themed clothing and other merchandise.

> **i** *Visitors to the Harley-Davidson factory floor must be at least 12 years of age. Younger children are invited to play at the Kids' Rally.*

Herr's Snack Factory
20 Herr Drive (Route 272 and Herr Drive), Nottingham
(800) 63-SNACK
www.herrs.com
It's always crunch time at this factory, but that's the way they like it—and you won't

hear any complaints from visitors either. Potato chips have been a primary product here since 1946, when 21-year-old James Stauffer Herr bought a small factory that produced the crackling snack spuds for $1,750, then, two years later, moved the whole works into an empty tobacco shed on his family's farm. In 1952 Herr bought 37 acres and built a 4,500-square-foot manufacturing facility to accommodate the constantly increasing demand for his chips. Today, a 15,000-square-foot visitor center adjacent to the plant is the first stop on a one-hour tour of the Herr's factory, where 340 different snack items, including pretzels, tortilla chips, cheese curls, popcorn, crackers, nuts, pork rinds, onion rings, meat sticks, and, of course, potato chips, are made. The tour starts with a 27-minute film starring Jim Herr and his puppet pal, Chipper the Chipmunk, in the visitor center's 140-seat theater. Free tours are offered Monday to Thursday from 9:00 A.M. to noon and from 1:00 to 3:00 P.M. (Friday tours may be available from 9:00 A.M. until noon if the factory is in production.) Advance scheduling is required.

Hope Acres Fully Robotic Dairy Farm
2680 Delta Road, Brogue
(800) 293-1054
www.hopeacres.com
Look ma, no hands! One of only 10 fully robotic dairy farms in the nation, Hope Acres is a bastion of bovine-oriented technology, featuring a fully automated milking process and a "cow spa" with waterbeds and back scratchers. The 75-minute tour includes a visit to the calving barn to take a peek at the farm's littlest residents and concludes with a scoop of made-on-the-premises ice cream. Hope Acres offers tours on Tuesday, Friday, and Saturday at 10:00 A.M., noon, and 2:00 P.M.; reservations are required, and the facility is wheelchair accessible. No cameras are allowed. Adult admission is $6.00, $5.00 for seniors age 60+, and $3.00 for children age 3 to 11.

Martin's Potato Chips
5847 Lincoln Highway West
(U.S. Route 30), Thomasville
(800) 272-4477
www.martinschips.com
Harry and Fairy Martin began making potato chips in their farm home kitchen way back in 1941. It wasn't long before they were delivering their crispy cargo fresh daily to local market stands and mom-and-pop grocery stores. In 1971 the Martins sold the business to Ken and Sandy Potter (the Martins remained as employees), and distribution has since grown to more than 50 markets, including Pittsburgh, Philadelphia, New York, and Virginia. Each month, the company produces 1.5 million bags of chips in its 75,000-square-foot York County plant. The product line has expanded, too, to include popcorn.

Free, 45-minute tours are available Monday and Tuesday from July through March; reservations are required. At the conclusion of the tour, you can sample Kettle Cook'd Potato Chips fresh off the production line. The tour is wheelchair accessible. Cameras are permitted, and visitors are required to wear closed-toe shoes.

It takes 10,000 pounds of potatoes to make 2,500 pounds of potato chips.

Perrydell Farm Dairy
90 Indian Rock Dam Road, York
(717) 741-3485
Okay, so it's not technically a factory, but the "employees" on this 171-acre organic dairy farm really know how to moo-ve production along. Since 1922, three generations of the Perry family have owned and operated Perrydell, which is best known for its hormone-free milk (it's available in chocolate, strawberry, and vanilla flavors, too) and ice creams. You can stop in just about any time of day from 7:00 A.M. (11:00 A.M. on Sunday) and take a free self-guided

If you love crispy, salted snacks, make the trip for the chips at Martin's. YORK COUNTY CONVENTION & VISITORS BUREAU

tour. Depending on the time of day, you might be able to watch the cows being milked or the milk being bottled. Or maybe it will be feeding time for the calves. You're welcome to bring your camera.

Snyder's of Hanover
1350 York Street, Hanover
(800) 233-7125, ext. 8592 (tours),
(717) 632-4477
www.snydersofhanover.com
In 1909 Harry V. Warehime, nicknamed "Gramp Harry," began this company with his "Hanover Olde Tyme Pretzels" recipe. But things really geared up 14 years later when William and Helen Snyder, along

with their sons Edward and Bill, broke into the baking business and expanded into potato chips.

At Snyder's, you actually get two tours for the price of one—and even that one is free—because you'll be able to peruse both its pretzel and potato chip production lines. The one-hour guided tours are offered on Tuesday, Wednesday, and Thursday at 10:00 and 11:00 A.M. and 1:00 P.M.; reservations are required 24 hours in advance. (Some stair climbing is involved in this tour.) Everyone gets a free bag of pretzels at the conclusion of the tour. No cameras are permitted.

Utz Quality Foods
900 High Street, Hanover
(800) 367-7629, (717) 637-6644
www.utzsnacks.com

i *Snyder's uses 300,000 pounds of local flour per day to produce pretzels.*

Get a bird's-eye view of potato chip production from the glass-enclosed observation gallery above the factory floor. Utz turns out 14,000 pounds of chips per hour, and you can watch the entire 30-minute process from start to finish on this free self-guided tour (with the assistance of a push-to-talk audio program and closed-circuit TV monitors). That's a far cry from how things were in 1921, when founders Bill and Salie Utz used hand-operated equipment that made about 50 chips an hour in the summer house behind their Hanover residence (they called their product "Hanover Home Brand Potato Chips"). These days, the third generation of the Utz family is in charge of this major regional snack source (the line is distributed as far north as Maine and as far south as southern North Carolina). No reservations are required. Tours are offered Monday to Thursday from 8:00 A.M. to 4:00 P.M. (call ahead if you're thinking of coming on a Friday). Cameras are permitted on this tour.

Wolfgang Candy Company
50 East Fourth Avenue, York
(800) 248-4273, (717) 843-5536
www.wolfgangcandy.com
Founded in 1921, Wolfgang, one of the oldest family-owned and managed candy companies in the United States, manufactures millions of pounds of candies for retail and fund-raising sales for schools, clubs, and other associations. Now operated by the family's fourth generation, the company has expanded from a home-grown operation in North York to three buildings. You can watch the Wolfgang candy makers produce boxed chocolates, chocolate bars, and other confections during a free, one-hour, guided tour available Monday to Friday from 10:00 A.M. to

The Wolfgang Candy factory requires walking ¼ mile, including three flights of stairs.

2:00 P.M.; reservations are required. Cameras are permitted. Footwear must have closed toes and flat heels. All jewelry except a plain band must be removed. Wolfgang provides hair and beard nets that must be worn during the tour. Visitors must be at least six years of age.

Airville

Indian Steps Museum
205 Indian Steps Road (at junction with Route 425)
(717) 993-3392, (717) 862-3948
Ten thousand Native American artifacts found on or near the southern York County site (some dating back as early as 2000 B.C.) are embedded in patterns, some of which represent birds, animals, and reptiles, in the masonry walls of this Victorian-style building constructed in 1912 by York attorney John E. Vandersloot. The "steps" (now submerged in the Susquehanna River) were carved centuries ago in Susquehanna River rocks to make it easier for the Native Americans to fish for shad. Open mid-April through mid-October; call for hours. Donations are welcome.

Ma & Pa Railroad Heritage Village
Ma & Pa Railroad Preservation Society
699 Frosty Hill Road
(717) 927-9565
www.maandparailroad.com
It was only 45 highway miles between Baltimore and York, yet the Maryland (Ma)

You can pick up a self-guided Walking Tour of Historic Downtown York with a map indicating 34 landmark sites booklet for $1.00 at many of the area's attractions, restaurants, shops, and visitor centers. Or you can order a copy by sending a self-addressed stamped envelope and $1.00 to Main Street York, 14 West Market Street, York, PA 17401.

& Pacific (Pa) Railroad took a 77-mile roundabout route to get between the two cities when it first began chugging along in 1901. You can still ride that train, not for 77 miles, but for 5 scenic ones through Muddy Creek Valley. There you'll disembark to tour an 1890 roller mill and grain elevator and visit the re-creation of the village of Muddy Creek Forks circa 1914. Costumed interpreters, a general store from 1900, and other historical exhibits and equipment help you to make the time transition. Trains run Sunday from July through September from 1:00 to 5:00 P.M.; call for fall foliage excursion schedule. Tickets are $4.00 for adults, $2.00 for children.

City of York

Avalanche Xpress at Heritage Hills Golf Resort
2700 Mount Rose Avenue
(877) STAY–PLAY
www.avalancheexpress.com
Open from November through March, this snow tubing and boarding terrain park has activities for all ages. Eight downhill tubing runs (six "Xtreme" lanes for the experienced and two for kids and beginners) and snowboarding slopes with rails, jumps, and other features for all skill levels from beginner to intermediate are available. Hours are Monday through Thursday from 4:00 to 10:00 P.M., Friday until 11:00 P.M., Saturday from 11:00 A.M. to 11:00 P.M., and Sunday until 10:00 P.M. (during March, the park is open on weekends only). All-day admission, including tubing and boarding, is $15 Monday to Thursday, $20 Friday to Sunday. Half price after 9:00 P.M.,

---

> **i** *Parking in downtown York is available in city-operated parking garages (rates are $2.00 for one hour, $7.50 for four hours, $25.00 for 13 to 24 hours). Metered street parking is also available.*

$10 for kids under age 6. Snowboard rentals are $20. Snowboard boot rental is $5.00.

The Shoe House
197 Shoe House Road
(717) 840–8339
There's no old woman living in this shoe, a York landmark built in 1948 by local shoe entrepreneur Mahlon Haines as a promotional gimmick. Once a cozy guesthouse hideaway, this 48-foot-long, 17-foot-wide, and 25-foot-high shoe-shaped structure (its wood frame is covered with wire lath and coated with a cement stucco) is now a museum and still a real eye-catcher. (The shoe theme is carried out in the stained glass windows, doghouse, and wooden fence surrounding the property.) The museum is open Wednesday through Friday from 11:00 A.M. to 5:00 P.M., Saturday and Sunday until 6:00 P.M. Admission is $3.00 for adults, $2.00 for children age 4 to 12; children 3 and under are free.

York County Heritage Trust Sites
250 East Market Street
(717) 848–1587
www.yorkheritage.org
One ticket (adults $6.00, students and seniors $5.00; children 12 and under free) covers visits to all of the York County Heritage Trust Sites listed below, which cover 250 years of the area's history. Available from mid-March through mid-December, guided tours depart from the visitor center on the hour, 10:00 A.M. to 2:00 P.M. Tuesday to Saturday. Strollers are not permitted, nor are cameras or video recorders. Included in the tour are the following sites:

The Gates House, Golden Plough Tavern, and Barnett Bobb Log House Complex—The circa 1751 stone and brick Georgian-style Gates House was the home and headquarters of General Horatio Gates in 1777 when the infamous "Conway Cabal" was foiled. Adjoining the house is the Golden Plough Tavern, a reminder of how taverns served as focal points for the community as well as for travelers in the early

days of our nation. The square-timber Barnett Bobb House gives a glimpse of family
life in the 1830s.

Historical Society Museum/Archives—
Over 10,000 square feet of exhibits of artifacts ranging from arrowheads to locally
made quilts are on display at this former
automobile dealership showroom built in
1921.

**Agricultural & Industrial Museum
(AIM)—**An 1830s grist mill, complete with
working waterwheel, player pianos, and
types of transportation from Conestoga
wagons to Pullman motor cars are among
the "Made in York" specialties on display in
this 12,000-square-foot exhibition space.

Colonial Courthouse Re-creation—
Tour a replica of the courthouse where the
Continental Congress met in York for nine
months in 1777 to 1778.

Fire Museum—Uniforms and equipment (including hand-pulled fire carriages
and vintage fire trucks) representing more
than 200 years of firefighting history in
York County are on display.

Bonham House—This Victorian town
home of Horace Bonham, a painter of
genre, narrative, and portrait art, contains
original furnishings and many of the
artist's works. Bonham's family lived here
from 1875 to 1965.

**York Heritage Rail Trail
York County Parks
400 Mundis Race Road
(717) 840-7440
www.yorkcountytrails.org**
Twenty-one miles long and covering 176
acres, Heritage Rail Trail County Park runs
north from the Maryland border (just
south of the Borough of New Freedom)
through the heart of York County. The
park is open year-round from 8:00 A.M.
until dusk. The trail, with its 10-foot-wide,
compacted stone surface, is four-season
friendly for hiking, bicycling, running,
horseback riding, cross-country skiing,
and snowshoeing. Pets on leashes are
permitted on the trail.

About 1½ miles from the Maryland
state line is the New Freedom Train Sta-

*For more information, maps, area
guides, and locations of visitor centers,
call the York County Convention and
Visitors Bureau at (888) 858–YORK from
9:30 A.M. to 5:00 P.M. daily, or check out
www.yorkpa.org.*

tion, built in the mid-1860s and one of the
two York County railroad sites listed on the
National Register of Historic Places.
Located at the highest point on the trail,
the station has been restored to look as it
did in 1935, and it contains a model of a
K-9 steam locomotive along with other
historic artifacts. About 10 miles north of
New Freedom is the other National Register railroad site, the Hanover Junction Train
Station. A museum on the first floor re-
creates the year 1863. Continue on the trail
for a little over 5 more miles and you'll
pass through the 370-foot-long, brick-lined
Howard Tunnel, the oldest operational tunnel in the nation, opened in 1838.

**York's Central Market
34 West Philadelphia Street
(717) 848-2243
www.centralmarkethouse.com**
Built in 1888, this neo-Romanesque, five-
towered brick building is a site to see,
even from the outside. Inside is a working
market featuring fresh-from-the-farm produce, meats, and cheeses, along with bakery products and other local specialties.
The market is open Tuesday, Thursday,
and Saturday from 6:00 A.M. to 3:00 P.M.

BRANDYWINE VALLEY

The land along the Brandywine was originally inhabited by an Algonquin Native
American tribe called the Lenape. Swedish
and Dutch fur traders arrived in the early
1640s, followed by Welsh settlers, then
English Quakers under the auspices of
William Penn and his successors. There
are still a substantial number of active
Quaker (or "Friends," as they are also

CLOSE-UP

The Murals of York

York County Heritage Trust
Throughout York's Historic Downtown area, 20 murals, ranging in size from large-scale to mini, painted on the sides of buildings, depict the city's history and achievements. Begun in 1996, this "open air gallery," as the city describes it, commemorates a range of subjects, from the drafting of the Articles of Confederation to York's agricultural roots and the industrial accomplishments of Harley-Davidson and other locally based manufacturing firms. You can pick up a self-guided mural tour booklet with a map at the York County Heritage Trust Gift Shop (250 East Market Street; 717–848–1587; www.yorkheritage.org) for $1.00. Groups of 10 or more can arrange for a guided tour. Be sure to check out the murals depicting the following:

The Art of Lewis Miller—16 mini murals represent the works of 19th-century folk artist Lewis Miller.

Conway Cabal—hoping to secure military support from the French for a cabal (secret plot) to overthrow General George Washington as commander of the revolutionary forces in 1777, some colonial Congressmen and army officers hosted a dinner for the Marquis de Lafayette at the York home and headquarters of General Horatio Gates, who had recently led a victorious campaign in Saratoga, New York. It is said that the conspirators realized their efforts were doomed when the marquis drank a toast to the health of General Washington.

William C. Goodridge—one of York County's first entrepreneurs in the years leading up to the Civil War, Goodridge had been born into slavery in 1805.

Muscletown U.S.A.—Georgia-born Bob Hoffman was a weightlifter (he was nicknamed "The Father of Weightlifting"), U.S. Olympic coach, and entrepreneur who not only started the York Barbell Company (which is still in operation) in 1932, but worked to promote York as "Muscletown U.S.A." Iron-pumping enthusiasts can also visit the Weightlifting Hall of Fame at York Barbell Company (3300 Board Road; 800–358–9675; www.yorkbarbell.com). This 8,000-square-foot free-of-charge attraction traces the history of

known) meetinghouses throughout the Brandywine Valley. Back then, they worked the land, developing large farms to grow grain and raise cattle. To grind the grain, mills were established along the creeks of the Brandywine.

In 1777 this area was the site of the largest battle of the Revolutionary War, the Battle of Brandywine, in which Continental troops and local militia led by George Washington and the Marquis de Lafayette clashed with British and Hessian soldiers on their way to capture Philadelphia. It was the Brandywine Valley's beauty, though, that has inspired and provided subject matter for the art of three generations of the Wyeth family, from patriarch N. C. to Andrew and James. Another locally born artist, Howard Pyle, was the father of the Brandywine school of American illustration, the influence of which can be clearly seen in the works of Frank Schoonover,

The colorful history of York County is illustrated on murals displayed throughout the downtown area. YORK COUNTY CONVENTION & VISITORS BUREAU

strength sports from mythology to the early Olympic Games to the present through exhibits, art, and equipment displays. Located 2 miles north of York at Exit 11 of Interstate 83.

The Breath of Life: Dr. George Holtzapple—to save the life of a young pneumonia patient who could not catch his breath, York County physician Dr. George Holtzapple put together a primitive apparatus to extract oxygen from chlorate of potash and black oxide of manganese in 1885. He had the extracted oxygen fanned into the patient's face, allowing him to breathe more easily and, eventually, recover. Dr. Holtzapple served on the staff of York Hospital for more than 50 years.

Maxfield Parrish, and others who came after.

Practitioners of the culinary arts are inspired by the abundance of mushrooms that grow in the Brandywine Valley. In fact, mushroom cultivation in the United States began right here in Kennett Square in 1896, when two local florists were exploring different ways to more efficiently use their greenhouses and decided to use the area beneath their ornamental plant shelves to grow some of these fabulous fungi. For many years, Kennett Square has been known as the "Mushroom Capital of the World" and has hosted an annual Mushroom Festival in September for the past two decades (for more festival information, call 888-440-9920, or visit the Web site at www.mushroomfestival.org).

Kennett Square

Named for a village in England (the original one was spelled with only one *t*), Kennett Square sprang up at a busy intersection, where the road from Chester, Pennsylvania, to Baltimore and one from Lancaster to Washington, D.C., crossed. In 1735 the spot was the site of the Unicorn Tavern. By 1810 a village of about eight dwellings had grown up around the tavern.

If you would prefer to take a self-guided tour of Kennett Square's Underground Railroad sites, you can find a complete annotated map on the center's Web site.

Kennett Underground Railroad Center (KURC)
History Station: 505 South Broad Street
(610) 347–2237
www.undergroundrr.kennett.net
With more than two dozen Underground Railroad sites within an 8-mile radius of Kennett Square, each documented at KURC, this area may have had the largest concentration of stations in the nation. Open from May 1 through September, Saturday and Sunday from 1:00 to 3:00 P.M. or by appointment throughout the year. Admission is free. KURC also offers narrated Kennett Underground Heritage Tours in passenger vans on the third Sunday of each month from June through August (wheelchair-accessible vans are often available). The one-hour tours cost $8.00 for adults, $5.00 for children. Reservations are required.

Longwood Gardens
U.S. Route 1 at Pennsylvania Route 52
(610) 388–1000
www.longwoodgardens.com
Longwood Garden's roots (sorry) go back all the way to 1798, when a Quaker family named Peirce began planting an arboretum on farmland purchased from William Penn almost 100 years before. In 1906 Pierre du Pont (great-grandson of the founder of DuPont Chemical Company) bought the property with the purpose of preserving the trees. With the arboretum as his foundation, du Pont created Longwood Gardens, which today features 1,050 acres of gardens, woodlands, and meadows. Every year, about a million visitors come to stroll through the 20 outdoor and 20 indoor gardens and four acres of heated greenhouses with their displays of 11,000 different types of plants, fountains, and hundreds of special horticultural and performing arts events, from organ and carillon concerts to outdoor folk and chamber music to open air theater productions. Summer fireworks and fountain displays are worth the trip all by themselves. Wheelchairs and a limited number of single-person electric scooters are available free at the information desk in the visitor center to be borrowed on an unreserved first come, first served basis. Photography is permitted; noncommercial photographers may use tripods on weekdays at specified times after receiving a permit at the visitor center. Longwood Gardens is located on U.S. Route 1 at Pennsylvania Route 52, 3 miles northeast of Kennett Square via Route 1. Longwood is open every day of the year from 9:00 A.M. to 5:00 P.M. and until around 10:00 P.M. on Tuesday, Thursday, and Saturday evenings from Memorial Day to Labor Day. General admission tickets cover an entire day of regular displays and concerts (some special events require separate tickets).

Cost for adults is $14.00 ($10.00 on Tuesday) April through the day before Thanksgiving, $12.00 ($8.00 on Tuesday) from mid-January through March, and $15.00 (no Tuesday discount) from Thanksgiving through early January. Admission for youths ages 16 to 20 is $6.00, children ages 6 to 15 are $2.00, and children under 6 are free.

Among the most popular annual special events at Longwood Gardens are the Festival of Fountains (weekends from Memorial Day through Labor Day), Garden Fest (early to mid-September through early October), Autumn's Colors (October), Chrysanthemum Festival (late October through mid-November), and Christmas (late November through early January), which features 400,000 outdoor lights.

The Mushroom Cap
114 West State Street
(610) 444-8484
www.themushroomcap.com
Not surprisingly, the focus here is on fungi, beginning with a free 10-minute video on how Kennett Square became the "Mushroom Capital of the World," along with the growing and picking processes. Owner Kathi Lafferty knows a lot about local mushrooms. Her husband, son, and brothers-in-law operate a mushroom farm that has been in their family since 1946. In addition to being an educational experience, the retail store carries a nice variety of fresh-picked locally grown 'shrooms, including white button, "baby bellas," shiitakes, oysters, and maitakes. You might even want to purchase a kit to grow your own white button or portabello mushrooms at home. Open seven days a week (closed Sunday in January, February, March, and July).

Chadds Ford

The Brandywine River Museum, located at the crossroads of Routes 1 and 100 in Chadds Ford, is generally considered to be the "heart of the Brandywine Valley." There's been an age-old dispute about whether Chadds Ford is located totally in Chester County or party in Delaware County as well, but, either way, it's historic, beautiful, and definitely worth a visit. To add a little more mystery to the mix, the village is named after 18th-century settler John Chads (whose father's surname was Chadsey). Why the extra *d* was added to Chadds Ford, no one is really sure.

Brandywine Battlefield
Route 1, about 2 miles
south of Route 202
(610) 459-3342
www.ushistory.org/brandywine/brandywine.htm
Looking for a way to cross the Brandywine River into the Colonial capital of Philadelphia on September 11, 1777, the British army under the command of General William Howe engaged Continental troops under the command of General George Washington and the Marquis de Lafayette in what would turn out to be the largest battle of the Revolutionary War. Start at the visitor center, which houses exhibits of uniforms, weapons, and artifacts found on the site and presents an 18-minute film giving battle background. You can also visit General Washington's headquarters (the Ring House) and Lafayette's quarters (Gideon Gilpin's farmhouse).

The grounds and historic houses are open Tuesday to Saturday 9:00 A.M. to 5:00 P.M. and Sunday noon to 5:00 P.M. The houses are accessible to groups and individuals by guided tours only; call for times. Cost for the tour is $5.00 for adults, $3.50 for seniors age 60+, $2.50 for children age 6 to 17.

If you would prefer to tour the Brandywine Battlefield area by car (the park is 50 acres, but the actual battle encompassed a 10-square-mile area), you can find three different self-guided routes on the Web site.

From April through November (Wednesday to Sunday), you can take a tour of the house where patriarch painter N. C. Wyeth raised his family and the studio in which he worked. Both have been restored to reflect the year 1945, when N. C. Wyeth died. For the house and studio tour, add $5.00 to the regular Brandywine River Museum admission price.

Brandywine River Museum
U.S. Route 1 and Creek Road
(610) 388–2700
www.brandywinemuseum.org
A former Civil War gristmill on the banks of the Brandywine River is home to an extensive collection of the paintings of all three generations of the Wyeth family, plus other outstanding examples of American illustration, landscape, and still life by renowned artists including Maxfield Parrish, Charles Dana Gibson, Rockwell Kent, Jasper Cropsey, George Cope, and Jefferson David Chalfant.

Individual handheld wand audio tours (there's one for adults and a special one for kids) of the museum are available for a rental charge of $3.00. The Brandywine River Museum is open daily from 9:30 A.M. to 4:30 P.M. Display areas are wheelchair accessible. No photography inside the museum. Admission is $8.00 for adults, $5.00 for seniors 65+, students, and children age 6 to 12; free for the under 6 crowd.

Chadds Ford Historical Society
1736 Creek Road (Old Route 100,
¼ mile north of U.S. Route 1)
(610) 388–7376
www.chaddsfordhistory.org
Your first stop is "The Barn" (the society's headquarters and visitor center, designed to look like a Colonial-era fieldstone and frame Pennsylvania bank barn), where you can see various exhibits of art and objects pertinent to the area's history. A single $5.00 admission covers your visits to the society's two other sites, the circa 1725 John Chads House and Springhouse and the 1714 Barns-Brinton House. The Barn is open Monday to Friday from 9:00 A.M. to 2:00 P.M. and weekends May through September from 1:00 to 5:00 P.M. The John Chads House is open May through September from 1:00 to 5:00 P.M., and the Barns-Brinton House from May through August from 1:00 to 5:00 P.M.

John Chads House
Five years after ferryman and farmer John Chads built this bluestone bank home, he brought his new bride, Elizabeth, here to live. Chads died in 1760, leaving the house and 40 acres of land to his wife. It is reported that, from her attic window, Elizabeth was a firsthand witness to the Battle of Brandywine and protected her most valuable possessions in the only way she could—by hiding "her silver spoons in her pocket." The home still has its original oak floors, paneling, and woodwork.

Barns-Brinton House
Originally William Barns' Tavern from 1722 until 1731, this authentically restored and furnished brick structure had a private side for the family as well as a barroom and sleeping quarters for travelers. The building and farmland were purchased in 1753 by James Brinton and remained in his family for more a century.

WEST CHESTER

Originally named Turks Head after a local inn that had been operating since the late

1680s, the city of West Chester has been the Chester County seat for more than 200 years. The Turk's Head Inn is still considered the center of this extremely walkable town, where more than 3,000 buildings have survived since the Colonial era (the downtown district is listed on the National Register of Historic Places).

American Helicopter Museum
1220 American Boulevard
(610) 436-9600
www.helicoptermuseum.org

See the evolution of rotary wing aircraft from the earliest helicopters to a V-22 tilt wing Osprey, which are among the more than 25 civilian and military helicopters, autogiros, and convertiplanes on display at this museum. There are plenty of opportunities to climb aboard and try your hand at the controls. Most of the helicopters are displayed inside, so this is an all-weather attraction. It is also wheelchair accessible (there is one wheelchair available for the convenience of visitors). Museum hours are 10:00 A.M. to 5:00 P.M. Wednesday to Saturday, noon to 5:00 P.M. Sunday. Tickets are $6.00 for adults, $5.00 for seniors, $4.00 for children and students with ID, and free for children under two.

Northbrook Canoe Company
1810 Beagle Road
(800) 898-2279, (610) 793-2279
www.northbrookcanoe.com

Ride the Brandywine River in a canoe, kayak, tube, or splash boat for scenic journeys that can range from one to six hours long. Designated as a Class 1 waterway, the Brandywine is slow and calm, with some light rapids, but easygoing enough for even first-timers. Tours are self-guided, preceded by an explanation of the waterway's course and, if needed, a basic canoeing course. Fido is welcome to join you, and you can bring along a small (up to 6-quart) cooler filled with snacks and beverages (no alcohol) to sustain you through the journey. Footwear must be worn at all times. Be sure to bring a dry

change of clothing for the trip home.

Canoe rentals (each can carry up to three adults or two adults and two children) range from $33 for one hour to $70 for six and a half hours. Single-person kayaks are $22 for one hour to $55 for six and a half hours. Bring your own canoe or kayak, and they'll transport it for $25. Single-person tubes rent for $12 for two hours, $17 for three. Privately owned tubes can be transported for a fee of $5.00. Northbrook is open daily from May to the end of September from 9:00 A.M. to 5:00 P.M., weekend trips through October 31 from 9:00 A.M. to 4:00 P.M.

Northbrook does not recommend kayaks for children under the age of 10 or under four feet tall.

ℹ

QVC Studio Tour
1200 Wilson Drive
(800) 600-9900
www.qvctours.com

Founded in 1986, QVC is the world's largest electronic retailer, broadcasting live 24 hours a day, reaching over 80 percent of all U.S. cable homes and three million satellite dishes. Recent sales figures topped $5.7 billion. It all happens at QVC Studio Park in West Chester, and you can watch the action during a guided walking tour of the 20,000-square-foot broadcasting facility, including a view from the observation deck 50 feet above the studio floor. Walking tours are available every hour on the hour, seven days a week, from 10:00 A.M. to 4:00 P.M. Admission is $7.50 per adult, $5.00 for children ages 6 to 12.

Viking Horse,
Icelandic Horses of Chester County
P.O. Box 3151
West Chester, PA 19381
(610) 517-7980
www.vikinghorse.com

In the ninth century, the Vikings brought gaited horses (gaited describes the way

---

Although just about anyone who has ridden a horse before can ride an Icelandic, management cautions that the experience is not appropriate for first-time riders or children under the age of 15.

---

they walk) from the British Isles, Ireland, and Norway along with them when they settled in Iceland. Only the hardiest of these equines survived the harsh winters, eventually evolving with shorter legs and necks and longer winter coats more suited to the below-zero environment. Small but extremely sturdy, these horses can carry up to 275 pounds and are sure-footed in even the roughest terrain. Icelandics are a relatively rare breed; there are only about 200,000 in the world.

A 90-minute trek (total time with tacking, training, and riding is about 2 hours) costs $75 for one rider, $70 each for two or more riders. A 2½-hour trek (total time approximately 3 hours) is $125 for one rider, $110 each for two or more riders; and for a 3½-hour trek (about 4 hours), it's $175 for one rider, $150 each for two or more riders.

Viking Horse has ASTM/SEI standard helmets in all sizes. You are also welcome to bring your own. Payment must be made by cash or check. Viking Horse is open seven days, year-round.

RELOCATION 🏠

It's about 90-minutes (80 miles) from Philadelphia to the heart of Pennsylvania Dutch Country and just a few minutes more (83 miles) from Baltimore. But proximity to these major urban centers is only one reason why Lancaster County is such an attractive relocation destination. Even more alluring are the unique combinations of town and country, earthy and edgy, picturesque and progressive that characterize this charismatic area.

Of Pennsylvania's 67 counties, Lancaster ranks sixth in population, says a published report by Lancaster Newspapers, Inc. Nearly half a million people live here, according to the Lancaster County Planning Commission. Since 2000, the number of residents has increased by more than 27,000, and is expected to grow by close to 28,000 more within the next five years. Employment is a major lure, with more than 11,000 companies, pretty evenly split among the manufacturing, service, and retail sectors. Unemployment here is generally well below the national average.

For retirees, Lancaster County and the surrounding area offer a range of communities that meet their individual needs for independent and assisted living. Health care institutions include Lancaster General Hospital (LGH), which has been named by *U.S. News & World Report* among the top 50 hospitals in the nation in five specialties: orthopedics, heart care and heart surgery, urology, hormonal disorders, including diabetes, and ear, nose, and throat. (LGH is also the county's leading employer.)

Penn State Milton S. Hershey Medical Center, another Pennsylvania Dutch Country landmark institution, has also been recognized by *U.S. News & World Report* as a top hospital, specifically in the areas of cancer, cardiology, endocrinology, gastroenterology, geriatrics, gynecology, HIV, orthopedics, otolaryngology, rheumatology, and urology. Pediatric Intensive Care Unit Evaluations ranks the Pediatric Intensive Care Unit at the center's Children's Hospital as one of the best in the country.

APARTMENTS

Just about everywhere you look—from the urban centers to the outskirts of the tiniest towns—construction of apartments and town homes is booming in Lancaster County and its surrounding area. Many developments offer a host of amenities ranging from elegantly furnished clubhouses for tenant use, swimming pools, and fitness centers to nature paths, play areas for children, and resort-like landscaping. For those who prefer to inhabit something with a bit more history behind it, a number of landmark buildings such as former factories, warehouses, and schools have been renovated for apartment living.

A garden apartment is defined as one that is in a building with a garden or lawn. Some units may actually have access to the garden or lawn. Ask the property manager for clarification.

ⓘ

B&F Properties
Corporate office: 2938 Columbia Avenue, Suite 1202, Lancaster
(717) 293-9200
Leasing office: 100 Wickshire Circle, Lititz
(800) 292-9380
www.bfproperty.com
B&F Properties manages luxury apartment rental communities in Lancaster County, including the following.

The Crest at Elm Tree
100 Crestwyck Circle, Mount Joy
(888) 663-4881
One-, two-, and three-bedroom garden
apartments with garages on either the
first or second floor.

The Highlands at Warwick
100 Wickshire Circle, Lititz
(866) 749-9227
One- and two-bedroom apartments and
multilevel two- and three-bedroom town
homes.

Boyd/Wilson Property Management
711 Olde Hickory Road, Lancaster
(717) 569-0484
www.boydwilson.com
Boyd/Wilson manages modern apartment
and town home communities in Lancaster
County and Hershey, including the following.

Donegal Crossing
Bradfield Drive, Mount Joy
(888) 572-4680
Conveniently located just off Route 283,
Donegal Crossing features two- and three-
bedroom town homes.

Hershey Heritage Village
1330 Wabank Road, Lancaster
(800) 292-7207, (717) 299-4317,
(717) 392-4166
www.hersheyheritagevillage.com
One- and two-bedroom garden apartments and two- and three-bedroom town
houses.

Newport Commons
600 Creekside Lane (off Newport Road),
Lititz
(717) 626-7368
One- to three-bedroom apartments, two-
to three-bedroom furnished town homes.

Pioneer Woods
9 Lampost Lane, Lancaster
(717) 464-2701
One- to three-bedroom apartments and
two-bedroom town homes.

The Village of Olde Hickory
725 Olde Hickory Road, Lancaster
(866) 224-2048, (717) 569-3231
One- to three-bedroom garden apartments and town houses.

High Real Estate Group
1853 William Penn Way, Lancaster
(800) 638-4414
www.highrealestate.com
High Group manages high-end apartment
and town home communities in Lancaster
County, including the following.

Bentley Ridge
650 Bentley Ridge Boulevard, Lancaster
(888) 330-8880
One- to three-bedroom apartments and
town homes.

Greenfield Estates
799 Patriot Drive, Lancaster
(866) 275-1116
One- to three-bedroom apartments and
town homes.

Horst Realty
205 Granite Run Drive, Suite 280,
Lancaster
(717) 735-6100
www.horstrealty.com
Horst manages apartments and town
homes in Lancaster County, including the
following.

Ashlea Gardens Apartments
150 Ashlea Gardens, New Holland
(877) 340-0943, (717) 354-4421
www.ashleagardens.com
Efficiency to three-bedroom garden
apartments in a Tudor Village–style setting.

Meadows East
13 Morning Glory Lane, Manheim
(717) 665-6864
www.meadowseast.com
One- to three-bedroom garden apartments and town houses.

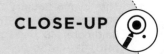
Residential Revivals

Historic Landmarks for Living
230 South Broad Street, Suite 1501
Philadelphia
(800) 563-6754, (215) 567-0701
www.historiclandmarks.com
This company rehabilitates landmark properties such as old railroad stations, warehouses, schools, and factories, maintaining their old-fashioned character, and turns them into upscale urban apartments with a full range of contemporary amenities. Examples of their properties include the following.

Peach Alley Court
155 South Poplar Street, Elizabethtown
(877) 563-6751
Built in 1905, this former shoe factory is a well-preserved example of "mill building"

architecture common in the early industrial era. Rehabbed by Historic Landmarks in 1983, the 72-unit building offers studio and one-bedroom apartments with 11-foot ceilings and oversized windows.

Shoe Factory
201 North Chestnut Street, Palmyra
(717) 838-5481
Shoes were big business in Palmyra (just a few minutes from Hershey) back in the day—1886 was the year this brick building was constructed. Historic Landmarks rehabbed this factory into 41 apartments in 1982 with care to preserve such industrial-era features as oversized windows, exposed brick walls, and timber beams and columns.

Mill Creek Manor
43 Baron Drive, Lancaster
(888) 398-1698
Three-bedroom rental town homes located a few minutes east of Routes 30 and 462.

The Village of Rivermoor
379 Rivermoor Drive, Marietta
(888) 314-2719
www.villageofrivermoor.com
One- to three-bedroom apartments.

RP Management, Inc.
301 East City Avenue, #140, Bala Cynwyd
(610) 667-5105
www.rpmanagementinc.com
RP Management manages residential apartment communities throughout Lancaster County, including the following.

Cherryhill Villas Apartments
560-02 Estelle Drive, Lancaster
(888) 693-9420
Studio and one- and two-bedroom garden apartments and town houses.

Cloister Gardens Apartments
845 Dawn Avenue, Ephrata
(888) 693-9432
One- to three-bedroom apartments.

Sweetbriar Apartments
1917 Oregon Pike, Lancaster
(866) 882-1969
One- and two-bedroom apartments in two-story Colonial brick buildings.

Windsor Court Townhomes
1831 Hidden Lane, Lancaster
(888) 693-9434
Two- and three-bedroom models.

The Town & Country Trust
300 East Lombard Street
Baltimore, MD
(410) 539–7600
www.tctrust.com
Town & Country is a Baltimore-based
management company with apartment
properties in Lancaster County, including
the following.

Lancaster West
190 Colonial Crest Drive, Lancaster
(866) 828–8755
One- and two-bedroom standard and garden apartments and two-bedroom town
homes.

Oakview Estates Apartment Homes
77 Foal Court, Lancaster
(866) 828–8754
One- and two-bedroom garden apartments and two-bedroom town homes.

Westminster Management LLC
c/o Kushner Companies
18 Columbia Turnpike
Florham, NJ
(866) 350–5222, (973) 822–0050
www.westminster-management.com
Lancaster County properties managed by
Westminster include the following.

Chelsea Village
25 Bradford Drive, Leola
One-bedroom apartments, two- and
three-bedroom garden apartments, and
two- to three-bedroom town houses.

Meadow Green
L-2000 Swarr Run Road, Lancaster
One- to three-bedroom apartments within
walking distance of Park City Mall.

Willow Woods Apartments
94 Willow Valley Drive, Lancaster
(888) 595–0540
One- to three-bedroom apartments and
one- and two-bedroom town houses
located 3 miles south of Lancaster on
Route 222. The Willow Valley Golf Course
is just across the street.

REAL ESTATE AND RENTALS

Advantage Realty Inc.—Greg Weaver
1560 Lititz Pike, Lancaster
Office: (717) 391–7000, ext. 2
Direct: (717) 314–8275

Apex Realty of Lancaster, Ltd.
100 Highlands Drive, Suite 200, Lititz
(717) 625–APEX (2739)
www.apexrol.com

Dennis Beck Real Estate
120 East Main Street, Lititz
(717) 627–2325

Beiler-Campbell Realtors
229 West Fourth Street, Quarryville
(717) 786–8000

Brownstone Real Estate Co.
1840 Fishburn Road, Hershey
(717) 533–6222, (717) 279–6222
www.brwnstone.com

Buyer's Edge Realty Ltd.
600 Olde Hickory Road, Lancaster
(717) 569–7396
Buyer's Edge Realty is part of a national
network of real estate companies offering
exclusive representation to home buyers.
As the name suggests, Buyer's Edge
Realty works only with buyers. This means
that they do not accept listings of homes
for sale.

Century 21
American Gold
2201 Columbia Avenue, Lancaster
(717) 397–2021

Century 21 Park Road
1825 Oregon Pike, Lancaster
(717) 560–4877
www.rissergroup.com

Fagan & Associates
1361 Fruitville Pike, Lancaster
(717) 397–7400

Lipka Group
434 West Fourth Street, Quarryville
(717) 786-9999

Neighborhood Realty, Inc.
705 Old Harrisburg Road, Gettysburg
(717) 334-9131

Clover Inc. Realtors
2603 Lititz Pike, Lancaster
(866) 425-6837, (717) 560-9495
Properties in Denver, Elizabethtown,
Ephrata, Hempfield, Lancaster, Leola,
Lititz, Manheim, Millersville, Mount Joy,
New Holland, Quarryville, and Strasburg.

Coldwell Banker
Elizabethtown Office: 155 East High
Street
(717) 367-3500

Ephrata Office: 5 Old Mill Road
(717) 738-9986

Gettysburg Office: 1270 Fairfield Road
(717) 334-7636

Hershey Office: 1135 West Governor
Road
(717) 533-8181

Mount Joy Office: 65C East Main Street
(717) 653-2646

Quarryville Office: 330 West State Street
(717) 786-1300

Willow Street Office: 2845 Willow
Street Pike
(717) 464-4700

Coldwell Banker Homesale Services
Relocation Division
111 Centerfield Road, Lancaster
(800) 965-2748, (717) 392-2717
www.cbhomesale.com

Coldwell Banker Homesale Services
Group
500 Delp Road, Lancaster
Business: (717) 560-9100
Direct: (717) 468-7277 (Mike Skillman)
www.mikeskillman.com

Dan Diller Realtors Gallery of Homes
58 Keller Avenue, Lancaster
(800) 743-7356, (717) 393-1311
www.dandillerrealtors.com

Ed Diller
131 Centerville Road, Lancaster
(717) 393-0100
Specializes in lots.

Donegal Real Estate
27 West Market Street, Marietta
(888) 471-8927, (717) 426-4530
www.resource.realtor.com
Specializing in Marietta.

For Sale by Owner Real Estate
2821 Willow Street Pike North, Willow
Street
(717) 464-9500

Gateway Realty
160 North Pointe Boulevard, Suite 200,
Lancaster
(800) 765-3247, (717) 560-5500
www.gatewayrealtyinc.com

Jack Gaughen Realtor ERA
224 Baltimore Street, Gettysburg
(717) 334-6283
www.jgr.com

Homes by Owner
Web site of homes for sale by owners. For
Lancaster County, look on www.homesby
owner.com/lancaster/home.asp.

Hostetter Realty
321 East Main Street, New Holland
(717) 354-6416

Kingsway Realty
(888) 454-6499, (877) 345-3886
www.kingswayrealty.com
Lancaster office: 1770 Oregon Pike
(717) 569-8701

Akron office: 112 South Seventh Street
(717) 859-2001

Lancaster County
Association of Realtors
1930 Harrington Drive, Lancaster
(717) 569-4625
www.lcar.com

Lancaster Real Estate
626 North Duke Street, Lancaster
(717) 399-8010
www.resource.realtor.com
Properties in Columbia, Ephrata, Lancaster, Lititz, Manheim, Marietta,
Millersville, Mount Joy, New Holland, Quarryville, and Willow Street.

John Mattilio
177 Linestown Road, Willow Street
(717) 464-8930

Mastros Real Estate
216 East Walnut Street, Lancaster
(717) 393-5090
Buys, sells and rents homes.

Murry Realty GMAC Real Estate
1630 Manheim Pike, Lancaster
(800) 555-7660, (717) 560-0755
www.drsgmac.com

Olde Heritage Inc. Realtors
142 East Main Street, New Holland
(717) 354-4071
www.oldeheritagerealtors.com

Pennsylvania Farms & Land
Kenneth H. Greider, Broker:
374 Donnerville Road, Lancaster
(717) 872-9002

John Mattilio, Realtor:
177 Linestown Road, Willow Street
(717) 464-8930

Preferred Realty Group, Inc.
48 South Market Street, Elizabethtown
(717) 367-6200
www.preferredrealty.com

Prudential Commonwealth Real Estate
1574 Lititz Pike, Lancaster
(877) 291-9101
Business: (717) 291-9101
Direct: (717) 239-5555
www.homesonline.com

Real Choice Real Estate, Inc.
730 North Duke Street, Lancaster
(717) 392-6222
www.realchoicerealestate.com

Realty 1
www.realty1.com
Ephrata office: 250 North Reading Road
(717) 721-7011

Lancaster office: 1547 Oregon Pike
(717) 295-1515

Realty Select
www.realty-select.com
Hershey office: 905 West Governor
Road, Suite 300
(717) 534-2442

Lancaster office: 217 Granite Run Drive
(717) 569-0608

Re/Max Associates of Lancaster
www.lancasterhomesforsale.com
Ephrata office:
116 North Reading Road
(717) 951-9621

Lancaster office:
100 Foxshire Drive
(800) 572-2338, (717) 569-2222

Willow Street office:
2929 Willow Street Pike
(717) 399-SOLD
www.thewilfongteam.com

Re/Max Realty Specialists
336 West Miller Street, Strasburg
(800) 706-SOLD, (717) 687-7300
www.lenferber.com

John Smith Real Estate Group
1255 South Market Street, Suite 101,
Elizabethtown
(717) 367-8310, (717) 367-2400, (717)
533-1100
www.johnsmithteam.com
Specializing in central Pennsylvania,
including Hershey and Lancaster.

Town & Country Realty of Lancaster
2547 Lititz Pike, Lancaster
(717) 299-4885
www.jeannevanhekken.com

Weichert Realtors Engle & Hambright
2122 Marietta Avenue, Lancaster
(717) 291-1041

RETIREMENT AND CONTINUING CARE COMMUNITIES

Accommodations and activities abound
for active adults looking for the good life.
For individuals who require special care at
any level, the options are equally impressive. Assisted care facilities can provide
otherwise independent residents with
bathing, dressing, meals, medication,
and/or other daily activities.

Audubon Villa
125 South Broad Street, Lititz
(717) 626-0211
A Victorian-style mansion is the centerpiece of this 42-bed skilled and intermediate care nursing facility. Residents have
individual rooms and share a large living
room, dining room, and sunporch in the
building. Medicare and Medicaid-certified,
Audubon Villa offers 24-hour nursing care,
social service, and nutritional support,
including accommodation of physician-
specified special dietary needs. A variety
of activities and social programs for residents and their families are available.

Brethren Village
3001 Lititz Pike, Lancaster
(717) 569-2657
www.bv.org
Active adults have the option to "retire a
little or a lot" in this independent living
community. Continuing care is available to
support residents through injuries, sudden
illness, or long-term disabilities. Residents
age 62 and up are eligible for assisted living services, if needed. Situated on 160
acres of green fields, Brethren Village,
which has its origins in 1897, is home to
more than 800 community members, who
live in residential suites and rooms
(monthly fees include meals, weekly
housekeeping, and laundry service), apartments (over 50 floor plan choices), and
cottages with professional grounds maintenance and options for weekly house
cleaning, laundry, and meal plan. Short-
term rehab services are also available.

*For information about continuing care
facility licensing and accreditation, contact the Pennsylvania Association of
Nonprofit Senior Services (PANPHA)
(717-763-5724; www.panpha.org) and
the American Association of Homes and
Services for the Aging (202-783-2242;
www.aahsa.org).*

Ephrata Manor
99 Bethany Road, Ephrata
(717) 738-4940
www.ucc-homes.org
Sponsored by United Church of Christ
Homes, Ephrata Manor is a nonprofit facility
that offers independent one- and two-
bedroom apartments with full kitchens and
washer/dryers, building maintenance, and
optional laundry, housekeeping, and meal
services. Assisted living (certified for
Medicare and Medicaid) in partially private
rooms is available, and, at the Health Center, nurses and other professionals provide
24/7 care in private and semiprivate rooms.

Garden Spot Village
433 South Kinzer Avenue, New Holland
(717) 355-6000
www.gardenspotvillage.org
Affiliated with the Lancaster Mennonite Conference of the Mennonite Church and Mennonite Health Services, this nonprofit residential community, founded in 1990, serves individuals of all faiths and backgrounds. Residence options include carriage homes, cottages, and apartments offering a variety of floor plan designs. Assisted living and 24-hour long- and short-term care in private and semiprivate rooms are available. For the safety and security of residents with Alzheimer's disease or other memory impairment, Garden Spot offers private and companion suites in three connected neighborhoods. Special short-term respite programs are designed for adults with Alzheimer's and other forms of dementia and/or physical challenges.

Homestead Village
1800 Village Circle, Lancaster
(717) 397-4831
www.homesteadvillage.org
Residents in this 33-acre community may choose from more than 20 different two-bedroom cottage and villa floor plans or apartments that range from studios to two-bedroom units. Emergency call systems provide additional security. Assisted living is available in studio apartments, skilled care in semiprivate and private accommodations. The facility offers on-site medical service and rehabilitative and restorative programs. A full-time activities director plans travel, social, and other programs for residents.

A number of the area's retirement communities also offer short-term residency and rehabilitation services for individuals who have been released from the hospital but are not yet ready to return to their regular homes.

Landis Homes
1001 East Oregon Road, Lititz
(717) 569-3271
www.landishomes.org
Accommodation options on the 100-acre campus range from cottages, apartments, to suites to assisted living and 24-hour skilled care rooms. Founded in 1964, Landis Homes accommodates around 645 residents. Adult day services (available Monday through Friday from 7:30 A.M. to 5:00 P.M.) allow nonresidents who live in their own homes to participate in day programs of social, recreational, and health activities. A special day program is designed for participants with memory impairment. Daily fees may be subsidized through the Lancaster County Office of Aging.

Luthercare
www.luthercare.org
Two senior living communities in Lititz and Columbia are affiliated with the Lower Susquehanna Synod of the Evangelical Church in America and with Lutheran Services in America. Both of these nonprofit facilities serve individuals of all faiths.

Luther Acres
600 East Main Street, Lititz
(717) 626-8376
Independent cottage and town home living for active adults age 65 and over, plus an entire continuum of care from assisted living through skilled nursing (mostly private rooms) and memory support for residents with early- to late-stage cognitive impairment, is available on this 60-acre campus. Luther Acres also offers rehabilitative services. Short-term rehab stays with physical, occupational, and speech therapies are available.

Luthercare at St. John Herr's Estate
200 Luther Lane, Columbia
(877) 999-0039, (717) 626-8376
On this 40-acre campus, two-bedroom cottages and one- and two-bedroom town homes offer maximum independence with minimum maintenance. Resi-

Landis Homes offers a range of programs to the general community, including aquatics classes for individuals with arthritis or Parkinson's disease (717–581–3998); a free memory loss support group sponsored by the South-Central Pennsylvania Chapter of the Alzheimer's Association of America; a Parkinson's support group (717–509–5494); and respite care (24-hour notice is required; call 717–581–3939).

dents may also receive assisted living services. Respite care in private rooms and suites is also available.

Masonic Village at Elizabethtown
One Masonic Drive, Elizabethtown
(877) 753-3228, (717) 361-4522
www.pagrandlodge.org/villages/
elizabethtown/admpol.html

Built in 1910, the stately granite buildings and well-groomed gardens of this not-for-profit continuing care community provide an elegant living environment for its 260 residents. Apartments (efficiency through two-bedroom floor plans) and cottages are offered for independent living, private rooms and suites for individuals requiring assisted living or 24-hour nursing. Specialized care options are designed for individuals with Alzheimer's disease and related dementia. Short-term subacute care and rehabilitative services are available on a short-term basis.

Mennonite Home
1520 Harrisburg Pike, Lancaster
(717) 393-1301

Woodcrest Villa
2001 Harrisburg Pike, Lancaster
(717) 390-4100
For both: www.mennonitehome.org

Woodcrest Villa has residential accommodations that range from studios in five styles to one- to two-bedroom apartments (some with dens). Special activities, entertainment, and trips are scheduled each month.

At the Mennonite Home, four levels of care are offered, from residential, with basic meal, housekeeping, laundry, and short-term illness assistance, to special care, for individuals with Alzheimer's and other forms of dementia. Round-the-clock nursing care and supervision are available.

Moravian Manor
300 West Lemon Street, Lititz
(717) 626-0214
www.moravianmanor.org

More than 300 adults make their home in a full range of accommodations, from the independence of cottages and apartments to assisted living (private and semiprivate rooms), skilled nursing, and special programs for memory impairment. Rehabilitative, subacute, and hospice care are also available.

Pleasant View Retirement Community
544 North Penryn Road, Manheim
(717) 665-2445
www.pleasantviewrc.org

Pleasant View offers fully equipped efficiency- to two-bedroom apartments and cottages for residents age 60 and over, assisted living (private and shared rooms), 24-hour skilled nursing, and structured living for residents with cognitive impairment on 108 acres in northern Lancaster

If you care for an aging loved one at home, some facilities offer short-term respite services to ensure your peace of mind should you choose to travel or simply take some time for yourself.

County. Founded in 1955, this community is faith-based but not church affiliated. Short-term rehab and respite care (no fewer than 3 days and no longer than 18) are available.

Quarryville Presbyterian Retirement Community
625 Robert Fulton Highway (Route 222), Quarryville
(717) 786-7321
www.quarryville.com/apart.html

For more than 50 years, this continuing care retirement community in southern Lancaster County has offered senior care services and independent living in one- and two-bedroom apartments on a 17-acre campus surrounded by 200 acres of countryside.

United Zion Retirement Community
722 Furnace Hills Pike, Lititz
(717) 626-2071

Known as the United Zion Home for nearly 100 years, this community has undergone an extensive program of expansion and renovation to provide even higher levels of comfort, care, and service. Cottages offer independent living in a private environment; studio and one-bedroom apartments in the main building allow individuals and couples to enjoy the security, services, and companionship of a full-service community. Personal- and nursing-care accommodations and services are available for residents who find

Prospective residents age 55 and over who might like to experience the Willow Valley lifestyle prior to making it their home may do so for a nominal monthly fee as members of the community's Discovery Club, which offers access to cultural programs, the day spa, cafe, and fee-for-service fitness classes. Membership can be upgraded to provide unlimited use of the fitness and aquatic centers.

themselves in need of additional assistance. Local area residents may also utilize the services of therapy and rehab specialists on an outpatient basis.

Willow Valley
60 Willow Valley Square, Lancaster
(800) 770-5445, (717) 464-6800
www.willowvalleyretirement.com

Services at nonprofit Willow Valley's four communities offer life-care service levels that increase with the individual needs of their residents. Independent living options include apartments, single-story villas, and two-story town homes. All "supportive living" services such as nursing care, assisted living, and memory support services are available on-site at no additional charge. Monthly residence fee includes two meals daily (including special diet or tray service); housekeeping and linen; 24-hour security; water, electricity, heating, and air-conditioning; landscaping; transportation; heated indoor pool and spa; preventive health care services; nursing care if ever needed; and all social and recreational activities. The premises also feature a fitness and aquatics center, full-service day spa, rehab facilities, and cultural center with 500-seat theater, ballroom, broadcast studio, art studio and gallery, and other amenities.

HEALTH CARE

Ephrata Community Hospital
169 Martin Avenue, Ephrata
(717) 733-0311
www.ephratahospital.org

Full-range inpatient and outpatient services, including preventive, primary, acute, and rehab care, are available to residents of northern Lancaster County and surrounding communities at this nonprofit center. Specific programs are available for cancer patients, women's health, active wellness, pain management, and home health care. The hospital's emergency department is open 24 hours a day, 7 days a week.

Each year Lancaster General Heart Center performs more than 600 open heart surgeries, and approximately 4,700 babies are born at Lancaster General Women and Babies Hospital annually. More than 5,000 people come to the Lancaster General Health Campus for medical services each weekday, and Lancaster General orthopedic surgeons perform more than 1,100 joint replacement surgeries a year.

Gettysburg Hospital
147 Gettys Street, Gettysburg
(717) 334-2121
www.wellspan.org
For more than 80 years, Gettysburg Hospital has been providing comprehensive care to Gettysburg and Adams County. Beyond acute care, the facility now operates family health centers across the region, including ones that specialize in maternity and cardiac care. Home health and 24-hour emergency services and preventive health education and screening programs are also available. The Transitional Care Center offers patients the extra care they need between the time of hospital release and return to their home or nursing facility. The hospital is operated by WellSpan Health, a community-based, not-for-profit, integrated health system serving the greater Adams–York County region.

Heart of Lancaster Regional
Medical Center
1100–1500 Highlands Drive, Lititz
(717) 625-5000
www.heartoflancaster.com
Staffed by more than 300 physicians and specialists, Heart of Lancaster offers private patient rooms with intensive-care, step-down, and dedicated pediatrics units; all-on-one-floor outpatient services; fully equipped surgical suites; and dedicated orthopedics and cardiology facilities. The Women's Place features comprehensive diagnostic and gynecological care as well as deluxe birthing suites. Heart of Lancaster is operated by Health Management Associates, Inc. (www.hma-corp.com), a

Naples, Florida–based organization with acute care hospitals primarily in the Southeast and Southwest.

Lancaster General Hospital
555 North Duke Street, Lancaster
(717) 290-5511
www.lancastergeneral.org
Open 24 hours a day, 7 days a week, this 563-bed facility is staffed by more than 4,600 people, including more than 470 physicians and surgeons. Its emergency department treats more than 68,000 patients a year (averaging more than 180 visits a day).

Inpatient services are also available at **Lancaster General Women and Babies Hospital** (690 Good Drive, Lancaster; 717-544-3700).

Outpatient services are available at the following locations:

Columbia Health Center: 306 North Seventh Street, Columbia; (717) 684-1500 (lab and pulmonary function testing, physician services, radiology/x-ray, rehab services)

Crooked Oak Medical Services: 1671 Crooked Oak Drive, Lancaster; (717) 569-5109 (laboratory and radiology)

Kissel Hill Health Center: 51 Peters Road, Lititz; (717) 627-2400 (lab and pulmonary function testing, radiology/x-ray, rehab services)

Ephrata Community Hospital offers a physician referral service at (717) 738-2777.

Lancaster Cleft Palate Clinic: 223 North Lime Street, Lancaster; (717) 394-3793

Lancaster General–Norlanco: 424 Cloverleaf Road, Elizabethtown; (717) 928-2001 (imaging and rehab services, lab and pulmonary function testing; Norlanco Medical Associates next door at 418 Cloverleaf Road)

Lancaster General Health Campus: 2100 Harrisburg Pike, Lancaster; (717) 544-5522 (cancer center, endoscopy, eye diagnostic and laser, lab, and pulmonary function testing, hyperbarics and wound care, neurocenter, occupational medicine, pain management, radiology/x-ray, rehab programs, renal dialysis, same-day surgical center)

Therapy Services at Cherry Street: 609 North Cherry Street, Lancaster; (717) 544-5770 (rehab services)

Walter L. Aument Family Health Center: 317 South Chestnut Street, Quarryville; (717) 786-7383 (physician services)

Willow Lakes Medical Services: 222 Willow Valley Lakes Drive, Willow Street; (717) 464-9173 (lab testing, radiology/x-ray, rehab services)

Penn State Milton S. Hershey Medical Center
500 University Drive, Hershey
(800) 243-1455, (717) 531-8521
www.hmc.psu.edu
Staffed by over 200 specialty physicians, the Milton S. Hershey Medical Center offers a full range of advanced medical and surgical diagnostics, procedures, and treatments. Special care centers, institutes, and programs focus on arthritis, bones, and joints; cancer; heart and vascular health; hemophilia; biomedical engineering; clinical, cancer, retina, and technology development research; shock and trauma; sports medicine; and women's health. For physician referrals, call the main number. Penn State Children's Hospital, a part of the medical center, is widely renowned for its inpatient (including intensive care) and outpatient medical and surgical care for infants, children, adolescents, and young adults

EDUCATION

Public Schools

According to the 2005 *Guide to Lancaster County,* published by the League of Women Voters of Lancaster County and Lancaster Newspapers, Inc., 16 school districts provide free education to more than 68,000 young people in this area. The average student population per district is about 4,200, ranging from 1,500 in Columbia to more than 11,000 in the city of Lancaster. Among the educational facilities are 83 elementary schools and 17 senior high schools. Special programs are avail-

The Northern Lancaster County Medical Transport Service Cooperative (717-355-0303) offers routine, nonemergency transportation for individuals moving from one health care facility to another or from the hospital to home. The service also provides rides to physicians' offices and physical therapy facilities.

able for youngsters with special behavioral, emotional, or academic needs. For vocational studies such as construction, manufacturing, health care, and transportation technologies; visual communications; culinary arts; and office and maintenance skills, the Lancaster County Career and Technology Center (717–653–3007) offers courses in five locations throughout the area.

To date, only one charter school, which was established in 1998 for students in grades 6 through 11 who are at risk of dropping out of the educational system, is in operation in the county.

Private Schools

The Roman Catholic Church operates six elementary schools (total enrollment is over 1,700 students) in Lancaster County. Lancaster Catholic High School has an enrollment of about 700 students. Lancaster Mennonite schools include 11 elementary schools (total enrollment of 2,500) and a high school (over 800 students). Other private institutions include Lancaster County Day School (college prep for kindergarten through grade 12), Linden Hall (primarily a boarding school for girls in grades 6 through 12), and Janus School (for students of high potential who have specific learning disabilities such as dyslexia).

Home Schooling

An estimated 2,700 children in Lancaster County are currently being home schooled, toward the goal of being awarded a Pennsylvania Homeschool Diploma, which is accepted by colleges and the military. Support and communication for home-schooling families is available through the Coalition of Homeschoolers Across Lancaster County (P.O. Box 480, Leola, PA 17540; 717–661–2242; www.chalc.org).

Colleges and Universities

Elizabethtown College
One Alpha Drive, Elizabethtown
(717) 361–1400
www.etown.edu
Founded in 1899 by members of the Church of the Brethren, this four-year residential college offers 45 major programs plus more than 60 minors/concentrations in 20 humanities, arts and sciences, and professional disciplines. Enrollment is approximately 1,850 full-time undergraduate students (85 percent live on campus). Average class is 25 students, with a student/faculty ratio of 13:1 (about 90 percent of the 180 full- and part-time faculty members hold a Ph.D. or other terminal degree in their field). Off-campus opportunities include study abroad programs in Europe, Asia, and South America (including a summer at Oxford University). Extracurricular athletic and cultural activities are also abundant, with more than 80 student clubs and organizations and a variety of sports teams.

Franklin & Marshall College
P.O. Box 3003
Lancaster, PA 17604
(717) 291–3911
www.fandm.edu
When it first opened in 1787, this educational institution was named solely for Benjamin Franklin, then the president of the Supreme Executive Council of Pennsylvania. In 1853 Franklin College merged with another small institution, named for Chief Justice John Marshall, that had been in operation since 1836. Four years prior

The nonresidential Center for Continuing Education and Distance Learning at Elizabethtown College offers degrees in business administration, accounting, criminal justice, computer science, and communications.

to becoming the 15th president of the United States, James Buchanan was named president of the first Franklin & Marshall board of trustees.

Privately funded, this liberal arts college, situated on 170 acres, enrolls about 1,980 full-time undergraduate students who are taught by approximately 175 full-time equivalent faculty members (99 percent of tenured or tenure-track faculty have a doctorate or equivalent terminal degree). Student/faculty ratio is 11:1. An average of 25 percent of the junior class participates in off-campus study abroad and affiliated American programs.

Gettysburg College
300 North Washington Street
Gettysburg
(717) 337-6000
www.gettysburg.edu
Chartered in 1832, this independent, residential, coeducational college of liberal arts and sciences is located on 200 acres adjacent to Gettysburg National Military Park.

Of the nearly 2,500 students (enrollment is almost evenly divided between men and women), about 96 percent live on campus to pursue more than 30 majors as well as a variety of special interest areas of concentration (dual degree programs are available). Of the more than 180 full-time faculty members, about 95 percent hold a doctorate or highest earned degree in their fields. Average class size is 18 students, with a student/faculty ratio of 11:1. Each year over 300 Gettysburg students spend a semester or a year abroad and nearly 50 percent will study abroad before they graduate. About 25 percent of students participate in the school's intercollegiate sports programs.

Lancaster Bible College
901 Eden Road
P.O. Box 83403
Lancaster, PA 17608-3403
(800) 544-7335, (717) 569-7071
www.lbc.edu

Since its beginning in 1933, Lancaster Bible College (LBC) has grown into a venerable institution with a cumulative enrollment of 1,058 students (more than 850 of whom are undergraduates) on its 100-acre campus. An additional 1,082 students attend LBC's Evening Institute. Close to 25 undergrad (and about a dozen graduate-level) professional ministry programs combine classroom study with practical real-world applications under faculty supervision. The college also offers undergraduate, graduate, and certificate programs in Bible studies and other areas. Of the total 90-person faculty, 42 are full time (25 with doctorates) and 48 are part time. At the undergraduate level, the student/faculty ratio is 16:1, at the graduate level 10:1. A variety of athletic programs are also available.

Lancaster General College of Nursing and Health Sciences
410 North Lime Street, Lancaster
(800) 622-5443, (717) 544-4912
www.lancastergeneral.org
Affiliated with Lancaster General Hospital, this private college offers its 450 students two-year programs of study, including experience in actual hands-on health care settings, designed to prepare them for entry into nursing and other health care professions in hospitals and other institutions. Since 1903 the School of Nursing has graduated over 3,000 professional nurses. In 1952 the first allied health education program in medical technology was added. Today, five applied science degree programs and two diploma programs in health sciences are available, including studies in clinical care services, clinical laboratory science, diagnostic medical sonography, invasive cardiovascular technology, nuclear medicine technology, radiography, and surgical technology. The nursing program is accredited by the National League for Nursing Accreditation Commission (www.nlnac.org) and approved by the Pennsylvania State Board of Nursing.

Millersville University
1 South George Street
P.O. Box 1002
Millersville, PA 17551
(717) 872-3024
www.millersville.edu

Located 3 miles from the city of Lancaster on a 250-acre campus, Millersville is the largest educational institution in Lancaster County. It was founded in 1855 as a teachers' college, but today it offers a variety of undergraduate and graduate majors in science and math, education, humanities, and social sciences to a total of almost 8,000 full-time undergraduate and graduate students. The average class size is 25 students, with a student/faculty ratio of 17:1. Undergraduates may apply to Honors College. A center of community culture is the university's Lyte Auditorium, a 700-seat performing arts center.

Pennsylvania College of Art and Design
204 North Prince Street, Lancaster
(717) 396-7833
www.pcad.edu

Students study with professional working artists (student/faculty ratio is 11:1) and designers to earn a bachelor of fine arts degree in fine art, graphic design, and illustration. The curriculum is approximately 65 percent art studies focused, with the remainder concentrated on literature, art history, philosophy, and math or science. Founded in 1982, the college also offers professional programs in digital design for the Web and print, mural painting, and folk art studies, as well as a variety of credit and noncredit studio and computer courses for youngsters and adults.

LIBRARY SYSTEM

Lancaster County Public Library
www.lancaster.lib.pa.us

Lancaster County Library has four locations in Lancaster County.

During the July 1863 Battle of Gettysburg, Gettysburg College's Pennsylvania Hall served as a hospital, treating more than 700 wounded Union and Confederate soldiers.

Duke Street Library
125 North Duke Street, Lancaster
(717) 394-2651

Eastern Lancaster County Library
11 Chestnut Drive, New Holland
(717) 354-0525
www.elancolibrary.org

Leola Branch Library
46 Hillcrest Road, Leola
(717) 656-7920

Manheim Township Branch Library
401-A Granite Run Drive, Lancaster
(717) 560-6441

Other Libraries

Adamstown Area Library
3000 North Reading Road (Route 272)
(717) 484-4200
www.adamstown.lib.pa.us

Columbia Public Library
24 South Sixth Street
(717) 684-2255
www.columbia.lib.pa.us

Elizabethtown Public Library
10 South Market Street
(717) 367-7467
www.etownpubliclibrary.org

Ephrata Public Library
550 South Reading Road
(717) 738-9291
www.ephratapubliclibrary.org

Hershey Public Library
701 Cocoa Avenue, Hershey
(717) 533-6555
www.hersheylibrary.org

Lititz Public Library
651 Kissel Hill Road
(717) 626-2255

Milanof-Schock Library
1184 Anderson Ferry Road, Mount Joy
(717) 635-1510
www.mslibrary.org

Moores Memorial Library
326 North Bridge Street, Christiana
(610) 593-6683
www.christianalibrary.org

Pequea Valley Public Library
3660 Old Philadelphia Pike, Intercourse
(717) 768-3160
www.intercourse.lib.pa.us

Quarryville Library
357 Buck Road, Quarryville
(717) 786-1336
www.quarryvillelibrary.org

Strasburg-Heisler Library
143 Precision Avenue, Strasburg
(717) 687-8969
www.strasburglibrary.org

CHILD CARE

Child Care Resource Developers (CCRD) of Pennsylvania
CCRD is a statewide initiative, created by the Pennsylvania Department of Public Welfare, to enhance community-based solutions to improving the quality and increasing the capacity of child care services in the state. CCRD of Central Region (800-346-3020) serves Adams, Dauphin, and Lancaster Counties. One way CCRD assists families seeking quality child care is through its Keystone STARS program, which rates participating providers according to specified levels of standards, training, assistance, resources, and support (STARS). The ratings range from Star 1, for these who meet minimal health and safety standards required by licensing, to Star 4, which is similar to meeting accreditation standards developed by the National Association for the Education of Young Children. For a list of Keystone STARS participating child care providers and their ratings, visit www.dpw.state.pa.us and click on "Child Services."

MEDIA

Magazines and Newspapers

Central PA Magazine
WITF
P.O. Box 2954
Harrisburg, PA 17105
(717) 236-6000
centralpa.org or witf.org
Every month approximately 40,000 households read *Central PA* to learn about local people and regional events as well as the programming offered by the WITF television and radio stations.

Lancaster County libraries are linked via a computerized catalog and an interlibrary loan service that allows materials to be shared throughout the county and borrowed from libraries across the nation.

Many of the libraries offer a variety of programs such as book discussion groups, author visits, art exhibits, and special activities for youngsters, including summer reading programs and activities.

Gettysburg Times
1570 Fairfield Road
P.O. Box 3669
Gettysburg, PA 17325
(717) 334-1131
www.gettysburgtimes.com
Published Monday through Saturday (circulation 11,000).

The Hershey Chronicle
513 West Chocolate Avenue, Hershey
(717) 533-2900
Weekly newspaper, published every Thursday (circulation is about 4,000).

***Lancaster County* Magazine**
200 Hazel Street, Lancaster
(717) 392-1321
Sleek monthly magazine filled with locally oriented features and advertising.

Lancaster Newspapers, Inc.
8 West King Street, Lancaster
(717) 291-8639
Publisher of two daily newspapers and one Sunday edition.
   Intelligencer Journal: morning newspaper (circulation more than 44,000) is published Monday through Saturday.
   Lancaster New Era: afternoon paper (circulation about 52,000) is published Monday through Saturday.
   Sunday News (circulation 100,289)

Merchandiser Newspapers
Engle Printing and Publishing Co, Inc.
1425 West Main Street, Mount Joy
(800) 800-1833, (717) 653-4300
Local news and advertising are the focus of these weekly newspapers. Manheim Township, Hempfield–Mountville, Elizabethtown–Mount Joy, Columbia–Wrightsville, and Manheim–Lititz editions have a total circulation of over 70,000.

Where & When
1425 West Main Street, Mount Joy
(800) 800-1833, ext. 2544
Published four times per year, this seasonal local travel magazine is available at tourist centers, chambers of commerce, state parks, museums, colleges, and some selected retail locations.

Local TV Stations

In addition to its own local stations, Lancaster County receives stations from Philadelphia and Baltimore.
WGAL-TV (Channel 8)—NBC affiliate
WITF-TV (Channel 33)—PBS
WLYH-TV (Channel 15)—UPN affiliate
WPMT-TV (Channel 43)—Fox affiliate

Local Radio Stations

In addition to its own local stations, Lancaster County receives stations from Philadelphia, Baltimore, and Harrisburg.
WDAC-FM (94.5)—Christian music, news, and issues programs
WFNM-FM (89.1)—Franklin & Marshall College
WGTY-FM (107.7)—Classic and contemporary country music, Nextel Cup racing
WIOV-FM (105.1)—Regent Broadcasting of Lancaster, Inc.—country music
WITF-FM (89.5)—Classical music and National Public Radio news
WJTL-FM (90.3)—Creative Ministries—contemporary Christian
WLAN-AM (1390)—Clear Channel—"timeless classics"
WLAN-FM (96.9)—Clear Channel Broadcasting Licenses, Inc.—Top 40
WLCH-FM (91.3)—Spanish American Civic Association—licensed as a public educational station and broadcasts in Spanish and English 18 hours a day
WLPA-AM (1490)—Hall Communications, Inc.—Fox and local sports; broadcasts WGAL-TV News
WROZ-FM (101.3)—Hall Communications, Inc.—soft rock

EMERGENCY CONTACT INFORMATION

Fire, police, and ambulance emergency: 911

Nonemergency police: (717) 664–1190

Nonemergency fire: (717) 664–1180

Central Pennsylvania Poison Control Center: (800) 222–1222

Lancaster County Office of Aging (150 North Queen Street, Suite 301, Lancaster; 800-801-3070, 717-299-7979; www.co.lancaster.pa.us/lanco_aging) has staff on call 24 hours a day to respond to and investigate elder abuse cases.

INDEX

ABOUT THE AUTHOR

Born, raised, and educated (she has a journalism degree from Temple University) in Philadelphia, Marilyn Odesser-Torpey is a travel and feature writer who regularly contributes to many regional and national magazines. When she was growing up, Pennsylvania Dutch Country was synonymous with Amish fairs and food.

It was while researching her first travel guide for Globe Pequot Press, *Quick*

Escapes Philadelphia, that Marilyn had the chance to really explore this section of her home state and began to discover its true diversity and virtually limitless possibilities. During the research for *Insiders' Guide to Pennsylvania Dutch Country,* she began to regard the area as her home away from home. With a move to the village of Lititz, she now calls it just plain home.